GATHERING
NO MOSS

Memoir of a Reluctant World Traveler

DON FEENEY

Printed in the United States of America

ISBN: Softcover   978-1-63871-965-6
          eBook   978-1-63871-966-3

Republished by: PageTurner Press and Media LLC
Publication Date: 02/10/2022

To order copies of this book, contact:
PageTurner Press and Media
Phone: 1-888-447-9651
info@pageturner.us
www.pageturner.us

CONTENTS

<u>PHOTO REFERENCES</u>

PART III *Reinvention and Pragmatism*

PART IV *Diplomacy and Restartment*

To my wife, Andrea Lee Feeney (née Moran), who means more to me than life itself. And to my dad, Earl Lawrence Feeney, who had a short and painful life, and whose generosity and self-sacrifice were underappreciated by the Feeney family. And finally to the Dead Man of Illopango, whoever you were.

A Rolling STONE gathers no moss

An old proverb, credited to Publilius Syrus (Latin writer of maxims), with many different meanings. In this book, I choose the interpretation that moss equates to inaction, or stagnation. The "rolling" is simply movement. Like Wiki-pedia states, "Such a proverb can also refer to those who keep moving as never lacking for fresh ideas or creativity."

INTRODUCTION

This is a book about a shy, inner-city kid from the north side of Pittsburgh, and how he managed to stumble from one part of the earth to the other. With literally no plan, guided or misguided by others, his life was laid out before him. He was a slow learner, pulled along by people and events into an exciting but lonely life. By 2014, he had moved twenty-four times. From childhood (nuns, Catholic schools, guilt), through adolescence and college (not much difference in maturity), into the air force (from a security police "two striper" who deserted his post, full circle to an assistant professor of aerospace studies at the Air Force Academy), and ultimately into the Department of State (unlikely diplomat, to say the least), this reluctant traveler went where he was told to go.

This traveler was me, Don Feeney, married four times and divorced three times. That leaves a remainder of one—my current and final bride, Andi. As the old adage says, "Even a blind pig finds an acorn once in a while." I'm holding onto this acorn for life, or at least as long as she'll have me.

The purpose of this book is to provide some understanding and closure for myself, my wife, my family, colleagues, and friends. (Of course, this was one of the most difficult things I have ever done.) The wide range of experiences that I hope to share with you may evoke several conflicting thoughts about my sanity. This is normal. But like most people, the aging process tends to simplify things and bring conflicting life experiences into focus. I now reside on the beach in Florida, have been married for well over twenty years, and live a relatively "normal" life, teaching graduate school part-time, traveling with Andi, reuniting with family and friends, and so on.

Why write this book? (I have never desired drawing attention to myself before.) Over the last ten years or so, when our travel experiences came up in conversation, there seemed to be a high level of interest. I am not sure why. It definitely caught me off guard, and planted the seed that ultimately led to this book. Maybe curiosity is contagious … I don't know. But if there is a chance that you might enjoy the ride, then it's worth a try.

A quick word about the writing style. I don't have one particular presentation. Instead, I decided to write this narrative not as an author but as a friend, talking about travel and about human stories good and bad, while desperately trying not to bore you to death! I've also tried to avoid too much detail, while at the same including things that hopefully will interest you. If this writing style provokes thoughts and experiences about your life, I've accomplished my purpose. After all, reading is really about the interpretation of the reader, and not so much about the writer. When this book becomes published, I'd love to discuss stories and ideas about your life that may have surfaced from reading about mine. There would be no bigger thrill for me. (If you do read this book, track me down. I'd love to hear about your unique stories.)

My approach is quasi-chronological, but I'm not adamant about it. I'll work around time lines if I think it might be of interest to you. I'll attempt to put a good story together, using an approach I call "steering the blob." If you're like me, you can't remember all the details about your life. Therefore,you try to interpret a mass of personal experiences (the blob) and guide them toward your hopes and dreams (steering) as you go from point A to point B, or from youth through old age. Put simply, all of us try to direct our lives toward goals, be it educational, marital, job-related, and so on. We use our intellect to manage this daily process, knowing that life always gets in the way (the "fog of war," as Clausewitz would say). But our experiences (blob) can get out of hand at times and even overwhelm us. So we constantly strive to make sense of our lives (steer) as we move through time. But why do we do this? My theory is that humans are the only animals that know they're going to die. Because of this, they plan everything, from attending preschool to purchasing a cemetery plot. And all the stuff in between, for lack of a better theory, entails steering the blob.

As you read this book, try to keep your spirit light, and travel with me to the five continents that I have called home. I will expose a lot about myself, reluctantly and self-deprecatingly, with the hope that you enjoy its intent, that is, to tell a simple story, using a little humor, dealing with a little grief, and hopefully entertaining you along the way. In order to do this, I had to trick myself into pretending that I'm writing about someone else— the only way I could justify putting much of this memoir down on paper.

I'd like to introduce what I believe is the true secret to life (got a pencil?). Here it is: "The more you know, the more you don't know sh*t!" or TMYKTMYDKS. This adage will show itself many times throughout the book. I have learned the hard way to follow this mantra. It helps to explain how a person could live this "homeless" life without throwing himself against the wall (Warren Zevon reference). I have been an airman, an officer, an instructor, a commander, a trainer, a consular officer, a manager, and a diplomat. I have also swept streets, sold paintings on the street corner, washed dishes, worked in a paper mill, flipped hamburgers, painted houses, and bartended. I have used drugs, drank too much, fell in and out of love like daydreams, went AWOL in the US Air Force, been shot at three times, survived a brain aneurysm, and beat colon cancer. In all of these situations, every time I learned five new things, I had ten more unanswered questions.

Simply put, the human mind will never let you understand the human mind. Is it cognitive dissonance on steroids or TMYKTMYDKS? Who knows? Maybe someday you can explain it to me.

To avoid undue embarrassment, lapses in memory, and/or unintended consequences, I used fictitious names for many people in this book. At other times, like with family and certain colleagues I admire and respect, I decided to use real names. We'll see how this works out going forward.

Finally, if you enjoy this book, I think it says two things about you. First, your life is not that different from mine. The common core experiences that we share will bear this out. We're all out there steering the blob. Second, and more importantly, you'll have used my words to rediscover thoughts about your own life, hidden just below the surface. I believe you will find many of these gems stuck in the back of your mind, just like I did. This is my major intent—to use a style of writing that makes this book more about you and less about me.

So, here goes …

PART I

Immaturity and Low Expectations

CHAPTER ONE

"Come home when the streetlights come on."

———◆○◆———

It was 1960, and I didn't know that we were poor. We lived on the north side of Pittsburgh, 52 Norman Street, about a mile from downtown. My parents, Earl and Theresa, were depression children who lived through World War II and had the scars to prove it. Each dropped out of school at a young age to enter the workforce and raise a family. With five kids (I'm in the middle) and no education, it's not hard to imagine that economics would become an issue throughout their lives.

I, however, was the happiest child on the block. There were kids to play with everywhere, and each day was full of wonder and excitement. Economics was not important to me as a kid (still isn't), and I couldn't wait to get up every day. It never occurred to me that receiving free food from the Salvation Army or buying clothes from secondhand stores or eating a constant array of leftovers were anything but normal. In fact, things were so tough that we had a fellow named Bob, a rail yard worker, living in our house to help with the bills. He was quiet, kept to himself, and had his own room (I shared a room with two brothers). We called him Uncle Bob, but we all knew he wasn't our uncle.

None of these economic limitations really fazed me. The way I looked at it, I had a house to live in, a strong family foundation, tons of friends, and could stay out every day after school until the streetlights came on. Decades later, during a Department of State retirement seminar, a lecturer said that over 90 percent of one's personality is developed by the age of four. If this is the case, I couldn't have received a better start to life. My foundation for the future was strong. In many ways, I still have that little kid inside me who's eager to go out and play.

Church was a huge part of my early life in Pittsburgh. I attended Annunciation Grade School, on the corner of Norwood and North Charles Streets, and started every school day attending early Mass. I was the model cherub, a little gift from God, for the first couple of years at Annunciation. Then for some reason, I began to get in trouble, and discovered the fun

1

of rebellion and class clownmanship. The normal scenario would go something like this:

"Sister, is it true that if you don't go to church on Sundays, you go to hell?" "Yes, that's correct, Mr. Feeney," said Sister Mary Catherine.

"So if I go to church every week my whole life, miss one Sunday Mass, and die, then I go to hell for eternity?" I asked.

"That's correct, my son."

"That doesn't make sense," said I as Sister Mary Catherine was moving swiftly toward me with a cane, fully believing that smacking me a few times was God's way of handling smart alecks.

Or:

"Sister Mary Oswald, is God so powerful that he can design a rock so heavy that even he can't pick it up?" asked I.

"Yes, that is correct," she said.

"Sister, do you mean he can design a rock bigger than he can pick up, or that he can pick up any rock, no matter how big?" I said with mock seriousness, as I was greatly amusing the rest of the class.

"You little mope. You slivery dick!" she exclaimed. (These are her true words—not poetic license.)

But instead of a cane, Sister Mary Oswald perfected the "Ozzie hold," as we affectionately called it. She would grab your jaw with her hand, thumb on one side, the other fingers on the other, and wriggle your face back and forth.

One time I really got in trouble when I overheard Father Benedict and Father Matthew discussing the issuance of penance after receiving confession. For those of you who don't follow the Catholic sacraments, confession is where you go to a booth in church—aptly called the confessional—and tell your sins to the priest. He evaluates the seriousness of your digressions and gives you penance, usually in the form of prayers, like Our Fathers, Hail Marys, and Glory Bes. You could be given a small penance (say, three of each), or a large one, depending on the priest. Well, I heard Father Matthew say that he thought Father Benedict's penances were too harsh and suggested he ease back a bit. I couldn't wait to tell my classmates which priest gave the easier penance. But someone squealed on me, and it was off to the principal's office again for a series of whippings. For years afterward, when I went to confession, I always chose the longest lines, which usually meant the priest in that confessional gave the easiest penance.

On all these occasions, the spanking ritual was the same. First, our homeroom nun would take a few whacks at me in class, ensuring that all my classmates knew who was in charge. Then it was off to the principal's office, which led to another spanking. But that's not the worst of it. The school would call home and inform Mom of my latest antic, so she was always waiting at the door with the pancake turner, poised for beating number three. I was a stubborn kid and could handle all the spankings from the nuns, and even my mom, and would never let them see me cry. But the main event was ahead. I still had to deal with my dad. All of the beatings together were nothing compared to the anticipation of my dad's leather-belt spankings. Every time I endured his wrath, I swore I'd never get in trouble again. But I was enjoying my newfound celebrity in the classroom too much, and being the class clown who was not afraid of the spankings made me pretty popular.

Then, when I least expected it, the neatest thing happened. After another run-in during class, it was off to the principal's office for yet another round of discipline. But this time, it went quite differently:

"Mr. Feeney, are you here again? What am I going to do with you?"

"I'm sorry, Sister Grace, I'll do better next time," said I with no conviction whatsoever, since these meetings always ended in a series of spankings anyway.

"I'll tell you what. We need a few things from the store. Take this money, and run a few errands for me," she said.

"Excuse me, Sister Grace?"

"Run to the store and buy these items for me. Can you do that?" "Yes, Sister." "Promise not to tell?"

"Yes, Sister," and off I went. No spankings, no calls home, no pancake turners, and no leather belts. This was the beginning of a symbiotic relationship that lasted on and off for two years. I could continue to pursue my goals as the class joker, get in trouble regularly, and win the admiration of my schoolmates for not backing down from the beatings, and at the same time get out of class to run errands for the principal's office. This setup was one of my earliest singularly significant events (SSEs), that is, meaningful strategic points along the road of life. In fact, looking back, I now realize that Sister Grace knew exactly what she was doing. The spankings weren't working, and my alienation was growing. Giving me some responsibility and showing me a little outside-the-box compassion really did the trick. In addition, trusting me with her secret—I never told a soul until now —was exactly the right formula to get me back on track. (Note: The Church of the Annunciation was founded in 1893 and had a stalwart parochial school in the community. But over time, the population of the parish began to drop. A merger with the Incarnation of the Lord parish in 1993 didn't help, and it closed in 2001.)

The North Side was a bustling neighborhood, crammed with baby-boomer kids. We had great street games. My favorite was called Tin Can Alley. Everybody would hide, and the person who was "it," that is, the hunter, started the game with a tin can, placed on a manhole cover at the top of Overlook Street. He or she would carefully stray from the can, identify a hidden kid, and run back to the manhole cover, tapping the lid and crying, "One, two, three on Billy, hiding under the red Pontiac." Billy was caught and had to stand embarrassingly by the manhole. This went on until all the kids were found. As you might expect, it was very difficult to find everyone, especially since the hunter had to stray farther and farther from the tin can to locate the hiding places. The absolute thrill of this game—I still get goose bumps thinking about it—was when the hunter missed my hiding place and walked past my secret spot of the day. Then, with a great sense of achievement, I could run like hell to the tin can, kick it as far as I could down Overlook Street, and scream, "Olly olly in free." I was the liberator; everybody would cheer me and then run off to another hiding place. Wow, what a feeling.

A great thing about being a Feeney kid was that our parents gave us tons of autonomy. All five of us became independent faster than most other kids. For example, I remember my mother allowing me to go to a Pirates game with my buddies, with no adult, at nine years old! She gave me two dollars, and off I went:

- Round trip via streetcar, with transfers, from downtown to Oakland— fifty cents
- Ticket to the bleachers in Forbes Field (aptly named for the sunburn that I would ultimately get)—one dollar
- Candy and soda—The real trick was to maximize the amount of food and drink you could buy. Should I choose two Cokes and two candy bars? Or a hot dog, one Coke, and cotton candy? These were tough decisions, and usually required me to wander around awhile and compare options. (I learned this technique from my brother Larry, who usually got stuck taking me to the games.)—fifty cents
- The actual Pirates game—priceless.

In 1960, I distinctly remember Bob (Dad's friend who lived with us for a while) taking my brother John and me downtown in his pickup to celebrate the Pirates winning the World Series. In one of the biggest upsets in history, the Pirates beat the Yankees in seven games, with a bottom-of-the-ninth home run by Bill Mazeroski. There were "Beat 'em Bucs" signs everywhere, and people singing, "The Bucs are going all the way, all the way, all the way, the Bucs are going all the way, all the way this year."

I also remember my dad taking me to a Pittsburgh Steelers game (1965?). They were playing the Chicago Bears. Back then, the team played at Pitt Stadium, and they were not a very good football club. But on the opening kickoff, Gale Sayers bolted 102 yards for a touchdown, weaving and cutting around defenders the whole way. He was a legend. The Steelers eventually won the game, and Dad was predicting they would make the playoffs. But the Steelers were the Steelers back then, and only won one more game that season, ending up with a 2–12 record. (It took forty years for the team to win its first playoff game.) But I didn't really care who won the football game. For me, the cherished memories with my dad helped to embed sports into my personality for life.

There were no parks or ball fields near our neighborhood. But there was an open field a few blocks from our house, across Buena Vista Avenue, that we all called the Quarry. None of us knew what the term *quarry* meant; we just knew it was our place to play baseball. I remember countless times lining up in front of the older kids who would pick sides, praying that I would get selected. It was very stressful. No one wanted to walk home unselected, mitt in hand. I saw many kids crying as they left the Quarry having not been chosen.

Luckily for me, I was a pretty good hitter, so I usually made one of the teams. But I came with a high price. Since I was the only left-handed batter, my tendencies were to pull the ball down the right field line. The Quarry sat on the edge of a steep, heavily wooded ravine, about ten yards from the first baseline. For some reason or another, I hit a lot of foul balls down into that ravine. This meant we all had to stop playing and start combing the hillside trying to find the ball. Many times, we never found it and had to cancel the game. Man, I hated it when that happened. I tried as hard as I could to hit the ball to left field, or even up the middle, but I couldn't do it. (To this day, my older brother Larry still talks about how frustrating it was to climb up and down the ravine looking for lost balls.) I guess old habits die hard. I played baseball up to the age of eighteen, and softball for twenty-five more years after that, and still have never hit a ball to left field. (The irony? I hit nothing but slices on the golf course, which means the golf ball goes to the left. The similarity? Lost balls were a common theme in both sports.)

Of course, neighborhood games were excellent preparation for organized sports. To me, organized sports are as important as social/ learning skills for young kids. You deal firsthand with winning and losing, you compete for team goals bigger than yourself, and you have fun doing it. In my travels, I occasionally ran into colleagues who never played sports. Many times these people envisioned games as beneath them or unworthy of their time. In my opinion, they underestimated how sports can provide valuable contributions to personality growth. As Michael Mandelbaum says in his book *The Meaning of Sports,* sports "are powerfully attractive forms of entertainment because of another feature: coherence. It is easy to underestimate the importance in human affairs of coherence, which is the property of making sense, of hanging together. Coherence is not necessary to sustain life, food or shelter. It is not a cause for which people have fought or died. But it is evidently a basic human need. All cultures have methods for making life intelligible to those who are living it."

Along with baseball and softball, I played football, basketball, and track and field, joined a swim team, bowled in several bowling leagues, and played tons of tennis in college. (Not to mention intramural sports from flag football to golf.) Given a few moments to reflect, I can find a sports analogy for almost any life situation. But even more importantly, my childhood development was affected more by sports than any other stimulus, short of my family and my church. (You know, I never realized this until right now.) I can still smell the grass and feel the pop of the ball when it hit my mitt in the Quarry.

Unfortunately, not all was rosy on the North Side. Although Pittsburgh is one of the nicest cities in America today, this was not always the case. Providing steel products for almost half the world was a big job, and the environment definitely suffered. In *Pittsburgh Now and Then*, Arthur G. Smith writes the following: "In 1868, James Parton wrote in the *Atlantic*

Monthly that looking down upon Pittsburgh from one of its hilltops was like looking into hell with the lid taken off." And the pictures from this publication definitely bear this out. At the Point (confluence of the Allegheny and Monongahela Rivers, forming the Ohio River), for instance, were smokestacks, factories, rail yards, blasting furnaces, hundreds of barges full of coal and steel—you get the picture. As Smith says, "Sometimes the river [Ohio] was so congested that one could almost cross it by jumping from barge to barge." It really did look like hell.

But like the Phoenix rising from the ashes, Pittsburgh had a renaissance like no other in American history. By the mid-eighties, the effects of this transformation began to become known. In 1985, Rand McNally listed Pittsburgh as "the most livable city in America." In 2000, the millennium edition of *Places Rated Almanac,* by David Savageau, ranked it twelfth out of 354 metropolitan areas. The rankings were based on a wide range of criteria, from jobs and education, to crime rates and health care. Not to be outdone, when the twenty-fifth anniversary edition of the same publication was released in 2007, the town of Pittsburgh, the "lidless hell," was rated the number-one city in America! The Point is now a beautiful park, and there are green spaces with trees everywhere; you can even catch bass in the Ohio River. And from the south side of the city, up on Mount Washington, the skyline view of Pittsburgh is a unique panorama.

But for those families who grew up amid the steel mills before the transformation years (the Feeneys, for instance), things were not so good.

We were exposed to a daily onslaught of deadly air pollution, and the physical results were staggering. My mom (Theresa), Pat (older sister), Larry (older brother), myself, and John (youngest brother) all got cancer in the coming decades. Only Susan, the younger sister, avoided the same fate. This may be because we moved from the North Side shortly after she was born. In addition to the environmental risks, things in the neighborhood really began to deteriorate. Crime and poverty were changing Norman Street, and those simple days of yore were evaporating fast. So the Feeneys picked up and moved to Avalon, a North Hills suburb, about eight miles west of downtown Pittsburgh. Sadly, my parents tried renting their small duplex, but the tenants trashed the place and disappeared. Dad had to pay hard-earned money to condemn the place, and later to tear it down. Good-bye, Norman Street, and good-bye to the innocence of an unknowing childhood. Once we moved to 313 Fisk Avenue in Avalon, it was time to adjust to a new environment. And just like Norman Street, the Roman Catholic Church (Assumption) was a major part of that adjustment. I became thoroughly enmeshed in the daily business of the Catholic Church, sans the class-clown antics. My brother John and I sang in the choir, ranging from weddings, funerals, and the Stations of the Cross on Good Friday, to Midnight Mass on Christmas Eve. We both did stints as altar boys, and I was a lecter for the reading of the Epistle (biblical verse) during daily Mass. Being a lecter was the coolest gig. I would be called from class (yeah!) to report to the church and read a few verses from the Bible for Mass. And the nuns couldn't do anything about it—I was serving the Lord! Here I was, a sixth grader, reading God's word to hundreds of people! Not only did I get out of class, but the priest would sometimes give me some unblessed hosts, which I used to practice giving communion to the neighborhood dogs. I still hold the record for sticking fifteen hosts to the roof of my mouth at the same time! I also remember taking my first sip of red wine, not yet the body of Christ—I'm not that stupid—when no one was looking. (I'm still addicted to red wine— *it's the church's fault.*)

The transition to Assumption School and Church, and to Avalon, was pretty seamless. After losing my old friends and meeting new ones, I began to settle into a pretty good pattern in Avalon. Some of the best memories of my childhood were during this period.

Bob had a hunting camp up in northern Pennsylvania (Marienville), part of the Allegheny National Forest. It was called the Little Indian (no one knew why), and was a place of countless wonders for me. It was a one-room dwelling, with bunk beds lined against two of the four walls. The rest was a meager collection of oil furnaces, gas stoves, a couple of refrigerators, deer and rifle racks hanging everywhere, and a large table in the middle of the camp. Our family would usually go up in the summer, when the weather was nice, and hang outside all day long. There was a lake nearby, where I learned how to canoe and where all of us kids loved playing on the "spillway," a runoff area from the lake to the creek. (I later learned the lake was called Buzzard Swamp—what an image killer.) At the camp, we shot bows and arrows, hunted down critters in the woods, caught baseballs and footballs, held our breath when using the outhouse, and generally were kids being kids. Little things like spotting deer, lifting rocks to find turtles and salamanders, or just wandering off into the forest were precious activities for us city kids.

My dad, who used to hunt every winter at the Little Indian, was never able to land a buck. I remember Bob, and Dad's other hunting buddies, kidding him all the time about his ineptitude as a hunter. When I asked Dad why he never bagged a deer, he said probably because he wasn't a very good hunter. Years later, I went to the camp with my dad and the gang right in the middle of hunting season. One morning at dawn, I took off with him to go looking for stags (I was unarmed). What I saw was amazing. Showing an acute skill to read hoofprints in the snow and judge the proximity of a buck by the freshness of its spoor, he led me to an area where a twelve-point buck was grazing just twenty-five yards away. (Spoor refers to any signs of a creature, like tracks, trails, and droppings.) I was really excited. My dad would finally show all the guys that he was a good hunter. He watched the buck for a moment or so, rifle in hand, but didn't shoot. He lowered his weapon, spun around silently, and we walked all the way back to camp without saying a word. When we arrived, we could hear Bob telling everybody about the deer he just shot. At the same time, my dad announced to everyone that again this year, he didn't land a deer. And they all laughed.

Another favorite childhood "institution" was the weekend trips to Grandma Feeney's house. Wow, what an Irish experience. Grandma had seven sons, all semipro football players, and one daughter. (Unfortunately, Aunt Ellen died during childbirth, so her daughter, Darleen, lived with Grandma.) All of her sons, loaded with spouses and children and beer, converged on Grandma's little house in Dormont, on the east side of the city, every Sunday. For us kids, there was nothing better. Two of my uncles, Al and Joe, lived on the same street. So we moved from house to house like a swarm of bees, trashing everything in our wake, making games out of everything, eating everything in sight, and loving every minute of it. Uncle Al and Aunt Rita had nine boys. As the story goes, after the seventh child, they decided to try for a girl one more time. They had twin boys! I still remember the picture in the *Pittsburgh Press*, with all nine boys wearing Pirate hats, and the caption reading "Who's on first?" Not to be outdone, my Uncle Jack and Aunt Florence had thirteen children. My mom, with only five kids (and two miscarriages), was considered practically barren in our clan.

The adult section of the "grandma" experience, the kitchen, was something else—with Mom and Dad and all the aunts and uncles firing down Iron City beer and whiskey in record quantities. I remember there were three refrigerators—one for food and two for beer! Cases upon cases were stacked like cordwood all around the room. Every so often one of the uncles would take on the duty of opening another case and rotating cold beer forward, warm beer in the back. And of course, everyone smoked, so the kitchen looked like Pittsburgh when it was a "lidless hell." They would talk for hours, laughing and blowing off steam pent up from a week of mindless work. There would be toasts to everything from Grandpa (John Feeney, who passed away very young with throat cancer) to the homeland of Ireland, with sad songs being sung amid constant shouting and cursing. Throw in the occasional fight, followed by quick apologies involving hugs and tears—all intensified with the constant flow of alcohol—and the routine weekend at Grandma's was complete. Even though this kind of activity may sound dysfunctional, it really wasn't. They loved each other and rarely missed a Sunday at Grandma's. I sometimes wish all of my brothers and sisters hung around with each other and developed that kind of camaraderie. It would have been priceless to be closer to them in the adult years. There's no way around it—my geographical separation, created by a hectic nomadic lifestyle, took its toll on this Feeney.

Grandma Feeney was a wonderful, caring woman. But she was a big woman. To be honest, she was very fat. I still recall with appalling clarity the size of her triceps fat (don't know what else to call it). It hung down at least seven inches under each arm. One time when I was around nine years old, we arrived at Grandma's, and she pulled me into that giant bosom to give me a hug. I felt the slapping of triceps fat against my face. It initially came in waves of warm flab hitting my cheeks, and then the tempo slowed until the fat stopped moving altogether. At that exact moment, I wished I was dead. In fact, this SSE has been haunting me my entire life. I really believe my discomfort with obesity, which I still have today, is in part because of that experience.

Back in Avalon, participating in sports, developing an interest in girls, and attending regular church activities kept me pretty busy entering junior high. With finances a real problem in the Feeney household, my parents decided to move me from Assumption to Avalon High School in ninth grade— making it the first public school I had ever attended. The initial thing I noticed about Avalon was how far behind it was compared to Assumption (public vs. parochial school). This was both good and bad. Good, because I rarely had to study to keep up with my classmates; bad, because I fell into some lousy study habits that I took to college with me.

It was about this time in my life when I started to notice that not all was well in the Feeney clan. In comparison to my life, which was relatively incident-free, my parents' existence was fraught with marital, health, and financial problems. I didn't have to look very far to find examples—starting with my dad, Earl Feeney. He worked over thirty years for Otto's, a local dairy, making ice cream. I didn't realize until decades later that he never made more than $9,500 in annual salary. How he managed to feed five children, I'll never know. (I can recall many times when we had no food to eat, but a freezer full of Nutty Buddy's, ice cream sandwiches, gallons of chocolate and vanilla ice cream, and so on. It was weird eating ice cream for breakfast, but hey, you got used to it.) Dad was up every morning at 5:00 a.m., and out the door by 5:45 a.m. I remember listening to him brew coffee, head outside to warm up the car, scrape ice from the car windows, and then drive off for work. (I could time his actions to the minute, using the rumbling of the streetcars roaring down California Avenue every fifteen minutes as my alarm clock.) It was a backbreaking and monotonous life, and I would give anything to have just one day to thank him for giving up his life for mine. (Ironically, after his thirty years with Otto's, the company went bankrupt and the local Teamster union disbanded, leaving him with nothing.) He was 99 percent pride and 1 percent everything else. Case in point—although he was eligible for welfare for the first time in his life, he refused to register because he was afraid someone might see him. Compare that sentiment to today's nanny-state mentality.

My dad was quite the enigma. At a recent family gathering, I was astounded to learn how little my brothers and sisters remember about him. He was branded, exiled if you will, from the family for one very grave reason—he physically assaulted my mother on more than one occasion. To my brothers and sisters, he was an afterthought. We rarely, if ever, even talk about him. Although I will never forget the physical abuse, I have come to terms with it and have forgiven him. (I learned an important lesson during my travels: sometimes good people do bad things. I believe this applies to my father.)

I never met anyone more generous than my dad. When he married my mom, he willingly accepted her mother and her sister in one package deal! My aunt Fran (mom's sister) adored my dad and considered him to be her father. Her husband, Uncle Sonny, felt exactly the same. Devastated by his inability to fight in World War II (heart murmur), Dad did an excellent job supporting the Feeney clan while his brothers were off to the front.

9

But to them, Chub (nickname in his younger days) was the nursemaid who stayed behind and watched the womenfolk, while they were saving the world from Hitler. A huge blow to his pride, this ate at him his entire life. Pile on five completely different children, little money, lost job and pension, condemned house, horrible health, war stories from his brothers, and a feisty wife that could drive him crazy, and it's not hard to imagine how a trapped and desolate man could hit the ceiling, even if it resulted in occasional violence.

His escape was an oasis—a bar called Yonk's. At Yonk's, Dad wasn't a failure. He was just one of the guys. Armed with a few bucks (purse strings tightly controlled by Mom), I soon learned why he enjoyed it so much. His gentle-giant personality and humble demeanor made him very popular there. Through the years, I don't know why, my dad gravitated toward me. I became his favorite. I saw a side of him at Yonk's that disappeared when he entered our house. (My dad never drank at home. When he stayed in, he was always sober. I think there is a difference between a drunk and a person who drinks to avoid deep-rooted pain. To be honest, my mom never gave him enough money to get drunk.) In some respects, he lost his family forever when he beat my mother. I believe the real reason she tried to stop him from going to Yonk's was simple—he enjoyed it there, and she didn't want him to enjoy anything. When my mother used to send me to the bar to get him, I felt horrible nagging him to come home. In my opinion, Mom held all the cards and knew how to play them. She could say things to my dad that were hurtful. I thought he was going to burst a couple of times. He didn't become violent because of his drinking. His outbursts were generated by a desperate sense of failure, to the point that the consequences of his actions didn't matter anymore.

That said, there was no excuse for what he did. I remember one time when he rammed Mom's head into the wall, breaking her nose. She hid under my bed, but Dad found her and dragged her out. It was one of the most frightening things I ever witnessed. I saw the worst firsthand and hated my father for years for beating my mother. But I couldn't hate him forever. It required real forgiveness, but I was determined to let him back in my life. Unfortunately, out of stubbornness or procrastination, I waited too long to settle things. His health was an issue, and he became very ill in his mid-forties, living a lonely life in and out of long-term care facilities. With his body pounded by several strokes, and ultimately a final heart attack, he died at age fifty-one. He left a legacy of nothing. My family can barely remember anything about him. He was a ghost, who provided food and shelter, and then got out of the way. Over time, we slowly released Dad from our thoughts and let him disappear like a coin falling into a lake.

Theresa Feeney definitely kept life interesting for us kids. She worked off and on throughout my childhood as a waitress and a bartender. She had the good combination of frugalness and common sense, and miraculously raised five healthy, law-abiding siblings in spite of her marital problems. Believe me, this was no easy feat, given the declining economic and social standards of the old neighborhood where we grew up. (Many of my best childhood friends from the North Side ended up on the wrong side of the justice system.)

I can't remember exactly when it happened, but my mother and I drifted apart while we lived in Avalon. There are several theories for this. First, being favored by my dad had to definitely weigh against me. She never liked that. Second, I stood up to her barrages against him, not because none of it was true, but because some of it was *not* true. And third, I was truly offended by her continual disinterest in my life. For example, I can't remember one time when she showed any interest in my education. She never asked about my schoolwork or cared what my grades were—as long as I passed. She showed no interest in the many sports I played, and never attended an athletic event that I participated in. When I considered attending college, she told me I wasn't college material and that I should get a job. When I got accepted to Clarion University, paid my own way, and graduated four years later, she never visited once. And when I dropped out of college after my first semester, she wasted no time reminding me about my limited potential. In spite of her doubts about my potential, I returned, and graduated on time. I'll never forget how weird it felt to have no guests at the ceremony. (I chose to skip it out of embarrassment.)

The straw that broke the camel's back? When I asked her why she named me Donald, she couldn't even remember.

To be fair, my mom had a tough childhood. After she was born, her father disappeared, leaving her and her mother, Lottie Jones, alone. He reappeared several years later. They had another child (Aunt Fran), and then he took off again. That had to be difficult. On her sixteenth birthday, she spent the morning visiting Aunt Fran in an orphanage, and the afternoon visiting Grandma Jones, who by this time was committed to May View Hospital, a state mental institution.

I'm not a counselor, but maybe this deep-rooted pain—coupled with a strong dislike for her father, who abandoned her—may have led her to mistrust men in general, and my dad in particular.

When my mother passed away in 2009, at age eighty-two, quietly in her sleep, we all knew she was ready to leave this world. It was a long, hard road, and she was ready to close her eyes for good. *Good-bye, Mom. I love you, and I'm sorry I wasn't what you wanted me to be.*

CHAPTER TWO

"The future ain't what it used to be." — *YOGI BERRA*

———◆○◆———

In 1968, Mom and Dad were still around. The Vietnam War was in full display on television everyday, and I was growing up faster than I wanted to. Pat, a brilliant student, left for Mount Mercy College on an academic scholarship. But life gets in the way, doesn't it? Pat met Frank, a navy man who served in Vietnam, fell in love, and chose raising a family over a teaching career. They're the proverbial yin and yang, and are still married today—it must be at least a hundred years by now … And Larry was off to attend Indiana University of Pennsylvania, working on his business administration degree. That left yours truly as the eldest, holding down the fort.

High school was a whole new universe for me. I was an adult, or at least I thought of myself that way. With all this responsibility came lots of decisions and dilemmas. Do I want a car? Will I need to get a job? Will I find a date for the prom? Will I be part of the cool kids who hang out on the "Wall" in front of the grade school? Where is this acne coming from? How did I end up as the captain of the football team? As one of the "crazy Catholic kids who came down from Assumption," will I ever fit in? Who hears me anyway?

First things first … I continued with sports, especially football, which was a mainstay for me throughout high school. As a sophomore, I was the starting tight end, a rare feat under the guise of our maniac head football coach, Mr. Isenberg. I use the term *maniac* in the best sense. He was motivational, intimidating, irascible, and funny all at the same time. (Ask my brother Larry, who was the team captain, about him.) During our two-a-day practices in August, he would drive us to the peak of exhaustion, constantly reminding us that we weren't good enough. But just when we thought we couldn't take it anymore, he'd offer a word or two of encouragement, and we'd be reenergized to do it all over again. He departed after my sophomore year and was replaced by Mr. Sullivan, who was an entirely different type of coach.

After Coach Isenberg, Coach Sullivan didn't have much of a chance. He was a deeply religious man, and nowhere near the motivator that his predecessor was. I was amazed then, and still am today, by the change in atmosphere that permeated the locker room during my junior and senior years. Our sophomore year, we'd explode onto the field after an inspiring pregame rant from Coach Isenberg. In the next two seasons, we'd say a prayer or two, and it was up to one of the players (sometimes me) to get the team motivated. None of us could motivate like Coach Isenberg, especially not Coach Sullivan —he just wasn't cut out for this job. In a way, maybe neither one of us was cut out for our jobs.

In 1971, by the time our senior year came around, everybody in the North Boroughs was picking Avalon to win the conference. We had a predominantly senior-based team, with lots of really good players. I was mildly surprised and really concerned when I was selected as one of the tri-captains, primarily because things were getting tougher on the home front. (Dad's emphysema was very bad, and his first lung operation was fraught with complications. In addition, as the oldest at home, I became the designated driver to take my mother from medical hospital to mental hospital on a regular basis. A teenager's dream, right?) These were among the toughest years of my early life. I was angry that I had to spend countless hours in hospital rooms, watching my dad suffer, or worse, watching my grandma struggle with sanity. Looking back, I probably took a lot of anger out on my mom. I think both of us were overwhelmed with different kinds of responsibilities, which could have contributed to the aloofness that grew between us. With all of these things going on at home, I was crushed when Coach Sullivan removed the other two tri-captains for cause just before the season started. That left me, and Coach Sullivan, to run the team. I was scared shitless.

All I wanted to do was to play football. If being one of the tri-captains was in the cards, fine. I would have been happy to take a backseat behind either of the other two. But being "the" captain was never in my plans. This position placed too much responsibility on me. I could barely keep my attention on football with all the other issues eating away inside me. Plus, I already had more responsibilities than any other player. I played every down, offense and defense, snapped punts, returned punts, was on the kickoff and kickoff return teams, and called all the defensive signals. This meant that I never left the field, not even for one play. Pile the captain's responsibilities on top of me as well, and it was too much.

We ended up with a record of four wins and five losses. Devastating. As the captain, I accepted some of the responsibility. I was no motivator—I wasn't Coach Isenberg. But on the positive side, I was very proud of our defense. We shut out four teams in a nine-game schedule. Our defense adjusted well to my signal calling and made me look good with excellent execution. If our offense had been anywhere near as good as the defense, we would have been very successful.

Like most high-school kids, I gravitated to certain teachers and administrators, and ran from others. At Avalon, we had a very eclectic mix of educators. The top of the list was Mr. Bradley, our English teacher. Smart, modest, funny—he encouraged your best effort, but never demanded it. You wanted to do well for him. He was, and is, the teacher I have emulated for the past twenty-five years, and still do when I walk into a classroom today (I teach graduate school part-time). I remember one class where he gave us an assignment to write a short paper and make it as creative as possible. It was outside-the-box thinking for the early 1970s. Taking a big leap, I wrote a paper about waking up in the morning and finding myself standing on the ceiling instead of the floor! I then described the difficulties of getting showered, dressed, and ready for school. The paper ended when I realized that I couldn't leave the house without falling upward. I remember another time when Mr. Bradley gave us an assignment to write a poem. I thought, *football players don't write poems*. But because it was him, I gave it a try. I came up with a poem that dealt with the infinite lack of permanence in life, and used a metaphor—something like "to explain life is like writing on water; the thought disappears the moment it is written." I know, not inspiring, but not bad for a jock.

Several years ago, Avalon held a reunion for all graduates from the 1960s and 1970s. It was held at nearby North Park, in one of the picnic groves. Pat, Larry, John, and I were all present. It was there I learned that Mr. Bradley was not only my favorite teacher; he was also the favorite teacher for every one of my brothers and sisters. We have a group photo of him with all four Feeneys that I will keep for the rest of my life. (Mr. Bradley was also the track coach, and he was still upset with me for not going out for track my junior year. But I needed to work, and issues at home took priority. However, I did come back my senior year and had a pretty successful season.)

Another one of my favorite teachers—but for an entirely different reason— was Miss Van Duzer, who taught Spanish. As a sixteen-year-old boy, with raging hormones, I had the biggest crush on her. Her cute outfits, with the flimsy, see-through blouses, drove me crazy. On many occasions, I messed up my Spanish tenses on purpose, just to have her come to my desk, lean over my shoulder, and help me get it right. In my daydreams, we traveled to Spain together, arm in arm, and I spoke perfect Spanish to everyone we met. But she got married my senior year, much to my dismay, and changed her name to Ms. Mashuda. So it was adios and *vaya con dios* for this hombre.

And then there was Mrs. Gollmar, our guidance counselor. At the beginning of my junior year, I was scheduled to see Mrs. Gollmar as part of a program for students nearing graduation. With no plans after high school except for a nebulous career at the steel mill or paper mill if or when the Teamsters came calling, I didn't expect much from this meeting. I couldn't have been more wrong (TMYKTMYDKS?). She had done her homework. She had reviewed my grades, had talked to teachers and coaches, was knowledgeable about my church contributions at Assumption, and also knew that Pat and Larry both went to college. She told me to take the Standard Achievement Test (SAT) and plan on continuing my education.

She gave me a bunch of college brochures and told me to come back in two weeks. We would discuss possible degree paths then. During this fortnight, without a word to my parents, I convinced myself that I could be a college man. Why not? I returned to Mrs. Gollmar's office and opted to apply to three universities (Pitt, Penn State, and Clarion), and also decided that, just like Larry, I wanted to seek a career in business administration. I took the SAT, did pretty well, and submitted all three applications. Then, and only then, did I tell my mother what my plans were after high school. (Note: I got accepted to all three schools. Penn State was too expensive, Pitt would mean living at home—ugh!—so I selected Clarion State College, now Clarion University —the exact school that Mrs. Gollmar had recommended months earlier.)

Of course, Mom was not too crazy about my decision to attend college. I guess I should have expected her reaction, since I was still stinging from her comments about forgoing college and looking for a job. To me, if Pat and Larry were good enough for college, so was I. Perhaps my mother was afraid of being left behind by another kid, or worried about how to handle all the family problems with less support from her children. Or maybe she couldn't possibly imagine how they could afford to pay the tuition. (Dad was ill, Otto's had closed and left us in a tight spot, so the pressure was on.) But I made it clear to my mother that I would pay my own way and seek as much financial aid as I could find. I also promised that I would get a job and start saving right away.

This was also about the time I began to drift from the Catholic Church. I still went to Mass on Sundays, but that was about it. The world was changing; there was fighting in the streets over the Vietnam War, boys were burning draft cards, and girls were burning bras. The "new normal" was to disagree with all types of authority, from parents and military, to politicians and religion. Alcohol and drugs—mainly marijuana—were also on the rise, bringing about a whole new set of realities for kids in the 1970s. It became very uncool to talk about religion, so I didn't. I began to skip confession and communion altogether, and purposely showed up late for Mass, which meant that I had to sit or stand in the back. This was by design—from there, I could sprint out of the church as soon as the body and blood of Christ was consecrated. It was commonly known to Catholic kids that if you stayed through the consecration, you got credit for attending an entire Mass. And if you stood in the back, you could slip out of the church without any nuns or ushers seeing you. Finally, with the Catholic Church's opinions on birth control and abortion so unpopular, it's easy to see why there was a mass exodus of young Catholics from organized religion. In the end, I became part of the disenchanted.

Energized by Mrs. Gollmar, I needed money for college. So I hit the workforce pretty hard during my last two years of high school. I had already been delivering papers (*North Hill News Record*) and also had my regulars— mowing lawns in the summer and shoveling snow in the winter. I tracked down and filled out every type of grant and loan application I could find. (One good thing about a low-income family: the chances of getting financial aid were greatly improved.)

Determined that I would pay my own way through college, I found a job at Winky's, a McDonald's-type clone. It was located on Ohio River Boulevard in Avalon. I became quite the food handler, running the register, flipping burgers, chopping up salads, and making doughnuts. (Making doughnuts was not as easy as you might think.) But I also cleaned toilets, swept and mopped floors, and emptied and scoured deep fryers. Cleaning a deep-fryer vat is a disgusting chore. The oil goes everywhere, and you *never* get all of it off the floor. When Winky's closed my senior year (oil-spill incident?), I was lucky enough to find another job right down the street in a carpet warehouse. My job was to draw carpet from the shelves, cut it to specifications, and load it onto trucks. It was good work and decent pay. My savings account at Mellon Bank was beginning to grow. Although the warehouse is gone, there is now a restaurant there, owned by the same guy, called Anthony's. I think one of our high-school reunions was held there. (I'm not sure which one, because I missed the five-, ten-, fifteen-, twenty-, and twenty-five-year reunions; the only one I ever made was the thirtieth—the one with all my brothers and sisters. I guess I wasn't much of a nostalgic type.)

I wasn't much of a ladies' man in high school either. Between sports, church activities, work, and class, there wasn't much time for dating. Lucky for me, I met my first girlfriend, Nancy Novak, in tenth grade, and we dated until after my graduation. She was one year younger than me, sweet and pretty, and was one of the Avalon High Letterettes (similar to majorettes, with school flags instead of batons). Looking back, we were definitely naïve about sex and moved very slowly in high school. Low on money, most of our dates were hanging around the Novak household, watching TV and waiting for her family to retire for the evening so we could fool around on the couch. Rarely getting past second base, it was very exciting because it was new for both of us.

I was very shy and felt more comfortable away from the spotlight. For example, as the captain of the football team, I had the pleasure of escorting Gail Lucas, our homecoming queen, to the homecoming dance. She was gorgeous, and I was so nervous that I almost threw up walking her through the crowd. My shyness really held me back with girls. For instance, well before I met Nancy, I had a crush on a fellow student named Diane James. But I never got up enough courage to speak to her. She was one of the cool kids, and I wasn't. Even now, decades later, when Tom Atkinson (reunion organizer) contacts me about an upcoming event, I always ask if Diane will be there. If I ever do run into her, I'll probably be a babbling idiot anyway. Why is it that things in high school stay with us for so long?

By the time graduation day arrived, I was in full rebellion mode and dead set against attending the ceremony. When I got accepted to Clarion State College, located just twenty-five miles south of Bob's Little Indian hunting camp, I enrolled in summer classes that started around the same time as my graduation. I had already been to the campus for orientation, secured a dormitory room, and landed a work-study job in the library. Coming back to Pittsburgh just for the ceremony was the last thing I wanted to do. But believe it or not, my parents wanted me there, so I showed up. During a practice run, I was advised by one of the administrators that my hair was too long, and if I didn't get it cut, I would be removed from the procession. Of course, I refused. To me, it was too late to tell this student what to do. High school was over; my head, and my hair, were elsewhere. I held the cards either way — in or out of the ceremony, it really didn't matter to me. But after listening to a lecture or two about appropriate dress standards, I was ultimately allowed to participate. (For the record: Tom Dominytus, "TD" as we called him, had the longest hair.) Just to stir the pot, right before the procession started, I took off my dress shoes and put on my black-and-white Converse tennis shoes. *I'll teach them a little about dress standards* ... Man, I really enjoyed pissing off the graduation committee. It was one last antic to top off the special day. Of course, upsetting my parents was also fun—in fact, it was sort of my primary job in those days.

So long, high school.

CHAPTER THREE

One Hundred and Ninety-Two

————————◆○◆————————

Being on my own in college was one of the most uplifting experiences of my early life: no parents, no curfew, no dress code, no football practice, no fryers to scour, no Mass to attend, no lawns to mow, no snow to shovel, no bathrooms to clean, and so on. I was on my own—*I'll show everyone that I can be a college guy.*

There were two sessions in the summer semester at Clarion State College, and you could take up to two courses each. I was assigned Accounting I and Accounting II for the first session, and Economics I and Economics II in the second session. As I look back on this schedule, I wonder why in the heck I didn't change classes. How are you supposed to know Accounting II principles when you are learning Accounting I terminology at the same time? And studying macroeconomics and microeconomics at the same time is crazy. But everything else was going great, so I decided to go with the flow. Clarion was predominantly a teachers college, with a large School of Business Administration. And the majority of teaching majors were female. That meant that the girl-to-guy ratio was excellent if you were a male. The fraternity parties were never-ending, the beer was cheap, and the girls were a blast. Slowly at first, then more and more over time, I began to shed my shyness and became much more outgoing (maybe the ratio and the beer helped). Nancy and I had drifted apart. Avalon was a thousand miles away, and I felt like the proverbial kid in a candy store. The summer flew by; I had the time of my life, and ended the semester with a whopping 1.5 GPA (two Cs and two Ds).

From graduation to probation in three months! Suddenly I had to face the fact that my mom was right and I wasn't college material. *Am I slated for a life working in a Pittsburgh mill after all? It could be a good life,* I rationalized, *with decent pay and incentives. I still have my family and many friends there. The humiliation and loss of face will recede over time, right?* So, with a huge swallow of pride, I headed back home to live with my mother and await the Holy Grail of opportunities—a nebulous job at an unspecified mill—to define my life.

Back at home in Avalon, I needed a job as soon as possible. I had to get out of the house and wanted to avoid the "I told you so" innuendos I was getting from my mother. Lucky for me, Larry was in the middle of a management trainee program with Sears and Roebuck, and was assigned to the store in Allegheny Center Mall in Pittsburgh. He was able to get me a job as a stock boy, and I was glad to have it. I didn't want to think about what had just happened at Clarion or where I was going in the future. For now, stocking shelves and unloading trucks was my life. And it wasn't half-bad. Sure, the pay sucked and my back was killing me at the end of each shift, but I had a job, that is, some kind of purpose. There were two of us: Manny, a middle-aged Afro-American guy, who had been working there for years, and me. Over the next few months, we started to get friendlier and talked about everything from sports to the new girls in the store. (One of the girls, Helen—from the optical shop—was of special interest to me. We dated off and on for a few years. She was great—cute and funny.) One day during a break in the little lunchroom, I asked, "Manny, how long have you been doing this job?"

"Thirteen years. Why?"

"I don't know. I mean, how can you do this every day, you know, the same thing over and over?" I said, with as much tact as a freight train.

"I have three kids, and a wife. It all happened so fast—and here I am. Anyway, I like it here. Decent pay and benefits, short commute, and low stress most of the time. What about you?" Manny asked.

"I was going to college at Clarion, went on academic probation my first semester, and decided to quit and face the fact that I'm not college material." Then Manny paused, just a little too long, and said, "Listen to me, boy. You're crazy. This isn't your life, working at Sears. Get your ass back to school. You don't want to spend the rest of your life feeling like a quitter, moping about what could have been. I took this job out of necessity, and I'm stuck with it. Don't put yourself in the same situation. Think about it, okay?

Come on, let's get back to work."

As I was riding home that afternoon on the #16 bus (the streetcars were gone—so much for progress), I couldn't get Manny's advice out of my head. (It wasn't just his words; there was a quiet desperation in his tone that sounded familiar, but from where?) *Will I spend the rest of my life unhappy, thinking I'm a quitter? Do I want to humiliate myself again by going back to school and failing?* I can recall exactly how lonely I felt that day.

Weeks later, still feeling alone and confused, I went up into my makeshift bedroom in the attic and cried for only the third time in my life. My dad heard me and came up the stairs.

"What is it, Don?

"Dad, why should I care about college? You know Mom thinks I should get a job and start a family."

"Look at me," he said in a tone I had not heard before. "Do you really want your life to be like mine? Do you see these hands?" (Note: His hands were always full of cuts, scrapes, and burns from all the hot machinery.) "I've been employed in the same job, working on the same machine, and doing exactly the same thing every day for thirty years," he said. "Is this what you want in life? Go back to school—make something of yourself. You don't want this life, Don."

Bam! The SSE hit me right between the eyes. I don't ever recall my dad letting his guard down like that. He was one tough Irishman. The only similar event I can remember was the time we went hunting at the Little Indian. But this was different. He opened himself up and basically said the last person in the world I wanted to be was him. And then it hit me. The silent desperation I mentioned—it was him. It was *his* life all along that caused me to feel this emotion. A cold wind ran through my bones. I knew how much it must have hurt him to denigrate himself in an effort to motivate me. And it did. I'll never forget it. I swore that day—right there in the attic—that I would complete my degree if it was the last thing I ever did.

With Dad's singularly significant event permanently filed away in my head, I bolted back to Clarion. (As I look back over my life—*this book is forcing me to do this*—I consider Dad's self-deprecating advice to be among the most important moments of my life. (I *was* college material! My dad said so!) Loaded with resolve, I hit the books, got off probation the following term, and never had to worry about that again. The next three and a half years of college went by quickly, filled with arrested adolescence. My life, like that of many college kids, was a combination of school, work, and partying—not necessarily in that order. College was a blur of beer and pot, and friends and teachers. My friends and I attended all the fraternity rush parties, pretending to be interested in pledging. But that was never the case—we were GDIs (goddamn independents), and we never wanted to join a fraternity. We enjoyed the parties and met lots of girls that we invited to our own soirees. We were definitely not interested in living in a house full of rowdy guys. I was self-actualizing for the first time in my life, enjoying all of my new friends and doing pretty well with the ladies. Who needed fraternities? That whole setup always seemed a little weird to me. Groucho Marx said it best: "I refuse to join any club that would have me as a member."

The town of Clarion, located in Clarion County, is located along Interstate 80, exit 10, between Grove City and Dubois, Pennsylvania. The school is about a hundred miles northeast of Pittsburgh, and had a 2010 population of 5,276. It's a small, beautiful town, with rolling hills of green and the deepest, bluest river you've ever seen. The center of all activity is the university, with ivied walls and huge, beautiful trees. Clarion draws thousands of people each year for the Autumn Leaf Festival, a remarkable time to be there. The vibrant colors of the trees are legendary. The event also hosts a large parade, which culminates the festival. I remember one year, my buddy Nolen decided to enter a float in the parade. The theme was patriotism. So he made a large paper-mache head of Uncle Sam drinking a beer and mounted it on his old rusty car! (We tried to get him to at least wash it, but he wouldn't.) By design, it was an eyesore, to say the least. Of course, they wouldn't let him enter the float. But Nolen was not deterred. He waited until none of the officials were looking, and we bolted right into the procession. Imagine—the two of us, drinking beer, howling laughing, and waving to the crowd like we were stars in the Macy's Thanksgiving Parade. And just above our heads, Uncle Sam was getting smashed! Unfortunately, we had to bail before the end of the parade to avoid local authorities who were waiting for us.

My roommate Jake was also a little crazy, and I was proud to have him as my friend. He came from a wealthy family, and his dad owned a swimming and tennis club in Penn Hills—a very nice suburb of Pittsburgh. Jake loved to have fun and was an outrageous Pittsburgh Penguin hockey fan. His dad had four season tickets, right on the red line, just above the glass. We wined and dined with the VIPs during intermissions. Jake knew many of the players, and we even partied with them a few times. Jake was short and stocky, and a competitive swimmer (butterfly) for Clarion's swim team. I never saw him lose. He had the same pattern in every race, that is, he'd fall behind early, and then make a mad dash at the end of the race to eke out the win. He always denied it, but we thought he did it to show off in front of his friends.

I have a million stories about Jake, but I'll just mention a couple. He didn't go to class much, and was only there at Clarion to swim. His long-range plan was to take over his dad's club, and he needed some college swimming experience on his resume. So he was always trying to get me to cut class. It usually went like this:

"Hey, Don, let's go see the Penguins tonight."

"I can't. I have a test tomorrow and a paper due in two days," I said, knowing this was a losing battle. "Where are they playing?"

"Toronto," he said, and off we went.

On another occasion, we were on our way to Atlanta to watch a hockey game. (Yes, all the way to Georgia from northern Pennsylvania to watch one hockey game.) Jake had a brand-new 1973 canary-yellow Corvette Stingray, with the famed T-Top. Man, what a car. We were flying down Route 77 in West Virginia when a state trooper appeared out of nowhere, with lights flashing and sirens engaged. This was a problem, because we had already drank half a case of Stroh's, and the cans were all over the floor. (With no backseat, we had nowhere else to put the empties.) We pulled off the road and awaited our fate. With cans ankle-deep on my side of the car, we heard a door slam and saw the state trooper walking toward us. I remember thinking, *that's it—we're going to end up in jail somewhere in the backwoods of West Virginia.* And just like that, a vehicle suddenly shot by us going at least one hundred miles an hour! The trooper spun on his heels, ran back to his car, and roared around us in pursuit of the speeding car. (It was like getting a reprieve from the governor.) After a few moments of stunned silence, we drove the speed limit after that and stopped at the next rest area to dump beer cans. We vowed on the spot that we would never put ourselves in that situation again. That lasted until we crossed the West Virginia border. We celebrated our luck with a few cold ones.

The next escapade didn't directly involve Jake, but happened on the way to his house. It was my sophomore year, and I was on the parkway going east at night, heading to Jake's. Just before his exit, I noticed many construction signs directing vehicles to slow down to twenty-five miles an hour. Three lanes were being funneled into one. When I glanced in my rearview mirror, the only vehicle I saw was a tractor trailer about eight hundred yards behind me. So I slowed and guided my 1967 Firebird into the right lane. Moments later, I was horrified when I saw the truck immediately behind me—and it was barreling at full speed! The rest was kind of hazy. The impact was severe. I shot upward, then landed and began to roll over. And for some reason, I dove under the dashboard as the car began to roll. I don't know how many times it turned over, but it eventually landed on its wheels. Amazingly, with my adrenaline surging, I squeezed out of the car on the passenger side. The roof on the driver's side was smashed all the way down to the seat back. Had I been wearing a seat belt, I would have been cut in half.

I ran toward the truck driver, daring him to get out of his cab. I was ready to kick the shit out of him. Then the shock caught up to me, and I collapsed. He called the police, and soon there were all kinds of people and vehicles present, and an EMT checking me out. I was okay. The truck driver was very apologetic and said over and over he'd do whatever he could to make this right. We settled out of court, and he paid me handsomely for the totaled Firebird. (Since I got the car from my brother Larry, he insisted he should get half of the settlement. What could I do? I gave him half.) For years afterward, I thought about those few seconds of terror. And how close I came to dying. That fear was real, and it stayed with me for a long time. It reminded me of a quote by authoress Carrie Ryan, "Survivors aren't always the strongest; sometimes they're the smartest, but more often simply the luckiest."

Over spring break of that same year, Jake and I headed to his summer home in Apopka, Florida. It's located between Daytona Beach and Orlando. During our first day there, his dad called from Puerto Rico and asked him to come over and help with a construction project he was overseeing. Jake took off and left me the keys to the Corvette, a credit card for gas, and a house key. He said he'd see me in two weeks. (On the counter in the kitchen were two season passes to Disney World.) Man, I had a blast.

The work-study program at Clarion was an excellent way for students in financial need to ease the cost of tuition and board. I worked at the Carlson Library, located right in the center of the campus, until I graduated in 1975. It was a great experience. But you had to earn your stripes. The first year, all I did was shelve books for hours on end, using the Dewey Decimal System— we converted to the Library of Congress System later. By my second year, I got to work the circulation desk and the checkout counter. The latter was a gold mine for meeting girls. Since everyone came through the library, I had the ideal spot. I was required to review all college ID cards when checking out books and got to know many of my fellow students. When my roommates and I threw parties (which was a lot), I would keep fliers under the desk and carefully invite certain female students as they were leaving the library. We knew from past experience that when girls came to parties, guys would follow. And we had some great parties. In fact, I remember fraternity houses asking us when our next party would be, so they could avoid scheduling theirs for the same night.

By my third year, I was mainly on the circulation desk, and filled in occasionally in the reference library. This was where the real action was, and where I developed a deep affection for reading, and books in general. (When we left the State Department in 2013, Andi and I donated thousands of books to charity. Looking back, I really regret that we didn't keep them.) Without this job, room and board would have left me starving to death. I will always be grateful for that library job, and to the red-hot circulation-desk manager—a thirtysomething who taught me a thing or two about romance as well!

But not all was well in 1972. The war in Vietnam was still raging, and college deferments were revoked. As an eighteen-year-old, I waited with great anxiety for the draft selection numbers to start. Many of my friends and I stayed up all night drinking, but we sobered up fast when we walked into the student union. Up on the wall were 365 numbers, with blank spaces next to each one. In a few minutes, birth dates would be called and placed alongside each number, starting with number one. (It felt like a scene from the movie *Logan's Run*, where people were removed from society solely because of their age.) The theory was simple: the lower the number, the higher the chance of being drafted and sent to Vietnam. What really made this nerve-racking was the timing. By late 1972, no one really believed that Vietnam would end well. To be sent there at this stage would be outrageous and devastating. One of my friends, Charlie Hughes, drew the very first number! He left school soon afterward, and I never heard from him again. (Hope you're okay, buddy.) My roommate Jake drew a huge number, something like 362. Talk about opposite emotions! While Charlie was crushed and left the student union in tears, Jake was joking that the government "would send blind people and nuns before they'd send me." (In a cruel twist of fate, Jake died of cancer in his late twenties. I was devastated. The last time I saw him, he was in so much pain that he was prescribed medical marijuana. I pulled out my guitar; we smoked some grass and sang some songs together. I still miss him.)

Me? I was number 192, and the date was October 23. Over the next twelve months, the government drafted "lucky winners" who had to quit school and travel to beautiful Vietnam. This life-changing decision was based solely on random numbers drawn against birth dates. If you were under 122, you were drafted. My number was 192, so I dodged the bullet. Years later, while teaching at the Air Force Academy, I began every class on Vietnam with the number 192 written on the blackboard. I asked my cadets to guess what it meant. No one ever figured it out. I guess it was ancient history to them, but not to me.

With the draft out of the way, we could now concentrate on important things—like having fun. One of our favorite pastimes was smoking pot. It was everywhere. Anyone who tells you they didn't smoke pot in the 1970s— or didn't inhale—is giving you a crock of bullshit. It was new and exciting. It made you laugh so hard you had tears in your eyes. It made even a box of macaroni and cheese taste like a five-star meal. And it made music sound almost like a religious experience. It was relatively inexpensive, kept many underage students out of the bars, and was the catalyst for many stories. I remember one night hanging out in a buddy's apartment; we were smoking and playing chess. On a normal move, George took my pawn with his knight, and knocked it to the side of the board in a swinging gesture. The piece slid almost a foot and stood up on its side. This wooden pawn was shaped like a small bowling pin. It was rounded on the sides and had no fulcrum, or central point, to make it stop in that position. We stared at it for several moments. Finally, it fell back down. For the rest of our time at Clarion—over two years—we challenged anyone to make that pawn stand on its side. No one could do it. And forget about sliding the piece across the board; we even allowed challengers to place the pawn directly on the board. No dice. Maybe pot had something to do with it, but we talked about this incident for years. (I wonder if we would have noticed if we hadn't been stoned.)

In spite of all the fun, there were drawbacks to pot. I'm embarrassed to say this, but I remember more than once running to the window just to see if I got my car home okay. And we usually mixed beer with pot, magnifying the effect. I recall one situation where this combination almost killed us. I was dating a girl named Joyce, and my buddy Dan had just met a new girl (I can't remember her name). He wanted to go parking down by the Clarion River above a scenic lookout—more like a cliff —about two hundred feet above the water. We were all stoned and sipping on a few beers when Dan found a good spot on top of a hill and parked. Within moments, we felt the car moving ever so slightly. Joyce and I, lying in the backseat, were giggling and thinking Dan was making his move. Suddenly we realized the car was rolling downhill, toward the scenic overlook! It was pitch black outside. I jumped up from my seat and yelled at Dan to hit the brake. His girlfriend was lying on top of him, and he was scrambling to get up. I grabbed her by her waist, tossed her sideways into the passenger door, and screamed again for him to hit the brake. At this exact point, we heard gravel stones. We knew immediately what that meant. We were in an area near the cliff used by visitors to stop and enjoy the view—this was not good. An instant later, Dan finally hit the brake, and we began a long slide. We all froze and waited for one of two things to happen: either the car would stop in a grinding lurch, or the sounds of the cobblestones would disappear, which would mean that we were airborne. Mercifully, we finally came to a halt.

"Don't anybody move," I screamed. "I am going to get out of the car very slowly and see where we are." I eased out of my backseat position and exited the car. Starting at the front door, I slid my foot forward inch by inch along the side of the car. When I was still standing on terra firma when I reached the front bumper, I called to Dan, "Turn on the lights." He did. We were roughly *seven feet* from the abyss! Dan slowly backed up, and we sat motionless, not saying a word, for a long time. There are times in life when fear can be so strong that it freezes you in that moment. My hands are sweating right now. I can still feel the fear, that expectation of soaring into the air, and into the Clarion River, and finally into nothingness.

Of course, I was still heading home every other weekend or so to help Mom take care of things. Grandma Jones passed away, and my mother had her hands full with my dad. The second lung operation was brutal and placed very high stress on his heart. The strokes would soon follow. I finally began to see how tough my mother's life was, and tried to make things better between us. I knew I'd never be the "number-one son," her nickname for Larry, but I tried to improve our relationship. It just wasn't in the cards, though. We loved each other, but we just didn't love being around each other.

Summers in college meant one thing—time to head home and get a job. Ironically, I finally got that mill job I sought in Pittsburgh. It was at the Saint Regis Paper Mill, located in what was called the "strip district." The area was full of steel and paper mills, produce companies, trucking firms, endless warehouses, and rust—lots of rust everywhere. Its close proximity to the Allegheny River, and numerous rail lines, made it ideal for the movement of heavy cargo. Although the city was well on its way to renovating the downtown area, the strip district was still the pits. (Today it's a thriving tourist area, with eclectic shops and restaurants carved into the old buildings.) I worked on a machine called the corrugator, which was seventy-five yards long. It turned tree products into pulp, and eventually into cardboard. My job was to remove the finished cardboard sheets from the end of the corrugator and stack them on pallets. That's it. Nothing else. Here's how it worked: we labored in teams of two, exactly mirroring each other. We'd slide a pile of cardboard from the conveyer belt onto its side, and then stack it vertically, like a giant deck of cards. Then we'd swing the giant deck onto a pallet. If either man flinched or was off with his timing, the other would get sliced with paper cuts. (I remember many times feeling the intense pain of these cuts on my arms and hands, especially during a shower.) It was grueling and very hot, but I was finally a Teamster, and making more money than I ever did before.

We received incentive pay, or piecework, based on how much product we moved. So all the other stackers, who were mostly family men, ran like hell all day to earn additional salary. We usually skipped our breaks, but the shop steward made us shut down for lunch. As the only college worker in the group, I was the "gofer." Just before lunch each day, I would run— yes, run—a quarter mile to the parking lot, get my car, and wait at the front door. Exactly at 11:30 a.m., five stackers would hop in my car, and we'd drive a couple of blocks to Paske's, a local bar. The bartender would have the sandwich of the day and cold beers waiting for us. We had exactly eighteen minutes to eat our lunch, drink six beers each, and be back on the corrugator by noon! So here I am, half-drunk, handling razor-sharp cardboard, in a factory with the temperature over 120 degrees, trying to keep up with the other stackers. (In case you wonder why we didn't wear gloves or protective clothing, ask the shop steward, who lost several fingers in the conveyor belt when his sleeve got stuck.)

But I was making tons of money and was excited when my first payday arrived. I had worked lots of overtime, and even volunteered to come in on Saturdays to steam clean the corrugator. When I saw my check, I almost cried. It was $55.54. I immediately sought out the shop steward.

"Bob, there must be some mistake here. I worked a full two-week schedule, with overtime and piecework. This check can't be right."

"Welcome to the Teamsters, son," he said. "It's our policy to collect annual union dues immediately. Your dues are paid up for the year."

"Yeah, but I'm a summer hire and will be leaving in three months. I really don't think it's fair. What can I do about it?"

"You can quit," he said, and walked away. This Teamsters Local was a closed shop, which means you have to join the union or you're dismissed. When I asked one of the stackers why I wasn't told this before, he said they rarely say anything to college kids ahead of time, because they'll quit. He argued, and he was right, that no kid would quit after paying the dues. And the stackers needed me, not just to drive the getaway car at lunch, but to be there through the summer. This allowed them to stagger their vacation times, with yours truly as the backup plan.

When the summer was over, I headed back to school with some serious cash in my pocket, minus my union ID card, which was blowing around somewhere on Interstate 79. It was time for fun again, and I wasted no time finding it. I moved into an old restaurant, called Cherico's, just off the main street in Clarion. It was an eclectic place with restaurant tables, large open areas, and a kitchen full of refrigerators and ovens. The only heat came from one giant ceiling blower, so all the prefab rooms didn't have ceilings. There were five of us, and only four bedrooms. The kitchen was huge, so I strung up some rope in the corner and attached a few blankets— my bedroom was complete.

Cherico's was a fantastic place for parties. It was right in the middle of town and had an unusualness that was very popular. We had some legendary events there. By now, I had fine-tuned my skills at the library checkout counter, so our turnouts were huge. Drinking, dancing, smoking, meeting girls—it was a long way from the paper mill. We had a friend; I'll call him Paul, who was quite the womanizer. He had a fiancée at home, but managed to date constantly at Clarion at the same time. I asked him during one of our parties what he would do if he got caught fooling around. I'll never forget his response:

"Three things, Don," Paul said. "Deny, deny, deny."

"But what if you get caught red-handed, in bed, with another woman?" said I, with an acute interest in his reply.

"The same. I'm sure I'd be able to deny it happened."

You can guess what occurred next. A few months later, his girlfriend, call her Martha, drove up to Clarion to surprise him. Two guesses where she found him—in the sack with another woman. What did he do? He spun a story about comforting the girl because she was sick, and that he accidently fell asleep; he then convinced her that the girl was dating one of his roommates, and he would *never* turn on his roommate. Finally, he feigned disappointment that she didn't trust him, which really hurt his feelings, and so on. You get the picture. She was apologizing to him by the afternoon.

On another occasion, Paul and Martha were heading home from a club in Pittsburgh, and it was really late. Paul stopped for gas. At 8:00 a.m. the next morning, Martha's dad called Paul and was screaming at him for leaving her in the middle of the night! As it turned out, Martha went to use the restroom, and when she came out, Paul was gone. (Note: The area where he left her was not ideal.) Believe it or not, he drove home, went to bed, and never once remembered that he left his fiancée at a gas station at 4:00 a.m.!

The Cherico house was a blast, with tons of characters. One guy, George, was our resident drug pusher. His collection of weed and other substances was legendary. (Me, I was just interested in pot.) Another friend, Joe, the quietest guy I knew, could take massive amounts of LSD and never show any outward change in behavior. Until one night, when he climbed on top of the furniture and screamed, "I am God, and you are all my disciples!" We teased him mercilessly for a long time about that. Then there was Nolen, the "Uncle Sam" parade crasher. Of course we had Charlie, before he got drafted, who was a big guy, but not muscular. His forte? He was unbeatable at arm wrestling. At a fraternity party one time, we had money on Charlie. His opponent was a jock, with muscles everywhere. We cleared out the room and put a small table and two chairs in the middle. Someone called "go!" and the match started. For a few seconds, they appeared to be in a stalemate. Then Charlie said, "Are you pushing?" and slammed the guy's arm so hard onto the table that you could hear it pop. We grabbed our spoils and ran, narrowly avoiding an all-out brawl.

But all good things must end. It was time to leave my crazy friends. Graduation was right around the corner. I had all the credits I needed to get my degree and couldn't afford to hang around for the five-and six-year programs that many of my buddies pursued. Of course, I skipped the graduation ceremony, mainly because none of my family was interested in coming to it. It was time to go back to Pittsburgh and begin my working career.

CHAPTER FOUR

"Maybe I should have called tails."

———◦———

Returning back to Pittsburgh in 1975 was really rough. I had no money, so I moved in with my mother. My dad was very seriously ill and would pass away in a year. Unemployment and inflation were at double-digit rates, and my degree didn't seem to mean anything to potential employers. I tried a short stint with Rite Aid, the pharmaceutical firm, as a management trainee. They sent me to Somerset, Pennsylvania, near Seven Springs, to begin my training. The pay was horrible, and the hours were long. (How ironic that I ended up working for a drug company after getting high almost every day for three years. Even better, I passed a polygraph test as well.) Luckily for me, I used to date a girl in Somerset, so I was able to get a cheap rental there. She was no longer around, but her family was glad to help out. Unfortunately, this management-trainee program was nothing but a glorified stock-boy position. I worked the register, swept up and down the aisles once in a while, cleaned the bathrooms—wait a minute, *am I back at Winky's again?* I quit after six weeks.

Left with few options, I started painting houses for a local subcontractor back in Pittsburgh. Good use of my degree, right? In the introduction to this book, I talked about living on five continents. But here I was, a house painter, twenty-two years old, never living anywhere but Pittsburgh, settling into a life of quiet desperation—much like my dad—and fully expecting to live and die in western Pennsylvania. Getting the big union job "someday" was still the ideal. The majority of homes in Pittsburgh were older, very large, and constructed almost entirely out of wood. That meant using all kinds of ladders and painstakingly scraping paint off the exterior inch by inch. This was backbreaking work, and especially difficult on a freezing winter day. Other than Sachon, Korea (a bare-base operation during my military service—more details later), I have never been colder in my life than when I was dangling from those ladders.

In the introduction I also mentioned that I was a slow learner and needed to be "pulled along by people and events." One day in the fall of

1975, at a nearby bar called Sunny Jim's, I experienced the first small tug—a woman named Jill Richard. She was at the pool table, beating everybody in the room. I had played tons of pool at Clarion and was on top of my game around that time. We played, and I beat her two out of three. She was not happy. (In later years, she would win air force–wide billiard competitions. Glad I wasn't playing her then.) Not only beautiful, she was confident and very competitive, which definitely attracted me to her. We started talking and really hit it off well. She had graduated from Avonworth High School, in Ben Avon—one borough west of Avalon. Although we never met in high school, we knew each other through mutual acquaintances. We fell into a serious relationship quickly, and loved to shoot pool, play tennis, and party with our friends. It was a great diversion from my dad's health problems and my woeful painting career. She was waitressing at a nearby restaurant, and like me, not enthusiastic about her life thus far. After a few months, one thing led to another, and we discussed getting a place together. We had fallen in love and wanted to take the next step.

With limited income, we found a second-story apartment on Grant Street in Bellevue, which is the borough just east of Avalon. (Quite the rolling stone so far, right?) It was a dump, and our jobs sucked —but we were young and living on love. After a long day of working *nothingness*, we really enjoyed our evenings together, either alone or with friends. We partied almost every day, mostly drinking and smoking pot, and life was relatively uneventful. But things were about to change.

Jill's family was not happy about their daughter "living in sin" with a pot-smoking housepainter. They were really putting the heat on her to move out or to get married. I remember once Jill told me that if she didn't move out, her family would consider her dead! This put me in a tight spot, because Jill was very close to her parents. There were other dynamics in play as well. *How do we handle an ultimatum like this? Shouldn't there be a middle ground? Do we have enough money to get married? Would either one of us want to get married if we weren't being coerced? Shouldn't we wait until we find more reliable employment?*

In early 1976, after discussing this issue over and over again, we finally reached a decision to get married. I never proposed. She never accepted. We just mutually agreed, based on the facts laid out in front of us, that matrimony was the solution, that is, the path of least resistance, sort of like the flow of running water. In retrospect, we should have realized right then and there that a decision of this magnitude should have been made solely by us, without interference from family members. (To this day, I resent Jill's parents for pressuring us into marriage.) We set the date for July 3, 1976, and planned for the reception to run past midnight and into the bicentennial— the two hundredth birthday of the United States of America.

We got married in her family's Lutheran church (and yes, I was back in the good graces of the Richards). Although I just excommunicated myself from the Roman Catholic Church by marrying elsewhere, I really didn't care. In my mind, I did what everybody wanted me to do—get married to Jill. I was off the hook. The reception was a blast, and many of our friends stayed well past midnight. The men in the wedding party donned red-white-and-blue bow ties that blinked off and on to commemorate the bicentennial. And unlike most receptions, this bride and groom stayed around until the last guest left, which happened to coincide with the closing of the cash-free bar.

Okay, the deed was done. I was a married man, with a good woman, and our honeymoon was just around the corner. We bought a car and headed to the west coast to visit Jill's relatives. It was a wonderful experience! Just some of the memories included visiting the Space Needle, and walking along Discovery Park in Seattle; touring the Olympia brewery, and pounding down beers at the end of the tour; dining at a restaurant on Fisherman's Wharf in San Francisco; walking down Rodeo Drive in Los Angeles, and wondering how anyone could afford that stuff; people watching and chilling at a café on Santa Monica Beach; and navigating around Tijuana, Mexico, looking for deals. I also remember how warm it was driving through Montana, shirtless, with windows open, even though the entire horizon was covered in snow. And finally, traveling to Yellowstone National Park, where we rented a couple of horses. I have very fond memories of a driving rainstorm, and the two of us riding those horses as fast as they wanted to run and holding on for dear life!

But it wasn't a glamorous trip. We mostly slept in the front and backseats of our car, or used our sleeping bags and crashed off the road somewhere. When we did get a hotel room, it was usually a Motel 6 or equivalent. It was the first time we ever did any traveling together, and it was exciting. One night while we were passing through Utah, we found a good place to crash well off the highway. Just as we were settling into our sleeping bags, the following happened:

"Who goes there?" a voice from the woods exclaimed.

"Uh, um, hello," I said with great glibness while scrambling to pick up our things and toss them into the car.

"What are you doing on my property? I could have you arrested for trespassing. I'm asking you again—what are you doing on my property?"

While I had visions of pellet guns and angry dogs, Jill took control of the situation. She was the kind of beauty that never paid traffic tickets. She said; "We are very sorry, sir. We just got married, and we are on our honeymoon. We don't have much money, and we were hoping to avoid paying for a hotel tonight by using our sleeping bags. We'll leave right away." Then she dramatically started to pack up our gear, cleverly making the farmer feel guilty for tossing newlyweds out into the dark night.

"Get your things together, and follow me to the main house," he said gently. And we did. The house was gigantic. He put us in a huge guest bedroom, with a private shower and bath. He told us to clean up and come down for dinner. We shared a beautiful meal with him and his wife, two elderly Mormons, and slept like babies that night. In the morning, when we came downstairs, there were fresh coffee and homemade muffins on the counter. But the Mormon couple was gone. They made a moral judgment about us and decided to leave complete strangers alone in their house! (To this day, I'll never forget how good it felt to be trusted by them.) We found a nice note encouraging us to help ourselves to breakfast—there were eggs, bacon, and so on in the refrigerator. After breakfast, we left a thank-you letter, took one last look around, and hit the road. I'm sorry I don't remember their names. But I'll never forget them. It was a random act of kindness, plain and simple, by a couple of good Samaritans, who asked for nothing from us in return.

Writing about this uplifting incident reminded me of a similar act of kindness that happened to me several years earlier. I was eighteen, and my brother John was in the army, stationed in Augsburg, Germany. He invited me to come visit, found me a cheap military carrier, and off I went. I had never been on a plane, so that was really something. (Note: The trip required me to stop for one day in Iceland, but I didn't mind. It was beautiful and cold.) John and I weren't real close in high school, so I was hoping this trip would help draw us closer. And it did—we had a blast. After a few days with John, I left Augsburg to bounce around Europe with my student Euro Pass. Sleeping on the trains, I saw a lot of Germany and parts of France and the Netherlands, and met some outrageous characters. When it was time to return to the United States, I arrived at Frankfurt Airport with pennies in my pocket and a duffel bag full of dirty clothes. And then the roof caved in.

The lady at the ticket window informed me that I was at the wrong airport and needed to get a fast taxi across town or I'd miss my flight! With exactly thirty-five cents to my name and no idea how I was going to get home, I sat down on my duffel bag and began to cry—the second time in my adult life that I remember crying. A middle-aged German, with broken English, asked me if I was okay. I explained my situation, and the rest, as they say, is history. He scooped up my bag, and we ran to his Mercedes. He shot across town, deftly using every shortcut possible, and we arrived at the correct airport terminal about nine minutes before the scheduled takeoff. He told me to head to the gate, grabbed my bag, and ran toward the ticket counter. I didn't have time to think or even worry about my luggage. I just yelled, "Thank you, sir," as he bolted down the corridor. He waved back, and I ran like hell. I arrived several minutes late. Luckily, they reopened the gate door, and the airplane door as well, and escorted me onto the plane seconds before it began to back up. I felt great admiration and gratitude for this man—just like the Mormon couple in Utah. He was my hero, and someone I would never see again.

Of course, I wasn't out of the woods yet. When I landed at JFK in New York, I still had issues. *Will my bag even make it to the United States? And how will I get to Pittsburgh with thirty-five cents in my pocket?* But amazingly, it all worked out in the end. My bag arrived safely, and I walked to the first road I could find. Then I spent the next two days hitchhiking all the way back home.

Our honeymoon ended, Jill and I arrived back in Pittsburgh, and we fell into our normal routines again. However, something had already begun to change. The trip gave us two weeks together, uninterrupted by jobs and friends, and we really learned a lot about each other. The excitement of the travel, along with hours of talks about hopes and dreams, may have been the beginning of the end for the chances of surviving our current lives in Pittsburgh.

A month later, on a chilly, rainy day, Jill had just gotten home from her waitressing job. I was sitting in front of the TV, beer in hand, watching sports. I had friends coming over, and everything seemed normal. Meanwhile, Jill sat down, got up and paced around for a while, and sat down again. I knew this maneuver. She had something to say. I watched, and waited.

"We can't keep living like this," she said.

"What do you mean?"

"I mean we can't get up every day, go to our stupid jobs, and then come home every night and party. Something's got to change."

"What do you have in mind?" I said, wishing immediately that I could take that question back.

She paused, started to speak, stopped a few times, and then said the words that would change our lives forever. "I want to join the air force."

Even though I knew we were going nowhere and that we could barely pay our rent, I said, "No chance in hell. You're crazy. Join the military?" I didn't know anything about military service. Where did this come from?

She went on. "We could get better jobs, learn new skills, travel to other places, and meet new people." I'd had enough of this talk, and left for Johnny's Hideaway to enjoy a cold beverage. But she was persistent and continued this argument on and off for weeks. Over time, her arguments grew stronger, and the current state of our lives didn't help. We were miserable in our jobs, with no future in sight. We couldn't even consider raising a family. But the military? I wanted no part of it. Then one day, she made one simple statement that would change the dynamics of our plight forever.

"I'll tell you what," she said. "Let's flip a coin. What do you think?" "You're on," I said. We set up a time that Friday night—with no one else around— and she tossed the coin into the air. I called heads. To say the result of this coin toss was an SSE would be putting it mildly. My life wasn't much, but it was mine. Like many young Americans during the mid-1970s, I hated the armed services because of Vietnam. The body counts, along with stories of razing villages and killing innocent people, didn't endear the military to me.

Here in Florida, where I am semiretired, I recently met a Vietnam veteran in a bar called Coconut's, in Cocoa Beach. He went through those hellish "Nam" experiences. I asked him point-blank:

"Did your platoon ever enter a village and open fire at the inhabitants?" "Yes."

"Did you ever burn down a village?"

"Yes."

I knew I was in a very sensitive area, but I pressed on. "Did you ever rape any of the women?" "Yes."

"But why? What made you do these things?" I asked.

He was silent for several moments. He was struggling with the impossible task of describing something to me that I'd never seen and would never understand. I was a stranger, asking too many personal questions. If he had thrown his beer in my face, I would have understood.

"We were going to die there anyway. We didn't care what happened to us, or anybody else for that matter."

Looking back, I know it was a big mistake to blame the soldiers for Vietnam, and I believe Americans have learned this lesson very well. The only reason I worked for the 1972 McGovern headquarters in Clarion was that he promised to end the Vietnam War in 120 days. But I couldn't comprehend a military lifestyle. I was comfortably numb in my world, and I wasn't ready to deal with any major changes yet.

I felt lucky, real lucky, about the coin toss. This couldn't happen. Karma was on my side.

"Tails," she said.

Over the next two weeks, we visited recruiters, got physicals, took aptitude tests, and discussed how our lives would change. She scored high on mechanical/electrical, and I scored high on administration/general knowledge. She picked missile maintenance, and I went with human resources. In late November 1976, just over four months after we got married, Jill and Don Feeney took the oath at the Federal Building in downtown Pittsburgh. We were now part of the world's best military arsenal.

Jill departed for basic training at Lackland Air Force Base (AFB) just after the new year. Upon graduation, she would go to Chanute AFB, Illinois, for a fairly long technical school in missile maintenance. I didn't depart Pittsburgh for basic training until early March, with my follow-on training slated for Keesler AFB, Mississippi. I never realized it at the time, but she and I would never live together again.

It was a very difficult separation. We kept telling ourselves that things would be great when we got assigned together and were able to begin our new lives. The air force had an assignment system that involved "dream sheets," which are forms designed to list your assignment preferences. We opted for a joint-spouse assignment that was designed to keep us together. Listening to the recruiter, this seemed like a sure thing. (Did I just say that?) While we were waiting for our final assignment, I visited her at Chanute AFB a few times. She was very busy and distracted. The long separation was wearing on both of us. Since our wedding, we'd spent more time apart than together. It was too much. We fell for each other too quickly, moved in together too quickly, married too quickly, and were separated too quickly.

The final death knell for our marriage came when our assignments were finalized. She went to Malmstrom AFB, in Great Falls, Montana. I was sent to Zweibrucken Air Base, Germany. I joked often (though it really wasn't a joke) that we got our first "dream sheet" choice—earth! After a few attempts at a long-range marriage, we gave up. Jill filed for divorce, and I cosigned without argument.

Maybe I should have called tails.

Divorce is the ultimate failure. It's black-and-white, and is known to everyone who matters to you. It stays with you for life, and you can never be un-divorced. I remember attending a stress-management seminar during my State Department career. Based on thousands of participants, the study rated divorce as one of the highest levels of stress, similar to losing a family member. This was prophetic, because right around the time our divorce paperwork was being drawn up, my father passed away.

Earl Lawrence Feeney—ice-cream maker and reluctant deer hunter—dead at age fifty-one.

PART II

Growth and Development

CHAPTER FIVE

"And their brains have been mismanaged with great skill." — BOB DYLAN

———◦———

So on a cold and gloomy day in March 1977, I boarded a plane for San Antonio, the home of Lackland Air Force Base. It's located just outside the beltway, in the southwest portion of the city. Lackland AFB is the sole location for all United States Air Force enlisted Basic Military Training (BMT). I didn't know it at the time, but I would never live in Pittsburgh again. I remember flying to Texas and thinking about the strange situation I had put myself into. First, I lost a coin toss and joined the air force with Jill. Second, before I even began BMT, my divorce was imminent, making the coin toss even more ridiculous. Third, my dad had just passed away. And fourth, knowing nothing about the military, I was a few hours away from seven weeks of brain mismanagement training! I felt like I was in a Fellini movie—with black-and-white scenes spiraling in circles, which caused my mind to actually experience vertigo.

In retrospect, maybe basic training was the best thing to happen to me, because as soon as I got off the bus at Lackland, all hell broke loose! The military training instructors (TIs) were everywhere, yelling and screaming at a nervous band of misfits, myself included. We were told to stand at attention (didn't know what that was) and march (huh?) to our new home, an open-bay barracks. Try to imagine this scene—a large rectangular room, maybe two hundred feet long, with a row of barracks on each side and an aisle down the middle. Each bed had one storage chest and one small locker. And I won't even discuss the latrine situation. That's it. No privacy whatsoever. I was assigned a bed and told by screaming TIs to be ready for the toughest seven weeks of my life. And they were right. (All of a sudden, my other problems were forgotten.)

The first day was surreal, to say the least. My hair was still pretty long, and kind of my trademark. It took thirty-five seconds to change that. I was now a bald recruit, lining up cattle-style for uniform and boot fittings.

And I had masking tape with the word "Feeney" pressed against my chest. Although we were harassed the entire day, we were still on edge because we hadn't met our assigned TI yet. We finally did. As luck would have it, my flight (a unit of the United States Air Force below a squadron) had the only marine TI. He was an asshole, and coveted the role. He ran our flight ragged, constantly telling us how soft the air force was, and reminding us we'd never make it as marines. Day after day, we marched for hours in the Texas sun, purposely avoided bus transportation when it was offered, and practiced endless parade formations. There were calisthenics, firings at the rifle range, navigations through the obstacle course, gobbling down chow-hall food in record time, and the endurance of constant personal and flight inspections. Each day would end with that magical escape called sleep.

SSgt Adams (not his real name—can't remember it) loved to set people back. A "setback" starts basic training all over again, and *no one* wanted that. It wasn't uncommon to wake up one morning and find the bunk next to you vacant. Everyone knew what that meant. I distinctly remember our last morning. We were all excited, ready to go on to tech school or get together with our families. It was 5:00 a.m., all the buses were loading, and many of us had airline tickets in our hands. Suddenly SSgt Adams showed up out of nowhere, grabbed one of our flight members by the collar, and yelled very loudly, "You're not going anywhere, airman. Get your stuff. You're starting all over again. And guess what? It's your lucky day—you get me again for seven more weeks." All of our hearts sank as we watched a grown man break down, sobbing as he was taken away.

Of course, some setbacks were warranted. We had this one guy in the flight, from Tennessee, who actually shit his pants one day while in formation! Everyone was hot and sweating, so you can imagine how "ripe" he smelled when the TI came by for inspection.

"Boy, you smell like shit"—the understatement of the day.

"Sir, I didn't want to break formation."

"Get outta here, and clean your ass up, boy."

He ran to the barracks for a well-needed overhaul. Later that same week, while we were shining shoes, making beds, and so on, he did it again! Only this time, the latrine was right down the hall. We had to do something, so several of us dragged him into the shower, clothes and all, and made him disrobe. We then used mops to wash him down. He was gone the next morning.

My squadron was 3711, and my flight was number 506. Every flight had a position called "dorm chief," sort of an intermediary between the TI and the basic trainees (no stripers, as we were called). For reasons unknown to me, I was selected as the dorm chief. My duties were to get the flight up, dressed, and ready for inspection each morning. Then, march them (we never walked) wherever they needed to be in a timely manner. I was also required to get Flight 506 in and out of the chow hall in exactly fifteen minutes every day and was tasked with leading our flight during the weekly military parades. Of course, all of these duties were in addition to the million and a half other things I had to do each day.

But my real job was to take abuse from the TI. Chewing me out in front of the flight was one of his favorite activities. I always got the most demerits on my uniform inspections and received more than my share of the *hated* middle-of-the-night dorm guard duty. He didn't like me, and I didn't like him. I really think it was a conscious effort by him to use me to terrify the others—kind of like a deranged management style. (Did he know I was only there because of a lost coin toss? Did he really think I was ate up about the military like him?) One day near the end of the training, I had my chance to get back at him, and I took it. We were lined up for inspection, standing at attention. SSgt Adams executed a right-face maneuver and was standing toe-to-toe with me.

"You're a mess, Feeney. Your name tag isn't on straight, your shoes look like shit, and your gig line is off." (A proper gig line vertically matches up your belt buckle with the seams of your trousers and your shirt.) "What do you have to say for yourself, Mr. Dormitory Chief?"

At that very second, I looked up at him and noticed a very large bird deposit on his shoulder epaulet. I couldn't believe my luck and decided to play this out.

"I'm asking you again, boy, why is your uniform such a mess?" *Not yet ... Not yet*, I thought. *Just a little bit longer.* "You have one minute to tell me why you don't have your goddamn uniform ready for inspection." *Perfect.*

In the loudest voice I could muster, I said, "Sir, you have bird shit on your shoulder." A sprinkling of giggles could be heard from Flight 506, standing right behind me. But I didn't laugh, because he was daring me to crack a smile.

"Say that again, boy," SSgt Adams said, moving even closer to me. He was fuming mad, but I didn't care. I was playing with fire and knew it.

"You have bird shit on your shoulder, sir," I repeated. But this time I couldn't control myself. I started laughing, the flight started laughing, and my TI was irate and embarrassed. He had called me out on my uniform, while his uniform had feces dripping from it. Classic. At this point, one of two things was going to happen. Either he would show his human side, laugh at himself, and share a bonding moment with the troops; or he would behave like a baby, lash out at me, and remove me from my position as dorm chief. I knew which one it would be.

"That's real funny, isn't it, Feeney? You're a goddamn comedian, ain't you? How would you like to start all over again? What do you think about going back to day one?" he roared. But at this point, the madder he got, the harder I laughed. I was doomed. "You disrespected this uniform and embarrassed me in front of my flight. You're no longer the dorm chief. Now get the hell out of my face, and fall in at the back of this flight."

Perfect—no more dorm chief duties, and I didn't get set back.

I finished the last few days of basic and graduated. We were all awarded the Basic Training Ribbon, our first official recognition. This was huge, since we had no stripes, and we looked more like skycaps than military men. In truth, I felt I deserved a second ribbon. I was able to get laid right in the middle of BMT—a rare accomplishment indeed! We (sorry, don't remember her name—hey, it was the seventies) found a hiding place under a jet-engine exhibit, covered by a tarp. Of course, with truth always being stranger than fiction, I found out later that she was training to be a jet-engine mechanic. You can't make this stuff up.

In later years, I often reflected on the effectiveness of these basic military training programs. I learned discipline, which had been in short supply so far in my life. As dorm chief, I had my first shot at a leadership role since high-school football—and I think I got better at it (if you don't count being fired). Even SSgt Adams—a real jerk—was able to develop a clever "us vs. him" mentality that we used to bond together as a flight. In short, our mutual dislike for our TI made us closer together. (I used some of this same technique as a flight training officer for ROTC cadets.) Basic training was a great confidence booster. I didn't know I was an expert marksman or that I could finish first in my squadron at the obstacle course races. I had no idea I could get so much done in twenty-four hours with practically no sleep. Who would have known that marching the flight around Lackland AFB, singing Jody calls in perfect rhythm and cadence, would be fun? (In the US military, cadences sung by marching or running soldiers are often called "Jody's" or "Jody calls." According to www.Army-Cadence.com, "The name 'Jody' refers to a recurring civilian character, the soldier's nemesis, who stays home to a perceived life of luxury. Jody stays home to drive the soldier's car, date the soldier's girl friend, hang out with the soldier's friends, and eat mom's great cooking.") Was my dad a reluctant Jody? Finally, I was in the best shape of my life—thanks to basic training. I was beginning to grab hold of that blob and was determined to steer it through the tough times.

Several of the other airmen from Flight 506 were also going to Keesler AFB, so the bus ride to Biloxi was fun. The pressure of BMT was over, and it was time for technical school. We even stopped in Louisiana for burgers and beer! Man, I don't ever remember a glass of beer tasting so good. Biloxi is near Gulfport, and right on the Gulf of Mexico. There were no casinos then, so the town was slow and easy. I fondly remember running there along the coast, where the sand was bright white and the shore, for the most part, was undisturbed. On base, under the Eighty-First Training Wing, there are several different technical schools for a wide variety of airmen, most of them coming from BMT at Lackland. Keesler AFB averages around 4,700 students at any given time throughout the year—roughly the size of a small to midrange college. It would prove to be a great location for a weekend jaunt to New Orleans, which is only about ninety miles west on Interstate 10.

The rigors of BMT made the adjustment to Keesler very comfortable. Although we were still marching to class, participating in parades, and doing physical training every morning, the way we were treated made all the difference. The harassment was gone, and most of the daily activities were led by senior classmates, not military training instructors. The emphasis on discipline and the air force way of life was still enforced, but attention to studies and development of student leadership became the first priority.

One of the coolest things about tech school was the "rope" leadership program. There were ropes assigned to different leaders. These ropes, which hung over your left shoulder and under your triceps muscle, identified your position. A green rope (this is what I wore) was a marching rope. You were responsible for marching a flight anywhere they needed to be. I reported to airmen with yellow ropes, who were responsible for all the flights in their squadron. At the top was the red rope, which was similar to a squadron commander. He or she worked with the green and yellow ropes on a daily basis. Although it sounds sort of hokey, it wasn't. We were all in this together, and our chain of command was clear and easy to follow. Having been a dorm chief in BMT, I really began to appreciate marching. I was nervous, but elated, when I was selected as a green rope. I can't explain the thrill of expertly maneuvering hundreds of airmen in and out of buildings, down long straightaways, and parking them exactly where they are supposed to be—on time, every day. It was almost spiritual.

The next nine weeks at Keesler passed rather quickly. I was learning all about personnel computers, government acronyms, and human resource programs of all kinds. After graduation, as a new recruit, I was slated for a lower-level entrance position in the Zweibrucken CBPO (Consolidated Base Personnel Office).

On some weekends, depending how well your flight did on inspections and honor flight competitions, you were free to leave the base. I remember my buddies and me going to New Orleans during one of our off-duty weekends. Yikes! What a city. There were bars and restaurants everywhere, and you could drink right in the middle of Bourbon Street. I really liked all the crazy entertainment going on in Jackson Square. Jugglers, musicians, clowns, human statues, unicycle riders, fire swallowers—you name it, it was there. I also remember going to Pat O'Brien's and partying in the smaller lounge with the dueling pianos. After a couple of hurricanes, we were singing along at the top of our lungs to everything from Irish songs to current ballads. It was truly special. After one too many, we'd drift over to the topless bars and act like big shots. But we fooled nobody —we were a group of young kids, all with military haircuts, who didn't know what we were doing. The dancers took our money very quickly, so it was off to the takee-outee window for some cheap Chinese food. On the way back, we crashed somewhere near Slidell, Louisiana, at a Motel 6, woke up hungover, and returned to Biloxi with tall tales of our experiences.

Looking forward, my ties to New Orleans grew even more. My sister Susan became a reporter for the *Times Picayune* and lived on Bourbon Street, near Esplanade Avenue. She generously allowed me to crash at her place for a couple Mardi Gras celebrations. (Note: My wife Andi went to college at Tulane and also had many great memories of New Orleans.)

Graduation day arrived, and for many of us, it was a sad event. We were really enjoying our tech school training, and we knew, for the most part, that we'd never see each other again. (This was the first time I was forced to face something that would happen many times in my life—dealing with the empty loneliness of continually moving from place to place, leaving behind friends and lovers.) But I had bigger fish to fry.

With my brain mismanaged with great skill, I headed to Germany.

CHAPTER SIX

Auf Wiedersehen, America

———◦———

The power of that coin toss continued to haunt me as I flew across the Atlantic Ocean. In just under five months, I went from a partying housepainter in Pittsburgh to an air force airman bound for Zweibrucken Air Base (AB), Germany. When I think of esoteric moments like this, I like to use a phrase I picked up from Andy—a boyfriend of my sister Sue—who used to say, "One never knows, does one?" Classic. It means nothing and everything. You can use that comment in any situation and sound like you know what you're talking about.

"What is the meaning of life? Where does space end? How does gravity work? Why can't the Cubs ever win a pennant? How did that pawn stand up on its side?"

"One never knows, does one?" I intellectually respond, with just the right amount of smugness.

My first impression of Germany was arriving at the airport in Frankfurt and standing outside the terminal awaiting the bus to Zweibrucken. On the sidewalk were rows of painted footprints, in some sort of formation, spread out over several hundred feet. Just as I started to wonder what they were for, out came at least 150 young men and women. I guessed they were US Army recruits. In seconds, they all "fell in" by standing on each of the painted footprints. Moments later, several buses arrived and came to a screeching halt exactly in-line with the formations. The buses had destinations like Garmisch, Kaiserslautern, Stuttgart, and Mannheim. It took me a few minutes, but I finally figured it out. Each recruit's first assignment was randomly selected by what footprints he or she was standing in! (I was thinking right about then that I was glad Jill chose the air force.)

The bus ride was uneventful, and I arrived at Zweibrucken two hours later, met my sponsor, and was taken to my dormitory room. Zweibrucken AB was a NATO air base in West Germany. It is about thirty-five miles southwest of Kaiserslautern, and just a few miles from the town of Zweibrucken. It supported reconnaissance missions for both the Royal

Canadian Air Force and the United States Air Forces in Europe (USAFE). It closed in 1992 and is now a civilian airport. In 1977, I was assigned to the CBPO, in the Twenty-Sixth Combat Support Squadron. Zweibrucken means "two bridges." For the life of me, I could never figure out where those two bridges were. The main weapon system was the RF-4C, which collected all kinds of reconnaissance information about our nemesis, the Union of Soviet Socialist Republics.

My first job in the USAF was as a records clerk, in the Customer Service Section. (As you can see, my college degree was really paying off.) It was simple work. I didn't mind it. It was my other job, called a "warskill" Air Force Specialty Code (AFSC), that I hated. I was assigned as a security police specialist. I was on call 24-7 to report for exercises, terrorist warnings, guard duty, chow relief, and so on. It didn't matter what I was doing in the CBPO; when they called, I went. More on this later.

Over the next few months, I really started to get into a rhythm. I finally received my first stripe and was no longer an airman basic. I didn't look like a skycap anymore. I was now a "skitter wing," or airman, and damn proud of it. Of all the ranks I would make in the military, this was the biggest one for me. I got out of the dorm and found an apartment in the village of Zweibrucken. Zweibrucken is a small town located in the Rhineland-Palatinate area on the Schwarbach River, and very close to the French border. Its population is about 33,000, and over 21 percent of its total land area was occupied by the US military. I found a small one-bedroom apartment in town, conveniently located right across the *strasse* from *der Gasthof* (tavern). I nailed down a second job (part-time) in the Noncommissioned Officers (NCO) Club as a bar waiter—an economic must in order to afford living off base. I made the base softball team, which allowed me to travel all over Europe. And I developed some good friendships in the CBPO, so there was always something to do after work. (The best thing about being enlisted was all the great friends I made—we were brothers-in-arms, watching out for each other.)

The base softball team was a really good deal. We would travel by bus and stay for free on military bases all over central Europe. We got paid to play softball! The memories of all those bus trips— watching the picturesque hills and valleys of Europe pass by—are still locked in my subconscious. And beer—man, we drank some beer. It seemed the more we partied before a tournament, the better we played. And we were good. Even though we were one of the smallest bases in the league, we finished high in the standings both years that I played. We came within one game of winning the European Division Championship in 1979—a heartbreaking loss to Ramstein AB.

Working in the NCO Club was really exhausting, but it was fun. In those days, the clubs were bustling with activity. On weekends, buses would bring local girls from downtown to the club. We always had live music, and it was always packed. These were simpler days, with no DUI patrols or MADD movements. Terrorism, although part of the equation in Europe at the time, wasn't a major concern for the US military. So the club was always packed, and I made pretty good tips. (I must say the female waiters did better than I. Guys usually preferred to sit at tables with female servers. Such is life.)

Away from the base, one of the greatest things about Europe is that you can go from country to country so easily. One of my softball-team members, Roger, had a brother stationed at Aviano AB, Italy. We visited him twice while I was posted there. The NATO base is located in northeastern Italy, at the foot of the Alps, near Pordenone. It was a real kick to get up in the morning in Germany, and be in Italy by dinnertime. And you couldn't visit Aviano without going to Venice, which was about thirty miles south, and sits right on the Gulf of Venice. What a city! It's made up of 118 islands, linked by countless bridges (similar to New Amsterdam), and is listed as a World Heritage Site. The Venice Lagoon that encompasses the city rests between the mouths of the Po and Piave Rivers. It's the world's only pedestrian city and is easily walkable. The Grand Canal runs through most of the districts in Venice and is accessible by water buses, private taxis, and of course, by gondola. I really enjoyed the Rialtime Islands—in the center of Venice— because you can walk end-to-end in about one hour.

The drive through Switzerland and Austria en route to and returning from Italy was also very impressive. I had never seen a large mountain range like the Alps before, and was awestruck by its size and beauty. (Later, when Andi and I moved to Colorado Springs, I felt the same reaction when I saw Pike's Peak for the first time.) We'd drive down through Stuttgart, Germany, and stop to relax and take in the city sights in Zurich or Vaduz, Switzerland. On the way back to Germany, we'd stop at Innsbruck, Austria, for a beer or two, and return to Zweibrucken through Munich. Not bad for a poor kid from Pittsburgh, huh?

Back in sunny Zwei, I bought an old VW van, poorly painted in red and purple primer, with a peace sign on the roof. The entire interior behind the driver's seat was carpeted, including the walls. It was butt ugly, but it was cheap. (The biggest drawback occurred when I went through the border crossings —it definitely looked like a vehicle out of a Cheech and Chong movie, and I really got harassed.) For the next two years, I drove that thing everywhere. It was especially great for weekend concerts. In the United States, rock and roll may have been slowing down by the late seventies, but it was in its prime in Germany. All summer long, there were mega outdoor concerts on scenic hilltops in places like St. Goarshansen and Heidelberg. They usually lasted all weekend, so we'd pack up the van with wine, cheese, and bread—the three basic food groups—and spend our time partying and listening to music. In just one concert, for example, the slate would include the Doobie Brothers, Jethro Tull, Black Sabbath, Aerosmith, Grand Funk Railroad, and Ted Nugent, among others. It was crazy good, and something I'll never forget. I saw many of these concerts with Sammy and Elaine, two of my fellow airmen from Zweibrucken. Sammy was an Afro-American, and of course, Elaine was female, so we called ourselves the Mod Squad (I didn't say it was original). I remember one concert where the mud was so bad that we had eleven strange people crashing in my little van! I had to sleep sitting up in the driver's seat. Come to think of it, I still don't know where Sammy slept. You should have seen that vehicle when we returned home.

My van was especially useful for the *volksmarsch* season, since it could hold more passengers than a normal car. *Volksmarsch* is German for "people's march." All over the country, these noncompetitive fitness walks were designed to take in all the beauty of Germany—forests, hills, rivers, and little villages. Of course, there were small stands along the pathways providing shots of schnapps, which were especially appreciated on freezing, snowy days. At the end of each walk, all participants would receive a commemorative award, usually a pin, patch, medal, or a *bier* stein. Many walkers had hundreds of pins on their hats or attached to their walking canes. Others had vests with countless patches sewn into the leather. Whether it's strolling along the scenic hills of Heidelberg and taking in the beautiful rhythm of the Rhine River or walking the wooded mountains of the Black Forest, *volksmarsching* was the perfect combination of fitness walking and educational travel. I have fond memories of all the scenic *volksmarsch* trails. (I wish I had saved all the awards that I collected. Where does stuff from your past go?)

Of course, the Germans are also well-known for their parties. In addition to all the concerts, wine fests were everywhere. According to Wikipedia, "There are more than a thousand wine festivals taking place every year in Germany's wine growing regions, from the largest in the world (Bad Durkheim), to local festivals in charming villages along the Rhine, Mosel, Elbe, and Main." What a blast—music, food, wine, people watching—you couldn't beat it. If you ever get the chance, try to make the winefest in Bad Durkheim. It's gigantic, and the wines are amazing. Just watch out for the young drunks who always seem to be looking for a fight.

And let's not forget *Oktoberfest*. It's a sixteen-day festival celebrating *bier*, held annually in Munich, Bavaria, Germany, running from late September into early October. Simply put, it's the world's largest fair, drawing in excess of six million people from around the world every year. But it's not just *bier*; it's brass-band entertainment on the grandest scale, and food! There were endless amounts of *wurstl* (sausages), *schweinshaxe* (grilled ham hock), *steckerlfisch* (grilled fish on a stick), *knodel* (potato or bread dumplings), and *hendl* (chicken), all with *brotchen* (fresh rolls) and sauerkraut. My favorite *Oktoberfest* locations were the Schottenhamel Tent and the Hofbrau Beer Tent, which were huge structures, capable of holding thousands comfortably. There were waitresses in *dirndl* outfits carrying impossible amounts of beer, and men in *lederhosen* playing music or just chilling out at one of the hundreds of large tables. The effect of this event can't be underestimated. Hundreds of cities and towns around the world celebrate *Oktoberfest* every year—I bet you know of one near your hometown.

Back at the CBPO, I was moved from the Records Section to the Assignments Section (Personnel Utilization) right around the time I got my next promotion to airman first class. I handled all the personnel actions for departing and arriving personnel. The CBPO was made up of four large divisions: customer service, quality control, personnel utilization, and career progression. Each division had different parts of the HR puzzle. (For instance, the records section fell under the customer service division.) The CBPO was usually run by a major—a walking god to new airmen—with the title of Chief, CBPO. Our CBPO Chief was a good guy, and I couldn't imagine one person having so much responsibility. (Years later, I would become a CBPO Chief.) I remember how stressed he was when the USAFE Operational Readiness Inspection Team came to Zweibrucken. A failed inspection could mean his career. We spent weeks preparing for the exercise, and were ready for the challenge. On the second day, after a ten-hour-day in the CBPO, I was ordered to report immediately to the Security Police (SP) Squadron for my warskill AFSC duty.

It was March 1978, and it was very cold. I was sent, without any winter clothing, to a post perimeter tower, referred to as a PP Tower. Since I was called on for "chow relief," I was told that I wouldn't be at the post very long. Several hours later, I was still there, freezing my ass off up in that windy tower. Each thirty minutes, during radio checks, I kept asking for relief, or at least for some coffee or food—I couldn't remember the last time I ate anything. Still nothing. Finally, with my hands and toes already numb and my patience gone, the following happened:

"Checkpoint one, checkpoint one, this is PP Tower 4, do you read me?"
"Loud and clear. Over."

"I request immediate relief. I have been at post for over twelve hours, and I don't have any winter fatigues, boots, or gloves. Do you read me?" I asked.

"We read you, PP Tower 4. Stand by."

Thirty minutes went by, then an hour—still no response. I'd had it. I was about to make a very serious decision. "Checkpoint one, checkpoint one, do you read me?"

"I read you loud and clear. Over."

"I can't feel my hands and feet. I have been on shift for almost twenty-two hours [counting my CBPO shift], and haven't been issued winter gear. I'm putting down my weapon, putting down the radio, and going home." And I left. The enormity of what I had done hit me as I hiked back to my car and drove home. *I went AWOL*—and worse, I left my weapon unsecured at my post.

Thirty minutes after I arrived home, the security police arrived. "Open the door, Airman Feeney. You are under arrest." I was placed in the back of a police car, thankfully without handcuffs, and taken to a retaining cell on base. After what seemed like hours, a legal officer entered. He explained to me that I had deserted my post and told me that a court-martial might be imminent. I was relieved of all my duties and taken home. I was ordered not to leave my house. And I didn't.

For two days, I sat there and let my imagination run wild. *Am I going to jail? Will I be busted to airman basic again? Why did I leave my post? What a jerk. I abandoned my weapon—a complete no-no for a security policeman.*

Oh well, I never wanted to join the military in the first place. I'm better off getting out, I rationalized. Finally, just after the base inspection ended, I was told to stand by for a vehicle and prepare to come to base.

When I arrived back at the SP squadron, I was escorted to a briefing room, not to a cell. A colonel, a full colonel—I had never spoken to one at that point—strode into the room.

"Do you realize why you are here?"

"Yes, sir."

"You abandoned your post and left a weapon unattended. Under the Uniform Code of Military Justice (UCMJ), these offenses can lead to a court-martial, and even jail time. Do you realize this?"

"Yes, sir." I learned all about the UCMJ in technical school.

"I'm going to ask you two questions, and I want honest answers. Were you issued any winter gear, like hats, coats, gloves, or boots? And how long were you at the PP tower?"

"No, sir. I didn't have any gear. And I was there for about twelve hours." "Did you complete an entire shift in the CBPO prior to deploying for chow relief?" "Yes, sir."

"Did any of the patrols bring you something to eat, or at least some hot coffee?" "No, sir."

I was told to report to my squadron commander the next morning. I had no idea what to expect. In fact, I was almost hoping I'd get kicked out. This military stuff wasn't for me after all. What was I doing in a PP Tower, in a foreign country, freezing my butt off? For the thousandth time I thought about that fated coin toss. I wanted to go home. So I had no expectations when I arrived in the commander's office.

But the strangest thing happened.

"Airman Feeney, you went AWOL and abandoned your weapon. That was dead wrong. You put your entire career on the line. There were serious discussions about a court-martial, did you know that?" I nodded. "However, because of the excessively long double shift and the fact that you were exposed to extreme weather conditions without winter gear, we have decided to take the court-martial off the table. I have been charged to decide what to do with you. I talked to your supervisor, and he thinks you have potential and should remain in the air force. Your CBPO Chief also felt that you deserve another chance. You are hereby reprimanded and will have a formal letter of reprimand placed in your permanent record. You are to report for road and grounds [base cleanup] at 7:00 a.m. every Saturday and Sunday for the next six weeks. You are grounded to your house during this entire period, and must travel directly to and from work. Do you understand?" my commander asked.

What? I'm not busted? No court-martial? Me, with potential? What are roads and grounds? "Yes, sir," I said, and was dismissed.

The next six weekends were a blur of sweeping, mopping, raking, painting, buffing, shoveling, and washing. But I wasn't complaining. Sure, I planned on getting out of the air force when my hitch was up, but I didn't want to be thrown out. Looking back, I had no idea how lucky I was. In today's one-mistake society, I might have been long gone. But in 1978, with the help of my supervisor, CBPO Chief, and squadron commander, I was given a second chance. They definitely *saw something in me that I didn't see myself*. With no punishable record and good performance evaluations, the blob was still steerable.

During one of my detention weekends, I was placed in the Airmen's Attic—a facility where donations from other military families were collected to help defray the cost of living for lower-ranking troops. We were told that General Alexander Haig, the Supreme Allied Commander of Europe, and his spouse were coming to Zweibrucken AB, and they wanted to visit the Airman's Attic. I spent the whole weekend scrubbing and painting, and was even on my hands and knees digging excess wax from hallway corners with razor blades. You could eat off that floor. It was such a big event, and everyone in the building was waiting for the Haigs. The volunteers were very pleased with my hard work, and asked me to be there when the General and Mrs. Haig stopped by. I had never met anyone important, so I showed up. We got word that the general and his entourage had completed their business with the wing commander and were on their way. We lined up outside the facility and watched as the motorcade raced by the Airmen's Attic at fifty miles an hour. Oh well, at least the problem of waxy buildup was solved.

Later in my tour, after I was cleared of AWOL charges, I became the model security police augmentee and volunteered for more shifts than anyone else. The way I figured it, I owed them for giving me another chance. In 1979, things really heated up in sunny Zwei. The Baader-Meinhof Gang —a real terrorist operation—bombed the Zweibrucken Courthouse! Our commander scrambled all his senior security policemen downtown to assist the local authorities. That left us experienced warskill SPs on the gates and aircraft hangars. I was placed just outside the main gate, up on a hill, with a full clip in my M-16. This was not a drill. Several of us were positioned in various locations, prepared to fire when we heard a certain code word on our radios. The rumor was that the gang planned to attack the base while our troops were responding downtown. They never showed. But it was very exciting lying there in the snow, ready to fire without hesitation when given the word. I guess our brains were well mismanaged, huh?

The months were passing by, and I had managed to get home on leave a few times. Mom was doing okay, even though she was a little lonely. She moved to a small house on Hiland Avenue, just off Ohio River Boulevard, in Ben Avon. She was working as a part-time bartender, and Sue was attending Avonworth High School. Although Mom and I we were still not very close, Dad had passed, and time has a tendency to heal all wounds. She installed a beer keg right in the small dining room (no kidding), and we spent many hours drinking beer and reminiscing about everything from childhood stories to tidbits about my father. They were some of the nicer times we had together.

I've always been an avid reader. I subscribe to the theory that reading isn't about the writer; it's about the reader. To me, there is not one sentence in any book that means a thing unless the reader decides that it does. The measurement of a quality book, in my opinion, is how well it integrates the thoughts and emotions of the reader into the dialogue. (I am basing this entire book on that theory.) The more common-core experiences I can weave into this book—not an American classic to be sure— the more successful it will be. After all, we all have to steer our own blobs. Why am I talking about books? Well, in the summer of 1978, I went to the base library looking for something to read. A young lady named Cheryl Sibley, whom I had never seen before, assisted me with the checkout process. When I left that morning, I had no idea that she would be my second wife.

As with Jill, things happened pretty fast. (Maybe I should have known better, huh?) I went back to the library a few days later and asked her out. I don't think either one of us ever dated anyone else after that day. She was cute and really enjoyed life. More importantly, she wasn't in the military. It was nice to date a civilian for a change. Her dad was a chief master sergeant, the highest enlisted rank in the USAF, and he worked in the Civil Engineering Squadron. As a military brat, Cheryl had traveled extensively, and I really liked that about her. We were inseparable, and after a few months, she moved in with me. Naturally, Chief Sibley wasn't crazy about Cheryl living with me. But she was already in her mid-twenties, so he took it pretty well. (Thank goodness the AWOL charges hadn't stuck.)

Over the last year of my assignment to Zweibrucken, we had a blast. Although the big mega concerts were slowing down, there were plenty of good bands to see in Germany. We saw Foreigner in Mannheim with a couple friends of ours, and Bob Dylan in Dortmund. They were both great. (Bob Dylan has been my favorite musical artist for over forty years. I've seen him in concert seven times, have at least twenty-five of his CDs, and can play upwards of forty of his songs on the guitar.) We also saw Cheap Trick—aptly named—in Hamburg, I think. It was pretty bad. The eighties were coming, and in my opinion, so were a slew of inferior bands. But there was a silver lining. The warm-up bank was Kansas! They were so good I was ready to leave during the intermission. But Cheryl would have none of that, so I gutted it out.

We also took an interest in the European Grand Prix circuit. I remember seeing the German Formula One Grand Prix in Hockenheim. The town was located in the Upper Rhine Valley, in the North Baden-Wurttemberg region, about twenty miles south of Mannheim. The actual racetrack was called the *Hockenheimring*. This track has hosted over thirty Formula One Grand Prix Races since 1970. In 1978, Mario Andretti, an American, was the point leader. When we arrived at the track, Cheryl and I decided to wander away from the main grandstand and found a spot up on a hill with a perfect view of a straightaway at the far end of the course. The race began, and we waited. First, we heard a low hum, barely above a murmur. Then, a higher-pitched rumbling, like a plane taking off nearby. And then an *explosion of sound* as the cars appeared seemingly out of nowhere. The roar of the Formula One engines was deafening as they shot past us. Then, instantly, they were gone. Silence. Wow—we couldn't wait for the next lap.

We spent the afternoon enjoying the race, eating, drinking, and rooting for Mario and his Lotus engine. He won, of course.

Later that summer, Cheryl and I took a Morale, Recreation and Welfare tour bus to the Dutch Grand Prix, located in Zandvoort, a municipality and town in the province of North Holland. The area is a major beach resort (North Sea) and hosts the race every year at the Circuit Park in Zandvoort. The race was just as exciting as the German Grand Prix, with Mario making a last-minute surge to win again. This time we sat in the grandstand with a bunch of friends from the base. Even after all these years, every time I see a Grand Prix race on TV, I still think about the roar of the engines stampeding across the Hockenheim countryside.

But the real excitement happened on the return bus ride from Zandvoort. Everyone was partying and drinking beer. We stopped at Gouda and loaded up on giant wax-covered wheels of cheese. (I bought one for my mom, but alas, I gave in and broke it open on the bus.) Anyway, someone in the back started smoking hashish. By 1979, even though pot and hash were still around, smoking in public was a stupid move. After a rest stop, the bus driver disappeared for a while. We found out later that he called the police and reported the drug use on his bus. As we approached the Belgian border (we angled through Belgium, via Maastricht, toward Zweibrucken), I noticed quite a commotion ahead. The border police entered the bus and ordered everybody to file out onto the street. For the next twenty minutes, they searched the entire vehicle, seat by seat, looking for drugs. When they stopped at my seat and called for the bus driver, I was getting a little antsy. When I saw the bus driver point at me, I knew I was in trouble.

As it turns out, whoever was smoking the hash (it wasn't me) dropped it under my seat as he or she was exiting the bus. The driver was merely telling police who was sitting there. The border police charged off the bus and headed straight for yours truly. With both arms secured by guards, I was marched to a cold, dank, metal-walled waiting room. They produced the hash and made it clear that I was in trouble (again?).

"Where did you get this hashish?" the officer asked. "We found it under your seat on the bus."

"It's not mine—I swear. I never saw that before," I replied, teeth chattering because of the cold. "Someone must have put it there." As I recall, I was sitting in the middle of the bus, right behind the side exit door. My guess was that whoever had the drugs dropped them under my seat on the way out.

"Take off your clothes." So in a freezing room filled with strangers, I stripped naked. After the guards took my clothes and possessions away, they left me alone, shaking like a leaf. Some time passed, and two creepy guys showed up with rubber gloves. This wasn't good. For the next fifteen minutes, I had fingernails scraped, teeth, ears, and gums searched, and fingers shoved up my ass. It was humiliating. And it was so cold that these invasions of my body seemed even almost surreal. Of course, they found nothing, and eventually I was allowed to return to the bus.

Once we were underway, I stood up and shouted, "If I ever find out who dropped that hash under my seat, that person will wish he was never born. I just received a full body-cavity search, with creeps sticking their fingers up my ass because of someone on this bus." In reality, at this point, I was just blowing off steam. I decided I was better off not knowing who did this, because I might have done something very stupid.

Back in sunny Zwei, the last six months of my tour in Germany went pretty smoothly. Cheryl and I really stepped up our travel plans. We decided to get out and see as much of Europe as we could before my tour was up in July.

We went to Paris a couple of times. It was really neat to get up in the morning in Germany and have lunch on the Avenue des Champs-Elysees in the afternoon. Not only is it one of the most famous streets in the world; it's also flanked by the Arc de Triomphe and the Place de la Concorde. The treelined avenue, with cafes, specialty shops, and expensive real estate, was very impressive. Of course, we climbed the Eiffel Tower—all 1,710 steps— and wandered around the Louvre for hours. (Be prepared for huge crowds, especially around the *Mona Lisa*.) We also visited one of my favorite attractions—the Parthenon. It's a very early example of neoclassicism, modeled similar to the Roman Parthenon, with a dome structure copied by many designers in France. Every time I think about this classic building, it reminds me of a TV interview with Shaq O'Neal during the Olympic Games in Athens. It went like this:

"Shaq, what did you think about the Parthenon?" asked the interviewer. "I don't know," replied Shaq. "We went to a lot of clubs."

There's everything in Paris, from the Notre Dame Cathedral to Moulin Rouge (Cabaret District). Another of my favorite stops is the Sacre Coeur Basilica, a Roman Byzantine church. The Savoyarde Bell itself weighs 18,355 kilograms! I enjoyed this spot for two reasons. First, it's at the highest point in the city, so you can see everything. And second, on a nearby hill— Montmartre—is the artist colony, packed with talented people, practicing their craft just like Van Gogh, Toulouse-Lautrec, Pissarro, and others did before them.

You've probably heard this joke before. (I heard it for the first time at the Gasthof across the street from my apartment.) Hey, if I can't use it here, when would be a better time?

"Why did the French put speed bumps on the Champ-Elysees?" "To slow down the Germans."

Cheryl and I also went to Amsterdam a few times as well. As I said before, the great thing about Europe is how quickly you can get from one country to the next. Known as the Venice of the North, Amsterdam has canals stretching over sixty miles, with 1,500 bridges connecting ninety islands. The absolute best thing to do in Amsterdam is to walk around and take it all in. Or ride one of the gondolas, and get some good local knowledge from the poler. For example, I learned that the canals were not just for picture taking. Over the last several centuries, the Dutch have been surrounded by some bad countries. Because of their small size, they had to devise a way to keep larger, more aggressive countries at bay. So they built the Dutch Water Line. According to www.thisblogrules.com, it's "a series of levies surrounding low laying land that could be flooded to stop any invading army before they reach Amsterdam. This worked against an army of Louis XIV of France, who some from history class may remember being the most powerful man on Earth at the time." Today, many of the flood plains are still there.

If you're up for something more risqué, check out the De Wallen area. It's one of the most famous red-light districts in the world. Again from www.thisblogrules.com, "Red light districts are places that glow red in the middle of the night because of all the lights coming from the shops, which cater to a rather, eh, raunchy crowd." Prostitution is legal there, and De Wallen is full of small apartments with working girls posing in the windows. There are also weird sex shops, pot houses, and crazy bars. It's kind of like Bourbon Street on acid. Even if you never tell anyone you stopped here, you have to try it once. It's a riot. (Note: There are male prostitutes as well—the Dutch are equal opportunity employers.)

Some of the other places we visited prior to the end of my tour were Luxembourg, a small, beautiful country with a fusion of Romance and Germanic Europe, and one of the nicest town squares I've ever seen; Cologne, Germany, where the largest Gothic church in Europe was built—a breathtaking structure, started in 1248, halted in 1473, and finally finished in 1880; and Stuttgart, with its fantastic main square, Schlossplatz, and its tremendous shopping along Konigstrasse, the longest pedestrianized street in Germany.

My tour was ending, and it was time to fill out my dream sheet again. I was determined to go somewhere warm, and listed preferences along the southern part of the United States. Florida, Texas, Arizona, and California were my choices. Considering my luck with my first assignment, I shouldn't have been surprised when my orders arrived—Loring AFB, Maine. Four hours north of Montreal. Hundreds of miles from any decent-sized city. And *cold*! Damn.

It was also time to say good-bye to my old VW van. I tried to sell it, but no one was interested. It had no heat and only one windshield wiper (luckily on the driver's side), and had to be started using pliers. I parked on hills nearby, so I could jump-start it when needed for my commute to work. So, a few weeks before I left Europe, with a heavy heart, I drove it to the junkyard and paid 75 *deutschmarks* to have it destroyed. (Note: I spent an hour going through photos looking for one picture of that old van. I didn't find any.)

There was one more "elephant in the room." What about Cheryl and me? I wasn't ready to get married again, but I thought it was love and wanted to keep seeing her (sound familiar?). She wanted to come with me, but I knew it would be a difficult adjustment. In the military, it's very hard to travel with a girlfriend. Cheryl would not be on my travel orders, could not live in base housing or use the medical facilities, and had no preference for job placement. She would have to be escorted on and off base every time and wasn't authorized to use the base exchange or commissary. But she was adamant. She wanted to come to Maine with me, and I didn't want to lose her. I acquiesced, but with one stipulation—that she didn't pressure me to get married. She agreed. *Let's see how that goes.*

So long, sunny Zwei ... Hello, frozen tundra.

CHAPTER SEVEN

Limestone, Maine, Known for Absolutely Nothing

———•○•———

O kay, you're still with me. That's good. The only thing that keeps me going on this project is the hope that people like you are still interested in reading it. So maybe I should share a few things about myself with you.

I'm nearing sixty, am six feet two inches tall, and weigh about 235 pounds. I have blue eyes, and brown (turning gray) hair. I was a Scorpio most of my life, but in later years, the experts tell me I'm now on the cusp with the Libras. Everyone tells me these two signs are opposites. So where does that leave me, astrologically speaking? I live in Indian Harbour Beach, Florida, with my wife, Andi, and our cat, Kismet. I'm semi-retired and teach graduate school part-time at a nearby university. My favorite color is yellow, I prefer sunrises to sunsets, I'm left-handed, and I'm an outrageous Pittsburgh Steelers fan. I have been shot at three times—once in a bar, once by an ex-girlfriend's boyfriend, and once randomly driving through New Orleans. But not once, ironically, in my military career. The three most influential public figures in my life are Thomas Jefferson, Bob Dylan, and Ayn Rand. My role models are Mr. Bradley, my high-school English teacher; Colonel Phillips, my boss in Stuttgart when I was stationed in Izmir, Turkey; and my older brother Larry. Since Andi and I have saved pretty well, I enjoy monkeying around with our retirement portfolio. I'm an avid red wine fan, mostly cabernet sauvignon, but won't pass up the opportunity for a nice, cold beer. (Everybody tells me I have a hollow leg. I'm Irish, and can hold my alcohol better than most.) I exercise almost every day (Andi never misses a day), and I know practically every good restaurant and happy hour in Brevard County. I love to read, and solve the most difficult crossword puzzles I can find. I absolutely *hate* to write, so I ground out this book one difficult page at a time. (I gave up several times, but my wife kept convincing me to continue.)

Okay, back to this nomadic tale ... We left Germany, stopped in Florida to visit Cheryl's family, and then finished our vacation in Pittsburgh. On a chilly day in June 1979, we arrived at Limestone, Maine—the home of Loring Air Force Base. Limestone is part of Aroostook County and has a population of 1,075 people. (The 2010 population of the entire county was 2,314.) The only other US town nearby is Caribou. The Canadian border of New Brunswick is about eight miles east. The land is predominantly flat, and there are lots of potato farmers. The population of four-legged residents greatly outnumbers the two-legged ones.

Since we weren't married, Cheryl and I had to find a place in town. Not an easy feat. The center of all local activity was the base, so everyone lived there. And with the brutal winters, the closer you were to work, the better—especially with Uncle Sam taking care of the heating bills. But we were lucky. We found an apartment right away, just behind a little gas station on Main Street. (I googled Main Street in Limestone, but couldn't find it.) The place was small—fully furnished with one bedroom—and relatively close to base. We bought an old Buick Skylark and moved our meager collection of stuff into our new home.

Loring AFB was the largest base in the United States Strategic Air Command (SAC). The main mission was 24-7 preparation for long-range bombing anywhere, anytime. It was our most important defense against an all-out nuclear attack. The two main weapon systems were the B-52 bomber and the KC-135 tanker. In tandem, they could travel almost anywhere without landing. I was assigned to the Forty-Second Combat Support Squadron in the CBPO. I was placed in the Quality Control Section and worked with employee evaluation reports. We did a myriad of functions with one overarching goal—to get all employee evaluations reports (EERs) for officers and enlisted personnel completed error-free and on time. A poorly written EER was the number-one reason for getting passed over for promotion.

But work was nothing more than a means to an end for me. I was counting the days to my separation date.

Softball season was just starting, and I was glad to join the squad. Playing softball was my way of making friends. Cheryl bonded with some of the wives and girlfriends of the players, and I developed a good rapport with several of the guys on the team. Since there was so little to do in Limestone, softball really helped pass the time. And we were pretty good. Entering the playoffs, our team was really confident. Maybe we were overconfident—we lost our first game in the base-wide double elimination playoff tournament. That meant that we had to go through the loser's bracket, play and win six games in a row, and then beat the winner's bracket team twice! On a cold night in September, with snow flurries coming down, we beat the Forty-Second Civil Engineering Squadron twice, and won the base championship. We played doubleheaders four nights in a row, and we were exhausted. We all piled down to the Rendezvous—a glorious pizza place just off the west gate—and wolfed down pizza and beer like it was our last meal.

Things weren't going well for Cheryl in Limestone. Her banishment from normal life on base really affected her. (Remember, she was an air force brat, and was much more comfortable living on base than I ever would be.) If Limestone wasn't the end of the earth, you could definitely see it from our apartment. I mean, there was nothing to do in town. We spent way too much time watching TV and drinking. That's another downside to the loneliness of lifelong travel: alcohol provides the slightest escape from reality when you need it most. I couldn't stand to see her like this. I figured, *hey, we're living together anyway, so why not get married? Maybe I'll get it right this time. Everything happens for a reason, right?*

We set a date for the end of September, reserved Chapel #1 on base for the wedding, and immediately got on the base-housing waiting list. I was twenty-six years of age and already going on my second wife. But I didn't care. We were in the middle of nowhere, and Cheryl dropped everything in her life to be with me in this hellhole. I owed her, and I had an easy fix that could integrate her into the base population, and at the same time, remove the embarrassment she may have felt as a live-in girlfriend. *After all, no one knows if a marriage will work or not. One divorce shouldn't have any effect on a second marriage, right?* I felt I learned a lot from my first marriage and would definitely do better this time. (TMYKTMYDKS.) So everything was in place. I'll never forget how excited Cheryl was when she found her wedding outfit at a tiny place called Lads, Lassies, and Ladies, in the tiny town of Houlton, Maine. Two days prior to the event, my buddies and I headed off to Quebec City for the bachelor's party. We hit the Old Town, near rue Saint-Jean, and drank until dawn. Since we didn't have money for hotels, we drove back to base—well over four hours—nursing huge hangovers the whole way. Thank God I had a day to dry out before the ceremony. The wedding was great, and all our new friends were there. One of my softball buddies and his wife allowed us to use their home for the reception, since our apartment was way too small. Everything was in place. I was a married man again. It felt right.

I'm not sure if most Americans can visualize how cold it gets up in northern Maine. Twenty or thirty degrees below zero was normal in the winter! We were issued electric blankets to place over our car motors at night. It wasn't uncommon for the engine block to freeze solid. Every spring, the authorities would find a few people dead in cars along the highway. The assumption was that their vehicle skidded off the road and wouldn't start, so they froze to death waiting for help. This was a serious concern to all travelers in Maine.

I remember returning from Pittsburgh just after Christmas and flying through Bar Harbor, Maine. I changed planes en route to Presque Isle and was flying on a small twelve-seat aircraft. The pilot was sitting right in front of me, and it felt like I was in the backseat of a car. I noticed we were weaving back and forth and not flying straight and level. So I asked:

"Excuse me, why are you weaving back and forth?"

"I'm following Route 1 toward Presque Isle," the pilot responded.

"So this aircraft doesn't have navigational equipment? Do you have to use ground reckoning to get to your location?"

"Yeah, it has navigational ability. But up here in Maine, we follow the highway. It's simple, really. In this harsh environment, if we have to force land for any reason, our only chance of survival would be the highway. Even with a black box, we couldn't last long in these blizzard-like conditions away from the road." For the rest of that flight, I made it my personal business to keep an eye on the highway below.

One night during the devilish winter of 1979, I went out barhopping with Bill, one of my CBPO coworkers. It was thirty below, and we were hustling to get into the car after leaving a local tavern. He took off his glove so he could pull the keys out of his pocket. While fumbling with the keys, he dropped them. Just as he reached down with his gloved hand to pick them up, he accidentally placed his other hand on the front fender. His hand instantly froze to the metal, and he couldn't move it. After several seconds of panic, he ripped his hand away from the car. Amazingly, it wasn't bleeding, and he said he was okay. So we jumped in the car and turned on the heat. Suddenly as his hand began to thaw, blood started shooting all over the place. He had to wrap a newspaper around it to keep it from totally trashing his car. At about the same time, he started screaming in pain. (Reflecting on this for a moment, I thought about how dangerously easy it would be to freeze to death. You don't feel pain, you don't bleed, and sooner or later, your body cries out for sleep. *Boom.* That's it.) Bill wore a bandage for months and had scars on his hand as a memento.

This area of the country was like the Wild West. There were lots of rugged types who weren't afraid to demonstrate their might. I remember once when my friend George convinced me to check out a new club just across the Canadian border near Grand Falls. We drove from Limestone to the border. When we arrived, the gate was entirely buried under a mound of potatoes! They were over two stories high, and you couldn't even see the guard booth. We found out later that there was a price battle going on between the United States and Canada, and one side wanted to send a strong message to the other. There were no police or border guards on the scene. No one even cared that the border was unprotected. Imagine this scenario in the post-9/11 world. We turned around and headed home. But George was persistent, and we decided a few weeks later to try to find the club again. We got lost a few times and were pretty frustrated when we finally located the place. It was called the Antler, or the Moose Head, or something like that. As soon as George opened the door, he got sucker punched right in the face and went flying backward down the steps. There was a massive bar fight going on, so we got the hell out of there and headed back to Limestone. He was okay, but his pride was hurt. First the potatoes, then a sucker punch. He made me promise never to mention this to anyone, and I didn't —until now.

Otherwise, things were going okay. We moved on base, and I made my third stripe (senior airman). Cheryl got involved in many of the base activities—one of her hobbies was belly dancing, believe it or not. Not far from her belly-dancing classes, in the CBPO, I was about to come face-to-face with the second biggest SSE decision of my life. (The coin toss still holds the number-one spot.) My CBPO Chief, Major Gray, approached me with a message (like a Western Union telegram) in his hand.

"Airman Feeney, have you read this message about Officer Training School (OTS) opportunities in 1980?" Yes, I read it. *Officer? Me? Who wanted to be a stupid officer anyway? I'm getting out at the end of this assignment, period.* So I couldn't care less.

"Major Gray, I really appreciate your interest, but I have no desire to make the air force a career. I am still planning to separate at the end of my tour here in Maine."

But he didn't move a muscle. After a moment, he said, "You have over two and a half years left on your enlistment, correct?" I nodded, yes, that was correct. "And you have a bachelor's degree, isn't that right?"

Again, I nodded, wondering why he was continuing this line of questioning. "I looked at your performance appraisals, and they are all strong," he persisted. (*He should have seen me going AWOL, and getting locked up in a cell.*) "Thank you, sir, but I really don't see myself in the military for the long term.

But thank you for your concern." *Now walk away,* I thought. He persisted. "Think about it. You can reduce your tour length while only adding a year and a half to your military service. Your salary will more than double, you'll get a chance to use your education, and you can get the heck out of Maine." I said nothing. "Just think about it, okay?"

"Yes, sir." And I did. I discussed it with Cheryl, and she supported anything that would get us out of Maine. And we could really use the extra money. But I was really torn. I got myself in this situation by letting other people (Jill) make decisions for me. Could I risk that again? What does it say about me if my most important career decisions were influenced by others, and not by me? (In my introduction, I talked about having no plan, and how much of my life was laid out for me by others.) Here was another singularly significant event staring me right in the face. But the real issue had to do with commitment. I was working hard, making my stripes, but I still hadn't bought into the military way of life. I was just shuffling along, waiting for my separation date. I knew, deep down, that I couldn't make it as an officer in my present frame of mine. Do I stay in Maine and freeze my ass off just to get out of the air force earlier? Or do I become an officer, extend my service time, and commit to a possible career in the military?

I was looking for answers when I ran into Major Gray the following week. It was his comments that day that finally helped me reach a decision.

"Airman Feeney, have you given any thought to our discussion about OTS opportunities? The final application deadline is only a week away."

"Yes sir, that's all I've been thinking about," I said. I shared my predicament with him and was taken aback by his concern for my future. He hardly knew me, yet he *saw something in me that I didn't see in myself—* déjà vu all over again, right, Yogi? But it was his final comment that sealed the deal.

"Look at it this way. Put in the application, and see what happens. You don't have to accept it if you change your mind," he said. That made a lot of sense—I still had all my options open.

So I spent all day that following Saturday putting together my application package, and asked Major Gray to review it. He added several improvements and also provided me with a nice letter of recommendation. I got my OTS package in just before the deadline. (I never told any of my friends, just in case I didn't make the grade.)

My life was changing fast—again. In less than six months, I had finished up my tour in Germany, moved domiciles twice in Maine, got married, and applied and was accepted into Officers Training School. Yes, I was selected! I was offered two choices—stay in human resources or become a navigator. I never had the flying bug and by now had learned quite a bit about military personnel systems, so the choice was an easy one for me.

As an OTS selectee, my grade was increased to staff sergeant. Sadly, my status among coworkers and friends changed almost immediately. For example, I now outranked my supervisor, who was a sergeant. He was very uncomfortable, and so was I. Little by little, my friends began to exclude Cheryl and myself from their inner circle. I was the enemy now. But I understood it. They felt uncomfortable hanging around officers, just like I did. The officers held all the cards—the system was designed that way. I realized quickly that I was no longer a peer, that is, an enlisted member of the air force. This stung a bit.

We had about seven weeks to get our affairs in order. Cheryl and I went through a flurry of activity, shipping household goods, scheduling flights, and planning our new life. She departed several weeks before me and would stay with her father (now retired) in Fort Myers, Florida. I would depart Loring Air Force Base, Limestone, Maine, and drive to Lackland AFB in late March 1980 and begin my training. (In 1991, the Base Realignment and Closure Commission recommended that Loring AFB be closed and its aircraft and mission be distributed to other bases around the nation. Even with Senator Muskie's strong objection, the base was closed in 1994.) When I exited the main gate for the last time, my thoughts were on new beginnings. I was determined to make this work. I vowed to make my wife and family proud of me.

I didn't know it at the time, but I would never live with Cheryl again. In fact, I would only see her one more time for the rest of my life.

CHAPTER EIGHT

"It's what you learn after you know it all that counts." — *JOHN WOODEN*

A s I was bouncing through Maine on Route 1 South in my Buick Skylark, somewhere between Caribou and nowhere, my mind started to race.

The flat, thinly treed, snow-covered tundra was luring me deep into my thoughts. In my mind, I was drawing a "T"—with a plus sign on one side and a minus sign on the other. After I placed the "T" on my imaginary refrigerator, I began assessing where the hell I was in my life. On the plus side: a steady job, a selectee for OTS, a good marriage (at least I thought so), and a chance to get out of Maine. On the minus side: a coin toss leading to a divorce, an unchosen career leading to unknown places, another SSE decision that was not my own idea, and a continual loss of friends along the way. But the real issue was much bigger. Although I had been doing a decent job and my performance appraisals were good enough for OTS, I still hadn't bought in to the military yet. This was a problem. The commitment to extend my stay in the USAF had to have some kind of meaning, right? Why did I always feel like I was in a play, but not really part of the cast? Was there some deep resentment of the military because of my divorce? Was I even officer material? Was my desire to leave Maine the sole reason why I was heading to Texas?

Somewhere near East Millinocket on Interstate 95, with the plusses and minuses in place, I finally came to a conclusion (my own SSE?) that would guide me for the next two decades. "Feeney," I said to myself, "you have to go all in. It doesn't matter how you got to this point in your life. You won't make it in this business if you're constantly second-guessing your decisions." I vowed at that exact moment to funnel all my energies toward positive career goals and stop living in the past. I couldn't wait to get out of Maine.

Back home, Mom was still living in Ben Avon, and Susan was attending college locally at Point Park on an academic scholarship. She would later transfer to Syracuse University, study journalism, and finish first in her class. It was hard to gauge how well my mother was doing. She was tough, and she was a survivor. We drank a few drafts from her beermeister, and I did some chores around the house. We talked a lot about Dad, my new officer career, and her bartending job. She had rekindled some old friendships and was trying her best to get by. Luckily, all of her kids visited her regularly (except me, because I was so far away). And her tally of grandkids and great-grandkids was growing, which really helped her loneliness. In the next few years, she would remarry.

It was surreal arriving at Lackland AFB, San Antonio, again. Three years earlier, I had been a fired dorm chief clawing through basic training. But this time around, I was assured by everyone I knew that OTS was not the same environment. And it wasn't.

The twelve-week program was not designed to be easy. The average day lasted eighteen hours and included many texts and academic assignments in addition to the already hectic military training schedule. Created in 1957, OTS offers commissioning opportunities to both qualified civilian college graduates and to active-duty enlisted personnel who have completed a bachelor's degree. The physical examinations were tough, and the security investigation was very thorough. (One negative comment about my AWOL incident would have instantly eliminated me.) The senior officer trainees (OTs) ran the school. The flight training officers (FTOs) were always nearby, but left the management of the day-to-day operations to the senior OTs. This proactive, hands-off approach was the exact opposite of basic military training, where every action was dictated and supervised by enlisted training instructors (TIs). This new approach was exactly what I needed.

I was assigned to Flight 612. We were one of six flights in Squadron 6. During any given encampment, there were three lower-class flights and three upper-class flights. Each squadron had about 125 OTs. I had a big advantage coming from BMT. I'd seen all of this before. I learned to *never* volunteer for anything. I knew that after graduation, the OT leadership positions were forgotten. My goal was to avoid extra duties and remain a low-ranked OT second lieutenant throughout the program. Cooperating and graduating was my plan.

During the first six weeks, the emphasis was heavily on training. Much of the training was familiar to me, like marching, calisthenics, parade practice, firing range, squadron inspections, and so on. The hardest part was the drill practice. They brought in enlisted TI's from Basic Military Training (BMT), and worked us pretty hard in that Texas afternoon sun, sometimes for hours at a time. It was commonplace for OTs to fall out from exhaustion or even faint in formation.

Everything else, to be honest, was pretty manageable for me. I was carrying out my plot to stay low-key with perfection. Everything was coming into focus—I could do this. I was steering the blob.

Of course, it didn't last. We were authorized weekly phone calls to spouses and families. Now that I was all in, I was excited about the prospect of beginning a new chapter with Cheryl, far away from the hellish cold of Maine. After about three weeks at OTS, during a conversation with her, this was the result:

"How are you doing, Don. All right?"

"Wow, it's really intense. But I'm doing good. Our flight is strong, and we're doing well in honor flight competitions," I said. "For example, yesterday at the leadership reaction course, we ..."

"Don, I need to tell you something," she interrupted. "This is very difficult." I waited. "I, uh, am seeing somebody else. I think I'm in love with him."

"In love! How in the hell can you be in love with someone else? You just left Maine eight weeks ago," I yelled. "Goddamnit, we just got married, for Christ's sake. Who is it? How did this happen so fast?"

"It's someone I've known for a long time. You know him too." I waited. "It's Richard" (not his real name).

"Your fucking cousin! You're sleeping with your cousin?" I was stunned. I knew Richard, and he seemed like a good guy. I remember asking him to keep an eye on Cheryl for me. (*Insert ironic joke here.*)

"Let me explain," she replied.

For the next few moments, as Cheryl spoke, I thought about the base library where I had met her, the travels around Europe, moving to Maine, and our wedding day just eight months earlier. I thought about the inevitable—two divorces at age twenty-six, with neither marriage ever having a chance.

There was no way out. I had stopped listening. The die was cast.

"Don't bother. I want a divorce," I said. Then I hung up. A few weeks later, she complied. We had nothing, so it was uncontested. The decree came in the mail. I signed it and sent it back to Florida. *Good riddance.* I thought of the fish I used to watch as a boy near the Little Indian. They would jump for joy in the lake. They looked so content. But they weren't. They were jumping for their lives, with predators just below the waterline. I wondered how long I could stay in the air and avoid the water below.

Perhaps it was the divorce or maybe the defense mechanism of avoidance, but I decided to turn all my energies toward my training and to block everything else out. Although the divorce was very painful, I couldn't allow myself to grieve during OTS—I didn't have the time. I was determined to stay in the air, like the fish, for as long as I could. I'd have to grieve later.

Luckily for me, I was really getting excited about OTS, and for the first time in my life, I felt like I belonged. The atmosphere was electric, and our flight training officer (FTO), Captain Lovell, was stern but pragmatic. Although I still wasn't interested in leadership positions, I did volunteer to be the flight athletics officer—and ate it up. We had two sports in OTS, flickerball and one-pitch. Each sport had tons of unique rules, and the key to winning was to maximize teamwork under pressure. For the first six weeks, we played one-pitch. It was similar to softball, except that each batter got only one pitch to hit. Everyone in the field was on the opponent's team, except the pitcher, who was your teammate. It was my job to ensure that every player competed, played at least two positions, and batted at least twice. This was very difficult, because we were always on the clock and had to run nonstop or get penalized. With a very good athletic team, Flight 612 went undefeated! We soundly beat every other flight for six straight weeks. I was beaming with pride. (Winning games kept you in honor flight competitions, which helped reduce demerits. Fewer demerits translated into off-base liberty. This was serious business.)

As I mentioned earlier, OTS was much different than BMT. Although the overall emphasis of both programs was military training and discipline, the former was more complex. In addition to the constant academic testing, OTS took the approach that you were an adult and didn't need constant supervision. It also gave you plenty of opportunities to succeed or fail. I didn't see it at first, but the training was carefully planned to develop leaders and encourage personal growth, not just to mismanage your brain with great skill. Offhand, I can think of three major differences between the two programs. First, the Leadership Reaction Course (LRC) . Second, the Officers Training School Open Mess (OTSOM). And third, the frequent chances to get off base.

Although both programs used an obstacle course (they actually shared the same one, and called it the Confidence Course), the LRC was developed for officer candidates only. The LRC was a series of life-sized puzzles, if you will, that required real teamwork to complete successfully. For example, you might have a series of low walls, ropes, a barrel/box to carry, wooden planks, and so on lying inside one of the LRC zones. The FTO read a scenario— crossing a river with important medical supplies, for instance— and you had to figure out how to use the available materials to accomplish the task, that is, get across the river while on the clock, ensuring that every person made it safely. It was fascinating to watch the different leadership styles. Some possessed good followership skills, while others raced into action. The stronger participants started lifting things and moving them around instinctively, while the quieter ones silently solved the tasks in their minds. There was lots of yelling and screaming, with too many type As trying to act without a workable plan. Captain Lovell observed all of us and recorded the events as they unfolded. At the end of each session, he would lead an "after-action" discussion that was very informative. Sometimes we solved the puzzle; other times we didn't. The amazing thing about the LRC was its ability to expose the leadership styles of all the participants. I learned not to plan too quickly, to pause a moment or two before jumping into action, and to seek out the quieter, thoughtful types who had a tendency to solve the problem first. (No one event did more to help me understand my management style than the LRC.) There were several visits to the LRC, and Flight 612 savored the opportunity to excel. And we did. Our success rate was the best in the squadron.

The OTSOM was an oasis in the desert and a great mental picture to focus on when you were marching in the one-hundred-degree heat. The daydream of a cold beer, together with the fun of meeting OTs from other squadrons, kept your mind in a positive place. The OTSOM was a bar, on base, that was open three or four nights a week. There you could swap stories about OTS and develop some lasting friendships. If you were lucky, like me, you could meet someone to help you recover from divorce #2. Her name was Rachel. She was from another squadron on the other side of the base. I raced to the OTSOM every chance I could, and was thrilled when I saw her there. We talked for hours. Her tremendous patience and humor helped me to slowly release the anxiety and embarrassment of my marriage. It took everything I had to swallow my pride and tell Rachel that my wife had left me for someone else. But I knew I had to confront the pain, or it wouldn't go away.

The theme song for the officer trainees in class 80-12 was "We Gotta Get Out of This Place," by the Animals. Every time it played at the OTSOM, we sang along as loudly as we could. It was our anthem and our therapy session at the same time. Imagine hundreds of young kids, overworked and in need of sleep, letting it all go at the same time. There were also dancing, darts, and heavily contested billiard matches. The laughter and excitement was infectious. In that spot, at that exact time, we were all one. I never felt that kind of camaraderie again. We were special, and we were accomplishing something great. To be an air force officer in the world's greatest military was humbling—it meant something. Tomorrow, it was back to reality. But tonight, at the OTSOM, we were dancing on the ceiling.

As Flight 612 approached the halfway point (six weeks) of our officer training experience, we started to realize how special we really were. We were crushing our sister flights in academics and athletics, and excelled in every flight competition. Our inspections were also going very well, so Captain Lovell had no choice but to cut us loose. Look out, San Antonio ...

Since most of us didn't have cars, we piled into cabs for the twelve-mile trip downtown. San Antonio, or Saint Anthony, is the seventh most populated city in the United States. It's in the American Southwest, in the south-central part of Texas. The River Walk, an urban river restoration, had numerous shops, bars, and restaurants. Small, flat, barge-like tourist boats passed by regularly. The food was amazing, the beer cold, and the music always playing. My flight buddies and I headed straight for Durty Nellie's, where we tossed peanut shells all over the floor and sang "When Irish Eyes Are Smiling" almost on key. (I remember during basic training, we were allowed to visit the River Walk for an hour or so. I told myself if I ever got back, I'd head directly to Durty Nellie's.) We sat outside and watched the real world go by. Sounds of folklorico and flamenco music wafted in the soft, summer air. And there was always some type of festival going on nearby.

After a few beers, we'd hit some of the local sites. The Arneson River Theater was just around the corner. It's an outside stage on the River Walk, with terraced seating on the opposite bank. We stopped and watched some folk dancers for a bit, then headed to the Alamo Mission. We marveled at the bravery of Davy Crockett, Jim Bowie, and 188 others who fought for Texas independence against overwhelming odds, and perished. (Years later, as a captain assigned to Randolph AFB, I was part of the Blue Notes, a USAF choir that performed in Alamo Plaza, right in front of the mission.) We climbed the 750-foot Tower of the Americas in HemisFair Plaza and took in the view. Finally, we circled the entire River Walk, returned to Durty Nellie's to chill for a while, and then returned to the base. It's hard to explain, but the rigors of OTS made every diversion—the OTSOM, the LRC, and the River Walk—more memorable.

Once a week, we had a Squadron Six Commander's Call, where Captain Lovell would brief us on upcoming events, honor flight results, and so on. Our class was finishing up its sixth week—the halfway point—and it was time to replace the wing and group staff. If you recall, my plan was to become a chameleon and volunteer for nothing. The OTs were asked to prioritize the leadership jobs they wanted, and then hand in their choices to the FTO. I left my list blank. I was confident there were enough OTs around scrambling for honor graduate to volunteer for the leadership positions. A few days later, the selections were announced. Flight 612 dominated the results. Of the fifteen members of our flight, three made the wing staff, including the wing commander position, and three made the group staff. There was no other flight even close. The word was out about Flight 612—we were really an exceptional group. (Note: We played flickerball—a cross between football and basketball —for the next six weeks and won every game. My flight never lost one athletic competition in twelve weeks!) There was one selection left— the best and most difficult position in OTS, the OT squadron commander. This job placed the leadership responsibility of the entire squadron, including academics, athletics, building and ground maintenance, parade formations, inspections, and so on on one person. Although the wing and group staff leadership positions were impressive, the selectees had limited opportunities to lead and were housed in a separate dormitory apart from the squadron. I was mildly curious about the selection of the OT Squadron Six Commander, because I knew the power that position had over all of us.

"And finally, the new OT Squadron Six Commander: OT Donald J. Feeney. OT Feeney, please step forward and accept the leadership role of squadron commander." I saluted Captain Lovell and was left standing in front of my new squadron.

"I'm honored to accept this leadership position, blah, blah, blah ..." To be honest, I don't remember what I said at that moment. But I know what I was thinking. *How in the hell did this happen? Is it the dorm chief saga all over again? Is it the return of the reluctant football captain? I left my leadership position list blank. Didn't that make my intentions clear enough? Have I lost control of the blob? Is it TMYKTMYDKS syndrome again?* Exactly one hour later, I was meeting with my executive staff, comprised of an operations officer (kind of like a vice commander), an administration officer, a material officer, and a standardization officer. We ground out a strategy for the upcoming weeks, relying heavily on Captain Lovell's helpful suggestions. A few days later, now part of the senior class, I was moved to the commander's dorm room, which I shared with the operations officer, OT Kelly.

That night, lying there unable to sleep, I pondered my situation. How is it that *people see things in me that I don't see in myself?* I got what I deserved, right? I was remembering the drive south from Maine, where I vowed to go all in. Although I didn't choose this path, the route was now clear. Dig in, and do the job; no excuses. I fell asleep moments later, resolved to accept any challenge that came my way.

The next six weeks were among the most productive of my young career. I was promoted to OT major and outranked every officer candidate in the building. I was no longer reluctant to lead. I laid out my vision at my own Commander's Call, felt very comfortable delegating to my staff as needed, and wasn't afraid of failure. I marched in front of my squadron with pride at our weekly parades, and took the heat when things didn't go right. I barely slept, and had to pay OT Kelly to make my bed and shine my shoes. I pulled unannounced inspections on other squadrons in the middle of the night, and was tough but fair. I kept a close watch on my new athletics officer, making sure we were as competitive as we could be. I kept a positive attitude and never missed an opportunity to recognize others for their achievements. I dedicated myself to be accountable and constantly reemphasized my vision—be relentless in everything you do. In short, I was becoming a leader. Like John C. Maxwell says in his book *The 21 Indispensable Qualities of a Leader,* "leadership truly develops from the inside out. If you can become the leader you ought to be on the inside, you will be able to become the leader you want to be on the outside."

But that doesn't mean I always did the right thing. I remember one week, when Rachel and I were both looking forward to getting off base and spending some time together. My squadron got a surprise inspection, and I was grounded for the weekend. We weren't ready for it, and it was my fault. I was upset that Rachel was heading downtown and I wasn't. I couldn't handle sitting in my room while she was out seeing San Antonio. I had to act fast. I put together a team of inspectors and headed to her squadron on Thursday around midnight. Long story short—when I got to her area, I gave her enough demerits to keep her on base for the weekend. I know; it was a shitty move. But in spite of that, we had fun at the OTSOM, and we laughed pretty hard about the whole thing. In a way, she was flattered that I would go through so much effort to be with her. (I even got to third base with her behind a maintenance building that night.)

Graduation day arrived. The last event was the final parade, in full military regalia. The parade grounds were packed with families and friends, and the VIP section was full of high-ranking officers, flight training officers, and various other OTS Staff. All of us were extremely excited and carried silver dollars in our pockets. (The tradition was to give a silver dollar to the first NCO you salute. None of us wanted to take the chance of saluting without coins, so we carried several to be safe.) The band was playing, we had a T-38 flyover, and all of us in Squadron Six saluted and stood proud when the national anthem played. It was exciting to call "eyes right" and salute from the front of my squadron for the final time as we marched past the reviewing stand. When the parade ended, all the squadrons returned to their positions. There was just one command left. The OT colonel, our wing commander from Flight 612, shouted:

"Officers Training School, Class 80-12. *Dismissed!*"

At that moment, around 1,500 service caps (the ones that look like bus-driver hats) went straight into the air. No one bothered to pick them up. In our dress-blue blouses, folded nicely to avoid wrinkling, were our flight caps, which we donned immediately. We then ripped our OT epaulets from our shoulders, and underneath were the gold bars of a USAF second lieutenant. Everybody was shaking hands, saluting, and passing out coins, and generally having a real nice time. Just then, I looked into the stands and saw Cheryl walking toward me.

"Congratulations, Lt. Feeney. You did it!" she said as she hugged me and kissed me on the cheek. "How does it feel?"

"Great. What are you doing here?" I said. My car was already packed, and parked next to the parade grounds. I was going to have lunch with Rachel, and then take off for Keesler AFB, Mississippi, for training. Cheryl's presence definitely made me feel uncomfortable.

"Don, I was hoping we could talk, you know, about maybe giving our relationship another chance." "What about your cousin Richard? How is that working out?" I really didn't want to know.

"We broke up. It didn't work out," she said very quietly.

Geez, what timing. I went from euphoria to anger in seconds. But OTS had given me strength, and a calmness I never felt before. There was no reason at this point to rub it in. "Look, Cheryl, I have someplace I have to be in a few minutes. And then I'm off to Mississippi for training this afternoon. I'm sorry things didn't work out for you, but it's time for me to move on." I walked to my car and never looked back. Two hours later, I was eastbound on the San Antonio Beltway.

The drive to Biloxi was uneventful. I thought long and hard about Cheryl, and tried to envision a scenario where we could repair our marriage and divorce. There wasn't one.

It was great to arrive at Keesler AFB again. Everything was the same, but different. The base looked the same, and the location was the same. However, everything about my training this time around was different. I was a commissioned officer now. The days of donning my green rope and marching flights to class were over. I had my own efficiency apartment—small, but with a kitchen and living room—and no roommates! The next nine weeks were liberating. For the first time in ages, I lived alone. I could come and go as I please. And I was not directly involved with anyone. Many of my fellow graduates also came to Keesler AFB, so there were ample opportunities to have fun. And I didn't miss many of them.

The classes were challenging. As an airman basic, the human resources curriculum was straightforward, concentrating on regulations, policies, and so on. The emphasis in the course syllabus was very specific, concentrating on entry-level personnel functions. This time around, as a second lieutenant, the approach was much different. The instructors concentrated on intangibles like evaluating performance, supervisory skills, and leadership. We had many in-class exercises and follow-up discussions that were really valuable. I took good notes and was thankful that I had three years of HR experience under my belt. I felt that my prior enlisted time gave me a big advantage in the classroom, and an even bigger advantage when I began my officer career. My plan was to use the best of both worlds to steer the blob.

My social life was great as well. The Keesler Officers' Club was fantastic— packed with new members like me. I was unattached and loving it. I also took a couple of trips to New Orleans with friends—taking in the aura of Bourbon Street once again. The nearby beaches were awesome, and I had the best tan of my life. My friend Rachel graduated from OTS and was training to be a weapons controller at Hurlburt Field, in Okaloosa County, Florida, which is part of the greater Eglin AFB reservation. I went to visit her over a long weekend. We were both nervous. We were inseparable at the OTSOM, but really didn't know each other that well. Our attempt at romance didn't work out that well. That's okay. We were buddies, and we were there for each other when we needed it most. I'll never forget her.

On the way back to Biloxi, I was passing a little nightclub in Pascagoula, Mississippi, when I saw a marquee that read:

SPECIAL GUEST—IRON BUTTERFLY. TODAY ONLY. 6PM.

It was 6:45 p.m., so I slammed on my brakes, made a U-turn, and headed into the club. Sure enough, there they were, playing on a small stage, with maybe fifteen to twenty people in the entire place. That evening, in a sparsely filled bar, I watched Iron Butterfly perform "In-A-Gadda-Da-Vida" in its entirety. It lasted over twenty minutes, and the drum solo blew me away. Yes, they were past their prime at this point. But I didn't care. That album was one of the all-time rock-and-roll classics, and sold more than thirty million copies (I had one stashed away somewhere).

The following week there was a big day at Keesler for new recruits like me. It was assignment time. All of us were nervous and eager to find out where we were headed. I was slated to Kirkland AFB, in Albuquerque, New Mexico. At first, I was very happy with this location. But after discussing the position with my assignment counselor, I learned that the CBPO was already overmanned by two officers. I wasn't about to start my career as the officer in charge of making coffee. I wanted my own section. I knew enough about CBPO operations to understand how awkward serving in an overage position could be. I was given a choice: either keep the assignment, or accept the first position that became available. (Kind of like a coin toss, right?) Without hesitation, I gave back the assignment. My friends thought I was crazy. I had opened myself up for worldwide duty, which included remote sites in some desolate places. But I didn't care. I wanted my own section.

Graduation came and went. My colleagues were off to begin their USAF careers. But I was still in Biloxi. It had been almost two months after I turned down my assignment to Kirkland AFB, and I still didn't have a clue where I was going. I was in what they call "casual status," that is, they didn't know what to do with me. It wasn't bad—I was working in one of the student squadrons, helping out the instructors and enjoying the pace. But inwardly, I was definitely on edge. It's the not-knowing that will drive you crazy.

And then I got the call:

"Lieutenant Feeney, this is Captain Williams, your assignment officer." (*Like I don't know who he is.*) "We've made a final selection for your initial assignment." I waited. "You have been assigned to the Fifteenth Air Base Wing, as the Chief, Customer Service Section." (*What base, man? Come on, I'm dying here.*) "You will report to Hickam Air Force Base, Honolulu, Hawaii, not later than 30 September, 1990."

That's right—Hawaii!

From a senior airman in Limestone, Maine, to a second lieutenant in Honolulu, Hawaii, in less than six months. Talk about a career change!

Maybe tails was a good choice after all.

CHAPTER NINE

"The most beautiful fleet of islands ever placed in any ocean ..." — *MARK TWAIN*

———◆◇◆———

When I departed Biloxi, I was on top of the world. I had risked losing a great assignment to New Mexico, but it didn't matter. I wanted a real job, even if it meant a lousy location. For the rest of my USAF career and my State Department career, I continued this trend. The position always came first. To me, the more challenging the position, the better. Ending up in Hawaii was a great break. I planned on capitalizing on it.

My orders allowed me to drive the Skylark to San Diego and ship it to Hawaii from there. That gave me ten days of paid travel and per diem pay, and I used all of it. I went through San Antonio and visited friends who ended up being stationed there. I stopped in Albuquerque, New Mexico, mostly out of curiosity, hung out one afternoon in Santa Fe, then moved on to check out the Grand Canyon in Arizona. And of course, I went through Los Angeles on the way south to San Diego. (I'm not a big LA fan, but I can never get enough of Santa Monica Beach.) It was a very relaxing trip, and the first time in my life I traveled that many days on my own. And I loved it.

I recall flying into Oahu like it was yesterday. It was early morning, and the sun was bright and clear. The landscape from Pearl Harbor to Diamondhead was laid out below me like a magic carpet. When the airplane wheels hit the threshold, it became a reality—I was home.

My sponsor picked me up at the airport and took me to the temporary officer housing facility on Hickam AFB. That afternoon, top down in her convertible, she took me around base, then to the Officers' Club, and eventually to downtown Waikiki. We ended up at her place. Welcome to Hawaii...

The next several weeks went by fast. I found a nice house in Halawa Heights, overlooking Pearl Harbor and Aloha Stadium, positioned just below the southern perimeter of Camp Smith. (Camp Smith is a US marine installation, and the headquarters for the US Pacific Command.) My backyard had several fruit trees and a view you couldn't believe. The filming of the Pearl Harbor attack in *Tora! Tora! Tora!* took place just above my back fence. If you remember the scenes, then you'll know what it was like to stand in my backyard. The landlord, Mr. Lee, was ninety-two years old when I met him. He worked at the Pearl Harbor Shipyard, and had every other Sunday off. On Sunday, December 7, 1941, he had watched the whole thing from his backyard. It must have been very frightening when the Japanese Zeros split the Waianae and Koolau Mountain Ranges, and buzzed directly over his head to begin the surprise attack. It must have been worse to watch as the bombers killed 2,117 people, with fifty-seven of the dead being fellow employees of his. (The awakening of the sleeping giant changed the face of America and the world. The quick American ascent from an isolationist country to world superpower probably started on that very day.)

My first officer position as the Chief, Customer Assistance Section, couldn't have been better. I had twenty-two airmen and NCOs under my supervision, and one very capable civilian secretary. I managed three distinct work centers in support of six thousand active-duty personnel and their dependents. My prior service in the CBPO was a great help when dealing with enlisted coworkers. I supervised several NCOs with much more experience than myself, including a senior master sergeant who was twenty-five years older than I. I gave him tons of latitude, stayed out of his way for the most part, and allowed him to slowly warm up to my management style. I knew I had no chance to reach the younger troops if my senior NCO wasn't in my camp.

But it was all good. I found it ironic that my position was responsible for the Records Section—the very first place I had ever worked as an airman basic in Zweibrucken. I oversaw all customer reception responsibilities, from in-processing to retirement, along with personnel, health, and immunization records. I also administered the base awards and decorations program, and dual-hatted as the air force aid officer. (The Air Force Aid Society is the official charity of the USAF. Founded in 1942, it's a nonprofit organization whose mission is to help relieve financial distress of air force members and their families and to assist in financing higher education goals. All funding comes from active-duty contributions.) In my first year alone, I approved loans and grants well over $75,000—a lot of money in 1990.

One night, after a few months living in paradise, I had another singularly significant event (SSE) that put to rest all the flak surrounding my military career this far. Sitting on the roof outside my living room, watching the sunset, it hit me. Even though I fought with Jill about coming into the military, moped about a lost coin toss, went AWOL in Germany, refused to even consider applying for OTS on my own, and pissed away two marriages, I was now an air force officer living in Honolulu. And through it all, guess what? I was happy. I couldn't believe how lucky I'd been and how fortunate I was to be around people *who saw something in me that*

I never saw in myself. My health was excellent, and I had some money in my pocket for the first time in my life. I was single, with no new ex-wives in the queue, and I planned on keeping it that way. My job was great, and I'd met a few really good friends already. To quote Bob Dylan: "May your hands always be busy, may your feet always be swift. May you have a strong foundation, when the winds of changes shift."

Thank you, Mom and Dad. And thank you, God, for my solid foundation. I met my best friend, Errol Gard, at the Officers' Club around this same time. He was also a second lieutenant, or "butter bar" as we were called, and worked in the HQ Pacific Air Forces building with me. He was a management analyst, soft-spoken with quiet confidence, living his dream as an air force officer. Unlike me, Errol had enrolled in Junior Reserve Officers Training Corps (JROTC) at a young age, attended military school in high school, and received his commission in college through ROTC. I really admired his single-mindedness of purpose, that is, knowing exactly what he wanted to do. We bonded quickly and were practically inseparable for most of the next three years. When the apartment downstairs opened up, Errol moved in. We were both very avid runners. After work we used to run from work, across the base down to Hickam Harbor, and then around the back of the Honolulu International Airport. The full circuit was about fifteen miles. We ran 5, 10, and 15K races anytime we could find one. Two races stick out in my mind. We traveled to Molokai, with our dates for the weekend, to run a 15K there. Molokai is a cigar-shaped island approximately thirty-eight miles long and ten miles wide. The terrain is very rugged, and arable land is in short supply. There was a leper colony (now vacant) located on the small north shore of Molokai—a place where sufferers of Hansen's disease, or leprosy, were forced into quarantine by the Hawaiian government. The race was brutal, with extreme changes in altitude and relentless wind. I finished around thirty seconds behind Errol and was very happy with that. He was thin and very quick. I was a block with a head (6'2" and 225 lbs.). Physics was not on my side. Afterward, at a nearby pub, we enjoyed the scenery and our company, had some great food and ale, and watched the sunset. The other race was in Kona, on the Big Island, aptly named Hawaii. Kona is a beautiful tourist town, with outstanding beaches and social life. The 10K was mostly flat and devoid of wind, so the race was uneventful. So we took off in our rental car. First, we drove to the top of Mauna Kea, over 13,796 feet above sea level. The view was amazing—from lava and desertlike terrain to green valleys and seascapes. After that, we headed to Kilauea, perhaps the most active volcano in the world. You can stand right on the edge and look down into the bubbling, hot center. Although it didn't erupt while we were there, we saw the results of recent explosions on the south side of the peak, located in Hawaii Volcanoes National Park.

But the real center of Hawaii is definitely Oahu, or "the gathering place." There was so much to do there—I don't know where to start. I was more active on Oahu (1980–1983) than any other time in my life.

I had already begun my master's degree with the University of Southern California. It was a very tough program, and I had to really study to keep up. I was also coaching and playing on our squadron softball team, holding down the anchor spot on the CBPO bowling team, running every day, and preparing for deployment as part of the CBPO PERSCO (Personnel Contingency) Team. I was the Base Family Services Center advisor and a member of the Child Advocacy Board, won an officer-of-the-year award, and served as Air Force Hawaii's Combined Federal Campaign Manager. For the first time in my life, I was self-actualizing, and it felt good. I was steering the blob.

Errol and I hiked Diamondhead and took some amazing pictures of Waikiki and Koko Head (next headland to the east), and of the beautiful coastline on the southeastern side of the island. We hit the North Shore Pipeline—Haleiwa, Waimea, and Sunset Beach—many times to swim in the gigantic waves. I learned how to water ski and sail at Hickam Harbor and how to surf at Ewa Beach. We hung out at Bellows Air Station, an MWR facility for the American military and their families. The beach was the best in the world—period. It was used for the *Magnum, P.I.* television series. (Note: We met Tom Selleck at the Honolulu Club. He was pleasant and cordial, and even bought us a drink.) Framed by Makapuu Point to the south and Kailua to the north, it was a conifer-lined beach, with perfect sand and waves. We spent many weekends staying with friends in the beachside cabanas there. At Hickam, we hung out at the Officers' Club, which rested on the narrow entrance to Pearl Harbor. It was a very popular spot, especially when aircraft carriers squeezed through the entryway. The ships felt so close you could almost touch them; and the sight of thousands of sailors in formation, donned with dress whites, was impressive.

I finally traded in my Buick Skylark and bought a two-seat Ford EXP. The interest rate was 19 percent! I guess the US economy was still recovering from the Carter administration. Errol and I had our house on Halawa Heights set up pretty nice and started to have parties there. We both played guitar and spent lots of nights honing our skills. The Hawaii Islanders (Pittsburgh Pirate AAA baseball team) played right below our house in Aloha Stadium. I thoroughly enjoyed taking in a game every once in a while. All and all, it was an idyllic life in one of the most beautiful places on earth.

We met some friends who lived close by while learning to water ski. Their place was kind of a commune—several people coming in and out, music playing, and pot smoke in the air. Believe it or not, we were still smoking pot once in a while. (The urinalysis program hadn't started yet, but was coming soon.) We called the place Crazy Tom's house. I can remember Errol getting high and meeting a girl near the swimming pool. Ten minutes later, they were screwing in the water, oblivious to those sitting nearby. One of the residents (can't remember his name) was a slothful type with no drive or direction. But, man, could he play guitar. After a few joints, he was ready to go. I was usually assigned basic rhythm, while Errol and he carried the melodies. We'd have the place rocking, with beer and pot everywhere, and occasionally, even a swimsuit top would come off.

And yes, there were girls, and the escapades that came with them. One comes to mind immediately. I met a girl named Mandy—half Chinese and half Sri Lankan—at the Illiki Nightclub in Waikiki. She was cute and very sweet. We dated for months, and I really liked her. She was living in one of the high-rises in Aiea, just a few miles from our place. It was a nice apartment, well-decorated and feminine. One day after hanging out at Crazy Tom's pool with us, she asked to borrow my car. I gave her the keys, and we agreed that I would pick up the EXP the next day. When I arrived to pick up my car, the following happened just after I rang her doorbell:

"Hello," a male voice answered. I was stunned.

"Who is this?" I asked. "Is Mandy there? I came to pick up my car keys." "I'm her husband, you asshole. Who is this? And what is my wife doing with your car keys?"

I was thinking—*this ain't good. What's going on here? I'd better act fast before he chucks them down the toilet.*

"Look, sir, I had no idea Mandy was married. She never told me. I swear." I heard him grumbling something about coming down to kick my ass. I needed my car, so I had to wait for him. Reflecting back, I realized that Mandy must have taken all his stuff out of the apartment and put it in storage while he was away. There was nothing masculine in that place.

The door opened. A big guy in a navy uniform appeared, with tears welled up in his eyes. "I should kick your ass," he said as he lunged toward me. I didn't move. I kept my hands to my sides. I was going to let him take a swing at me without defending myself. But he stopped. "How long were you seeing my wife?" It was just over five months—about the same length of time a sailor would remain at sea. Duh.

"Sir, I am very sorry. I would never have dated her if I knew she was married. There's nothing in the apartment to suggest she had a husband. Look, give me my keys, and I promise you, you'll never see me again." I waited. He growled. Then he threw the keys in my face. (I had heard about navy wives having affairs while their husbands were at sea. But it would never happen to me, right?) Driving home, I felt awful on two fronts. I had assisted Mandy in committing adultery and hurt someone I never met before. In addition, I was really starting to like her, and now it was clearly over. My sterling record with women continued.

Errol and I headed down to Duke's Canoe Club, on the beach in the Outrigger Waikiki—between the Royal Hawaiian and the Moana Sheraton— where I could lick my wounds for a while. Of all the bars in the world, this is and will always be my favorite. It's located right on the beach, with great food and live music on weekends. It's an eclectic mix of tourists and locals. In my opinion, both groups are essential for a world-class hangout. Locals bring all kinds of charm and experiences with them. And tourists are great because they choose to be there, they're always in a good mood, and they aren't afraid to spend money. After a few brews and some encouraging words from my pal Errol, I began to relax. After all, I really hadn't known Mandy was married. And it was fun dating her, even though it ended badly. Pretty soon we were laughing out loud, and I was returning to normal.

A few weeks later, Errol and I left for Kauai, where we had decided to hike the Na Pali Mountains. We spent five days along that crest line, observing the greenest greens and the bluest blues we'd ever seen. Living on trail mix, cheese, and fruit, we drank fresh rainwater in abundance and scaled some tricky and dangerous trails. According to Wikipedia, "The Kalalau Trail from the end of Hawaii Route 56 provides the only land access, traversing 11 miles and crossing five major valleys (and many smaller ones) before reaching Kalalau Beach at the base of the Kalalau Valley." It was very strenuous traipsing up and down those valleys and peaks, but worth every minute. When we finally completed our circuit, we hitchhiked to Princeville and thoroughly enjoyed a feast of pizza and beer. I'll never forget the beauty of the "Garden Isle."

During a Friday happy hour at the O' Club, we met Al Malero, another junior officer like Errol and myself. We got along well, and the three of us started to hang out together. Al was handsome, similar to my buddy Paul at Clarion, and the girls swooned around him. He was shy with women and had no idea how attractive he was. Al was an orphan, with no family. He always had that hangdog look like an adorable puppy—girls ate it up. The three of us continued to run daily and enter 10K and 15K races in places like Kaneohe, Pearl City, and Mililani. The races were fun and a great place to meet girls. Al also joined Errol and me for the Carole Kai Bed Races in Kapiolani Park in Waikiki. This charitable event involved five people—one bikinied girl in the double-bed frame with wheels, and four guys using the bedposts to push it as fast as possible down a raceway. We qualified at Hickam in the preliminary rounds and then went downtown for the big race. It was a blast, and there was plenty of food and beer afterward. (We weren't even close to winning; the Samoans dominated every year.)

The three of us would bolt to the O' Club happy hour on Fridays for Mongolian barbeque. I never had a better meal in my life. You were given a large bowl, about the size of a helmet. Then you perused a wide array of meats and vegetables and selected as many of each as you wanted. After adding frying oils to your masterpiece—there must have been at least twenty different types—your concoction was weighed, and you paid by the ounce. But the best part came next. The Mongolian cooks would take your bowl and splash its contents onto large, circular wooden cooking surfaces, which sat on top of open flames. You would watch all your selected ingredients meld together in taste and aroma. Then the scalding-hot repast was dumped over rice, and away you'd go. The reason we raced to the happy hour was simple. The retiree population in Hawaii was huge. If we didn't move fast, we were SOL. (Today, as a retiree myself, I refuse to step in front of an active-duty military member for any reason. It's their day—not mine.)

My Hawaiian experience was going too fast. I made first lieutenant, and life was good. My mother and her sister (Aunt Fran—part of a package deal when my dad married my mom) came to visit. Although they stayed in Waikiki, I caught up with them every day for dinner, a luau, or a show. One night, I surprised them with tickets to see Don Ho, the biggest star in Waikiki, at the Hilton Hawaiian Village. The tickets were expensive, but they were for my mom. Mr. Ho's performance was, in a word, terrible. He was so badly coked out, he could barely stand up. I remember this scenario:

"And what is your name, young lady?" he said to a fan on stage with him.

"Mary," she replied.

"And where are you from, Mary?" he asked.

"Los Angeles, California, Mr. Ho," she replied in excitement. Don Ho paused for a few seconds, struggling to keep his balance, and asked, "And where are you from, Mary?"

He was so wasted that he forgot he had just asked the same question! But his music was even worse. During "Tiny Bubbles," his only hit, he was too stoned to sing the song. So he mumbled the words, and the audience sang the song for him. He'd say "Tiny bubbles," and the audience would sing, "Tiny bubbles"; then he'd say, "in the wine," and the audience would sing, "in the wine," and so on. What a rip-off. But it was great seeing my mom, and she looked pretty good. Susan, the youngest of us children, had left for Syracuse University, and Mom was now living alone. But she was doing okay, and we got along great during her visit.

Speaking of Susan, she came to live with me during my second summer in Honolulu. I found her a General Service (GS) administrative job on Ford Island, which was located in the middle of Pearl Harbor. In 1992, the island could only be reached by ferry, and it supported several naval administrative facilities. Her best friend, Andy (the "one never knows, does one?" guy), was also on Oahu, so it worked out well for her.

The summer flew by, and I must admit, I don't remember a lot about Susan's visit. She spent much of her time at work or with Andy. His dad, by the way, was the conductor of the Honolulu Symphony. One of my best memories involved driving Susan to the dock each morning for her ferry ride. (We could see the ferry leaving Ford Island from our living-room window.) At first, we'd arrive early, making sure Susan wouldn't miss the ferry. But as the summer wore on, we departed a few moments later each day. It was driving Susan crazy. But I was determined to time the drop-off perfectly, with Susan boarding the ferry just as it was pulling out. Every morning, I'd watch through the window and let the ferry get closer to Pearl Harbor before we departed. Each day, it moved even closer. Susan was a nervous wreck. I was really enjoying the challenge. One red light at the wrong time and she'd miss her ferry. Near the end of the summer, I finally did it—the perfect drop-off. It involved speeding down Halawa Heights, catching all the lights, and screeching to a halt at the pier. I watched as Susan ran for the boat and literally jumped from the pier to the ferry just as it was pulling away. Priceless.

Andy had a sister on Kauai who was studying the patterns of rare birds. Susan, Andy, and I went to visit her one weekend. Kauai is the oldest Hawaiian island and has the wettest spot on earth, a place called Mount

Wai'ale'ale. Andy's sister was living very austerely at a nearby encampment, and loving it. She showed us all types of rare birds and happily related the history of their development. But leave it to man to mess up a good thing. She also explained that the island had a rat problem—which had been introduced by passing ships over the last three centuries. In an effort to thwart this invasion of rats, locals released mongoose into the area. The idea was simple—the mongoose would eat the rats, and everything would be hunky-dory. However, these Einsteins failed to realize that mongoose come out in the day and that rats are nocturnal. The rest is obvious. The mongoose gorged on the eggs of rare birds, wiping out several species forever. And since the birds had no predators, they laid their eggs right on the ground, making it an easy feast for the mongoose. Millions of years of evolution erased by the animals with the brains.

As you may recall, I mentioned that I had to deploy on occasion with the PERSCO (Personnel Contingency) Team. I went to Korea a few times in support of Team Spirit, which was the largest military exercise in the world. (In 1981, the United States sent over 167,000 participants to Korea for the exercise, which also included 107,000 South Korean personnel as well. Since the Korean War never officially ended, these exercises were designed to let North Koreans know we were serious about protecting our ally.) Twice I went to Osan Air Base, near Songtan Station, in the city of Pyeongtaek, South Korea. My job was to support the reception and bed-down of thousands of troops and to support the mobility lines that prepared to deploy in-country. Part of my job was to travel via star flight, or bus, to the various locations and evaluate how well the PERSCO teams were doing their job, that is, tracking the total number of troops under the commander, including injuries, fatalities, MIA, and so on. I visited Suwon, Kunsan, Kwangju, Pusan, and Taegu, among others, and really enjoyed the experience.

During my last full summer in Hawaii, circa 1982, I was asked to support Team Spirit as an observer. This sounded good to me. No deploying responsibility, and comfortable billeting on Osan Air Base instead of the usual tent city. I was happy to oblige—I knew exactly what to expect. But during our indoctrination, one of the PERSCO Team chiefs failed to show up, so yours truly was pulled from the comfortable position of observer and sent to Sachon, a bare-base operation on a mountaintop (TMYKTMYDKS). Damn. *Bare-base* means just what it sounds like—the Seabees or Army Corps of Engineers went to Sachon for a week or two, put up some sleeping, office, and mess tents, and then split. For over seven weeks, I froze my ass off up there. No kidding—that was the coldest I have ever been in my life. And that includes winters in Limestone, Maine! Cold mud during the day, frozen mud at night. No trees or structures within miles to hide from the wind. And a very limited amount of hot water. Showers were scarce and fast. Since it was too remote for aircraft, supplies were always behind. When provisions arrived around week four with an assortment of different foods and cases of beer, I almost cried with excitement. From an operational perspective, we weren't getting much accomplished. We lost power all the time, prepared dozens of reports no one read, and were pretty much convinced that Osan Air Base had forgotten all about us. Then one night several Korean buses arrived, and we were taken to one of the palaces of President Rah Tae-Woo. With fine china and crystal glasses, we dined in elegance, scruffy beards and weather-beaten fatigue uniforms notwithstanding. It was quite the comedown to return to Sachon after that feast. But finally, the exercise ended, and I was headed back to Hawaii. Man, it was sweet to see Diamondhead on the horizon again.

Back in the CBPO, I was promoted and moved to a new position—Chief, Personnel Utilization Section. This was the biggest job in the CBPO. I had forty-six people working for me and ran four distinct subunits: Manning Control (inbound assignments), Outbound Assignments, Personnel Readiness (military deployments), and INTRO (employee orientation). It was a very satisfying position, and I became the focal point for base-wide contingency operations. My Team Spirit experience, plus a few other temporary-duty (TDY) deployments dealing with contingency operations were the perfect segue into this job. My office was also the focal point for every departing and arriving family on base. My team was the "first face" for hundreds of employees and their families. I took it very seriously. First impressions make all the difference.

After the 1982 Christmas season was over, 1983 began without incident. (I left my silver Christmas tree up until May. Why? Because I could.) It was my last six months in Hawaii, and everything was going fine. I was single and unattached and enjoying it. I finished my master's degree in systems management, now called management information systems, and felt a great sense of accomplishment. I'm pretty sure I became the first in the Feeney clan to get a master's degree. The USC graduation was great, and I brought along four friends to enjoy the commencement festivities, which included a nice dinner and an open bar. We got our money's worth.

A few weeks later, after several discussions with my assignments officer back in Texas, I decided to apply for a special-duty assignment as a Reserve Officer Training Corps (ROTC) instructor. I needed a break from the personnel sections in the CBPO. Since I was still a first lieutenant, I also needed a grade waiver. My application was accepted, and I was chosen to teach ROTC at the University of Missouri-Rolla. The unit was technically attached to the University of Missouri, but would eventually become its own ROTC detachment. (More on this later.)

What was the old *Candid Camera* line? "When you least expect it, you're elected; it's your lucky day." Well, my lucky day happened during a base-wide picnic, when I ran into Sherie Jennings. She was a sergeant (E-4) and worked in chapel management. Ironically enough, we had arrived in Hawaii on the same day twenty-eight months earlier. She was with her husband at the time. (Now divorced, but who wasn't?) I remember seeing her then and thinking that she was attractive. We started dating, and things began to move fast. But there were complications. Although fraternization policies restricting officers and airmen relationships were not established, they were coming soon. We knew it was problematic, so we stayed low-key and spent most of our time away from Hickam. Sherie was a real California girl—tall, slim, and a little quirky—and fun to be around. We were falling in love, and I was sick inside about it. With my track record, this was the last thing I needed. We dated for the rest of my tour in Hawaii. Sherie wanted to get out of the USAF and follow me to Missouri. Since she had another year left on her enlistment, I doubted whether our new, long-distance relationship would last. But I decided to let things play out anyway...

All in all, I really enjoyed my time in the Hawaiian Islands. It would be impossible to include all the madcap times I had over there. I visited Lanai, Kauai, Molokai, Maui, Kahoolawa, and the big Island of Hawaii. Each is beautiful, and each is unique. Oahu has 85 percent of the state population and the large city of Honolulu, which includes the legendary Waikiki area. Maui has the road to Hana, a small untouched village on the eastern coast. To get there, you travel on one of the world's most scenic drives. The whaling village of La Haina is historic, and also a lively hot spot for tourists. Molokai is rugged and steep, but has an enchanting aura that's different from the rest. And the leper colony is located in a beautiful valley of greens and blues. Kauai is by far the most beautiful of them all. From the lush Na Pali Mountains to the perfect beaches and forests, it truly was the Garden Island. The big island of Hawaii is the youngest, and the largest, and it's still growing. It has the world's most active volcano (Kilauea) and the tallest sea mountain in the world (Mauna Kea). Remarkably, it has all but two of the world's climate zones on one island. Even Lanai, which was mostly pineapple fields in the 1980s, had simple charms, including its one hotel. (Billionaire Larry Ellison bought 98 percent of the island, which today is home to over three thousand people. Where have all the pineapples gone?) I even enjoyed Kahoolawa, a deserted island used as a navy bombing range. I volunteered to help search for unexploded ordinance on the island. We walked in wide lines, ten yards apart, and held up a flag when we saw anything metallic or unusual. The experts would mark the spot, and we'd move on. Weird, but interesting ...

But not all was rosy with my two pals Errol and Al.

I'll start with Errol. Remember the girl that he screwed in the pool at Crazy Tom's? Well, she was still in the picture. She stayed at our house often and always had tons of marijuana. (She stole money from me and ran up my phone bill as well. A real gem.) Errol was smoking more and more, and I started to get concerned. When our wing commander announced that a random drug urinalysis program would begin soon, I quit smoking immediately. My career was too important to let it go up in smoke. But Errol continued to get high. He told me his girlfriend had connections at Tripler Medical Center, where the drug tests would be analyzed. If he was tapped to give a sample, she would make sure it came back negative. I told him he was crazy, but he wouldn't listen to me. At this point, our great friendship began to wane.

A few months later, Errol was selected to give a urine sample. (I don't believe it was random. I think he was targeted.) Everyone knew we hung out together, so I decided to offer an unsolicited sample. My results were negative, but Errol's were not. He tested positive for pot. Our CBPO chief, who honchoed the program, knew of Errol's result. He burst into my office and suggested that I get tested as well. He was caught off guard when I told him I already gave my donation.

Luckily, Errol was a favorite of the wing commander. He was slated to fill the executive officer position in the command section. This was a very promotable job, consisting of managing all the day-to-day operations of the wing commander. Errol convinced him that there must have been some mistake and claimed that he never used drugs. The wing commander gave him a second chance. Meanwhile, back at the house he was *still smoking* with that loser, and was convinced that the glitch in the drug lab at Tripler Medical Center was fixed. What a fucking idiot. I loved him as a friend, but I started to hate him for his gullibility. No woman was worth this much. Sure as hell, he was selected again for a urine test. Guess what happened? You're right. He was positive again. He lost his commission and was separated from the USAF. It was a long and painful process. He might as well have been wearing a scarlet letter. Eventually he left Halawa Heights and departed Hawaii; I never saw him again.

But Errol's story pales in comparison to Al's. In early 1993, Al met a lady we'll call Karen, who was on vacation from the States. They became inseparable. She traveled back and forth from Kentucky several times to see him, and eventually moved in with him. A few months later, they decided to get married, and Al asked me to be his best man. The wedding was nice, and he seemed very happy. Shortly afterward, everything changed. I had a friend living in the same Pearl City high-rise as Al. She called me one day frantically screaming about his behavior. He had cut Karen's face out of a wedding picture and stuck a knife into her abdomen (in the picture)! I scrambled to his apartment and found him crazy with anger. I had *never* seen this side of him. He was always the "too cool for school" type. Karen was back in the states visiting family, so we spent hours talking him down and making him promise to see the base psychologist. He apologized for his ranting, said he was okay, and promised this wouldn't happen again. He also assured us that he would definitely get some help.

Two weeks later, after missing his appointment with the psychologist, Al called his wife in the United States from his apartment. He told her he was going to kill himself and that it was her fault. Then he threw down the phone and jumped from the twenty-third story of his building!

Since he had no family, Al identified me as his next of kin. I had to identify his body. Have you ever seen a body after it landed on solid concrete from twenty-three stories? I hope not. The first gruesome thought that came to my head was strawberry marmalade. The second was anger. *How could you do this to yourself? Your new bride?* And the third was pity. What was going on in Al's head? Was the loneliness of being an orphan too much for this life? Did the movement from foster home to foster home break his spirit? The mental and physical images were too much to handle. I didn't sleep for six months.

I was charged with escorting the body, in full military regalia, back to Puerto Rico, where a distant relative (actually a maid from one of his many foster homes) would receive the remains. It was brutal. I traveled 17,000 miles in five days. I stood for hours at parade rest on the tarmac in Los Angeles and in Dallas, baking in the hot sun. Our regulations required that I never leave the casket. I was the first one off and the last one on each plane. The burial was uncomfortable. Karen flew down, and we hung close. Neither one of us really knew this man (or each other for that matter). The whole affair was an eerie experience, almost like a Hitchcock movie. We never told the guests what Al said when he dropped the phone and jumped. Karen was a widower, scarred for life by his death, just months after her wedding. And I had lost a friend I never really knew…

These events drove Sherie and me closer—almost an "us against the world" kind of thing. The last few months were long, and in my head, I was already gone. In June 1983, I finally departed for Academic Instructor School in Montgomery, Alabama. I would meet Sherie after graduation in California. Then she would return to Hawaii and continue her crusade for early-out approval from the air force so she could join me in Missouri.

Before I end this chapter, I think it's important to point out how difficult it has been to write this book. For decades, I have been able to bury the bad things that happened to me, from crushing divorces and loneliness, to lost coin tosses and Al's suicide. From my dad's early death, to the painful cancer that killed my best friend Jake. From the brain aneurysm that almost killed me, to the colon cancer that was ripped from my body. I had blindly kicked my way through life's doors, and slammed them absentmindedly shut behind me. I liken it to the classic line in *The Gumball Rally*, where the driver is explaining his philosophy on racing. "It's like Italian driving," he said as he removed the rearview mirror and threw it away. "What's behind you is not important." The demons that were put away a long time ago came back. The rearview mirror was reattached, and the roadway was full of thoughts once buried or forgotten. In the long run, I suppose it's good to face down your fears. It just hurts more than I expected.

If I had my way, I would have chosen Bob Seger's "Against the Wind" mentality at this point of my life:

"I wish I didn't know now what I didn't know then."

CHAPTER TEN

Scarcely Acres

———◦———

But life, as they say, goes on. I guess it's really not about where you came from or even where you are going. It's about each day—God's gift of a fresh start—that helps one adjust to almost anything over time.

Hawaii was behind me now, and it was time for the next step in my career—becoming an assistant professor of aerospace studies. I took some leave en route to Maxwell AFB and went home to visit my mom. Everything was about the same—she was living in the same small apartment and still bartending at a place called Kate's—and her life was relatively calm. I had worked it out so my Ford EXP would arrive in California and then be transported overland to Montgomery, Alabama, so it would be waiting for me when I started Academic Instructor School (AIS).

On the plane ride from Pittsburgh to Montgomery, I remember trying to sort out what had happened with Sherie. I didn't think she'd be able to get out of the air force early. I was pretty sure we'd drift apart over time, and that would be that. Did I invite her to come to Missouri because I didn't think it would happen? Did I really think this through? Or was it a web that was spinning tighter and tighter?

Maxwell Air Force Base is the home of the USAF's Air University. According to the website, the "Air University provides the full spectrum of air force education, from pre-commissioning to the highest levels of professional education, including degree granting and professional continuing education for officers, enlisted and civilian personnel throughout their careers." AIS is simply the teachers college for the air force. "It is widely acclaimed throughout the DOD for its role in satisfying the requirements of the air force for educated instructors and for its unique contributions to the field of education." Only six weeks long in 1983, AIS was packed with everything from basic principles of learning and instructional design, to developing curriculum and evaluating the achievement of learning objectives. The homework was intense, because you were evaluated by your actual in-class instruction skills. AIS taught me a valuable lesson about being an instructor. Like F. Lee Bailey, the famous defense lawyer once said, "You win the case before you enter the courtroom." To be an effective instructor, the same adage applies. If you're not prepared prior to class, you won't be effective in the class.

Montgomery, Alabama, is an interesting town, with a combination of old Southern charm and modern-city allure. The food's great, and the weather is always warm. I enjoyed walking around in the nineteenth-century South area of Old Alabama Town. On base, Maxwell AFB felt like a college campus, with large walkways and colorful landscaping. The golf course was top-notch, and the Officers' Club remained one of the best in the world. My class went quickly, and I learned a lot about my teaching style. I carefully studied my strengths and weaknesses and appreciated all the feedback I received from instructors and fellow students alike. But just like that, it was time to leave. Two days later, I was flying to California to catch-up with Sherie and to meet her family.

Her parents ran a halfway house for homeless kids. They had a big place near Livermore, with lots of space for transients. Even though they knew we were coming, they had no room for us. So we had to sleep on the floor in the basement! There were drugs everywhere—not a good sign for a halfway house. At dinner that night, we had to wait until all the "guests" ate before we could sit at the table. During the night, there were couples fornicating on the floor next to us. In the morning, we realized that we'd been robbed. (No wonder Sherie's childhood was so mixed up. By the way, she was also sexually assaulted as a teenager. But she refused to discuss it with me, so I don't know much about it.) Needless to say, after a few days of this arrangement, we were feeling creeped out. So we headed to San Francisco to enjoy the sights. While at Fisherman's Wharf, we decided to cut our visit short. She returned to Hawaii to continue her early-out efforts, and I headed to Montgomery to pick up my car and drive to Rolla, Missouri.

As soon as Sherie arrived back in the islands, she was pulling out all the stops. She convinced her health professionals that she was unable to function without me (say what?) and that the trauma of this separation was causing her to lose weight. In short, not being with the one she loved was catamount to an illness. (I should have noticed right then—especially with her strange home environment—that she was a very volatile person. But I had completed AIS and was ready for a new life in Missouri. And having her with me seemed like a good idea at the time.)

When I arrived in Rolla, I went directly to my job location. My unit, Air Force ROTC Detachment 440A, was in a small building on campus at the University of Missouri-Rolla (UMR). Since the operation was very new, there were only two officers assigned, the commander and one other instructor. I was the third. UMR is part of the University of Missouri system. It is made up almost entirely of engineering and sciences students. UMR ranks in the top twenty-five nationwide for the number of engineering degrees awarded annually and has an enrollment of approximately 6,800. My first job was to develop a new leadership and management course for juniors. (Up until this point, 440A didn't have any junior cadets.) I had free rein to take the course in any direction I chose.

According to Wikipedia, "AFROTC is the largest and oldest source of commissioned officers for the U.S. Air Force." The detachments "are located in 144 colleges and university campuses with 984 additional institutions participating in cross-town agreements that allow their students to attend AFROTC classes at a nearby host college or university. Most colleges and universities will designate the AFROTC Detachment as the Department of Aerospace Studies."

The professor of aerospace studies (PAS) serves as the detachment commander, and usually has two or three assistant professors of aerospace studies (APAS) on his or her staff, plus a few enlisted administrative staff. The cadets are set up in a functional wing format, that is, one consisting of wings, groups, squadrons, and flights. There are two main divisions in a ROTC detachment: the General Military Course, consisting of the first two years of training; and the Professional Officer Course, consisting of the last two years of training. The cadets have two distinct training functions as well: the Academic Classroom Program, and the Cadet Activities Programs, which includes leadership lab, physical training, and other training. My APAS job was to concentrate on the academic classroom side of the operation.

The next weeks—and months—were fun, and vastly different from anything I had done previously in the air force. The detachment was growing fast, and I was right in the middle of it. The air force needed science and engineering grads, and we were there to develop and commission them. My initial contribution was to ensure that these gifted students understood that management and leadership abilities are necessary to function effectively as an air force officer. (My mental analogy for engineers and science students was simple. I knew they could design a paper bag, but could they find their way out of a paper bag? I would use this same mental picture with my Air Force Academy cadets.)

Rolla, Missouri, is a very small town, about halfway between Springfield and St. Louis. It's located in Phelps County, about sixty miles south of the main University of Missouri campus in Columbia. The town is full of springs, forested hills, and rivers. The park system alone is over 304 acres, with ten miles of walking trails. But there were very few rental properties available. So for the first time in my life, I became a landowner. I bought a ranch-style home—three bedrooms, two baths, and a two-car garage—just south of the campus, on Route 72. The house sat on three acres, with most of it wooded. (This Pittsburgh boy was *definitely* out of his element. But when in Rome ...)

I became the epitome of a Midwesterner. I bought a driving mower and bounded around my large lawn donning a cowboy hat for shade and toting a beer in my hand for refreshment. I felt like I was on The Ponderosa, and half expected Hoss to show up on horseback, reminding me that Hop Sing had dinner on the table. I cut down, chainsawed, split, and stacked my own wood, only removing trees that had fallen or died. I planted new trees and gardens, and even built a shed for my new rural equipment. My furniture from Hawaii had arrived, and the house looked pretty good from the inside as well. I named it Scarcely Acres. (A year later, Meshell, my closest friend in the world before I met my wife Andi, made a Scarcely Acres plaque for the front door. I still have it.)

It was final. Sherie received her early discharge and was coming to Missouri. I didn't know what to think. On the one hand, I missed her and wanted to see her. After all, Rolla wasn't exactly Manhattan. The off-duty options were very limited. On the other hand, I was thoroughly enjoying my job, all the cadets, and my house. I was a big fish in a small pond. Did I want to lose that? Would she be devastated when I would *refuse* to get married again? I must have told her a hundred times—no more marriages for me. But would she accept this arrangement? After all, she had given up her USAF career for me. Was I too stupid to see where this was going, or was I denying it?

When Sherie arrived in Rolla, things started out very well. She was beginning to gain a little weight, and her attitude was good about the future. I was hoping I was in love, and she was killing me with kindness. As expected, the discussion about marriage began to arise slowly, until it was the main topic of our lives every day. She couldn't live this way. She needed to be married. So in record time —less than two months in Missouri—we were married. We said our vows quietly at the City Hall in Salem, Missouri, a town just south of Rolla.

It was a mistake.

Almost immediately after the wedding, Sherie began to deteriorate. Her calm demeanor had been replaced by a sense of paranoia that really surprised me. She would constantly complain about how boring Rolla was and how unhappy it made her. She would disappear for hours at a time and never tell me where she went. She rustled through my old photos and cut off the heads of my ex-wives and girlfriends. (This freaked me out and rekindled thoughts of Al's suicide.) I sent her to a psychologist, and it didn't seem to help. (I found out later that she never showed for her appointments.) Sherie thought that enrolling in college would help. I agreed. So she enrolled in some classes at UMR. For weeks, she told me about her classes, discussed her homework assignments, and generally seemed to have a purpose in life. I thought, *maybe school will get her back on the right track*. No chance. Several weeks later, a friend called me from the registrar's office, explaining that Sherie's GPA was 0.0. As it turns out, she never attended any of the classes, and it was too late to drop them. This broke the camel's back for me. How could she sit there, day after day, and lie incessantly about her imaginary college courses? How could she talk about teachers and fellow students for hours? Why didn't she care about the wasted cost of tuition? And how did she ever expect to get away with this charade?

Sherie was too much for me to handle, and she knew it. She called her parents, who had promised to set a room aside for her, and we made plans for her to leave Rolla. They weren't surprised that she was coming back home.

A few days later, we loaded all her personal belongings into a rental car, and off to California she went. Our entire marriage lasted less than eight months. We should have annulled the wedding, but we never got around to it. There was nothing to settle, so the divorce was simple.

I was now on my third divorce. The embarrassment was stifling. I told no one I was married three times. Reflecting back, my ex-wives were all completely different, in appearance and personality. Jill, the first, was strong as an ox, with an athlete's figure. My brother-in-law thought she was the most beautiful woman he had ever seen. Her homelife was very strong. Our divorce wouldn't even slow her down. She was fine. Cheryl, the second, was smaller, daintier, and just plain weird. She was a daddy's girl, well-adjusted but somewhat quirky. No one in my family liked her. My brother Larry called her a "dolt," and he was right. She met someone else just a few months after our wedding. We agreed that divorce was the only option. And then, months later, just as I was picking up the pieces, she showed up at my Officers Training School graduation ceremony attempting to patch things up. No chance. I rarely, if ever, think about Cheryl. Good riddance.

But Sherie was an entirely different story. She was the tallest, with a thin, model-like appearance. She wasn't as strong mentally, and her life was chaotic. She lived an odd communal existence and had a rough time with a previous marriage. Before Sherie left Missouri, I could sense her resignation. She was slated to inherit a fortune from her wealthy uncle. I met him once in San Francisco, when he arrived by helicopter atop a nearby skyscraper! I think the promise of this expected windfall crushed her desire to accomplish anything constructive, and paradoxically made her feel even more resigned about herself. Many times during our last days together, in the middle of an argument, she would remind me that I would lose everything if we divorced.

She could not believe that I didn't care about the money.

Even with all her problems, I still worry about Sherie the most, and think about her on occasion. (I even tried to find her once.) How was she doing? Has she ever found happiness? Is she enjoying her inherited wealth? Or did she learn that money doesn't make you happy? Does she realize that our divorce was not just her fault—that I made my share of mistakes as well? That maybe my previous baggage doomed our relationship? Does she now realize that divorce was the best option? I guess I'll never know. Perhaps that's a good thing…

As bad as my personal life was going, my ROTC instructor duty was the exact opposite. Everything about this job was great. I was teaching college for the first time in my life and developed a love for teaching that I still have today. I was active on campus, heavily involved in the Academic Affairs and Student Planning Committees. I doubled the ROTC scholarships for UMR in my first year, then doubled them again the year after that. I put together an ROTC intramural sports program, with six established teams, involving 50 percent of the cadet corps. My teacher/student evaluations placed me eighth out of 431 instructors. And I was just warming up. The more the detachment grew, the more I grew. It was a symbiotic relationship. I was lucky to be a part of it.

To broaden my horizons (no pun intended), I decided that it was time to learn to fly. Although I really didn't have the flying bug, I figured once I got into it, I'd really enjoy it. After all, I was in the air force, right? So I completed ground school and started my flying lessons at Green Airfield in St. James, Missouri. At first, I really enjoyed it. My favorite part of flying was landing, and doing "touch and go's" on the runway. Takeoffs were pretty standard, and flying straight and level was, well, boring—especially since the Cessna 150 cockpit was so cramped. (Don't forget—I'm a card-carrying claustrophobic.) I remember "crabbing" (flying sideways) into the constant Missouri wind as I headed to the threshold to land. And just before touchdown, I'd pass two giant silos that would immediately block the wind and force me to quickly spin the aircraft so it was aligned with the runway. This was always tricky, and I must admit had my attention every time. Another exercise I enjoyed was flying directly vertical until the aircraft hit stall speed. The warning alarms would sound, and the plane would stall out. I would let go of the controls, and the plane would start a very fast tailfirst fall. Using gravity and the weight of the engine in front, the nose would eventually come forward, and the lift from the wings would stabilize the aircraft. I'll admit it: the first time I did this maneuver, I was scared shitless. Once I mastered the landings, did my solo flight, and flew some short cross-country reckonings, I realized that I had had enough of flying. I guess it was more important to know I could fly than it was to keep flying. I never finished the program.

With a few bucks in my pocket, I chucked my Ford EXP—it was falling apart—and bought a 1984 Toyota minivan. It was the first of its kind, and ugly as sin. It looked like a moon buggy designed by a committee. I couldn't resist buying it. Maybe I missed my old VW van from Germany. There was something outrageous about a single, oft-divorced guy driving a family van. Trust me, I was no soccer dad. (Little did I know it at the time, but I would drive that van for the next eighteen years!)

But my personal situation wasn't going as smoothly. For the first time in my life, I was lonely. Rolla was a very small town. Opportunities to meet someone in Phelps County were very slim. I was starting to believe that I would never meet anyone meaningful again. And if I did, I'd probably figure out some way to screw it up. I even tried a dating service. This was a desperate move for me. I didn't like the idea of putting my personal life on a hook and waiting for someone to bite. (*But I'm doing that now, aren't I?*) I still believed in fate—the chance meeting, the rush you get when that special person steps into your life. But I tried the dating service anyway. I went out on three dates, with three different women. All were divorced, and all had children. There was one girl, "Joan," whom I liked. But I couldn't help feeling that she was looking for a replacement father and a paycheck. I smelled organized desperation. That's the problem with prefab dating— there's no spontaneity. If we had met in the traditional way and I really got to know her, the issues of children and economics would have worked themselves out. I don't want to read about someone's favorite color or that she likes walking on the beach at sunset. I don't want to read that someone considers herself a "people person." I'd rather find that out on my own. I decided to drop out of the electronic romance department.

And just like that—it happened. There was a dance at the local Holiday Inn in Rolla. (I think it was a Holiday Inn. I googled it, but it's no longer there.) I was watching the band and saw an attractive blond girl standing by herself. My confidence was at an all-time low, so I decided to just stand there and watch the show. At that moment, I noticed a guy walking toward her. Just seconds before he said something to her, I reached over a few people standing in front of me and tapped her on the shoulder. She turned around, and I asked her to dance. My psyche was like eggshells. I felt foolish. I didn't know how to date. To this point in my life, I spent more time getting out of relationships than trying to start one. She said yes.

Her name was Meshell Murray. She was from Crocker, Missouri, a tiny town west of Rolla. She was five feet tall and looked like a Barbie doll. She had beautiful dancing brown eyes, and a curiosity to her personality that I really liked. She was a licensed practical nurse, and single. There were no children. We talked between dances, had a few beers, and generally had a very nice time. When I returned home, I debated whether to call her or not. Meshell was nice, but probably not my type. She was an easygoing country girl. I was a train wreck. She had never been married, and I— well, you get the picture. Had this been a computer date, it would have been a disaster. But it wasn't, so I decided to let fate play itself out, and I called her. We went out to dinner and began a relationship that lasted over four years, which was longer than all three of my earlier marriages combined!

Meshell became my best friend, and we were inseparable. We spent countless weekends at my house, barbequing in the summer and sitting in front of the fireplace in the winter. We smoked pot once in a while, but I was losing interest in it. And we traveled the Midwest as much as we could. When the Pirates came to St. Louis, we'd get a hotel and check out a few games at Busch Stadium. If you ever get a chance, you have to climb the St. Louis Arch. At 630 feet, it's the largest man-made monument in the United States. When you reach the top, the ceiling is very low, and you have to lie down to look through the glass under your feet. It's really eerie to see nothing but air below you. And don't miss the Anheuser-Busch Brewery. The tour is great, and the free beer at the end is even better. Make sure you visit the Clydesdales while you're there. We also headed to New Orleans for Mardi Gras and stayed with my sister Susan. There's something for everybody at Mardi Gras. I didn't sleep for three days. Later that summer, we went to Branson, fifty miles south of Springfield, and enjoyed a nice dinner cruise on Table Rock Lake. They had some great seafood there. I also enjoyed the Lake of the Ozarks, located in the Midwest's premier lake resort destination. It's about fifty miles northwest of Crocker and has everything from golf, shopping, and boating, to hotels, restaurants, state parks, and live Vegas-type shows. But one of my favorite trips was to Memphis—the home of Beale Street. For over 150 years, Beale Street has hosted blues music and entertainment. In just three blocks, it packs in thousands of bands, major blues players, and fans. Greats like Elvis Presley, W. C. Handy, Johnny Cash, and B. B. King played there. My favorite places are the Rum Boogie Café and B. B. King's Blues Club. You can also take the monorail across the Mississippi River to Mud Island. When you arrive, you'll see an amazing hydraulic scale model of the lower Mississippi River, from Cairo, Illinois, to New Orleans, etched in the island floor. It opens into the Gulf of Mexico, and you can walk the entire model, visiting several cities along the way. Everywhere we went, nothing else around us mattered. I had never felt anything like that before. Could it be that I was finally in love?

But not all of our travels went well. While we were in Cancun on vacation, I developed a serious case of amebiasis, which is amoebas growing in your body. They live by eating and digesting bacteria and food particles in the gastrointestinal tract. I read online that about 40,000 to 100,000 people worldwide die of this disease annually. For months, I couldn't shake it. I tried everything the doctors could prescribe, and nothing worked. My system was a mess, and the amebiasis was spreading. Finally Meshell found a Mexican product which was not yet cleared by the FDA. I didn't care. For three days, under this medication, I basically blanched my body. I looked like Casper the Friendly Ghost. It sucked the strength out of me, and I was tired and ashen the whole time. But it worked, thank goodness. I was lucky that my girlfriend was a nurse and knew how to track down an illegal medication that finally destroyed the amoebas. That's one thing about worldwide travel—it comes with risks. I've been exposed to hepatitis multiple times and picked up a dormant strain of tuberculosis as well. It's a dangerous world out there, kids.

Back at the detachment, I received a promotion to captain, and I was completing my first full year as an instructor. I was also slated to go back to San Antonio—Lackland AFB again—for ROTC field training. Only this time, I was the field training officer (FTO), not an airman basic or an officer trainee. I was assigned to "D" Flight, consisting of twenty-three aviation cadets. I felt like I had been preparing for this encampment all my life. Between basic training (enlisted) and officers' training, I had learned quite a bit about motivation and development of future leaders. In addition, I had already developed my FTO strategy in my head. In short, I knew this stuff.

The ROTC Flight Training Program, in many ways, was similar to Officers Training School. The major areas of training included physical conditioning, marksmanship, survival, confidence course, aircraft and crew orientation, human relations, drill and ceremony, leadership studies, and air force specialty orientation. (The last activity was designed for cadets to meet and work with officers in careers that interested them.)

But unlike OTS, the ROTC cadets are still in college (between their sophomore and junior years). Some are on scholarship, and some are not. They have no formal commitment to the air force and can walk away afterward if they desire. So field training is the fork in the road. Upon completion, they return to their detachment and decide whether to become part of the professional officer corps—which includes a four- to six-year commitment— or move on to something else. It's our job to really test them during the training and weed out those who aren't optimal for military service. Another big difference was the layout of the training facility at Lackland AFB. For OTS, the cadets shared a room with a roommate; in ROTC, it was an open bay, just like basic training.

To help my cadets make tough decisions as a team, I decided to become the dedicated asshole. In other words, I was going to be so tough on my flight early on that they wouldn't have time to do anything but band together. Once they were working as one, I'd start to ease up on the gas pedal. I rationed that it was better for my flight to bond against a common enemy than to have dissension among them. I figured if they worked together and accomplished things as a team, they would have an easier time making decisions. (In essence, I borrowed a page from my marine training instructor in basic training.)

On the first night, well after lights out, I purposely avoided my flight. I wanted them to feel comfortable, to relax, and to think this training wouldn't be so bad. At 2:30 a.m., I barged into the common bay area and tossed a large buffer down the center aisle, clanking and banging its way to the far end of the building.

"Get up. Get your asses out of bed! I want this floor so clean you can eat off it. Oh, and one more thing. If you aren't the best flight in this encampment, I will make this the longest seven weeks of your life." Then I left. No introductions, no small talk. I scared the hell out of them. My work was done for the night. (Many of the cadets later shared with me how powerful and intimidating that first meeting was. Put simply, they hated my guts—which was part of my master plan.)

The camp was amazing, and my flight was terrific. They excelled at survival training, finding roots, berries, and an occasional armadillo for sustenance; they won practically every athletic, drill, and/or inspection competition; they solved all the Leadership Reaction Course challenges; they ran more miles for honor flight points than any other flight; and of course, they won the overall honor flight award. (Interesting story about survival training: the following year, I had a female cadet from Harvard's ROTC detachment. She was very fragile, and I was worried that she might break a nail during survival training. But I couldn't have been more wrong. She completed the training and came out of the woods wearing animal pelts, donning camo face paint, and slinging a hunting knife from her waist. She looked like Rambo's sister!)

Anyway, my plan worked. They rebelled against me at first and pulled together as a team. Soon, as they started crushing all the other flights, I began to ease up on the gas pedal. When D Flight realized its potential, they understood why I used the designated asshole approach. There were too many other FTOs who started soft—trying to be friends—and couldn't turn their flights around when they needed to improve. While FTOs were grinding to get their flights back in the race, I was on the golf course. In fact, we had clinched camp honor flight with more than two weeks remaining!

Of course, I never told them. I wanted a 100 percent effort all the way to the finish line. "Be relentless" was my mantra. I reminded them often that "Only the concentrated effort of mind, body, and spirit completes the winning cycle, exposing the unavoidable need to win that is within us all." (I quoted an anonymous article entitled "To the Best within You," which was published in a previous yearbook. I never told anyone until now, but that anonymous writer was me.)

The final banquet was a blast. I sat with my flight and was no longer the adversary. I felt more like a parent, who was proud of what my kids accomplished. We respected each other. The entire encampment gave me a standing ovation when I accepted the Honor Flight Award for D Flight. My flight gave me a signed plaque that simply said: *Be relentless.*

Back at work, things could not have been better. The months were flying by. Meshell and I were happy, and my job in the detachment was fun. I was recruiting at area high schools and college fairs, and loving it. Sometimes I'd set up a table, with fliers and videos. Other times, I'd speak in front of hundreds of people in an auditorium. My beat was from St. Louis to Springfield. In addition, I was selected by my PAS to be the commandant of cadets. I now had the responsibility to develop and implement the Professional Military Training Program for 145 cadets. (Our enrollment was higher than the University of Missouri. We earned full detachment status and officially became Detachment 442. The staff grew from three to eight— we were no longer a subset of UM.) I was also selected for Squadron Officers' School, and completed the nine-week Air University course in Montgomery, Alabama. I could go on, but you get the picture. Even my designated-asshole handle was appreciated by our area commander. By popular demand, I was asked to go back for another field training encampment the following summer.

My tour in Rolla was winding down, and I was sorry to see it end. I had been in an excellent relationship with Meshell for over two years, and I didn't want it to end. I was still single—she never pushed me to get married—and she understood me better than anyone else I had ever met. (Looking back, if it weren't for my wife, Andi, I'd say it was the best relationship I ever had.)

After long discussions with my assignment officer at the Air Force Military Personnel Center (AFMPC), he convinced me that it was time to come there. He rationalized correctly that all human resource management officers needed to do at least one air staff tour. I agreed (anything was better than the Pentagon). So I accepted a job at AFMPC as the Chief, Aircrew Training and Scheduling Section, Randolph AFB, Texas. I was heading back to San Antonio.

I kept Scarcely Acres, and rented it for the next several years. Meshell and I were too close to separate. She would come to San Antonio a few months later and live with me in Universal City, just a few miles from the Randolph AFB main gate.

I departed Rolla in 1986 on a rainy, summer morning, driving in my space buggy. I felt very proud of what I'd accomplished there. To this day, I still can't believe how well this inner-city kid adjusted to that little Midwestern town. I figured if I could go from Zweibrucken, Germany, to Rolla, Missouri —with tours in Maine and Hawaii in between—I could live anywhere.

So long, Scarcely Acres. The designated asshole has left the building.

CHAPTER ELEVEN

"Progress always involves risks. You can't steal second base and keep your foot on first."
— *FREDERICK B. WILCOX*

———◦———

O kay, I know what you are thinking … San Antonio again? Yes, it's true. Texas just keeps drawing me back. First, it was basic military training, followed by Officers Training School, and then AFROTC Field Training. I now had direct experience with three of the four USAF entrance programs. (The Air Force Academy was coming up, and would be the fourth.)

The Air Force Military Personnel Center (AFMPC), or the "puzzle palace," as it was sarcastically called, was a huge organization in 1986. Located on Randolph AFB, it had over three thousand military and contactors' positions, making it one of the largest HR operations in the world. Our job was to develop the air force's most valuable weapon system— airmen. I was assigned to the directorate of assignments, whose mission, according to the Air Force Personnel Center website (name changed when it combined with the Air Force Civilian Personnel Management Center in 1995), was to "develop, coordinate, and execute Air Force assignment policies and procedures to insure effective utilization and professional development of enlisted active duty personnel and officers." As the Chief, Aircrew Training and Scheduling Section, my job was to directly manage the programming and assignment of over 29,000 class seats annually—in support of Headquarters Tactical Air Command, Strategic Air Command, and Mobility Air Command— with a total value in excess of $1 billion! I had eight NCOs in my shop, and it was our responsibility to ensure that the USAF didn't waste any of the appropriated training dollars. For example, just one B-1 bomber training seat had a total cost of $500,000. And there were 29,000 other class seats—all requiring constant vigilance to ensure the right airmen were in those seats. Our DOD contracts were very clear; we paid for the training whether the student showed up or not. This put a lot of pressure on my section, and we were always scrambling to fill last-minute vacancies.

After spending a few weeks in temporary housing, I found a place on Crystal Canyon Road, just behind the Universal City Sports Park. I could jump the fence next to my yard—which was connected to the baseball/softball complex—and be in right field. It was a great location, and close to Randolph AFB. When all my stuff arrived, Meshell packed up from Rolla (she didn't live in Crocker anymore) and headed to Texas to be with me. I couldn't have been happier. My job was great, and AFMPC was full of young captains and majors. There were plenty of friends to hang out with, and every kind of intramural sport you can imagine. During my time there, I was involved in flag football, softball, golf, bowling, and 10K races. In no time, my sadness from leaving the detachment in Rolla was replaced by the excitement of a new job, a chance to live in a big city again, and the joy I felt about Meshell coming to stay with me.

The sports teams were the best I ever played on—including the base team at Zweibrucken and my college track and field experience. In all the years of playing softball, I was always the number three or four hitter. I had good power and usually led the team in offense. At AFMPC, I tried out for team #1, and didn't make it! So I played for team #2. We beat everyone we played and finished second in the league behind team #1. The domination of AFMPC forced the base to change the home-run rules. My second year, when a team reached five home runs in a game (which was every game for us), the next homer was an out. So in order to preserve our limited quota of home runs, we decided to assess a fine of one case of beer for homers hit with less than two runners on base. I got stung with a couple of cases during that season. It's not as easy as you think to keep the ball in the ballpark. Sometimes a line drive just goes over the fence.

It was the same thing with the bowling league. I carried a high 180s average, near 190 almost every year I was there, but still didn't make the AFMPC #1 tryouts. I did make the team #2 squad, and we were pretty good as well. In fact, during my third year, team #2 won the base championship over team #1. I'll just give you one example about how good some of these guys were. There was one bowler on team #1 (I can't remember his name) who rolled two 300 games on the same night. Even more amazingly, he did it with different balls, on different lane conditions, in separate bowling alleys! I wonder if that's ever been done before.

Meshell arrived and moved in with me. As an LPN, it didn't take her long to find a job in the nursing business. We were having a blast. Our weekends were full of softball tournaments, visits to the River Walk, trips to South Padre Island, treks to the Astrodome to see the Pirates and Steelers, and eating and drinking at many of the fine establishments nearby. The greater San Antonio area had over fifty festivals a year. We went to many of them, including Wurstfest in New Branfels, the Wine and Music Festival in Kerrville, and the gigantic Folk Life Festival on the River Walk. All were full of merriment, music, and refreshment. There were others, but I've forgotten many of them.

I also landed a job teaching business and management courses for Texas Lutheran University. Although they were based in Seguin, Texas, they held classes at Randolph AFB, which made it very convenient for me. Originally founded in 1891, it was called the Academy of the First German Evangelical Lutheran Synod of Texas. (Imagine having that on a T-shirt.) It changed its name to Texas Lutheran College, and eventually to Texas Lutheran University. As an adjunct instructor, I was able to keep doing something I loved, while at the same time make a little extra cash. Things were good—I distinctly remember the warm feeling of happiness I felt during that time of my life.

But why can't those positive feelings continue? Why don't relationships last in my world? Why am I always waiting for the other shoe to drop? And how come I can't apply my "steer the blob" philosophy to personal relationships?

It started slowly. We weren't married, and that was not going to change. Little disagreements grew to bigger arguments, with the following subliminal messages: What are we doing here? What's next in this relationship? If we're never going to get married, what does that say about how we feel about each other?

I will state right now that I really did love Meshell. I will also state that I don't have the slightest idea why we didn't get married. I will state that until I met Andi, she was the longest relationship I ever had and was with me for over four years. I will also state that my previous baggage may have had a lot to do with my indecision. And through it all, Meshell dealt with my personal psychosis and never prodded me into marriage like the others. And now, after all those years—sitting here writing this story—I finally figured out why. She knew that if she pressured me to get married, I would have agreed. She decided she'd rather risk losing me than to pressure me into something I wasn't capable of doing.

Eventually Meshell moved out, got a really good job, and began working on her RN license. We dated on and off for the next two years. We were both crazy—breaking up and making up. It was nuts. For the first time in my life, I became very jealous. I would see her at Kramer's—a popular dance club— with someone else, and lose it. But when we got together, all we did was argue. We were hot and cold like Latin lovers, saying hurtful things to each other one minute, and apologizing and making up the next. It was insane.

Back at work, things were going well. I was transferred to a new job— Chief, United States Air Force Academy (USAFA)/Air Force Institute of Technology (AFIT) Assignments. It was probably the best job in the entire Support Officers Assignments Division. I managed the selective duty assignment of 840 instructors at the Air Force Academy. In addition, I assigned exchange instructor positions to West Point (the United States Military Academy) and Annapolis (the United States Naval Academy), as well as over two hundred AFIT instructor positions at Wright-Patterson AFB, Ohio. I regularly escorted high-ranking generals and colonels from all the service academies around AFMPC, and was treated like royalty when I visited their academies. But it wasn't an easy job. If the best candidate for an assistant football coach was an F-15 pilot, I had to battle the fighter pilot assignment guys to get him released. If the best aeronautical engineer instructor candidate were a top-notch aircraft maintenance officer, I had to negotiate an assignment that would remove the officer from the flight line and place him or her into the classroom. Every time the USAFA gained a staff member, the assignment teams lost a resource. This position required a combination of hardheadedness, tact, and diplomacy. (I needed all of those skills later in the State Department.) Luckily for me, the USAFA lobby was strong, and many of our senior leaders were graduates. The academy department heads had extensive, high-level contacts as well, which I nudged on occasion to get an officer released from his or her primary duties.

During early 1989, while Meshell and I were broken up for the latest time, I was out on the club scene with my two buddies Billy Garcia and Dave Benson. I met Billy during one of my ROTC summer camps. He was permanently assigned to the Lackland AFB staff in San Antonio. When I arrived at AFMPC, we started hanging out together. My best running mate Dave was an Office of Special Investigations Assignments Officer, working in the same division as I. We were in "the attic," a colloquial name for the windowless top floor of AFMPC. Billy was a local guy and knew all the best spots for dancing, and generally where the girls were. And Dave was a true networker—he knew who would be where and was always trying to date more than one girl at the same time. In my opinion, his approach demanded way too much work and required constant vigilance not to screw up his system. I was always telling him to ease up and just let it happen. (As it turned out, shortly after I started dating Andi, Dave got engaged and later married. Guess who introduced him to his fiancée— me! So much for his networking skills.)

The third biggest SSE of my life happened around February 1989. Dave and I agreed to meet at a place called Raffles. It must have been ladies' night or something, or Dave wouldn't have suggested it. I arrived shortly afterward and found him standing at the bar with a date. I shouldn't have been surprised; he'd done this before. One of his best tactics was to plan a night with the guys and invite a date at the same time.

"Don, this is my friend Andrea Moran. She likes to be called Andi."

"Hi." I stepped away and said, "Dave, do you have a moment?" We moved to the side of the bar. "What's up here, man? I thought we were hanging out tonight."

"I just started dating Andi, and she seems really nice, so I invited her to Raffles." I realized very quickly that I was the third man out and left them alone.

I started wandering around the club, talking to people and having a couple of beers. Every so often, I'd swing by Dave and Andi, and they seemed to be having a good time. After the third time around, I realized three things. One, I had gotten stiffed by Dave—not unusual. Second, the crowd at Raffles was not doing it for me. And third, the best-looking woman in the place was with my best friend. I left and headed over to Kramer's.

For the next month or so, Dave, Billie, and I hit some of the nightspots and were generally having a good time. I kept wondering what happened to Andi and if Dave was working his networking scheme without her. Finally, I had to ask.

"Dave, how's Andi doing? Are you still seeing her?" "We've been out a few times, why?"

Okay, here it goes. "Do you mind if I give her a call?" I said with feigned indifference, realizing at that moment I really wanted to see her. "If it's nothing serious, I mean." (His next response began a relationship that has lasted twenty-five years and is still going strong.)

"No, it's not serious. I have her number back in the office. I'll give it to you on Monday."

A week or so later, I called Andi, and we met at a Chinese restaurant in Universal City, just off Pat Booker Road (I can't remember the name). We had dinner, polished off a bottle of wine, and really enjoyed ourselves. Andi was recently divorced after thirteen years of marriage. She worked in the administration section of the Coleman Company, in New Branfels, Texas; the company made everything from coolers to canoes. Her ex-husband, Stan, was an engineer who emotionally fell to pieces, dropped out of life, and disappeared. (She still doesn't know what happened to him.) She went to college at Tulane (New Orleans), was a little sister for Stan's fraternity, and partied her way out of the university without graduating. She was engaging and honest, and had a good heart. Andi was thin but shapely, and looked great (still does). Her personal life, like mine, was definitely in transition. I was surprised that she would be interested in Dave, with his methodical dating style. I wasn't disappointed when she told me that she hardly knew him and he really wasn't her type anyway.

The next several months were a blur of activity. We were inseparable. Whether it was trekking to Austin to party, or to South Padre Island for sun and fun, or to Houston to see my hallowed Pittsburgh sports teams play, we were always together. I was falling in love—and scared to death about it. With my track record, not to mention all the baggage I was carrying, I didn't see a good outcome in sight.

Since I *never* wanted to get married again and since I was expecting an assignment soon, I was subliminally planning my exit strategy. But at the same time, I decided to enjoy it while it lasted.

In the "attic," our senior division chief, Colonel Patrick, summoned me to his office the following week. I considered him a mentor and was motivated to help him when he asked. I didn't expect what happened.

"Feeney, I want you to volunteer for a CBPO Chief job for your next assignment. Go down to see Captain Baker (HR Assignments), and see what's available. I know it's a tough job, but I think you can handle it." I was stunned. I was flashing back. In 1977, I was the lowliest airman in the Zweibrucken Consolidated Base Personnel Office (and a deserter as well). Back then, the CBPO Chief was a god, with more responsibility than I could imagine at the time. There weren't many CBPO Chief openings, and with Colonel Patrick's blessing, I knew I had a good shot.

So I sat down with my buddy Capt. Baker. I called him "Bakerman." He ran through the openings and asked me if I were interested in going overseas. Of course, I said. Would I take a remote assignment? (A remote assignment can have many limitations, from austere weather conditions and family restrictions, to locations far from cities and towns.) Of course, I said. I was single, and ready for anything. My next assignment was decided in minutes and was probably one of the easiest placements Bakerman had ever done.

"How about Comiso Air Base, Sicily? It's in the south, close to the Mediterranean Sea, and it's the largest NATO base in southern Europe. The mission supports ground launch cruise missiles (GLCMs), and the CBPO oversees a base population of three thousand people," Bakerman said. "What do you think?"

I always wanted to be a CBPO Chief. I just didn't think it was going to happen. "Okay, Bakerman. I'm in." We shook hands, and just like that, I was on my way to Sicily.

But there was one big problem—Andi. Even though she was excited when I told her about my new assignment, the tension was there. We both knew she wouldn't be able to go with me. In the 1990s, you had to be married to get "command sponsorship" into a foreign country. Without it, you could not live or work on base, or use the recreational or medical facilities. In the back of my mind, the same image kept coming back to me. Remember early in this book when I said I could find sports metaphors for almost anything? Well, here's mine for this situation. I had my foot on first base (no more marriages for me), but I was considering stealing second (OMG, another marriage?). I was content at first base. But I knew deep down it was time to risk stealing second. I'd been single for almost six years. Surely by now my base-stealing skills had improved, right?

It was February 1990, and Andi and I went to Las Vegas on vacation. I love Vegas and really enjoy gambling on occasion. We stayed at the Aladdin Hotel and Casino. It was a classic casino and has since been razed. I watched it implode online and come smashing to the ground in seconds. (The older you get, the more things behind you disappear.) But it was open for business when we arrived. In my pocket, I was carrying a wedding ring. Andi had no idea I was contemplating the unthinkable— another marriage. I didn't tell her because I wasn't sure I could go through with it. If I chickened out, she'd never know. If I didn't, she might tell me to take a hike anyway. Either way, I was running out of time. I would depart for Sicily in less than three months. We checked in and began a great week of gambling, eating, drinking, visiting other casinos, and going to shows. Every night for almost a week, I thought about proposing. I'd check and recheck my pocket, making sure I still had the ring if needed.

Believe it or not, my mom and my brother Larry were both in Vegas at the same time! We found out by accident when I called home to Pittsburgh. No one in my family knew that I was considering proposing to Andi. Talk about an omen!

(Back in Pittsburgh, Mom had recently gotten remarried, to a guy named Bob Kachinko. She moved into his house in Ben Avon. He painted nuclear power plants and was widowed, with several adult children. Mom met him in the bar she worked in, and over time, they decided to get married. I'm convinced she never really loved him; it was more a marriage of convenience. They were both lonely, in their sixties, and found safety in each other. Bob was a very simple man, and his kids ran amok over him. He was an alcoholic, and his kids rolled him for his money on regular occasions. But my mother did a good job straightening out Bob's kids. They were never going to be great citizens, but she taught them something about accountability and honesty. And she also made Bob save his money, which really helped when he passed away years before my mother. The Kachinkos moved to a nice house in North Hills, just off Mt. Nebo Road, and were doing okay. Bob wasn't very popular with the Feeney kids—my brother John did not like him and wouldn't go into the house if he was home. But I think Bob really loved my mom, because he was willing to take a lot of harassment from her. It was a strange relationship. But I learned a long time ago, with my track record on relationships, to *never* give marital advice.)

It was our sixth and last night in Vegas. Larry and my mother went home. I was searching for reasons to avoid matrimony, but I couldn't find any. Not only was it a great omen to have my family there, but I was winning at blackjack every day! Seriously, I couldn't lose. In fact, it cost me exactly ninety-two dollars for the whole trip. I won enough to cover the flights, hotels, food, drinks, shows, and yes, the limo and marriage ceremony. I did it. I came through on the last night. Talk about your singularly significant event!

We were waiting for a cab to go to a comedy show. I had a stretch limo waiting outside, and paid a cabbie to come in and tell us our taxi was ready. (I also booked a wedding chapel down the street.) So when we walked through the doors, I softly guided Andi toward the limo and away from the cab.

"What's going on, Don?"

I motioned her into the limo. I wanted to save my comments until we were alone. The doors were closed, and I poured a couple glasses of champagne.

"Andi, you know I'm going to Sicily in a few months. You also know my horrendous record as a husband. But I love you. And I can't imagine a life without you. Will you marry me?" Andi started to tear up. I went on nervously, "If you don't want to get married, I understand. I have the limo for the whole night. We can cruise up and down the Strip, and enjoy the champagne." I had one thought in the back of my mind—this was the first time I had officially proposed in my life.

"Yes, Don, I'll marry you. I love you too."

We drove to the small wedding chapel I found through the concierge. With fake flowers, a seedy-looking fountain, and the tackiest altar in the world, Donald Joseph Feeney and Andrea Lee Moran became one. Our best man was the limo driver. The maid of honor was the clerk/typist who took forever to hunt and peck the marriage license one letter at a time. (The license took more time than the wedding ceremony!) It was 11:00 p.m. on February 7, and we were the last of eleven weddings that night. I'm not a big fan of kismet, but looking back, the stars were definitely aligned. My mother and brother magically arrived in Vegas, and I was on a six-day blackjack winning streak. Think about it; we got married on the seventh (lucky seven) and became the eleventh (lucky eleven) marriage of the day at 11:00 p.m. (lucky eleven again). And absolutely none of these events were preplanned.

The clerk was tired, and it showed. To add some levity, I said to her:

"You know, as our maid of honor, we'll be expecting anniversary gifts from you." She didn't think it was funny, but my "best man" was cracking up. We enjoyed the rest of the night in the limo and returned to our room in the Aladdin Hotel and Casino as husband and wife.

For the next few months, we prepared for our move to Europe. It was an exciting period in our lives. We were starting a new life together that would stand the test of time. From 1990 to 2014, we lived in the following places: San Antonio, Texas; Comiso, Sicily; Colorado Springs, Colorado; Honolulu, Hawaii; Izmir, Turkey; Norfolk, Virginia; Perth, Australia; Indialantic, Florida; Washington, DC; San Salvador, El Salvador; Manama, Bahrain; Willemstad, Curacao; Athens, Greece; and Indian Harbour Beach, Florida.

So we became a couple of homeless people, traipsing hodgepodge around the world. I hope very much that you decide to come along with us.

Feeney is stealing second. He slides ... safe!

CHAPTER TWELVE

"The first cut is the deepest." — ROD STEWART

———◦———

We loaded up the moon buggy and headed north to Pittsburgh, Washington, DC, and eventually to Newport, Rhode Island, to visit family. Things were relatively calm in "the burg," so we set out for DC, where my sister Susan and her family lived. They were all doing fine as well. On our way out of town, we decided to visit a few Smithsonian museums. So we parked in the mall and went walking. When we returned, our car had been robbed. We lost our passports, wedding pictures, clothes, money, savings bonds, some rare coins, medical records, and so on. In general, all the important things we were advised to hand-carry for safety were gone. We were crushed. We had just two days to leave our van at Larry's house in Newport, Rhode Island, and catch a flight from Boston to Catania, Italy. We both knew that Andi would be grounded in the United States without her passport. (I was okay, with a military ID and travel orders.) After we filed a police report, we headed to the nearest Department of State Passport Center and begged them to issue a same-day passport. We were denied three or four times, and each time I asked to speak to the next-level supervisor. Our case was unique; we're serving our country; blah blah blah ... The clock was ticking. I finally found an employee with enough "steelies" to agree to issue the passports. We walked around the city for several hours and came back just before closing, and they were ready. We had less than thirty hours until our departure for Italy, and we were still in DC.

In the back of my mind I couldn't help thinking—*what a bad omen for our first months of marriage.* I felt sorry for my new bride. She had been carrying all her clothes and personal items. And on top of that, she was staring down a totally new life—recent marriage, unfamiliar military lifestyle, first overseas assignment, and so on. And all her stuff was gone. I can't explain it, but we both felt violated. Some stranger, some punk, stole all our personal stuff. I had a coin circa 1873 that my mother gave me. It came from her great-grandmother. The only thing of value my mom had to remember her by. Gone. Not to mention all the other things.

(For the record, I received a call from the Capital Police about eight months later. They caught the thief trying to cash savings bonds using my passport. He was an African American in his fifties, about five foot six. I'm Irish-American, and was thirty-seven at the time. Not to mention that I'm six foot two. He was a real criminal mastermind... He got twenty-two months in jail.)

We arrived in Rhode Island in record time, and spent some quality time with Larry and Bonnie and the kids. Larry agreed to keep the moon buggy at his place while we were gone. The next morning, we exited the United States via Logan International Airport, albeit with plenty of space in our new luggage. We vowed not to spend time reliving the robbery. We decided to shift our energies to thoughts of Europe.

So, less than four months after handing the plastic flowers back to the uptight clerk/typist (and maid of honor) at Wedding Gardens #3 in Vegas— trust me, there were no gardens—we were landing at Catania International Airport. I had turned Andi's life upside down and indirectly caused her to lose everything. I was praying that she would adjust to living overseas, to the military, and most of all, to me. We found a gentleman in the terminal with a placard that said "Captain Feeney" and jumped into a van. We headed southwest to Comiso. The drive was mesmerizing, with idyllic little towns, rolling hills, wide-open two-lane highways, and many predominant views of Mount Etna. And the Italian drivers were crazy. I was looking forward to joining in the fun when Andi's Honda Accord arrived from the mainland.

We checked into a temporary lodging facility on base. We were both exhausted and ready to crash. But a few minutes later, we received a call from my predecessor—we'll call him Major Ryan— inviting us out to dinner. We tried to take a rain check, but he was leaving the next day, so we agreed to meet him at an on-base restaurant just down the street.

When we arrived, Major Ryan and my new boss, Lieutenant Colonel Handley, were waiting for us. Major Ryan started in right away. His litany of negative input was like a punch in the face. I could see stark terror in Andi's eyes. *Everything is broken* (to borrow a lyric from Bob Dylan). This wasn't right, and that wasn't right, and so on. If it wasn't for him, the whole place would collapse, blah, blah, blah. Lieutenant Colonel Handley tried to ease the onslaught, but the damage was already done. We returned to our room tired and dejected. What had we gotten ourselves into?

I'd like to address two things here. One, I think it's important to present some thoughts on adjusting to overseas living. The other? I'd like to add some suggestions on how to avoid creating negative first impressions.

I'll start by pontificating a little. Moving overseas is very traumatic. Like the stages of grief, you have to go through denial, anger, bargaining, depression, and then acceptance. It's especially tough the first time, when it cuts the deepest. I felt badly for Andi, who was thrown straight into denial after our meeting with my predecessor. She struggled for a few months adjusting to Comiso, grinding through the steps, but eventually she grew to enjoy it. (In fact, she found a great job in the Family Support Center, working as the Personal Financial Management Program counselor, helping families draw down debt, set up savings programs, balance checkbooks, and so on. Maybe I should have sent her to Washington?) Here's my advice to first-time residents overseas: it gets better each time. Although you can't avoid the stages, you can run through them faster. The cut isn't as deep the next time, and you're eager to get to acceptance as fast as possible. But remember, there's no way around the stages—the first time will be difficult. (My hardest adjustment was Zweibrucken.) The key is to focus on getting to acceptance in an expeditious manner. It's not easy, but it's better than languishing in an earlier stage for your entire overseas experience. For some, who remain angry and refuse to bargain, depression will dominate their tour in Comiso. I saw it all the time. For example, upon arrival at Comiso, everyone received an application for an Italian ID card. Without this card, Americans assigned to the base were not permitted to travel in-country. One day, my Customer Service NCO showed up in my office with a box full of envelopes.

"What's in the box?" I asked.

"These are Italian ID cards that have never been picked up. I have fifty-four of them. What should I do with them?" I couldn't believe my ears. These fifty-four people (many are family members) have never left the base! With all the beauty of Italy nearby, and several great restaurants just a three-wood shot from the main gate, they chose to hibernate for their entire tour! I called all of them, one by one, and urged them to come and get their IDs. Some did, and some didn't. You can lead a horse to water …

(Another example came later in my career while serving in Athens … In Greece, things went wrong on occasion. Strikes, poor housing, and traffic, just to name a few. Let's say 15 percent of the time. While most coworkers and families would concentrate on the other 85 percent—from the amazing Greek Isles to the beauty of Athens—others would let the 15 percent take them down. They just couldn't get past the anger stage. The die was cast. They'd be miserable for their entire tour, and there was nothing you could do about it.)

All through my career, I've also seen the effects of bad first impressions. Major Ryan knocked us for a loop. If you are ever in a position to welcome a successor or new employee to an overseas location, get organized. Talk up the positives, share the best stories you have, tell him or her the best places you've seen, give good examples about your job, and so on. There's a way to weave in the challenging issues without sniveling or complaining. Every place has problems. Do your homework. Discuss the tougher issues thoughtfully, and even offer up suggested improvements, if you have them. Be a leader. Be empathetic. Be a mentor. You'll help the employee and his or her family, and support the organization at the same time. On an even broader scale, you'll help our American team members adjust to living in a foreign land, which will lead to better overall relations with the host country.

For the record, Comiso ended up being my favorite place to live and work in my entire military career. Take that, Ryan.

Comiso is located in the Province of Ragusa, in the southeast corner of Sicily. It sits between Ragusa and Vittoria, just fifteen miles north of Marina de Ragusa, on the Mediterranean (Med) Sea. The area is mainly agricultural, with almond trees, carob trees, wheat, livestock, and wineries. Since Sicily is the biggest island in the Med, it has much to offer. Comiso Air Base (AB) was practically brand-new in 1990. Housing was still being built, and the on-base facilities were great. Andi and I moved into a brand-new Swiss-built townhouse on the west side of the base. I could walk or bike to work every day, because the weather was perfect year-round. I never grew tired of the mountain ranges that surrounded us. They welcomed me to Sicily every morning.

It's impossible to talk about Italy without talking about driving. By far, Italians are the most aggressive drivers in Europe. With literally no fear, they will do things on the road that leave you speechless. Speed limits, warning signs, and no-passing zones are irrelevant. For example, in Sicily there are tons of high-altitude hairpin turns, and narrow two-lane roads without guardrails. I learned very quickly that you were expected to place two wheels off the road, near the edge, every time you entered a blind corner. Why? Because crazy Italians were passing by driving directly down the middle of the road! The unwritten rule was simple: if the vehicles on each side had two wheels off the road, there was just enough room for a passing car to squeeze through. The first time this happens will scare the shit out of you. But believe it or not, you get used to it. In fact, I started doing it myself (when in Rome, right?) when Andi wasn't in the car. She didn't have the stomach for it. I thought it was fun.

The CBPO fell under the 487th Mission Support Squadron, which supported the 487th Tactical Missile Wing. It was a new, well-laid-out operation on the second and third floors of the Headquarters Building. As CBPO Chief, I had two officers, forty-six Airmen, and twelve civilians working for me. I was responsible for the management of eight branches—Military Personnel, Information Management, Family Support Center, Education Office, Civilian Personnel, Social Actions, CBPO Unit Administration, and the NCO Preparatory School. Talk about a big job. I spent more time with the wing commander than I did with my wife! (I know ... a slight exaggeration.) Most of my early days were spent trying to undo what Major Ryan had done. Andi and I weren't the only ones with a negative impression of him. One good thing about following a middle-of-the-road performer is that it can make you look better. My team responded quickly, and I was very thankful. I used everything I had in my toolbox to bring up morale. Empathy, empowerment, autonomy, delegation, humor, monthly social events, open discussion formats, open door policy—you name it, I used it. In a way, Major Ryan did me a favor. After listening to him, I was determined to prove him wrong. To this day, I never enjoyed a job more. Our CBPO came together as a team. It was a joy to go to work in the morning. Although Andi and I will not soon forget the lousy welcome we received, we vowed to *never* let anyone cloud our judgment again. The next cut wouldn't be as deep.

On base, life was very good to us as well. I was able to sign on with Maryland University and taught a few college classes while I was there. (As I mentioned above, Andi found a good job as well.) And of course, there was softball—the 487th Mission Support Squadron won the final base championship. Yours truly hit the game-winning, walk-off home run. (With the drawdown looming—more on this in a minute—it was the last pitch ever thrown in Sicily.) I just missed averaging 190 again in bowling—coming in at 189. The base had a great running and biking trail that circled the entire facility. Andi and I used it countless times. But the most important thing about Comiso were the people. We were thousands of miles from home. Many of my friends, teammates, and colleagues were stationed there without their families. We needed each other. We fed on each other's company. In many cases, our time together filled the ever-present void of loneliness and reduced the pain of missing husbands, wives, and children.

I could spend the next hundred pages talking about things to see in Sicily (Italy). But I'm not writing a travel guide. So, Andi and I sat down and listed the top ten. We've omitted so many good places to see that I had to include some honorable mentions. Drumroll please ...

Marina de Ragusa—Just because this is listed number ten doesn't mean it wasn't a great place. The village is a *frazione* of Ragusa, Sicily, and is located right on the Med, directly across from the island of Malta. The deep blue of the sea was almost unworldly. Of course, the local economy was based on tourism, with many bars, restaurants, and hotels. Andi and I had our share of great meals there. In the summer, this sleepy town of four thousand people exploded with activity, bursting at the seams with over 60,000 people. When Larry came to visit, we biked down to the coast, and he was amazed at the beauty and interesting terrain of Sicily.

Mount Etna—It's the highest mountain in Italy south of the Alps. As one of the world's most active volcanoes, it is in a constant state of activity. Even the elevation—10,922 feet—varies with each eruption. It covers 460 square miles and dominates the Sicilian skyline around Catania and Messina. You can drive halfway to the top, and there are a few brave restaurants carved into the mountainside. I remember driving through walls of snowbanks, sitting outside with heaters at our feet, and enjoying a glass of wine and some pasta. Magical.

Siracusa—Once the capital of ancient Sicily, this city is listed by UNESCO as a World Heritage Site. Siracusa was one of the major powers of the Mediterranean world and played a large role in the development of Europe over the millennia. Walking around town was very different, with Greek history, culture, amphitheaters, and hallowed architecture everywhere. The city is almost three thousand years old and is located in the southeastern part of Sicily. It was once called "the greatest Greek city and the most beautiful of them all" by Cicero. You can get lost in time there.

Pompeii—Pompeii is located about twenty miles south of Naples, with Mount Vesuvius in between the two cities. You probably know the story. In 79 AD, Mount Vesuvius erupted, and Pompeii was covered in ashes. The estimated casualties approached twenty thousand people, many "frozen" in time by the hot ash and preserved for thousands of years by the lack of air and moisture. During the excavation in the 1700s, according to Wikipedia, "plaster was used to fill the voids between the ash layers that once held human bodies. This allowed one to see the exact position a person was in when they died." Mothers hugging babies, men shielding their eyes, stark terror in the faces of children—all were plain to see. An eerie place, but very memorable. Today, over 2.5 million tourists visit Pompeii each year.

Agrigento—Someone once said, "If you want to see Greece, go to Agrigento." This apparent paradox is only a slight exaggeration. The Valley of the Temples, just outside Agrigento in the south central part of Sicily, is one of the most famous tourist attractions on the island. The archaeological park consists of eight temples built between 510 BC and 430 BC. My two favorites were the Temple of Caster and Pollux and the Temple of Demeter—both were well preserved and nicely presented. Imagine eight huge Greek temples in one place. Interestingly, the Valley of the Temples actually sits on a rocky crest just south of modern-day Agrigento, so it's really not a valley at all.

Amalfi Coast—The Amalfi Coast stretches along the coastline of the Sorrentine Peninsula, in the Province of Salerno in southern Italy. It's one of the most beautiful drives in the world. With a steep shoreline and little room for rural or agricultural growth, the coastline maintains its unbelievable landscape. There is just one road—*Strade Statale 163*—and it scales the cliffs for forty kilometers, weaving from *Vietri sul Mare* to *Positano*. Along the way, there's a smattering of little towns clinging to the cliffside. It's quite extraordinary, and I highly recommend it.

Aeolian Islands—These are the "seven sisters" that lie to the north of "their great mother," Sicily. The islands of Lipari, Vulcano, Salina, Panarea, Strombli, Alicudi, and Filicudi make up the island chain. Lipari is the most densely populated, and where most of the ferries arrive from Sicily. From there, you can fan out to the other islands. There were lots of restaurants and bars by the ferry docks, which were packed with lively tourists waiting for ferries. We rented mopeds on Vulcano, home of the legendary *Aephaestus* (the Greek vulture), and rode them to the edge of the volcano's great crater. Andi was scared silly when we came screaming down the crater at warp speed. We also went to Stromboli, home of the islands' only active volcano. By the sea line, at a place called *Sciara del Fuoco*, we saw the massive, but picturesque, flow of volcanic debris. Actually, the ferry rides from Cefalu (Sicilian coast) to the Aeolian Islands were almost as much fun as the islands themselves —beautiful scenery, crystal-clear blue water, and excellent views of Mount Etna.

Rome—There's no way to adequately cover all the things to see in Rome. I've been there four times and still haven't come close to seeing everything. However, here is a short list of can't-miss stops: the Vatican (Basilica of

St. Peter), Circus Maximus (Roman chariot-racing stadium), the Coliseum (obvious choice), Trevi Fountain (don't forget your coins), the Pantheon (a magnificent ancient structure), and the Spanish Steps (people watching extraordinaire). But while you're hustling from place to place, don't forget to slow down, have a glass of *vino locali*, and take in the city's beauty.

Isle of Capri—This mountainous island is located twenty miles south of Naples and is accessible by ferry. The limestone rock is famed for its unparalleled sea views, the Blue Grotto, and countless Imperial Roman villas. The entire cities of Capri and Anacapri seem to float on air, much like the Greek Isle of Santorini. The tiny streets, warm plazas, and fine restaurants made the visit even more memorable. Over in Anacapri, you can take a long, one-seat swing ride to the top of Mount Solaro (589 meters). It's incredible— you'll pass houses, farms, and vineyards during the first part of the ride. Then, the swing turns steeply upward, scales the mountain, and offers staggering 360-degree vistas all around you. I'll never forget how much fun that was.

Taormina—I think the website www.thinksicily.com says it perfectly: "What do Goethe, Alexander Dumas, Johannes Brahms, Gustav Klimt, D. H. Lawrence, Richard Wagner, Oscar Wilde, Truman Capote, John Steinbeck, Ingmar Bergman, Francis Ford Coppola, Leonard Bernstein, Marlene Dietrich, Greta Garbo, Federico Fellini, Cary Grant, Elizabeth Taylor, and Woody Allen all have in common?

"Simple—they all have sojourned in Taormina, the pearl of the Mediterranean." Idyllically perched on a rocky promontory high above the sea, Taormina has been the most popular tourist destination in Sicily for a couple of hundred years. Beautifully restored medieval buildings, breathtaking views around every corner, and a giddy network of winding streets strewn with shops, bars, and restaurants make it the perfect holiday spot.

Taormina's past is Sicily's history in a microcosm: Greeks, Romans, Byzantines, Arabs, Normans, Swabians, French, and the Spanish all came, saw, conquered, and left. Throw in the unrestricted views of Mount Etna, and the Straights of Messina below, and you get the picture. Andi and I went there several times, and it's one of the best places to walk in the world. The swayback roads to the top will give you goose bumps.

That leaves two honorable mentions. One is *Carney Park*, in Naples. It's a dormant volcano turned into a recreation area. There's a nine-hole golf course inside the crater. And all around the rim, thousands of goats with cowbells noisily feed on wild vegetation. It's almost a religious experience to play golf there, with the soft tinkering of distant "church bells" in the background. On a couple of occasions, a bunch of us drove to Palermo, took the overnight auto ferry to Naples, and played golf at Carney Park for a few days. It was really fun.

The other is *Chiarmonte Gulfi*, known as the Balcony of Sicily. You can drive from the rolling, semiarid terrain near the base to a mountainous and dense pine forest in thirty minutes! From there, you can see local towns like Comiso and Vittoria, and peer all the way to the Mediterranean Sea.

Of course, you can also take in Mount Etna and the Erean Mountains near Caltagirone. (Caltagirone almost made the list. I spent several hours in a local club one night singing and playing guitar. American music was very popular. So I reluctantly agreed to play one Dylan number, and it kind of skyrocketed from there. My fingers were bleeding pretty badly when I finished, but I didn't care. Deep down, I knew I'd never do anything like that again.) Anyway, the Chiarmonte mountaintop was where I started to develop my love for *vino locali*—which I still have today. That alone qualifies it for honorable mention.

(Even while Andi and I were running around Italy at breakneck speed, things were happening in our lives that would complicate things. When I married Andi, I knew she was a type 1 diabetic. She lost function of her pancreas at age twenty-five and requires several shots of insulin every day. Prior to our marriage, I didn't realize the full weight of her disability, nor how much it would take for her to function normally. She was falling into insulin shock on occasion, and it was scaring the shit out of me. Convulsions, inability to eat/swallow, sweats, swelled tongue, and so on. I was in way over my head. For some reason, I couldn't get her to eat enough to keep her blood sugar higher. Fast forward twenty-three years—and I still can't today. It's a mystery I've never understood. She'd bite me when I tried to feed her, and spit food at me when I was finally able to get some nourishment into her system. [She never remembers anything about her hypoglycemic incidents, which makes it difficult to chastise her about them.] Of course, I gave her dozens of glucagon shots, and summoned ambulances when I ran out of options. In short, I became a 24-7 health-care provider and slept with one eye open, which I still do today. Her disease put tremendous pressure on me. It also constantly reminded me how tough it was to be a diabetic and what a tremendous liability this disease created for my wife. I mention this because her diabetic condition would play a major role in our careers, and consequently, in the rest of our lives.)

The Ground Launch Cruise Missile (GLCM) program spearheaded by President Reagan was a great success. For the first time in the USSR's history, their nuclear weapons were neutralized. Here's how it worked. In Comiso, as well as Greenham Common AB in England, the GLCMs were pointed right at Russia. This meant that if the Union of Soviet Socialist Republics ever launched missiles, the GLCMs would strike them before their rockets left Russian airspace. In other words, they were rendered meaningless, because Moscow and other cities would be gone before they would know the results of their launches. The threat of a surprise attack was removed. Combine this with the cost of an escalating arms race, and Russia gave up. They signed every treaty the United States introduced, thus diffusing their arsenal.

In Comiso, this had an immediate effect. The wheels were in motion— the air base would be slated for closure. We agreed to remove the GLCMs from Europe if the Russians complied with our demands. They did. So, in late 1990, we started to remove the missiles. There were regular USSR helicopter visits checking our progress, just like we were checking theirs in Russia. In the CBPO, I was tasked to develop a comprehensive military personnel drawdown plan. This was a big job. I designed and implemented a detailed configuration plan drawing down every military position on base. This included plans to close every facility on Comiso—including the CBPO, early releases and reassignments, terminating and adjusting all services requiring manpower, reducing online computer capabilities, adjusting a slew of DOD contacts, and closing offices under my direct supervision—all the time assuring that the right people remained and eventually departed at the appropriate time. The plan was painful to develop, and even more difficult to sell to the wing and group commanders.

With much gnashing of teeth, the PROTAF Creek Resolve Plan (I have no idea what it stands for) authorized the military withdrawal of personnel from Comiso Air Base. Things were in place. All the planning was over. It was time to start the drawdown process. I was ready to move into action. I even received my next assignment during this time—we were going to the United States Air Force Academy—and we were very happy about it. What could stop us now?

But something did stop us—Desert Storm. I was tasked to support the Joint Staff at Incirlik Air Base, Turkey, just north of Iraq. The timing wasn't good. Andi was struggling with her diabetes, and I was leaving just as my drawdown plan was ready for implementation. And with open-ended orders, I could be gone indefinitely. Where would Andi go after the base closed? What if she had a hypoglycemic attack while she was alone in the house? It could mean her life. But when a military man is called, he goes. Period.

There was a nice send-off for me at Comiso, and I wondered if I would ever see Andi again. I traveled to Turkey and was in place on the flight line supporting Operation Proven Force as best I could. I was on the J-1 staff (manpower and personnel), working twenty hours a day and sleeping on the cot next to my computers. My job was to produce up-to-the-minute accountability statistics for General Jameson's staff. Who was in theater? Who departed? Injuries? Fatalities? Who's manifested on incoming aircraft? And so on. It was intense to say the least. Every few minutes around the clock, another aircraft took off. The noise was deafening. The war was afoot. SCUDs were fired at us, but thankfully, no direct hits. My open-ended orders meant my return was unknown. I couldn't help feeling that I was going to be there for a long time. I prayed that Andi would be okay.

But, thankfully to all involved, I was wrong. Our military might struck quickly, wiping out Iraq's ability to see (communications sites), and then bombing their runways into submission. With no eyes or the ability to launch aircraft, the Iraq Air Force was erased by our forces, opening up the floodgates for our ground troops to seal the deal. In just two weeks, the J-1 staff grew substantially at Incirlik, even though the offensive was already receding. I got on General Jameson's calendar and explained my situation in Comiso. He understood. I was released to return to Comiso. And Andi was fine—thank you, Lord.

The rest of my time in Comiso was consumed with drawing down the base. People were heading to the Catania Airport daily, housing units were getting "pickled," or closed, and offices were getting smaller and smaller. My CBPO staff was dwindling as well. It was an uneasy process, but one of satisfaction for a job well done.

From an historical perspective, the cost of building Comiso AB was gigantic. The entire base was brand-new. There were over seventy recently completed homes that were never occupied. And how about America's generous real estate investment? First, we built the base. Second, we rented it from the Italians. And finally, we gave it back to them when we left. (I would have liked to be in on that real estate deal.) On the upside, we took away Russia's one big stick—a surprise nuclear attack. Two countries—Italy and England—stepped up. It couldn't have been easy to convince constituents to place nuclear weapons in their backyards. Kudos to both for making the world a safer place.

It's impossible to leave Sicily without talking about the food and wine. When you arrive at a Sicilian restaurant for dinner, the first thing the waiter does is place a basket of bread and a jug of wine on your table. Not napkins or water or menus—but bread and wine. At a restaurant near Marsala, when a bottle of wine was brought to the table, we asked for the *vino locali* instead. Tourists liked the fancy bottled wines, but we learned early on that the local wines were much better. Anyway, we saw the server cross a small street and enter his house. Moments later, he came out with a ceramic jug (looked like a rooster—very common there) and brought it to our table. We were receiving his private, family stock. And it was great. As I mentioned before, my taste for red wine started in Sicily. I can't imagine a steak or pasta, or even a plate of cheese and crackers, without red wine.

One of our last trips was to Cefalu, a small town in the north-central part of the island. We knew it well, since it's the takeoff point for the Aeolian Islands. For the last time, we settled in for the usual three to four hour dining experience there. Unlike the United States, where people gobble down fast food or eat on the run, in Italy it's an enjoyable and deliberate process. With wine and bread already present, the meal usually consisted of five components:

antipasto

primo pasta

secondo pasta

contorno

dolce

The *antipasto* was usually meats, cheeses, and an assortment of marinated vegetables. The term *antipasto* means "before the meal," like an appetizer. But each restaurant/trattoria had its specialty, and you accepted what was offered.

The *primo pasta* was usually served in rich creamy sauces, like risotto, polenta, or penne. It was always good, and really whetted your appetite. The chef's concentration was on the perfect preparation of the noodles—with different seasonings and excellent "al dente" presentation.

The *secondo pasta* was the main dish—the specialty of the house. It usually involved different types of meats, with less spice, to compensate for the primo pasta selection.

The *contorno* can come after the main dish or alongside of it. The word *contorno* translates to "contours," and it could be a salad or a platter of vegetables. This component of the meal was to use vegetables to help define and shape the meal.

The *dolce* was the dessert—usually sweet.

But all good things must come to an end. It's hard to imagine, but our entire stay in Sicily only lasted thirteen months. The tour length was cut almost in half because of the base drawdown. But it didn't matter. We did more in that one year than in any other year of our marriage. Andi, after a slow start, was flourishing. She would never have trouble adjusting again, regardless of where we were headed. Yes, her diabetes was a challenge—is a challenge—but what can you do? If you love someone, you accept them, warts and all. I was a CBPO Chief—a job I admired from my first day in Germany and the best job in the air force as far as I was concerned. Even better, I was heading to Colorado to assume my assistant professorship at the United States Air Force Academy. And the cuts would never hurt us again.

Arrivederci, e grazie. (Good-bye, and thanks.)

CHAPTER THIRTEEN

Pikes Peak or Bust

———————————◦———————————

According to Wikipedia, "Pike's Peak is a mountain in the front range of the Rocky Mountains within Pike National Forest. Originally called El Capitan by Spanish settlers, the mountain was renamed Pikes Peak after Zebulon Pike Jr., an explorer who led an expedition to the southern Colorado area in 1806." (The Arapaho called it *heeyotoyoo*, or Long Mountain.) It's one of fifty-four "fourteeners," and has an elevation of 14,115 feet. When you arrive in Colorado Springs, it's the first thing you notice. Snowcapped year-round, Pikes Peak dominates the skyline. And like Poseidon's Temple watching over the sea at Cape Sounion, it sees all, and seems to welcome you to its domain.

We settled into temporary housing at the academy and began our search for a place to call home. We had shipped our Honda Accord from Comiso, and my younger brother, John, had brought my van back from Los Angeles. Upon arrival, I had several first impressions of Colorado. The air was crisp and clean—but there wasn't much of it! One flight of stairs could take your breath away. And surprisingly, the city of Colorado Springs is relatively flat, even though the terrain elevates over five thousand feet above sea level. But nothing left a bigger impression than the United States Air Force Academy (USAFA or AFA). The AFA is over 18,500 acres, and only about 2 to 3 percent of the base is developed. It was like working in a national park. I remember many mornings, while driving to work, seeing hundreds of deer crossing Stillman Field, just behind the cadet area. The base is located on the side of Rampart Ridge, an eastern section of the Rockies. It rests 7,258 feet above sea level. There were days when the snow was so outrageous or the fog was so dense that it felt like we were working in a cloud bank or on the north face of Mount Everest.

I couldn't believe my luck in getting an assignment to the academy. Over the next three years, I felt privileged to be part of the academy team. And I knew how tough it was to get stationed there—remember, I did AFA Assignments at AFMPC. I was slated to become an air officer commanding

117

(AOC) after my first year. AOCs are specially selected officers who command cadet squadrons and groups at USAFA. They have command authority over their cadet squadrons and are expected to train cadets in officership and military matters. These positions are highly sought after, very promotable, and rarely given to non-academy graduates or nonflying officers. I would serve one year as an instructor, learn the lay of the land so to speak, and then take over a squadron as an AOC.

My first job title was Instructor, Professional Military Studies (PMS— yeah, I know the inference), which fell under the Commandant of Cadets Division. I taught PMS 330, Joint Force Employment, a required university-level course for junior cadets. Just some of the curriculum included spectrum of conflict and instruments of power; National Security Act of 1947; the birth of the USAF; the DOD budget process; unified/ joint commands; military treaties; and an extensive review of dozens of military operations from the American Revolution to the Gulf War. It was an exhausting endeavor to bone up for this course, and the toughest class I ever taught. And I had no margin for error. My classes were full of the brightest young men and women in the country. Almost one-third of the students in my second-year class were valedictorians! They would be all over me if I tried to "mail it in." But I didn't mind the hard work. As I mentioned to Andi many times, I would have done this job for nothing.

I remember having one student who was seven feet two inches tall, the tallest cadet in academy history. One day my class talked me into asking him if he played basketball to see what he'd say. It went like this:

"Cadet Murray, do you play basketball?" said I, playing along with the class. With a deadpan expression, he answered, "No, do you play miniature golf?" He was in on the ruse.

The class cracked up. I was the bait.

You have to tip your hat to these kids. They take twenty-three to twenty-six credit hours per semester, not including labs. In addition, they have a continuous agenda of military training, physical conditioning, study requirements, dorm inspections, and various cadet programs. I swear, they never slept. (Except in my class—just joking.) And they get a whopping *two weeks'* vacation per year! That's it. After that, it's back to the academy to administer basic cadet training programs in the summer, and to attend classes the rest of the calendar year.

So if they can get a laugh setting up the instructor, more power to them. The mission of the Commandant of Cadets was to train and motivate 4,400 members of the cadet wing to become career officers in the USAF. Our goal was to direct the academy leadership programs and provide military and aviation instruction that would instill the character and dedication required for military professionals. The cadet area was gigantic, with the terrazzo (large open area) right in the middle, the chapel to the west, and Harmon Hall (classrooms) to the east. The terrazzo was the staging area for the cafeteria, which was called Mitchell Hall. It was an amazing spectacle to watch over 4,400 cadets enter, eat, and depart the cafeteria in less than twenty minutes! The place went from deserted, to full earsplitting capacity, back to deserted in minutes. The ever-present visitors on the balcony—senior officers, politicians, and so on—were never disappointed. It was a hell of a show.

Andi and I found a beautiful home on Crocus Lane, above the corner of Austin Bluffs and Union Boulevard, in Colorado Springs. It rested atop a high ridge, with perfect views of the Garden of the Gods and, of course, Pikes Peak. The Garden of the Gods is a 1,319-acre public park in Colorado Springs. It's full of rock formations, vegetation, and assorted wildlife. There are great views everywhere, and easy hiking trails in all directions. The vistas from Rampart Range Road, east of Balanced Rock, provided excellent views of downtown Colorado Springs and the Garden of the Gods. Our house had a master bedroom that encompassed the entire top floor, with a wide window that perfectly framed Pikes Peak. It was the first thing Andi and I saw every morning. The house was on a gravel, dead-end road. There were two other houses in the area, but they weren't located close to us. The place had hundreds of feet of decks and a wide variety of different-shaped rooms. A fireplace stood away from the wall, providing 360-degree heat. Simply put—it was modernistic, with unusual interior and exterior shapes of all kinds, and looked awesome from the street far below. Of course, the drawback was the garage. It was attached to the house, with a very steep driveway down to the road. There were snowy mornings where I literally skied down the driveway in my van, each time hoping to avoid crossing the road and vaulting downward toward the ravine below. On two occasions, the only thing that saved me was the snowbank between my house and the cliff.

Academy life was ideal, and we were settled into our new home. Andi was still struggling with her diabetes, and I was still sweating bullets. When she decided to go back to college and finish her degree, I thought it was a great idea—*if she promised she would do a better job managing her blood sugar*. We made a pact, and off to the University of Colorado-Colorado Springs she went. It bothered her for years that she had dropped out of Tulane and never really focused on her academics. This gave her a second chance, and she would maximize it. Before we left Colorado, she graduated magna cum laude with a bachelor of science degree in business. I was very proud of her. I always knew she was the smart one in the family. This accomplishment was hard-earned, and I knew she was proud of it.

One limiting factor about living in a place like Colorado was the weather. For many months per year, snow and cold temperatures limited outdoor travel options. Unless you were a skier or cold-sport enthusiast, winters meant lots of warm fires, cozy evenings reading a book or listening to music, and watching sports or shows on television. It was quite an adjustment from the year-round moderate climate of Comiso. But when spring arrived and the weather broke, it was a mad rush to get out of the house and enjoy the region. The rustiness of winter soon gave way to the excitement of expected activity. When the seasons started to change, we couldn't wait to kick the door open and enjoy the beautiful state of Colorado.

We started locally. The city of Colorado Springs is nestled against the eastern side of the Rocky Mountains and is located in El Paso County. The elevation is 6,035 feet, placing it well above one mile in altitude. Colorado Springs lies approximately sixty-five miles south of Denver and had a population of 416,000. One of our first priorities was to take the seventeen-mile drive up to the top of Pikes Peak. (I wanted to see if I could locate our master bedroom window from there—just kidding.) Most of the road is not paved, so it's sketchy navigating the hairpin turns. All along the way, you can't resist stopping and admiring the vista. We saw deer, mountain goats, and even animals we later learned were marmots. At the top, the air was very thin, and it felt like you were floating. We watched the Cog Railway Train grunting its way to the top, and even stopped in the Summit House for a hot cup of coffee. Wow—what a trip.

On a warm day, hanging out downtown on Tejon Street was one of our most relaxing pastimes. Sipping a brew at Old Chicago's or having a nice lunch at the Ritz Grill was always fun. For something different, we'd head over to the Broadmoor Hotel, the "Grand Dame of the Rockies." It was built in 1918 and has fifteen restaurants and cafes and three golf courses. I can also remember spending a few hours in the Colorado Springs Fine Arts Center, featuring Spanish Colonial and Native American pieces, and then heading to the Broadmoor for a late lunch. There are numerous other respites nearby. Here are just a few: the USAFA Visitor Center, with over one million visitors per year; the Olympic Training Center, headquarters of the US Olympic Committee and a world-class training facility; the Rio Grande Railroad, with restored 1950 Pullman coaches and scenic rides through La Veta Pass in the Rockies; and Cripple Creek, a former gold mining town on the slopes of the Rockies, with abandoned mines and retro casinos. A few years ago, I read in *Money* magazine that Colorado Springs was voted the number-one "Best Place to Live" in the United States.

But life, as we all know, can kick you in the gut sometimes. In this case, it was Andi's gut. In mid-1992, Andi's diabetes management was going south. She would fall into hypoglycemic shock within minutes, and she couldn't control it. After an ambulance incident at our house, we knew something was really wrong. So Andi went to a doctor. Although she was on the pill, the doctor ran a pregnancy test and found that my wife was five or six weeks' pregnant. He explained to her that with her health deteriorating so quickly, the chance of a successful pregnancy was very low. In addition, he warned Andi that it was dangerous and could be fatal. He spoke to me as well and told me the same thing. But he added one more element to his conversation with me. He stated adamantly that she needed a medical abortion. So Andi and I discussed this option. I was strongly for the abortion, because I believed the doctor. And also because I felt her life was more important than a dangerous pregnancy. But I wasn't the potential mother, so I left the final decision up to Andi.

So, on a cold drizzly morning a few days later, Andi and I went to a clinic in Colorado City, and the fetus was medically aborted. (Talk about a negative SSE.) Two weeks later, at Peterson AFB, she had her tubes tied. We didn't know what to say to each other afterward. Even though we weren't planning to have kids, the finality of it hit both of us. We would remain childless for the rest of our lives. But God does things in mysterious ways. I doubt if Andi and I would have had children anyway. Especially with our nomadic lifestyle. So this medical abortion took the weight off her shoulders. It was health, not personal preference, that would decide her fate. She was relieved of the pressure that millions of mothers and potential mothers have anguished over forever—whether to have children or not. Looking back, I can honestly say children were not in the cards for us. But I'd be lying if I didn't say that I sometimes wondered what it would have been like to have a child. But I'd also be an idiot if I'd pressured Andi to risk her life to find out.

We used this incident to strengthen our marriage. As Dylan says, "May you have a strong foundation, when the winds of changes shift." It was just us. We knew our foundation was strong. Our cards were dealt. It was time to move on.

Before we knew it, my first academic year at the academy was winding down, and I started to anticipate my next job as an AOC. But it never happened. Instead, I was offered the Deputy Chief, Military Training Division position. And I jumped on it. Although the AOC job was an excellent opportunity and a good career move, I saw the deputy position as a chance to direct a broader-based component of academy programs. Instead of just one squadron, I was responsible for all formal military training received by the entire 4,400 cadet wing! And the best part—I was promised that I could continue to teach my PMS 330 classes. It was a no-brainer.

My division had four huge training components: Basic Cadet Training (BCT); DOD-accredited Survival, Evasion, Resistance, and Escape (SERE) training; worldwide summer temporary-duty programs for cadets; and Combat Arms and Maintenance Training (firing range). Each program was separate and distinct, and each was a blast.

The USAFA website describes BCT as "a five week program that tests your mental and physical abilities and helps you make the transition from civilian to military life. You'll develop alertness, physical endurance, emotional stability, self-reliance, and individual initiative. The training is divided into two phases, and is administered by upper-class cadets, with officers and noncommissioned officers serving as advisors." (The program was similar to Officers Training School in Texas.) Again, from the website, "The first phase of BCT takes place in the cadet area and is devoted to military orientation programs. Emphasis is placed on learning basic military skills and responsibilities, improving conditioning and adapting to teamwork through competitive sports. The second phase of BCT consists of Field-Training activities conducted at the Jack's Valley encampment site, five miles north of the cadet area." The cadets erect tents and live there for eighteen days. The activities include military orientation, weapons training, and challenging mental and physical obstacles like the Leadership Reaction Course. "The training demands the most in stamina, determination and resourcefulness." Although the upper class did most of the work, my office oversaw the program. I dropped in on the proceedings every time I had a chance.

The Survival, Evasion, Resistance, and Escape (SERE) program at the academy was designed to provide training in evading capture, survival skills, and the military code of conduct. The academy training concentrated on wilderness survival under all types of conditions, including first aid, land navigation, camouflage techniques, methods of evasion, communication protocols, and how to make rudimentary tools. Cadets were released into the woods, tracked down, and brought to a mock POW camp. (The camp was very realistic, with cells, barbed-wire fences, cameras everywhere, and some minor—but effective—torture protocols.) They also dealt with a variety of mental and physical challenges, many of which are classified. The "enemy" used a wide array of techniques to try to break the cadet's will. I spent one summer as an advisor, and it was alarming to see some of the techniques that were used to induce POWs to talk, try to escape, or turn on their comrades. The camp was highly effective, but very controversial. It's a thin line between training cadets to handle the rigors of being a POW, and causing mental and physical harassment. (Note: The SERE program is no longer at the academy. It has been moved to Fairchild AFB in Washington, where the USAF Survival School instructors are permanently located.) Stuffing cadets in small, unlit boxes where they couldn't move for hours or denying sleep for long periods of time may be harsh. On the other hand, it's hard to imagine any worthwhile training dealing with the capture of POWs that wouldn't be difficult. For me, as a claustrophobic, I still get sweaty palms thinking about those small boxes.

The Summer Temporary Duty Program was the complete opposite of SERE. Our office worked with air force bases all over the world, setting up opportunities for cadets to see firsthand how operational wings carried out their missions. The goal was to place a cadet as closely as possible to his or her chosen career path, that is, pilots to flying units, engineers to field operation locations involving science, and so on. The toughest part of this program was logistics. Funding, housing, transportation, and such were all difficult issues. But it was worth it. The cadets usually came back to Colorado full of energy and excitement.

The Combat Arms Training and Maintenance Unit (CATM), also called the firing range, was a riot. The crew of civil service employees were highly proficient and fun to hang out with. They trained all the cadets and staff members, and most of the police and federal agencies throughout Colorado and the Northwest. But their facilities were lousy, and they didn't have enough people to meet all the demands on their time. I fixed that. Since I managed the budget for our division, I was directly involved in the annual appropriations of USAFA funds. I fought for additional staff at the firing range and was successful in getting four new positions. In addition, I invited the senior staff to visit the firing range, and had an opportunity to show them firsthand how inadequate the place really was. They agreed with me. Just before I left, construction began on a new $15-million facility.

Needless to say, I was pretty popular with the CATM guys. I remember hanging out after work, taking a shot or two of bourbon, and then firing whatever weapons they would let me fire. (I know, alcohol and guns, not a good combination. But it was a lot of fun.) When I left the academy, the CATM team gave me a briefcase, with a long-nose Smith and Wesson .22-caliber pistol, complete with a clip, rounds of ammo, and my name etched into the barrel. Inside the briefcase was a nice bronze plaque, thanking me for having the "steelies" to support the CATM team. I still have the entire set.

When Andi and I could get away, we concentrated our travels outside of the Colorado Springs area. Denver was our favorite escape, and we must have gone there at least fifteen times. We especially enjoyed the Mount Evans road to the sky. It's the highest paved road in North America, reaching 14,240 feet at the summit. You pass through three life zones, see mountain goats and bighorn sheep along the way, and view many changing terrains. The day we went, it was ninety degrees in Denver, but just forty-two degrees at the top. When the weather was nice, we'd drive up to Denver, and hang out in Larimer Square or the Sixteenth Street Mall area. There were plenty of shops, restaurants, microbreweries, landmarks, walking areas, and so on. And of course, we never missed a chance to see the Pirates at Mile High Stadium. Walking the 320-acre City Park was also a big thrill for us. It housed the Denver Zoo and had all kinds of recreational opportunities.

Each year we went to the Cherry Creek Arts Festival (CCAF), and the Renaissance Festival in nearby Larkspur. The CCAF has been bringing the world to Denver and Colorado since 1991. It is considered by many to be America's most popular art festival. Huge in scope, it's packed with content and presents a very festive atmosphere for over 350,000 visitors annually. The Renaissance Festival was even better. As the website says, "It's a weekend of riotous comedy, death-defying peril, and mouth-watering delights. When the cannon fires, the castle gate opens and you'll be transported to 16th Century Tudor England." The place was full of merchants, selling everything from leatherwork and blown glass to woodworking and pottery. There were pirates, wenches, jugglers, jesters, sword-swallowers, knights, kings, and queens all over the place. It was very imaginative and fun. We also went to Aspen and Vail on a couple of occasions, but never during ski season. In the summer, they were lazy towns, full of scenery and places to eat, drink, and shop.

Back at the academy, the unexpected happened again. Cruising along in my role as the deputy director of the Military Training Division, I was offered the job as Commander, Commandant of Cadets Squadron. No one turns down a commander job. It just isn't done. So even though I loved my current position, I headed over to the command section to take on my new responsibilities. (The AOC job was now off the table.) Thankfully, I was allowed to keep teaching, not just my PMS classes, but also a recently added leadership and management class in the behavioral sciences department. Looking back, maybe I was overreaching a bit. But for one year, I felt I could handle the double duty. I had command authority over 171 enlisted personnel, and morale, welfare, legal, and administrative authority over 170 officers and 390 civilians. A big job to say the least. In a given day, I could hold a commander's call in the morning and speak to my squadron about working together as a team, and that afternoon process an administrative discharge case or Article 15 punishment under the Uniform Code of Military Justice, effectively ending one's career. Simply put, a commander sees the best and worst of his squadron population.

I remember one case involving an airman who worked in the Mitchell Hall cafeteria. Let's call him Airman Smith. His roommate came into the command section one day complaining about a bad odor coming from Airman Smith's sleeping area. I sent my first sergeant to his room to investigate. Under his bed were dozens of crusty women's panties, which he had used to ejaculate into. The cumulative effect was a stench that his roommate couldn't bear anymore. It gets worse. We assumed he stole the panties from the women's laundry room, but we had no legal proof. So in order to verify our theory, we collected all the panties and laid them out on a table in a spare room for inspection. We then asked all female airmen and NCOs who were missing underwear to review the contents and let us know if any of the panties were theirs. When several identified their clothing, we had enough evidence to toss the pervert out of the air force. As I said before, you can't make this stuff up.

My days as commander were full of good and bad. On good days, I'd present awards, write positive airman performance reports (APRs), have a constructive commanders call, upgrade IT equipment, create new positions in the squadron, honcho a social function, and so on. On the not-so-good days, I'd carry out disciplinary cases resulting in loss of pay, loss of rank, or both. Or I'd sign an APR that would ensure an airman would never get promoted again. It was tough, but my prime directive—if I can borrow the term from *Star Trek*—was to uphold the standards of the squadron. Sometimes rehabilitation was effective, and sometimes it wasn't. When it wasn't, it was the commander's job, with legal advice, to take the appropriate steps.

Andi and I were really enjoying our off-duty time. We went to Boulder, Colorado—home of the University of Colorado—for a couple of concerts. We saw John Hiatt and John Prine there. And we never missed an annual state fair down in Pueblo, Colorado. It was eleven days of concerts, rodeos, livestock exhibits, horse shows, and so on. I'm a city kid, but I really got a kick out of the animals, as well as the rural flavor of Pueblo. We took our first cruise with two other couples on Norwegian Cruise Lines, and marveled at the decadence of the food and the great ports of the Eastern Caribbean. (I can't remember all the stops, but I do remember San Juan, Nassau, St. John, and St. Thomas.) We also vacationed in Puerto Vallarta, Mexico, and thoroughly enjoyed the "Old Town." Finally, we squeezed in a trip to visit my brother John in Los Angeles, did the Disneyland gig, and spent some good times on Santa Monica Beach.

It was almost time to leave the academy. My next assignment was up in the air, and the options weren't very good. I had already been a CBPO Chief and served at AFMPC, so it looked more and more like my next assignment would be the Pentagon. No one liked going to the Pentagon; you're buried in red tape and living economically beyond your means. There are layers and layers of people who outrank you. It's the little-fish-in-the-big-pond scenario—something I tried to avoid as much as possible. So when my assignment officer suggested Washington, DC, and I hesitated, he gave me one other option. He offered me a position on the Inspector General (IG) Staff in the Pacific Air Force Theater, which is located at Hickam AFB, Hawaii. For the first time in my career, I didn't have any great options. So it came down to Honolulu vs. Washington, DC. (This would be the second time I took a job that I didn't want—the *first* and the last.)

Going back to Honolulu was great news to Andi. For me, it was very mixed. I absolutely love the Hawaiian Islands (as you've seen earlier in this book). But the IG Staff were the bad guys, reporting on mission effectiveness and readiness and serving as the "policemen" between the air force bases and the Department of Defense. I was hoping that I'd warm up to this role over time. I never did.

The most dreaded statement any wing commander could ever hear? "We're the IG team, and we are here to help."

It was the final day in our house on Crocus Lane, and the last time we'd see Pikes Peak through our bedroom window. The van for our household goods had arrived, and we were migrating to the academy for our final days before departure.

See you in my dreams, Pikes Peak. Your power and beauty was the first thing I saw every morning, and the last thing I saw every night. Thanks for welcoming us to Colorado, and for watching over us from your throne atop the snowy Rocky Mountains.

CHAPTER FOURTEEN

"I've been in the right place, but it must have been the wrong time."— DR. JOHN

———————◦———————

It's always weird leaving a place you called home and starting all over again somewhere else. In this crazy life of ours, we kept "throwing away the rearview mirror" and driving blindly around that Italian corner— never knowing what to expect next. We were like a couple of sharks who had to keep moving to stay alive. So far, the yin and yang between our work and personal lives were in sync. But the law of averages was against us as we headed to Hawaii. Looking back, it would have been great to reattach the rearview mirror, shift into reverse, back up into Colorado, and start again. But of course, that was impossible.

As our plane lifted skyward from Denver International Airport, I shifted my thoughts to my mom. We were on our way back to Pittsburgh. My stepdad, Bob, had passed away. My mother moved out of the house near Mt. Nebo Road and into a small apartment in Avalon, just a few short blocks from my old high school. Although the transition must have been rough, I was thankful that Pat and John (my sister and brother) were there for her. They helped my Mom get settled, handled all her personal affairs, and pretty much remained "on call" when needed for the rest of her life. Eventually John actually moved into my mother's building, which gave her even more stability. I was an outsider, who passed through once in a while. I knew my role—number-five child—and accepted it. (Actually, I worked very hard to earn that title, and I expected to keep it.) The chemistry between my mother and me hadn't changed much over the years. I don't know if it was a carryover from childhood or the long periods of time between visits, but the distance still remained. But having Andi in the family definitely helped my standing. Everybody, including my mom, loved her. The jokes about my ex-wives stopped. Everyone in the family knew I finally got it right. "Even a blind pig ..."

It was great seeing Mom, and I was determined to be on my best behavior. We had long discussions about my dad—and not so much about Bob—that were very enjoyable. It was my mother's way of assuring me that she always loved Dad and didn't marry Bob to replace him. (I always knew this, but it was nice to hear anyway.) At some level, she was trying to patch up the relationship between mother and son by accentuating the positive things about Dad and easing up on the negative stuff. It was well received, and I appreciated what she was trying to accomplish for my sake.

John had moved back to Pittsburgh, and we usually stayed with him when we visited home. For most of our lives, John and I were not close. But in the middle years, around this time, we developed a pretty good friendship. After I married Andi, it got even better. They were like two peas in a pod. We were always welcome at his house, and I really appreciated it—especially with Andi and myself living so far away. Among us Feeney kids, John had the toughest life. He'd been sick for a long time, and fought it daily with massive amounts of medication. Being unable to work put economic pressure on him that the rest of us didn't have to face. We're eleven months apart, and are affectionately called "Irish twins" because we were born within the same year. Unfortunately, our relationship these days is on the decline.

Anyway, we all went out for lunch one afternoon (Mom, Pat, her daughter Denise, John, Andi, and me) and forgot about Bob's passing for a few hours. It was during these rare occasions that I actually felt like I belonged and that I was part of the family. They never lasted very long, though, because we were always gearing up to travel somewhere far away from the family. I'll never shake that hollow feeling of being part of the family, but not part of the family. I was a ghost. *A rolling stone gathering no moss ...*

Flying from Pittsburgh to Honolulu was long and very tedious. We were both happy to see Diamondhead appear through our airplane window. I was excited to be there for two reasons. I have always loved, and always will love, Hawaii. In fact, I tried talking Andi into retiring there. But the second reason was Andi. I selected the IG team in Hawaii over the Pentagon mainly because of her. I figured it this way. If both jobs sucked, I might as well pick the one that was in a better location. And since I knew quite a bit about the islands, I figured the chances of her enjoying Hawaii were pretty good. And I guessed right. Not only did she enjoy living in Waikiki (Oahu), but she had a chance to reconnect with her sister, Alison, who lived on Maui.

We checked into temporary housing on Hickam AFB, and I went to work. My office was in the HQ Pacific Air Forces (HQ PACAF) building, the same place I had worked as a second lieutenant. I was now a major, and assigned as the Chief, Mission Support Inspections. My job was to evaluate and report on the mission readiness and effectiveness of PACAF air force installations/ bases throughout the Western Pacific. Our area of responsibility ranged from Fairbanks, Alaska, to Okinawa, Japan. I specifically focused on contingency operations plans, mobility processing, and reception/beddown in the war zone, or Area of Responsibility (AOR). Over the next year, I would deploy nine times for Operational Readiness Inspections (ORIs). And they all sucked.

On a brighter note, Andi and I found an apartment in Waikiki, a high-rise at 1350 Ala Moana Boulevard. It was a two-bedroom, two-bath apartment on the twenty-second floor—smallish and *very* expensive. But the location was unbelievable. We were just across the street from Ala Moana Park and the Pacific Ocean. From our front balcony, we had unobstructed views spanning from Diamondhead to the east, all the way to Pearl Harbor looking westward. It was, in a word, stunning. Our side balcony had a perfect view of downtown Honolulu. I couldn't look at the city at night without thinking about the song "Honolulu City Lights," by the Beamers. It's a haunting, but beautiful, tune exposing the lonely feeling you get leaving home for whereabouts unknown. We were a short, ten-minute trek from all the famous Waikiki beaches and sights. And the Ala Moana Mall was right next door, which made Andi very happy. I remember taking long walks through Ala Moana Park, then along Waikiki Beach to Kapiolani Park and the Waikiki Shell, and then back down Kalakaua Avenue like it was yesterday. (Kalakaua is the main street through Waikiki, and it's full of great places to see.) The weather was always perfect, and the ocean-side bars and restaurants were always busy with excited tourists. On the downside, the traffic in Waikiki could get pretty intense at times. So we bought a couple of mopeds. We learned to zip in and out of traffic with the best of them, and never needed a parking spot.

As usual, Andi found a job quickly. She worked at a place called Office Pavilion, which sold medical furniture and equipment. It was located in Restaurant Row. The name was accurate, because the entire center of this mall was full of restaurants and clubs. It was an ideal place to meet up with Andi after work for happy hour. But it wasn't long before she was offered an even better job. The Aloha Tower Marketplace was just getting started, and Andi was offered a job as the accounts payable and payroll coordinator. It was better pay and a more challenging position. The Aloha Tower Marketplace is a waterfront shopping center in Honolulu. There are over one hundred stores and popular restaurants there, along with several national landmarks like the Aloha Tower, the Falls of Clyde Museum, and the Hawai'i Maritime Center. When her brother George came to visit, we jumped on the mopeds and headed over to the marketplace to meet Andi at Sloppy Joes. You should have seen George's face as we went screaming down Ala Moana Boulevard, cutting in and out of traffic. I'll give him credit, because he fought valiantly to keep up with me. Although he was tentative and nervous in traffic—and probably thought I was a crazy man—he was smiling the whole time.

Our Inspector General team was always on alert. We were 100 percent packed and ready to deploy at all times. No one, not even the inspectors, knew where we were going until the last minute. I can remember being awakened at 4:00 a.m. and being told to be at the Hickam flight line in two hours. And because the Pacific Region was so large, all of our flights were extremely long. Imagine flying twenty-three straight hours in a C-130 "rope seat" and then going directly to work. We did it all the time. It was mind-numbing.

Our Operational Readiness Inspections (ORIs) were made up of two parts. The first was a no-notice, surprise inspection. The function of this visit was to test the operational readiness of an air force base. Simply put, are they ready to deploy? Are areas set up for fast, reliable mobility processing? Are there medical, financial, legal, HR, and so on on the mobility line prepared to deal with last-minute problems? Who was on the manifests to deploy? Are travel orders completed? Are aircraft standing by? We measured all of these factors, and many others, and then left the country. Several weeks later, the IG team would return for the second portion of the inspection. This time, they knew we were coming. The base was required to set up a kind of tent city, simulating deployment into the AOR (war zone). The emphasis of our inspection changed at this point. We were now inspecting their ability to sustain operations in the AOR. We were now asking different questions: Do you have a reception/beddown operation in place when the troops arrive in theater? Are the manifests accurate? What about your replacement plans for returning personnel? How will you track injured, missing, and/or mortally wounded?

During the first part of an inspection, the aircraft manifests were the key. If you weren't identified as a deploying asset, you couldn't "play" in the second part of the inspection. To put it differently, you weren't there. You were back at your home base. I can't tell you how many times senior officers (who didn't belong) showed up in our simulated AOR ready to fight the war. As the inspector, it was my job to weed them out.

"Excuse me, Colonel. Can I help you with something?" I asked. "No thanks, Major. I'm the Group Commander of XYZ Air Base, and I'm here to get things done right."

"Yes, sir, but you weren't on the manifest during the deployment phase of the exercise," I added.

"But I'm here now. What difference does it make?" he'd reply sternly.

"All the difference in the world, sir. Now, please depart this area, or you'll jeopardize the results of this inspection." Man, they hated that. But it makes sense. You have to practice just like you'll play. So bases need to carefully plan who will deploy, and then get the right people on the plane. It's all about accountability. During any conflict, nothing means more to senior leadership than knowing where their people are.

I don't want to bore you to death trudging through stories of our many deployments. So I'll concentrate on one IG visit that was kind of different. One Sunday morning I got "the call." Here we go again. This time it was Eielson Air Force Base, in Fairbanks, Alaska. Eielson is the home of the 354th Fighter Wing. Its mission is to support Red Flag–Alaska, a series of PACAF commander-directed field training exercises for US forces. We arrived unannounced in the middle of the night, and it was freezing. For the next several days, everything we inspected was in perfect order. In fact, it was too perfect. Pallets were on the runway and ready for shipment to the AOR; final manifests were completed, even though they weren't tasked to deploy yet; and mobility lines were already set up and waiting for us. The wing passed with flying colors. I gave them an excellent rating for the mission support portion of the inspection. When we returned to Hawaii, our leadership was not happy. The feeling among the staff was that someone had tipped them off. They were waiting for us.

Before I continue with the Eielson visit, I'd like to explain the inspector's role in these visits. We would amass at Hickam, and then fly somewhere in the Western Pacific region. We would arrive at the front gate, notify the wing commander we were there, and then go to work. It was not uncommon to fly twenty hours, and then work continuously for the next eighteen to twenty-four hours. We didn't have the option to rest, because we were there to rate the no-notice posture of the mission's readiness and effectiveness. So resting until tomorrow was out of the question. Any delays would allow units time to artificially project their readiness capability. Seriously, I remember sneaking into the IG staffing room, sleeping sitting up for thirty minutes, and then going back out for another six hours of intense inspection. We were sleep-deprived and physically and mentally drained, and tried to stay objective. I can remember asking questions and forgetting the answers. Or writing things in my report that were nonsensical. Or not being able to answer a question that I knew the answer to. It was the hardest job I ever had. Nothing prepares you for this type of work.

On top of everything else—we were the bad guys. No one liked the IG. I was constantly asked why I would choose this job, and I had no response. In general, our morale was low, and most of us disliked rating our peers. The stark difficulty of the job—not to mention long separations from family — was too much. Andi and I spent thirteen months in Hawaii, and I went on nine inspections. I was never there. Thank goodness she was doing pretty well with her diabetes during that period. And every time the IG went "wheels up" and I was departing to somewhere and nowhere at the same time, the words of "Honolulu City Lights" hammered away in my already-lonely brain:

Looking out upon the city lights, and the stars above the ocean
Got my ticket for the midnight plane, and it's not easy to leave again
Each night Honolulu City Lights stirs up memories in me
Each night Honolulu City Lights brings me back again.

A few months after the team finished its Eielson AFB inspection, our Inspector General called a no-notice meeting involving the entire team. We were going back, and this time, there would be no leaks. We took commercial flights instead of military airlift and traveled in small groups. The team was carefully dispersed in different hotels in the Fairbanks area. This time, we arrived in rental cars and avoided military transportation. I would have loved to see the wing commander's face when he learned that the IG was back.

"Hello, we're the IG team, and we're here to help."

It was a different story this time. The overall IG rating was marginal, and I also gave a marginal rating for the mission support operations.

There were many stories from places like Misawa, Okinawa, Osan, Anchorage, and so on, involving impossible work schedules, dreadful flights, hours and hours of meetings and report writing, and the never-ending battle to stay awake. My boss, Colonel McCladdie, did the best he could to ease the difficulties of this job. He was excellent and expected a lot from me. And I gave it everything I had. In my thirty five years of government service in the Departments of Defense and State, this was by far the lowest point of my professional career. It would have been even worse without the strong leadership of Colonel McCladdie. I was depressed and really dejected thinking about spending two more years on the IG team.

Between IG trips, when I was home in Waikiki, Andi and I made the most of it. There were so many good restaurants, and we really enjoyed them. Just some of our favorites were Duke's Canoe Club, in the Outrigger Waikiki, the best beach bar and restaurant in the world; Compadres, an excellent Mexican place in Ward's Warehouse; Kincaid's, a fish, chop, and steakhouse on Ala Moana Boulevard; Horatio's Italian Restaurant, also in Ward's Warehouse; Sloppy Joe's in the Aloha Tower Marketplace; and the Shorebird, a great place for food and music in the Outrigger Reef on Waikiki Beach.

And since we were in the center of everything, there was always something going on. I remember one morning at 4:30 a.m. when flashing lights woke us up. We went to the balcony, and just below us were over 30,000 marathoners lining up for the race. The start line was right in front of our house! When the Thunderbird Air Show came to Waikiki, they opened their maneuvers by roaring right over our balcony. It was crazy good. Across the street, especially on weekends, Ala Moana Park became a small city, with locals setting up tents, selling wares, playing music, cooking Kailua pigs, and partying like crazy. You couldn't walk through the park without someone offering you food and drink.

We even took a seven-night cruise on the only American-owned liner in the United States, American Hawaii Cruises. The *S.S. Independence* hit five ports on four different islands—Oahu, Maui, Kauai, and the Big Island of Hawaii. Although not built for elegance, the cabins were big. And because of its smaller size, we could squeeze into ports like Hilo, Hawaii, that bigger ships had to avoid. It was the perfect cruise and served as a traveling hotel room. We disembarked every morning and reboarded for dinner every evening. No long days at sea, and no lining up waiting for small tenders to take us to shore (the worst thing about the big, newer ships).

Of course, since Andi wasn't with me the first time I was stationed in Hawaii, we were compelled to hit all the usual spots like Diamondhead, Bellows AFS recreation area, the North Shore, Punchbowl, every corner of Waikiki, and so on. We visited Alison on Maui, checked out Haleakala (a live volcano), went to the top of Mauna Kea, drove to Hana, and had a cheeseburger in Paradise on Front Street in Lahaina, the coolest town on the island.

It happened so quickly.

As I was preparing for my next trip, I got a call from Colonel Thomas Phillips, the commander of the USAFE-wide Joint Support Squadrons. He offered me a job as the commander of the Joint Support Squadron in Izmir, Turkey. The only drawback? I had to report within sixty days. Since I had only been assigned to Hickam for twelve months, I knew it would take a Secretary of the Air Force (SECAF) waiver to curtail my tour in Hawaii by two years. I didn't think that was possible. He told me to talk to my supervisor, and my wife, and call him back in two days. He would take care of the waiver. This was problematic. Andi loved Hawaii and had a really good job. In addition, it had taken me almost a year to become fully trained as an IG inspector, and I was about to abandon Colonel McCladdie and our Mission Support Team with no advance warning. But inside, my heart was racing —a chance to command my own squadron, and *get the hell out of the IG business.*

I started with Andi. She never ceases to amaze me. There's no way she wanted to leave paradise. Departing early would disrupt her career plans, and cut into her pocketbook at the same time. But she knew how much I hated my job. Without hesitation, she was on board.

One down, and one to go.

I knew I was taking a big risk talking to Colonel McCladdie about "jumping ship." If the SECAF waiver didn't come through, I'd burned my bridges behind me. But I had to take the chance. As I explained my situation, he was not happy. He had taken me under his wing, and he felt like I was abandoning him. And until they found a replacement for me, he was stuck with the additional workload. I had to plead my case quickly. I promised him I wouldn't leave if he didn't support the assignment. (This was a very difficult thing to say. I wanted out of there so bad. But fair was fair, and as my boss, his opinion mattered.) He slept on it, and called me to his desk the next day. *If* I got all my reports done, and *if* I developed a continuity folder for my replacement, and *if* I completed a couple of pending projects I was working on, *then* he would support me. No problem, sir.

I was ecstatic, so I called Colonel Phillips back. "Sir, I spoke to Colonel McCladdie, and he agreed to release me. Is the job still open?"

"Yes." Good news. I would have been crushed if he'd found someone else.

"Are you confident you can get the SECAF waiver, sir?" I asked.

"Yes." I believed him. I came to know Colonel Phillips very well over the next two years. He was the best there is in the USAF—an excellent mentor to yours truly.

"Just one more thing, sir. Why did you select me for this position?" I had to ask. A two-year waiver of assignment is very rare and usually requires specific justification.

"I asked your assignment officer for an 0-4 [major] with prior commander experience. I also wanted a previous CBPO Chief who had worked at AFMPC. It was a very short list." Bingo! This job had my name written all over it. True to form, an official message came for Randolph AFB a few days later, reflecting SECAF approval to curtail Major Donald J. Feeney's tour in Hawaii by twenty-four months.

It felt like a stay of execution from the governor. One week ago, I was dying inside trying to figure out how I was going to last two more years in this job. Now I was getting my own squadron and moving to Asia. We packed quickly, Andi gave her notice at work, and like a flash, we were gone. So long, fellow inspectors. Good luck with that.

I was in the right place, and it must have been the right time.

Earl and Theresa Feeney on their wedding day in 1945.

The oldest picture I have of my childhood.
Larry and Pat are in the back row, with John and me sitting in front. (Susan
would arrive a few years later.)

52 Norman Street: seven Feeney's lived in that little duplex.

My high-school graduation. This is the only picture I have with my father.

The Feeney kids at my college graduation.
Left to right: Pat, John, me, Larry, and Susan.

My first wife, Jill.
She of the famous "coin toss" that would change the course of my life forever.

Jill dancing with my dad at our wedding.
Alas, he passed away a few months later at the age of 51.

The "Mod Squad" in Zweibrucken, Germany.
Elaine, Jimmie, and me hamming it up at one of the many wine fests we frequented
throughout the summer of 1978.

Cheryl and myself at the Dutch Grand Prix.
(Number-two wife in the queue.)

Our wedding day in northern Maine.

The sprawling metropolis of Limestone, Maine.
Cheryl and I lived in a small place behind the gas station.

Hiking the Napali Coast of Kauai with my best friend, Errol.
Unfortunately, he would be involuntarily discharged from the Air Force 18 months later.

Al's wedding day.
He would commit suicide four months later.

"Scarcely Acres." My first home in Rolla, Missouri.
Three acres of country for this city boy!

Sherie, my third wife, and by far the most unusual.
I still wonder about her to this day.

Meshell, with a three-legged dog somewhere in Cape Cod.

The River Walk in San Antonio. I spent many "Hemingway afternoons" there.

An air force "dining out" shortly after I met the love of my life, Andi.

Our Las Vegas marriage in 1990. Notice the fake flowers and gardens. Luckily, this photo was not stolen from our van in DC.

Andi and me on the Isle of Capri in Italy.

Sampling the "vino locale" in Marsala, on the western coast of Sicily.

With some of my staff on Mt. Chiarmonte, in Sicily. The towns of Comiso and Ragusa are laid out below.

Our first home together in Colorado Springs, Colorado. (This is the only remaining picture from our Air Force Academy experience. The others were destroyed by water damage in my brother John's basement.)

View from the summit of Diamondhead, on the island of Oahu, in Hawaii.

*Hanging out with friends at a beach cabin near Barber's Point.
That's Diamondhead in the background.*

Dinner on the briny aboard the Hawaiian yacht Navatek.

*Kusadasi, Turkey. It's part of the Turquoise Coast, and one of our "all time"
favorite places.*

Ephesus. Home of St. John, and where Mary, the mother of Jesus, spent her final days. These immense ruins are the number-one tourist attraction in Turkey.

Mom, with the whole clan, celebrating her marriage to Bob.

My "pin on" ceremony to Lt. Colonel, with Larry and Andi doing the honors.

Our informal Hooters bus retirement ceremony. (From left to right: George, Andi's brother; Andi; me; Jim; Emily, Larry's daughter; Larry; unknown guy with moustache; and John, my ex-First Sergeant from Izmir). Not seen is my pal Joe, who took the picture.

The beloved Toyota Van, a.k.a. "moon buggy." I would drive it for over eighteen years!

Cappuccino Strip, Fremantle, Western Australia. Great people-watching place.

My crazy Aussie friends in Margaret River, Western Australia, enjoying the wine fests: Lisa, Melissa, Andi, me, and Damian. (Noe is taking the picture.) Can anyone sing "Seventeen bottles of Wine on the Wall"?

King's Hill, high above Perth, Australia, with the Black Swan River on the right.

The indoor waterfall in our "mini prison" home in Santa Elena, El Salvador.

146

The eclectic back yard. (Notice the tree where I befriended a mother song sparrow and her family.)

Antigua, Guatemala, where Andi and I traveled for an extensive Spanish-language immersion experience.

My mother's seventy-fifth birthday in Pittsburgh.

A ride on a Dhow in the old section of Dubai, United Arab Emirates.

The Pyramids of Egypt. (Look closely, and you can see Andi walking to the left of the Sphinx with a white blouse, and dark pants.)

Hanging out at the Taj Mahal, in Agra, India.

Our apartment on Pennsylvania Ave. in DC, just a short block from Georgetown.
(Top floor, left corner, just under the open window)

The famous backdrop of Willemstad, on the Island of Curacao. The Iguana Cafe
on the baai (right side) was one of our favorite hangouts.

Brad and me at the summit of Mt. Christoffel, Curacao.

John, Andi, Larry, and me before our day-long helicopter trip to Kleine Curacao, a deserted island.

View from the Acropolis in Athens, Greece. We lived on the side of Mt. Lycabettus (seen in the center background), which is the highest point in the city, and just northwest of the US embassy.

Andi and me chilling on the Greek Island of Hydra, where the only motor vehicles are trash trucks.

The outrageous beauty of Santorini, the jewel of the Greek Isles.

One of our last official diplomatic functions in Athens.

CHAPTER FIFTEEN

"For the traveler who is always on the lookout for the new and strange, Turkey in many ways represents one of the world's last frontiers."
— *FODOR'S TURKEY*

———◦———

To quote Giovanna Magi and Giuliano Valdes from the book All of Turkey, English edition: "Geographically, Turkey is sort of the gravitational center between the West and the East, a point of junction between continental and peninsular Europe and the immense mass of the Afro-Asian continent. ... Tourist literature often uses the terms 'Land of Contrasts' and 'Gate to the Orient' when speaking of Turkey, and while these phrases have a measure of truth to them, they are little compared with what the modern state of Turkey really is—an immense container of art, history and culture." It is also the birthplace of Homer, who wrote the *Iliad*. The famous Trojan War battlefield—with Helen, Achilles, Priam, Ajax, Paris, Nestor, and so on—lies to the north of Izmir.

For the next two years, living and working in Izmir, Andi and I would dedicate ourselves to seeking out the charms of this incomparable country.

Unlike Sicily, our first impression of Izmir was very positive. My first sergeant—top NCO in the squadron—met us at the Izmir Adhan Menderies Airport and drove us to the Mercure Hotel in the downtown area. (We used this hotel for temporary housing since there were no military bases in Izmir.) His energy and positive attitude were like a breath of fresh air. We were exhausted from the long trip, but quickly felt reenergized by the bustling activity of Izmir as we entered the city for the first time.

After we slept for a few hours, Andi and I went out touring. To this day, I still remember how exciting it was to walk past Ataturk Square—built to honor the leader mainly responsible for Izmir's Western influence—and down to Kanak Camii (kind of like a boardwalk) on the First Kordon. The Kordon (street) is a waterfront promenade lined with rows of outside cafes on one side and the Aegean Sea on the other. In the coming years, we would spend many lazy afternoons on the Kordon. I liked calling these relaxing moments HAs, or Hemingway Afternoons. Izmir (also known as Smyrna) is considered by many as the "San Francisco of Turkey." It is a Muslim city, but great effort has been made to separate religion from state. It always felt more like Europe than Asia; Izmir was very safe, and the people were among the friendliest we have ever been around. It's also very modern, due in part to the great fire of 1922, which destroyed most of the downtown buildings. We strolled Kultur Parki, which is an immense public park right in the middle of town. Then we checked out the *Saat Kulesi* (Clock Tower) in Konak Square, largely considered Izmir's iconic symbol. And of course, we shopped at the nearby Bazaar (*souk*), the heart and soul of Izmir, with hundreds of stalls ranging from gold and silver to caged birds and wedding dresses. If you're ever in Izmir, you don't want to miss the Bazaar. (They should have named it Andi's *Souk*.)

The next day, I went to work. It was a refreshing change to be in the military but not physically working on an operational base. The Joint Support Squadron was located right in the middle of town, in a high-rise known as the Akin Building. And because of the scattered terrorist attacks in and around Izmir, we were authorized to wear civilian clothes. Ask any air force person how rare that is. But my favorite part of the job? My boss was in Germany! That's right—Stuttgart, Germany. (Admit it. How often have you wished your boss was in another country?) I grew to really admire Colonel Phillips, who was now my boss. But I also loved having the autonomy and the freedom to act without direct supervision. This leadership opportunity liberated me more than any other job I ever had. And another nice perk? I had to attend staff meetings in Germany every few months. Not a bad gig, right?

As commander, I was responsible for the command and administrative support for over 550 military and dependents assigned to USAFE, Sixth Allied Tactical Air Force, HQ Allied Land Forces Southern Europe, and other NATO organizations in and around Izmir. It was a diverse job, to say the least. I directly supervised eighteen people and had Uniform Code of Military Justice (UCMJ) authority over 360 enlisted members and their families, given only to commanders, which allowed me to exercise a wide range of legal options. And I hit the ground running. Shortly after my arrival, Izmir was inundated with a massive flood. My office was involved in the relocation of families, procuring of medical supplies for inoculations to avoid disease, temporary lodging arrangements, setting up food distribution points, and so on. There were two more floods in the next twenty months or so that I was assigned in Turkey, and all three floods were very trying times for my squadron.

Turkey, with all its beauty, also had its warts. Terrorist incidents were relatively common, but thankfully not fatal. Power and water outages were regular irritants. And the traffic was—to put it bluntly—a pain in the ass. And just after I settled in, my first sergeant was sent TDY to Operation Joint Endeavor, a peacekeeping force located in Bosnia to minimize the murder of innocent people through genocide. Although I totally supported this deployment, his absence ratcheted up the workload for the rest of my command section. But I wasn't complaining. The 15 percent rule wasn't going to get us down. There was too much to do—and a blob to steer.

After three weeks in the Mercure Hotel, Andi and I finally found an apartment in Konak. It was a seventh-floor penthouse, located on Vasif Cinar, just south of Kultur Parki and three blocks west of the Akin Building. The First Kordon was minutes away. The building complex was older and very quaint. Our apartment had two small bedrooms and one small bath. We had the only apartment on our floor. When the elevator worked, it was a good day. The best thing about it? A working fireplace that was our main source of heat during winter power outages.

And there's nothing like walking to work. No commutes, no tolls, no trains or buses, no traffic jams, no developing ulcers, no lost hours, no wrinkled work clothes, no gas station stops, and so on. Believe it or not, my three- block commute passed through a place called Lovers' Lane every morning, where vendors sold local wares and couples cuddled on benches along the cobblestoned path.

At the beginning of Lovers' Lane, there was an empty lot that became a home for stray cats. (My wife is a cat freak, almost to the point of an obsession.) There was this one cat—Andi called him Sparky—who had an injured leg and hobbled around like he was really suffering. Andi took a liking to him and would bring him food every morning on the way to the Akin. He would slowly and dramatically limp up to her, she would feed him, and off we'd go. One morning, when I had to go to work early, I walked past Sparky, and he was running around as fast as the rest of the cats. That feline was acting injured to get Andi to feed him. What a scammer. Now that I think about it, he was definitely the fattest cat on the lot. I wondered how many other clients he had lined up.

We learned very early to develop a relationship with our *kapici*, the building janitor. He was always around to help Andi carry groceries up seven floors when the elevator was out, or to wash our Toyota moon-buggy van, or to fix a leak in the refrigerator, or to catch a mouse that snuck into the apartment. He lived in the basement, below sea level, so he really got wiped out by all the floods. God help him. He did so much for so little. He almost broke down and cried when we gave him twenty dollars for Christmas. That was more than a month's pay. And he adored Andi. During our twenty-four months in Izmir, she always brought him something from the market. (Andi used a Turkish guy named Charley, driving a horse carriage, to get her groceries to Vasif Cinar. It was wild to see them clopping down the busy street in the middle of all the automobile chaos. When I asked her why she didn't take a cab, she said Charley was always waiting for her, and she couldn't say no to him.) Or she'd give the *kapici* towels, small carpets, plates, utensils, and so on that were economically out of reach for him and his family. She also paid him well for standing in line at the utility companies to pay our monthly bills. This process could take hours.

One of the *kapici's* most important roles was to keep track of our automobile queue. Since parking on the street was almost impossible, the tenants would park single file in a small alley next door. It was his job to make sure your car wasn't trapped behind other vehicles when you needed it. This was a very important duty. For example, my first sergeant told me what happened to him the previous summer. His building also had similar parking conditions. One day when he went down to get his car, he was blocked in by another vehicle. When he contacted his *kapici*, he learned that the owner was gone for the summer! For the next three months, he could only stare at his car, which was unfortunately locked in the queue, and say good-bye to his summer plans.

When we left Izmir, we put aside tons of items for our *kapici* and his family. He was a good man, who worked very hard for very little. So long, *tesekkar ederim*, and *memnun oldum*. (Thank you—it was nice to have met you.)

Back at the Akin Building, things couldn't have been better. My staff was located on two different floors. My office, the command section, was on the third floor. It was a small five-person office. The main administration and personnel area, with thirteen employees, was one floor below us. From the beginning, we clicked. We worked hard, and we played hard. Since almost everyone lived within walking distance, we ended many a day on the First Kordon enjoying an HA. We took blue cruises together on the Aegean Sea (sailing, snorkeling, and dining), and formed a bowling team in a downtown league. Every Friday at 3:30 p.m., I held our staff meetings. They lasted fifteen minutes or so, and then the party would begin. Out came the dominoes, along with the beer and food. These games were *serious*. I have so many memories of those staff meetings. I didn't see it then, but I now realize how rare that kind of camaraderie really was. I would never experience anything like that again.

We were a team and worked very well together. I liken our staff unity to a Vesta A. Kelly quote: "Snowflakes are one of nature's most fragile creatures, but just look at what they can do when they stick together." With my boss in Germany, I was free to implement all those management and leadership principles I had been teaching for years. Izmir was my petri dish, that is, a place where I could grow the office culture at my own pace, using my own style. For some reason, I have never been afraid of making mistakes, or of failure. The way I looked at it, true leadership required you to make many hard decisions. It's unrealistic to assume every decision would be a flawless one. That's why I like the steer-the-blob mentality. Let's face it—in a blob, there will always be less-than-perfect decisions. It's how you steer through the imperfections that count. Reflecting back, what surprised me more than anything in my career was the large number of peers who couldn't make a decision. I think Lee Iacocca said it best: "If I had to sum up one word that makes a good manager, I'd say decisiveness. You can use the fanciest computers to gather the numbers, but in the end you have to set a timetable and act."

Of course, not everything was rosy. Over at *Scherzinger,* a Turkish NATO base, there were a couple of two-star US generals who commanded the Sixth Allied Tactical Air Forces and the HQ Allied Land Forces Southeastern Europe. The former, let's call him General Hanson, was a real pain in the ass. (Small-man syndrome—you know the type: little guy with the big ideas.) It drove him crazy that a major like me had command authority over all the enlisted USAFE and NATO personnel in and around Izmir. He was constantly trying to usurp my authority and became very belligerent when I wouldn't cooperate. During my first few days on the job, he contacted Colonel Phillips in Stuttgart, complaining about my handling of a major USAFE deployment. Since he wasn't the commander, it shouldn't have made any difference to him. But he was determined to use his rank to push me to the sidelines. Less than a week later, I had to discipline an airman by issuing him an Article 15, which is a form of nonjudicial punishment under the Uniform Code of Military Justice (UCMJ). As soon as General Hanson heard about it, he summoned me to his office.

"Feeney, who gave you the right to discipline my airman? I'm the one who makes the decisions around here. Do you understand?"

"Sir, the airman involved is a NATO asset, but he falls under my command authority," I said, expecting all hell to break loose soon.

"Are you refusing to follow my orders? Do you know who you are talking to? Get the hell out of my office." As I headed toward the door, I heard him yell over my head to his secretary, "Get Feeney's goddamn supervisor on the phone. I'll have him fired before he gets back to the Akin." I must admit, he had me rattled. Two calls to my boss in Germany during my very first week on the job. That's it, then… The shortest command in the history of Izmir. Two weeks.

When I returned to my office, I had a message to call Colonel Phillips. My guess was that he got reamed out by General Hanson and was pressured to remove me from my command. I was half-right. "Hello, Colonel Phillips. This is Major Feeney."

"Don, what in the heck is going on down there?" (He never used a swear word.) "This is the second time I've received an unpleasant phone call from General Hanson. And he really let me have it this time." At this point, I was thinking that maybe I should revise my decisiveness approach to management. But I knew I couldn't do it. Either way, I was going down with the ship.

"Sir, I issued an Article 15 yesterday. I bounced it off the legal staff and am confident that I did the right thing. General Hanson disagrees. He wants to make the command decisions for my squadron and has vowed to have me fired for disagreeing with him." I paused. The next few seconds would determine my future career and cement my relationship with Colonel Phillips forever. But I was prepared for any scenario at this point. Or at least I thought I was.

"Don, this is the second time you've had a confrontation with General Hanson. And it's only your second week." *Here it comes,* I thought. "I'm going to give you twenty-five chances, and you've used two of them already."

What? Say what? "I'm sorry, sir, I don't understand."

"You heard me. Keep doing what you're doing. Be the commander I expected you to be when I hired you. By my count, you now have twenty-three chances left. I've got to run. Good-bye, Don, and see you in Stuttgart in a couple of weeks." He hung up the phone.

I realized right then that I was in the presence of true leadership. It didn't matter how many stars an officer had, Colonel Phillips would do the right thing. He acted. He wasn't afraid of failure, and he wasn't afraid of me failing either. He stuck by me and made it clear to General Hanson that I wasn't going anywhere. From the first time I ever met him—he flew down to Izmir for my official change-of-command ceremony—I knew he was special. Soft-spoken and confident but not arrogant. My troops loved him. He went to the First Kordon with us for a few beers, even though he didn't drink. He sat around the table and quietly blended into our conversations. He could make young airmen feel comfortable, while at the same time function well among the highest leaders in EUCOM (European Command). He actively listened and gave great advice—but only when asked. My squadron was part of him, and he was part of my squadron. When General Hanson realized Colonel Phillips was in my court, he backed off quite a bit. I had very few run-ins with him after that experience. To this day, Colonel Tom Phillips was the finest mentor I ever had. Thank you, sir.

With General Hanson out of the way and twenty-three "get out of jail" cards to play, I was feeling pretty good about my Izmir experience so far. I started teaching management classes for the University of Maryland. As a commander, I got involved in community programs like Izmir's Financial Management Board, the Child Advocacy Committee, and the Family Action Information Board. I did everything I could to ensure that I was in tune with my community and to improve the management skills I needed to command. I was determined to prove that Colonel Phillips made the right decision to support me. I learned to scuba dive and continued to bowl in our office league—still unable to hit the magic 190 average I had sought for so long. I was still playing softball for our squadron team. And with a short right-field fence, I was in heaven at the plate.

And of course, Andi found a job almost immediately. She worked as an administrative assistant for the Chief, Mission Support Squadron. We added a new addition to our family—an abandoned stray cat, who lived under a car on a very busy highway. We named her Kismet (fate) and spent half a grand cleaning her up. She had ringworm and fleas, among other ailments, and was half-starved to death. We got all her shots, had her spayed, and introduced her to Vasif Cinar, her new home. (We refer to her as K1, since we later adopted another cat in the Middle East, whom we named K2.) The courage of this little animal was amazing. She darted in and out of fast-moving traffic, scrounged for food in alleyways, and managed to avoid the lethal programs designed to eradicate stray animals. We both grew very fond of her and were crushed when she disappeared years later in Norfolk, Virginia.

Nothing prepared us for the amazing beauty of Turkey. It would be impossible to list all the gems of this nation. So I'll just highlight some of our favorites: Istanbul, Ephesus, Pamukkale, and the spellbinding Turquoise Coast.

What can I say about one of the greatest cities on earth? Istanbul has been inhabited since 658 BC, and it rests on the dividing line between Europe and Asia. It is surrounded by the Bosphorus, with its green banks reaching thirty kilometers north to the Black Sea and its southern current emptying into the Sea of *Marmaris*. (We took a boat ride up the Bosphorus and were intrigued to find out we weren't in Asia or Europe. So where were we? Outer limits?) Most of the people (six million) live in the Old Town, or what was once medieval Constantinople, hemmed in by walls built centuries ago. The Blue Mosque dominates the skyline, with its cascading domes and half domes, and with all colors and forms in visual harmony. The nearby Hagia Sophia Mosque is almost as amazing. The "covered" Great Bazaar runs all over the city, most of it underground. It's the largest *souk* in the world, expanding over 200,000 square meters. After strolling around this vast network of tunnels and cisterns (there are twenty entrances), you can easily get lost when you come up to the street level. But who cares? It's a blast. Between the mosques lies the Hippodrome. It's also known as the *At Meydani*, or Plaza of the Horses, because it was used principally for horse racing in the Constantinople era. Full of ancient buildings, obelisks, and fountains, it's an astonishing place to sightsee. And you can't miss the Galata Bridge, which spans the Bosphorus. It sits on twenty-two pontoons, rotates for incoming ships, and connects Europe to Asia. You'll wear out your camera in Istanbul.

Ephesus is one of the largest archaeological sites on earth. It's also the number-one tourist attraction in Turkey. Ephesus is known for the preaching of the apostle St. John (he's buried there in St. John's Church), and as the residence of the Madonna (Mary) after the crucifixion of Jesus Christ. It was also a bustling commercial center during the Roman period. The Arcadian Way is full of an unbelievable array of ruins, including basilicas, columns, *odeions* (theaters), statues, houses, roads, and more. The nearby Temple of Artemis is one of the Seven Ancient Wonders of the World. Throw in the Temple of Hadrian, the immense Theater of Ephesus, and the unmistakable beauty of the Library of Celsus, and you get the idea.

Incredibly, this beautiful city was almost forgotten in history. Again from *All of Turkey,* English edition:

"Its decline began in the second half of the 3rd century when it was conquered and sacked by the Goths. During the long dark centuries of the Middle Ages it was little more than a village, subject to continuous raids by the Arabs and pirates. After the early years of Ottoman rule, it fell into complete oblivion. Abandoned and deserted, all trace of it almost disappeared until 1869 when the first of the archaeological excavations which were meant to restore to the world the ancient and unforgotten beauty of the city was undertaken." An inspirational corner of the world, to be sure.

Pamukkale, or Castle of Cotton, is located north of Denizli, Turkey, and is like no other place I have ever seen. The extraordinary actions of various mineral springs containing calcium oxide have created a petrified, cascading terrace of white, like a mountain of cotton. You can stroll among the unique formations or soak in one of the curative, natural spas. The ever-changing stalactites—and the constant effects of erosion—repaint this canvas over and over again. When you approach Pamukkale, the stark contrast of this phenomenon against the brown earth takes your breath away. As far as I know, there is no other place like it on earth.

But the real jewel of this country lies in the southwest corner—the Turkish Riviera, sometimes called the Turquoise Coast. Cesme, the first coastal gem west of Izmir, is a very popular holiday resort for well-to-do residents of the city. *Cesme* means fountain in Persian, probably because the town is full of Ottoman fountains. I learned to dive there and took many blue cruises from its modern seaport. There are ninety kilometers of coastline, with every type of resort available. The close proximity to Chios (Greek Island) allows many Turks to return from Western Europe using Chios and Cesme ferries. The Cesme Castle is in perfect condition and draws many tourists. My favorite thing about Cesme? It was the closest and fastest way to the water!

But for sun and fun, you can't beat *Kusadasi* . It's a well-equipped tourist destination, with lots of restaurants, bars, outside cafes, and hotels. It overlooks Kusadasi Bay, which reaches out to the Aegean Sea. Daily cruise ships keep the place jumping. Kusadasi's location makes it an ideal starting point for Turkish excursions, so there are always tourists milling about. Andi and I spent many HAs sipping wine with friends, people watching, and exploring the nearby ancient sights. It was a great place to snorkel, with jutted inlets and calm waters. And right in the middle of the bay, connected by a road to the sea, is the Kucukada Kalesi, an ancient fortress surrounded by turrets. In the sixteenth century, the fortress was used as a base of operations for the famous pirate Barbarossa. If I could only visit one place on the Turkish Riviera, this would be it.

That's not to say the others are not worth visiting. Next up for us along the Turquoise Coast was *Bodrum*. Like *Kusadasi* , *Bodrum* rests on an idyllic coast, with a charming bay admired by tourists. There are beautiful beaches just out of town, and great views of the Aegean Islands in the distance. It was always interesting to Andi and me that this town had a large percentage of German tourists. Many of the restaurants and hotels catered to them. That made *Bodrum* a unique sea town. It also has a large castle in the bay, the Castle of St. Peter, or the ancient Halikarnassos in Greek. I'm always amazed by Turkey's history. It's everywhere. In *Bodrum*, the Mausoleum (named after Mausolus to whom it was dedicated), another one of the Seven Ancient Wonders of the World, rests nearby. With just a few fragments remaining, you wouldn't even know it was there unless you sought it out. Imagine an ancient wonder of the world eroding away, and no one noticing. The Turks are an enigmatic people, to say the least. I never figured them out, but always enjoyed trying.

Marmaris doesn't beat around the bush. There are no ancient wonders of the world, or Greek or Roman ruins. Neither Achilles nor the Madonna comes up in conversation along the shores of this gorgeous beach town. According to *All of Turkey,* English edition:

"Despite the ancient origins and closeness of important archaeological sites which testify to a flourishing civilization on the coast in earliest times, *Marmaris* today is exclusively a tourist seaside resort. The town, site of the ancient Physkos of which barely the memory remains, spreads out around the picturesque circular bay, with green mountains on all sides. The safe harbor, opposite which lays numerous enticing islands, has always furnished ships and boats with an ideal landing place. Today the yachts of an international clientele who favor this stretch of southern Turkey for vacations or a base for interesting excursions into the environs are sheltered here."

That's a good recap of *Marmaris*. Like *Bodrum*, a large percentage of tourists are from a specific country. In this case, it's the United Kingdom. I'm not sure why, but it adds to the melting-pot tourism of Turkey. Andi and I rented a speedboat and barreled around the Bay of *Marmaris* one afternoon. We came across a huge yacht (we were told it was the Sultan of Brunei's) and couldn't believe how big it was. The back hydraulic door was open, and you could seek several cars on rotating palettes. It had a helipad, and a "dinghy" the size of a normal yacht. The ship had to be at least five hundred feet long. I counted two dozen men watching our every move, so we decided to get out of the area before we became fish bait.

Antalya has a few things different from the other beach towns. It's framed by the Taurus Mountains, which are snowcapped for much of the year. It also has a beautiful tourist port, small but quaint, with neat restaurants and cafes. The port is surrounded by castle walls, which give it a Camelot-type feel. *Antalya* has been around for over 50,000 years, making it one of the oldest cities on earth. If you still haven't had your fill of ruins, you can visit Hadrian's Gate, the famous Yivli Minare (grooved minaret), or the outstanding Archaeological Museum. *Antalya* is divided in two: the old town with picturesque glimpses of its past, and the newer area with treelined streets and tourist attractions. Both are worth seeing if you have the time.

Each location along the coast is different, and each location is worth seeing. If you ever get the chance, schedule a vacation to Turkey. Fly into Izmir and spend a day or two there, then hit the road from *Cesme* to *Antalya*. Stop in Istanbul on the way back. Some honorable mentions along the way? Aphrodisias, with the great Temple of Aphrodites; Cappadocia, with amazing villages carved directly into mountain rock; and Sardis, with one of the finest architectural masterpieces, the Gymnasium of Sardis, along with the Castle of Antiochus III. All of these locations, intertwined with centuries of historical input from all directions, have magically— almost secretly— emerged like Phoenix from the ashes to form modern-day Turkey. There's no other place like it.

But I don't want to give you the impression that Turkey was some kind of Shangri-La in the 1990s. It wasn't. There was much poverty, and heartbreaking treatment of man and animals. You didn't have to drive very far during Ramadan to see sheep slaughtered alive with their throats cut open. It was eerie to see the blood splashing on the sidewalk. And the

Izmir Bay really served as a huge septic tank. With no modern plumbing, massive amounts of human waste were dumped into the bay each day. Unfortunately, during the floods, the water level would rise and fill the streets with stench. It was terrible for the thousands of residents who lived on the first floor (or in the basement, like our *kapici*). The wastewater would get absorbed into their meager furniture. After a flood, it wasn't uncommon to see poorer families trying in vain to wash the crud and smell out of their possessions. Our softball fields were located in nearby Bayrakli Park. (Bayrakli is known as the ancient city of Old Smyrna and home to the Tomb of Tantalus.) I can remember the stench getting so bad that people actually got sick. We had to cancel softball games on occasion because of the awful smell.

But the Turks are anything but quitters. They will do any kind of job to take care of their families. They couldn't depend on the government to take care of them, or rely on immigrants to do their work for them. They welcomed each and every opportunity to earn a living. And the Turks were fearless. I remember coming home from work one day and noticing a guy hanging out of our seventh-floor window! When I got inside, I realized that he was painting the outside window frames. He had his big toe on the window ledge, and two fingers under the windowsill. The rest of his body was dangling—without scaffolding—over the edge of the building. With each brush of paint, he took his life in his own hands. But things like this were normal. For example, one day we noticed a gas leak in the apartment. The *kapici* came to our rescue. Using a lighter—that's right, a lighter—he tested the lines for leaks. Two explosions later, he located the leak, but lost half of his hair in the process. When our electric power went out, the *kapici* decided that he'd better get an experienced electrician. So how did the electrician test the power lines? By placing the wires on his *tongue*! After he was thrown across the room once or twice, he located the problem. When we received approval to place a stoplight on the roundabout near the commissary and Kultur Parki, next to the school buses, we felt a sense of accomplishment. However, the Turks refused to recognize it. No one stopped. After a while, it became as useless as an ocean to a thirsty sailor.

All of these things—and many others—speak to the philosophy of kismet. To the Turks, a better world awaits. The next life is the place to be. So if today were their day to perish, then so be it. Armed with absolutely no fear of dying, many Turks took large risks without hesitation. (Maybe that's why they are known as one of the toughest military armies in the world.) Andi and I spoke to many Turks about this philosophy. It's so contrarian to America, where we place a high value on human life. In a way, the Turks seemed liberated by this approach. Whatever works, I guess.

When I was stationed in Izmir, Turkish Airlines was one of the worst airlines in the world. On one of my trips to Stuttgart, I had a flight from Izmir, through Istanbul, then into Frankfurt. (I always flew into Frankfurt, so I could rent a car and beat the hell out of it on the autobahn.) During one trip, as I was boarding in Izmir, I noticed that the passengers were being seated row by row and packed tightly together. When I looked at the back of the plane, it was empty. Being the savvy traveler, I squeezed out of my middle seat and scrambled to an empty exit row behind the passengers. And just as I was thinking how shrewd I was, the back exit door opened. And in came the great unwashed: a slew of downtrodden people getting a free lift to Istanbul. There were chickens, acrid plastic bags full of meat products, rancid foods of every kind, screaming babies on every arm, and so on. At the Istanbul airport, we disembarked, and I piled into a bus with the rest of the cast of *Les Miserables*. When the bus screamed onto an outbound highway, I realized we were speeding away from the airport! I was panicking, since I had a connecting flight in fifty minutes. A few miles from the airport, the bus slammed to a halt. Sitting there, in the middle of nowhere, was a taxi. The driver boarded the bus, walked right up to my seat, and offered me a ride back to the airport for fifty dollars. It turns out that when I changed seats, the new location altered my status from an airport passenger to an Istanbul passenger. Of course, this was not explained to me. There must have been some serious giggles among the flight attendants after another dumb American moved behind the "magic row." I wasn't surprised that a taxi was conveniently waiting for me.

In retrospect, I wasn't that alarmed by this hoodwink. For any of you who travel and live abroad, you know that getting ripped off on occasion is par for the course. What doesn't kill you, makes you stronger, right? That fifty dollars taxi ride probably fed the driver's family for a month. US dollars were supreme in Turkey. In the two years I lived there, the Turkish currency went from 42,000 lira per dollar to 999,999 lira per dollar! That taxi driver blackmailed me for over 49,999,950 lira!

During the second half of our tour in Izmir, Andi and I took another run through Western Europe, and later did something else that was always on my to-do list—visited London and several parts of Ireland. As an Irish Catholic growing up in Pittsburgh, I used to listen to my uncles talk about the homeland, the "Old Sod," the "Emerald Isle," and so on. I heard more than once about our ancestors in the Galway area, near Salt Hill. I wondered how much was BS, and how much was true. We decided to find out.

For our European swing, we flew into Frankfurt, rented a car, and spent ten days touring through Germany, the Netherlands, Belgium, Luxembourg, and France. Of course, we enjoyed many beautiful places in the region. Just some of the best respites along the way included Amsterdam, Brussels, Luxembourg City, Paris, and my old stomping grounds of Saarbrucken and Zweibrucken in Germany. I've never ceased to be amazed how quickly you can travel around Europe. This trip was similar in length to driving around Texas for ten days. Whether it was riding a tour boat through the Amsterdam port canals, sipping an ice-cold Stella Artois on the plaza in Luxembourg City, wasting a full day browsing around the Louvre, or enjoying Brussels on the "Hop-on Hop-off " double-deck bus—it was all good. Andi and I were tired but energized from the trip when we landed back in Izmir. We thought it might be the last time we'd ever live in or near Western Europe, so we wanted one last trip around the neighborhood.

As good as the revisit of Western Europe turned out, our trek to London and Ireland a few months later was even better. Believe it or not, even though I passed through Heathrow many times, I had never been to London. Since our time in Izmir was winding down, we decided we couldn't pass up the opportunity. We set our agenda up in two phases— three days in London, and nine days touring Ireland via the bed-and-breakfast circuit.

London was a blast. We did all the normal touristy stuff—checking out Big Ben towering over the Houses of Parliament; visiting Buckingham Palace; exploring the Tower of London and all those Crown Jewels; and riding the London Eye, a huge Ferris wheel-like contraption with thirty-two high-tech glass capsules that takes you 804 feet into the air! We also took a boat down the Thames and under the Tower Bridge, passing the Old Globe Theatre, Eton, and the Tate Museum. And Andi and I loved walking through Soho and the theater district, and then down to Hyde Park. One afternoon, after strolling through the park for a few hours, we passed the original Hard Rock Café on the way back to our hotel. Believe it or not, on that exact day, it was the twenty-fifth anniversary of the original restaurant. All menu items were set at 1971 prices. We dined, had a few drinks, and listened to music for pennies on the dollar. It was fun. (And one of the only things in London that wasn't expensive.)

Content with our whirlwind tour of London, it was time for a short hop via Aer Lingus to Dublin, Ireland. We stayed in Temple Bar, Dublin's cultural quarter, which is in the heart of the city. The area boasts theaters, artist studios, small galleries, hotels, restaurants, bars, and shops along its cobblestoned streets. The streets are set up in a medieval street pattern, with two huge public squares —Temple Bar Square and Meeting House Square— framing the pedestrian area. We walked and walked, and ate and drank with abandon. There's something about the Irish—you feel unmanly if you can't go toe-to-toe with them in the drinking establishments.

For example, Andi and I were in a little pub on a Sunday morning, around ten thirty, having breakfast. (Most of the pubs serve breakfast.) We noticed several people drinking shots and beers all around us. Geez … And not only were they drinking, but all the customers were lining up rows of drinks in front of them. I found that especially troubling—until the clock hit 11:00 a.m. Then I got it. It turns out that it's illegal to serve alcohol on Sunday between 11:00 a.m. and 1:00 p.m., in respect for church and Mass services. The barkeep locked the door, shut off all the lights, and the place was now closed. We were suddenly eating our eggs in the dark. The rows of drinks were designed to last until the pub opened again. Andi and I were stuck inside, and the only ones without libation. After a while, the constable entered the pub and made sure no one was buying liquor. (It didn't matter that *everyone* except us was drinking liquor.) They're real law-abiding citizens, those Irish are.

After a couple of days of visiting galleries and shops, Trinity College, the Christchurch Cathedral, the Joyce Tower, Dublin Writers Museum, and a host of bars from the Brogan's and Auld Dubliner to Danger Doyle's and the Temple Bar, it was time to dry out and hit the road across the countryside. But before I move on in our saga, I have some good advice for Irish Americans like Andi and I who visit the Emerald Isle. Locals aren't keen on Americans boasting about being Irish and acting like they're James Joyce or something. Keep your cool. Eventually the locals will engage you, and when they find out you're a Feeney, for example, you won't be able to pay for another drink.

Our first night was spent in Waterford, about seventy miles south of Dublin. The most shocking thing about driving in Ireland is the colors. The greenest greens and bluest blues in the world, or at least on this side of Hawaii. Every turn was a postcard, and every cow was fat, dumb, and happy. Waterford itself consists of various cultural centers, like the Viking Triangle, surrounded by fortifications from the tenth century. The Quay, and also the John Roberts Square, are pedestrian walkways, which we normally seek out when traveling.

Of course, we had to go to the Waterford Crystal Factory. Watching the glassblowing process was interesting, and we bought a set of very expensive wineglasses to savor into our retirement. (However, they arrived in Turkey in pieces—what are you going to do?) I also tracked down Waterford's oldest pub, T & H Doolans, which has been officially active for over three hundred years. Local lore insists the pub is over five hundred years old, but there is no documentation to prove it. A part of the Viking Triangle, known to be at least one thousand years old, can be viewed from the lounge.

Next up—Cork… Like Venice, the town of Cork is built around water. In fact, the center part of the city center was built on an island, surrounded by the River Lee. The city was scenic, with bridges, peaceful backwaters, and hilly streets. We took the scenic Mardyke riverside walk starting from Fitzgerald Park, with pedestrian bridges and small inlets. The City Hall was formidable and huge. Being from Pennsylvania, I couldn't resist visiting the old Quaker Meeting House, where William Penn spoke last before heading to the new world and founding my home state. But the main event in Cork is unquestioned—the Blarney Castle. It's just outside town, about seven kilometers, and is of course famous for the Blarney Stone. For those lucky enough to kiss it, they will be conferred the power of eloquence. But it's not an easy thing to do. The steps to the castle are small and extremely slippery, and the stone is set in a wall below the battlements. In order to smooch the stone, people have to bend backward and suspend themselves in midair over the grounds below. No worries, though—there's a guy there who holds you in place, for a tip, of course. Andi is afraid of heights and almost backed out when we got to the top. But you can't turn around. The steps are too narrow, and the people behind you are stuck in the queue. So she bucked up, hung over the castle, and kissed the stone. (We even have a refrigerator magnet that says, "Yes, I kissed the Blarney Stone.")

Limerick, like Cork, is dominated by water from the River Shannon. The riverside walking tours were excellent and gave you a good feeling for the town. Limerick is broken up into three distinct regions. According to Wikipedia, "The city centre is divided between the traditional areas of

'English Town' on the southern end of King's Island, which includes the King John's Castle; 'Irish Town', which includes the older streets on the south bank; and the current economic centre further south, called 'Newtown Perry', built in the 17th century." I must admit, although we walked all around Limerick, I didn't realize the city has these diverse sections. And keeping with my Irish responsibilities, we sought out a couple of bars on Denmark Street— Flannery's and Smyth's—right in the heart of Limerick's entertainment area. (My goal to frequent at least one pub in every county was becoming a reality.)

Last, but *definitely* not least, was Galway—home of my ancestors... According to Ned Cully, an Irish writer, "If you went out the coast road from Galway city approximately 8 miles to Furbo and for the next 15 miles to Tully Cross, every third house would be a Feeney house ... there are simply scads of them there and most claim not to be related to their neighbors (folks across the road), but they're all related if you go back 3, 4, or 5 generations." Wow—scads of them. It sounds bad, huh? Kind of like locusts or something ...

But he was right—there were Feeneys everywhere, from hardware stores to post offices.

Galway is the jewel of southern Ireland. I have to quote www. galwaytourism. ie, which sums it up nicely:

"Galway City is a thriving, bohemian, cultural city on the western coast of Ireland. Along with being a popular beachside destination with beautiful beaches and long winding promenades, it also has a buzzing cosmopolitan city centre. The city is a joy to explore with its labyrinthine cobbled streets, colourful shop facades and busy café/bar culture." (We can definitely vouch for the latter reference.)

Whether it's Eyre Square for nightclubs or the Latin Quarter near Quay Street for the pubs and bars, you can't help but have a good time there. At sunset, we were drawn to the Spanish Arch, where you can watch fishing boats coming and going, and also enjoy the wild birds framing the backdrop for an unparalleled sunset over Galway Bay. I couldn't wait to test my "let them come to you" approach in some of the pubs there. It always worked. They love Yanks who don't present themselves as Irish, but are proud to call themselves Irish Americans.

The name Feeney in Galway is very well-known. I felt more at home there than anyplace I have ever been outside the United States. Even though I didn't know them, my ancestors were everywhere, and I could feel it in my bones. (Or maybe it was an extra Guinness or two that I was feeling.) Either way, it was special. We drove back to Dublin the next day, and departed for Izmir the following morning. What a trip! On the plane, I couldn't help feeling this connection with Ireland, that is, a link to something that I couldn't explain. There's a sadness that comes with gathering no moss, and I definitely felt it then. The blob wins on this issue. I have no power or ability to steer my past. Does it really exist then?

Things got back to normal in Turkey. I was sitting on the First Kordon one afternoon with a couple of buddies, and we were bantering back and forth about things we would remember after we left Izmir. Here's one discovery that stuck with me. At the risk of sounding like a chauvinist, I feel like I have to mention this fact about Turkey. In all the places I have been in the world—many more than most people—I can honestly say that Turkey has the most attractive women I have ever seen. (Except for my wife, of course.) The confluence of Asia and Eastern Europe, with a touch of Africa, provided the perfect ingredients for stunning female beauties. One of my jobs as commander was to counsel young airmen who decided to marry foreign spouses. The process was complex and involved Turkish laws, US law, immigration policy, military Status of Forces Agreements or SOFAs, and so on. At times I felt like a justice of the peace. I marveled at these young men, barely wet behind the ears, marching one beautiful woman after another into my office to start the matrimony process. In the back of my mind, I couldn't help thinking that most of these guys were in over their heads. But, hey, my thoughts didn't matter, did they? And with my track record in relationships, I had no room to talk. I wondered how many of those Turkish beauties stayed with their GI spouses after moving to the United States.

As our tour neared its completion, we were still enjoying Izmir. We loved taking the ferry over to Karsiyaka, located on the other side of the Gulf of Izmir. The first thing you noticed upon arrival was the giant Karsiyaka Monument, a salute to Turkish freedom. The Karsiyaka Souk on Bazaar Street was very large and modern, and the area around the port had a wide variety of restaurants. We used to enjoy walking along the bay and getting away from the large crowds on the First Kordon in Konak.

One of the best events of the year was the Izmir International Fair. According to Wikipedia, the fair "is the oldest tradeshow in Turkey, and considered the cradle of Turkey's fairs and exposition industry, and is also notable for hosting a series of simultaneous festival activities." It was held every year in Kultur Parki and usually drew up to a million and a half people.

The fair was huge—over 80,000 meters of exposition space. And since there were no yearly themes, you never knew what to expect. It was a crazy venue.

Right after the end of the 1996 fair, I was selected for promotion to lieutenant colonel (Lt. Col.). As I was reviewing the promotion list, I noticed that many of my peers, that is, prior-service majors, did not get selected. In the air force officer corps, a non-selection basically ended your career. Since I still had contacts at AFMPC, I queried the promotions section for a breakdown of selects vs. non-selects for prior-service majors. This information was usually available before the selectee list came out. I was appalled that less than 25 percent of nonrated majors were selected to Lt. Col. That was more than two standard deviations below the overall selection rate. In my mind, it was discrimination, plain and simple. And I saw this coming. With the DOD looking to reduce costs, one sneaky way to do it was to target prior-service officers. Their rationale was as follows: since the prior-service majors have already qualified for a pension, cutting their careers short could save money and avoid potential loss of pensions for newer officers.

Simply put—this was pure bullshit. You promote the best, period. Many of my cohorts were still in their early forties. To be penalized for overachieving as enlisted members and getting selected for Officers Training School was wrong. And the difference in pensions between a major and Lt. Col. retiree over a twenty-five-year retirement is several hundred thousand dollars. As hard as I tried, I couldn't get anyone to admit publicly that this happened. For the first time in my life, I was embarrassed to be in the USAF. Even though I did get promoted, I was also targeted. I felt like I needed a shower.

For most of my colleagues, a non-promotion was devastating. The fear of not getting promoted is much more powerful than the desire to get promoted. Non-selects become lame ducks, will never get considered for promotion again, and will immediately lose any opportunities for competitive jobs. They are assigned a mandatory retirement date and shuffled off into a corner to fade away. It is humiliating to the officer and his or her family. I watched this happen many times and never got used to it. Ironically, many of the non-selects wished they would have stayed in the enlisted corps. At least they would still have a job and a chance to compete for promotions in the future.

Controlling my rage, and pissed that so many of my peers were tossed aside, I called Andi with the news.

"Hi, Andi, it's Don. I have some good news and some bad news. Which one do you want first?" She paused. "Uh, I guess I'll take the good news."

"I made lieutenant colonel. The list just came out."

"That's great. Congratulations! You did it." As always, my number-one fan made me feel better—at least for a moment. But I was determined to push on. "What's the bad news?" After I explained what happened, I decided on the spot that I would never allow the USAF to use my enlisted time to discriminate against me again. Before I knew it, I said the following:

"The bad news? In exactly three years and one second from my date of promotion, we're getting out." There was a deep silence on the line. I couldn't believe I had just said that, and Andi couldn't believe how angry I was. But I knew then, as I did three years later, I was "already gone." (Note: I had to serve three years in order to qualify for a Lt. Col. retirement pension.)

We finished up our remaining months traveling to the Turquoise Coast a few more times and thoroughly enjoying the many restaurants and bars of Izmir. There were great domino games during our Friday staff meetings, excellent diving trips to the Aegean Coast, fun-filled bowling nights and softball days, middle-of-the-night raids on the Akin Building to watch sports, and a host of Hemingway Afternoons designed to remember and reminisce about our enigmatic days in Izmir.

I accepted a job in the US Atlantic Command (USACOM), a Joint Forces operation located at Norfolk Naval Air Station, Virginia. I was slated to be the Deputy Chief, Assignments and Personnel Programs Division.

Having a joint job (multiservice) was the next step on my upwardly mobile career path. I was becoming a "player."

But my thoughts were no longer focused on career aspirations or potential promotions. I would work hard in Virginia, mainly because of my family work ethic—and then get the hell out of the military. My USAF career had hit the wall. I decided that *no one* was going to tell me when to stay and when to leave. How close had I come to being passed over? Why did prior enlisted time punish my peers by requiring them to meet a higher standard than other majors? (While reading this paragraph on my computer screen, I was alarmed to admit how deeply this situation had affected me.)

As far as I was concerned, I was "Already Gone," just like the Eagles' song. I threw away the rearview mirror. The road behind me was forgotten. But I was still determined to get the most out of my last assignment. With no upward mobility to worry about, I was free to enjoy the final ride. And deep down, I was beginning to get excited about transitioning to civilian life—and to wherever that decision would take me.

So long, Asia…And thank you, Mother Turkey, for your beauty and hospitality. You were a good friend.

And I hope you find another matriarch, Sparky…

CHAPTER SIXTEEN

Willoughby Spit

———◆○◆———

I t was a long but memorable flight back to New York. The second leg from Istanbul to JFK was a cocktail flight—the first-ever nonstop Turkish Airline route to New York. They set up an invitation-only party area, complete with champagne, food, live music, and gifts for everybody. It was very nice. And we were carrying Kismet with us as well. Our plan was to forward her to Pittsburgh after landing in New York; my brother John would pick her up there. And once we got settled in Norfolk, we'd come back and get her. When we arrived at JFK two hours late, we were really panicking. Kismet had already spent eighteen hours in her carrier, and if she missed her connecting flight, she'd be looking at fifteen more before the next flight to Pittsburgh. This was unacceptable to me. So as soon as we cleared customs, I grabbed her carrier and ran almost one mile to the departing flight's baggage area. You should have heard Kismet squealing as she was bouncing around like a ping-pong ball in a lotto machine. When I arrived, the baggage door was closed, and I pressed my nose up against the window. I saw an employee and held up the cat so he could see her. I then formed my hands like I was praying and mouthed the word help. Come on, man. Please. Then he walked away. Seconds later, when I paused to realize how much I was sweating from the run, he returned.

"Sorry, I had to go get my keys. Where are you coming from?"

"Izmir, Turkey." I explained our predicament, and then asked, "Is there any way you can get our cat on the flight to Pittsburgh?"

"Hold on a minute," he said. Then he went back inside the baggage area. Kismet was disoriented, I was sweating like a pig, and I didn't remember where I was supposed to meet Andi. (She was also stuck, with several pieces of luggage that she couldn't possibly carry.) This wasn't looking good. He came back out. "What's her name?"

"Kismet. We found her abandoned on the street. Kismet means fate in Arabic." "Give her to me. I called my buddies on the tarmac. They'll keep the cargo hold open until I get her out there."

"Thank you so much, sir. You have no idea how happy you have made my wife." Later that night, we called John from a nearby hotel. Kismet arrived safely in Pittsburgh and was the first "baggage" off the plane. Fate was on her side.

The next day, we caught a cab to Bayonne, New Jersey, to pick up our Toyota moon buggy. Once we had everything inside, we headed south to Norfolk, Virginia. Two days later, we settled in a hotel in Hampton, Virginia, and began our new life.

Hampton Roads is the name of the body of water and the Virginia Beach-Norfolk-Newport News area that surrounds it in southeastern Virginia. It's one of the most interesting areas in the country for water enthusiasts. You have the James River to the northwest, and the Chesapeake Bay and Atlantic Ocean to the east. The Elizabeth River takes you south into downtown Norfolk, which connects to the Intracoastal Waterway and all points south. According to Wikipedia, "Hampton Roads is notable for its large military presence and its year-around ice-free harbor, for the United States Navy, Coast Guard, Air Force, NASA, Marine Corps, and Army facilities, shipyards, coal piers, and hundreds of miles of waterfront property and beaches, all of which contribute to the diversity and stability of the region's economy."

Although I was still on leave, I dropped by my new office, met everyone, and was feeling pretty good about things. My job was to manage all officer and enlisted assignment policy, programs, and procedures for over 1,200 joint service personnel. This meant I needed to become familiar with army, navy, air force, and marine service-specific policies. It sounded pretty interesting. I vowed to be at work soon. But first, it was house-hunting time again.

After several days of traipsing through rental properties, we found our place. It was a townhouse located on Ocean View Avenue, in Willoughby Spit. The back steps led right onto the sands of the Chesapeake Bay. It was a strange apartment—long and skinny like a bus—but you couldn't beat the location. The Spit was formed via the violence of Mother Nature. During a hurricane in 1749, the Chesapeake Bay rose by more than fourteen feet, creating a massive sand spit at Sewell's Point (just south of the Spit). Some fifty-seven years later, the Great Coastal Hurricane of 1806 finished the job, cutting away land on three sides and developing an isthmus later called Willoughby Spit.

Over the years there, we saw every type of watercraft imaginable pass by our beachfront. The procession included aircraft carriers, cruise liners, tall ships, submarines, yachts, and more, and I enjoyed every minute of it. Ocean View Avenue hugged the coastline for almost ten miles, so it was the perfect place for long runs. (And of course, for mopeds.) With our apartment now secure, we scheduled delivery of our household goods from Turkey, and then headed to Pittsburgh to visit family and pick up Kismet.

I never get tired of the "Steel City." PNC Park is the best place to see a baseball game in the country. Mount Washington offers some of the greatest urban views on the planet. The downtown is renovated, walkable, and safe.

The people from Pittsburgh are proud of their roots. As a Pittsburgh native, you can be gone for years, and then walk into any local bar and start up a conversation as if you never left. Pittsburghers—let me say it now so I won't forget—thank you for always welcoming me home. (Note: In all of my travels, I have *never* met anyone from Pittsburgh who didn't like it there.)

During this visit, we stayed at John's house in Belleview. He and I were pretty close in the late nineties. Mom was still Mom—driving us all crazy, but in a good way. I can't tell you how many times John, Pat, and myself would crack up talking about "Mom stories." The older my mother got, the more compelled she was to say anything she wanted to anyone she met. Unintentionally, my mother could say the rudest things to strangers and get away with it. She was quite comical at times ...Back at the Spit, with Kismet adjusting to the beachside very quickly, we settled in for our last round of military moves. There was a house next to us, a putrid-looking dwelling, reminiscent of the house on the *Addam's Family* TV show. But two of the residents, Joe and Jim (real names), became great neighbors and friends. Joe, an environmental engineer, was a local through and through, and had more BS than most. But he was fun and a very good person at heart. Jim, a manager at a local Hooters restaurant, was a Jimmy Buffett type, who loved grilling on the beach and dating as many women as possible. He was from northern New York. Each of us had separate backgrounds and thought differently on most issues. But that's why we got along so well. We liked each other for what we were and didn't care about changing anything.

In the office, I was grinding along, handling tons of joint policy issues. It was important work, but not super-challenging. My boss was good, and the office morale wasn't bad. Since I had never worked with the US Navy before, it took some time to adjust. For instance, when navy officers are on "shore duty," they consider it almost like a sabbatical. It's not "real work" like deploying at sea, so they can lose focus quickly. I had a submarine officer who was working for me. His stories about cruising under ice caps for weeks at a time made the hair on my arms stand on end. He was always jumpy and excitable. Living like that had to have something to do with it. In my first year at USACOM, I felt very lucky to be selected to attend Armed Forces Staff College. This twelve-week college was a rigorous joint professional military education course designed to educate officers and other leaders in the deployment, employment, synchronization, and support for joint and multinational forces. And of course, we had a softball team. Hitting home runs made me popular in my class—we were all type As and hated to lose at anything, including softball.

Around this same time period, I finally "pinned" on lieutenant colonel, my last rank as an air force officer. My brother Larry came to Norfolk, and with Andi, assisted in the ceremony. One on each side, they pinned the insignia to my shoulder epaulets. It was just the right touch. Then as well as now, they are the two most important people in my life. My wife is a godsend, and Larry has been there for me through the good and the bad.

Perhaps the highlight of our stay in Willoughby Spit occurred when we decided to buy a boat. It was a Maxum 2300SC Cuddy Cabin, with a

205-horsepower MerCruiser engine. Andi and I spent hundreds of hours on that boat. (We stored it a marina just one mile from our house. So it was "easy on, easy off," without towing and lining up at boat ramps.) The hull was deep, with a wide body. The cabin contained a galley, a head, and a large bed for overnight trips. We took it everywhere. I remember one weekend when my sister Pat and her husband, Frank, came to visit us with a couple of friends. All six of us spent the entire weekend on the boat. We headed up into Hampton to visit the Virginia Air and Space Center, and then stopped at a famous restored hotel on Fort Monroe for brunch. Afterward, we headed to downtown Norfolk, tied up the boat, and went sightseeing along the Elizabeth River. The next day, we headed across the Chesapeake Bay (under the Chesapeake Bay Bridge) to Rudee's Inlet. From there, we entered a whole new world of waterways, including Lynnhaven, Dauphin, and Broad Bays. After lunch at Bubba's waterfront restaurant, we eventually moored just one block from Virginia Beach, where we spent the afternoon on the boardwalk. I fondly remember how relaxing it was on the way back to the marina flying across the calm waters of the bay at dusk. That feeling of relaxation that comes after a day on the water is something I'll never forget. (Pat still reminds us that her friends said it was the best vacation of their lives.)

Of course, Andi and I took the boat down the Intracoastal Waterway, through the Great Dismal Swamp and several connecting locks, into North Carolina. Sometimes we'd stop at a "boatel" along the waterway for supplies or a clean shower. Other times, we'd head down the Pasquotank portion of the waterway into Albemarle Sound, and spend a day or two in Elizabeth City or Edenton. Many times as we were cruising through the open waterway, we wouldn't see anyone for hours. Our most common "neighbors" were the osprey eagles, perched high atop the mile markers. They kept a close eye on their babies, and on us as well. For a city kid who never saw the ocean until he was sixteen, I felt completely comfortable on the water in any situation.

But it wasn't just boating that was fun in the Tidewater area. The boardwalk at Virginia Beach was one of our regular stops. My favorite place was the Eighteenth Street Cafe and Grill. It sits right on the boardwalk, has great food, and is the perfect people-watching spot. (The more we traveled, the more we learned from people watching. It's a great educational tool.) Of course, as crazy Steelers' fans, we'd head to McFadden's in Hampton or Sneeky Pete's in Virginia Beach to watch the game and put back a few beers. For a unique place to shop or a different kind of dining experience, try the Ghent area of Norfolk. It also houses the Chrysler Museum of Art, the Virginia Opera's home stage, the Harrison Opera House, and the historic Naro Theater. To the north, we loved going to Old Dominion—an excellent amusement park—and visiting historic Colonial Williamsburg. And with Washington, DC, a few hours away, we visited my sister on occasion, and also enjoyed the tourist sites. To the south, we especially enjoyed the Outer Banks, taking Route 12 into North Carolina and winding through Nags Head and Kill Devil Hills, all the way to Hatteras. We'd ferry to Ocracoke

Island, spend the day, and then head to Cedar Island via another ferry, and work our way down to Cape Lookout. What beautiful country... The best part? The return trip was just as much fun, and included another stop in Ocracoke. At home, we had just as much fun hanging out on the beach, firing up the barbeque, and talking with neighbors and friends. But I don't want to mislead anybody either. It wasn't Waikiki, or even Colorado Springs for that matter. All and all, it was a fun part of our lives, and the people we met in Willoughby Spit were great.

On a sad note, Kismet's karma finally ran out. One day, she didn't come home. This never happened, and we feared the worst. We cruised up and down the Spit and walked every inch of the beach. She was nowhere to be found. Since she never wandered very far and was wearing a tag with our phone number on it, we had to accept the fact that she was stolen. (This Turkish cat was too savvy to be hit by a car or tracked down by another animal.) We drowned our sorrows at the Thirsty Camel, a pub nearby, and agreed that she had a good life. And we hoped that if she was stolen, she'd be okay.

But Andi couldn't give up the search. So we ran ads in the paper offering a five-hundred-dollar reward and posted missing-cat signs all over the place. Finally, we got a collect call from a truck driver, who had recently dropped off some furniture on Ocean Drive and just now realized there was a cat in the back of his truck. His explanation matched Kismet perfectly. He said he'd be glad to bring her back, but he lost his wallet and needed five hundred dollars up front to pay for the trip. Andi was ecstatic. I was skeptical. But what choice did I have? Andi absolutely loved that cat—from the first day she saw her crouched under a car in Izmir to now. We sent the money Western Union, and he promised we'd have Kismet back in three days. We waited. He never showed up. It was a con. There was probably a partner in Norfolk who read missing-pet ads and then relayed the information to an accomplice. It was the advertisement this punk had, not the cat. If I'd ever met this guy, I would have torn his head off and shoved it down his throat. It crushed my wife to wait, day after day, hoping against hope that a moving van would stop at our door and Kismet would walk out like the lost aviator's in *Close Encounters of the Third Kind.*

Not to pontificate too often, but things like this stir up a lifelong question: is man born good or bad? Is it the family, church, teachers, or mentors that help us "center" our personalities and develop a firm understanding of good and bad? And do they also teach us the harmful effects of sin and dishonesty? Or left unchecked, is man basically bad? Are the very instincts in our DNA selfish and animalistic? Have thousands of years of man's existence on earth created survival tools that are innately destructive? Is this whole discussion a subset of the heredity vs. environment argument?

I grew up Catholic, which had its pros and cons. But I couldn't steal ten cents without feeling guilty of thievery. But this schmuck, for five hundred dollars, lied to my wife about Kismet; then he hung up the phone and walked away. For weeks, every truck that passed our place triggered faint hopes that would never materialize. A great American, huh?

On to a happy place ... As I mentioned earlier, I had two great neighbors, Joe and Jim. We spent many weekends sitting on the beach and solving the world's problems. We usually hung at Jim's, because he always had Buffett music playing and something great sizzling on the grill. Once in a while, he'd invite several of the Hooters girls to his apartment. When that happened, the place would fill up in a hurry. Most of the time, we drank beer, took in some sun, and watched people pass by on the shore. Jim was one of the most generous people I have ever known. I tried for years to give him money for the foodstuffs and constantly volunteered to go out and buy him supplies for one of his shindigs. He always refused. I had to sneak in cases of beer, without telling him, in order to contribute to the parties. And Joe was also a blast. He was very political and had opposing views from mine on most issues. But the debates were legendary. I don't think we ever convinced each other of anything, but we had fun trying.

As a Lt. Col., I was reassigned, to the Joint Task Force (JTF)—Civil Support as the J-1. In joint terminology, J-1 means Director, Manpower and Personnel. We started as a small cadre of people (six or seven) and ended up with over two hundred by the time I retired. Our job was to develop playbooks for small, medium, and large nuclear, biological, chemical, radiological, and explosive-ordinance scenarios. We worked with all the military services side by side including NCIS, FBI, FEMA, Civil Service, State Department, CIA, and so on. Our goal was to anticipate any and all scenarios. When or if a certain scenario arose, we'd pull the playbook and go to work. This was 1999 to 2000, well before 9/11. But our planners knew all about Osama bin Laden. They regularly went to Washington for briefings and told anyone who would listen that he would attack the United States. But it fell on deaf ears. (After the attack, when I had already retired, my boss was sent to the White House to work with the Bush administration.)

I hadn't mentioned my plans to retire to anyone yet. I didn't want to be a lame duck, and I was determined to pull my own weight right up until my final day. But things were getting interesting. My boss, we'll call him Major General Lawson, was very fond of me. Something clicked when I met him. He was the perfect general officer—firm but compassionate. I'd run through walls for him. He had what was called a "definitely promote," that is, the ability to promote an officer to colonel without going to the promotion board. I would be eligible for consideration in eighteen months and was General Lawson's only eligible candidate slated for the next cycle. Although I never came out and asked him—I didn't want to know—I was sure he would support me. That's why it was so hard to tell him I was retiring. He wasn't happy. Remember, I began with him and a small cadre, and we built an entire organization in less than eighteen months. And since finding a replacement would take a while, I felt I'd better keep him up to speed. It went like this:

"General Lawson, do you have a moment?" "Sure, Feeney. What's up?"

"Sir, I guess I should come right out and say it. I put my retirement papers in today."

"I'm sorry to hear that. Can I ask why? You still have many years of service eligibility left."

"Sir, I just don't have my heart in it anymore. If I can't do my best, then I don't think it's fair to the air force or myself to continue. I've kind of hit the wall. Each day, it's become more difficult to keep my eye on the ball."

He waited for what seemed like a long time. He was intense and gentle at the same time—a very rare combination. "I understand. When are you planning to retire?"

"The end of July," I replied. Maybe I'm crazy, but I felt like I was letting him down. He picked up on my uneasiness.

"You served your country. You have a right to retire when it's best for you and your family. I can't say I'm happy you're leaving us, but I understand." As usual, class and empathy personified.

"Uh, on a side note, sir. Are you still planning to buy my boat?" I was concerned that he might change his mind. I wouldn't be around to show him the ropes, so to speak.

"Sure, Feeney, I'll buy the boat. Anything else?"

"No, sir, and thank you for supporting me. Not just today, but ever since I came to the JTF. It's been fun putting this organization together. And I promise, I'll find you a good replacement and will give a 100-percent effort up until my final day."

"I know, Feeney, I know. If you need any help with your retirement processing, come see me, okay?" I said I would, and left his office. I guess it's human nature, but we communicated a lot less after that day. He was looking long-term, and I was focused on the short-term. Many of our projects would extend well past my departure. In his own way, he was freeing up my time to concentrate on other things. And I appreciated it. He would be my keynote speaker at my retirement ceremony.

As each month passed by, I was even more eager to retire from the military. The anger that I still felt about the blatant discrimination of prior-service officers was still lingering. (They say that type As possess the anger trait. In this case, they're right.) So after considering all my options and realizing how much I enjoyed teaching, I decided to seek a doctor of education degree from the University of Notre Dame–Australia. (I had been researching this university for many months, and was enamored by the idea of living and studying in Australia.) I hoped Andi would be just as excited —she was. The campus is located in Fremantle, which is in the southwest portion of Western Australia. The application process was long, but eventually I got accepted. I lined up my GI Bill to coincide with the start of the fall 2000 semester, and counted the days until I was a free man.

My day finally arrived. The retirement ceremony was humbling, with hundreds of well-wishers. General Lawson made sure the event was set up perfectly and even emceed the festivities. He was such a natural speaker and captivated the audience by exaggerating my accomplishments almost to the point of embarrassment. As I sat there onstage in my dress blues, listening to him speak, I couldn't help reflecting back on my life so far. How in the hell did I get to this point? It seemed like only yesterday I was painting houses for a living. I thought of coin tosses, divorces, countries, lost friendships, and lost lives. I was also feeling vulnerable and afraid. Should I have stayed in the air force? All of a sudden, the idea of fleeing to Australia seemed trivial, even stupid. Who walks away from a chance to make full colonel? I felt like I was putting down my weapon and walking away from my post, like I did in Zweibrucken. Was I empathetic enough to Andi's needs? Did I even want to pursue a doctor of education degree? Where does space end?

It's hard to change your life. But nothing stands still, either. Everything has a life cycle, with a beginning and an end. This retirement was no different. Like Richard Carlson declares in his book *Don't Sweat the Small Stuff ... and It's All Small Stuff*:

"Every experience you have ever had is over. Every thought you've ever had, started and finished. Every emotion and mood you've experienced has been replaced by another. You've been happy, sad, jealous, depressed, angry, in love, shamed, proud, and every other conceivable human feeling. Where did they all go? The answer is, no one really knows. All we know is that, eventually, everything disappears into nothingness. Welcoming this truth into your life is the beginning of a liberating adventure."

Looking out into the audience, I reflected upon another one of Mr. Carlson's stress-reducing insights: *"Understand the Statement, Where Ever You Go, There You Are."* Simply put, focus on where you are today, and not where you think you should be or would rather be tomorrow. Don't let self-directed pressure win. Overcome it.

It was time to step to the podium. I thanked General Lawson for his kind words, and then asked everybody to please stand. After the rumbling of chairs stopped and the entire audience was standing, I asked them to please sit down. (I always wanted to do that.) Next, I recognized my very special invited guests. I talked about Andi and my brother Larry—the two most important people in my life. I thanked Larry's daughter Emily and my brother-in-law George for being there on this important day. I then introduced my beach buddies—Joe and Jim—and thanked them for their friendship and for helping me solve the world's problems. And I was grateful that my first sergeant from Izmir, Chief John Potts, was there to support me as well.

I can't explain it, but once I started to speak, all the tension and self-doubt faded away. I never looked at my carefully written speech. Instead, I just laid out the truth as I saw it. I spoke about losing the coin toss that placed me in the military, about being assigned to Germany while my new bride was assigned to Montana, about going AWOL as a airman first class, and about how lucky I was that people saw things in me that I didn't see in myself. I talked about leadership, and how the axiom "steering the blob" helped me to visualize my leadership role. I talked about the "box," my personal place for those things that nobody gets. They're mine, and mine alone. (I believe each person has this box, and it may contain things like religion, family, integrity, love, accountability, and so on.) The key is to treasure these gifts with passion, and never compromise any of them. You won't get them back if you do. I also talked about Dylan's line "You don't have to be a weatherman to know which way the wind blows." All my life people had been telling me what I couldn't do. But I never listened. (I guess I'm still not listening, huh?) The labeling of people has done more to screw up the world than practically anything else. I say this to you—don't search for the weatherman; be the weatherman.

I finally closed with a John Hiatt quote. Something like this: "Thank you very much for being here today. I wish you all 'a little joy, a little peace, and a whole lot of light.'"

Then I sat down, a civilian for the first time in twenty-three years.

The applause was very loud, and I was thankful I didn't use my written speech. I left the auditorium with Andi and waited outside to shake the hand of every person who took the time to watch my retirement ceremony. The responses to my speech were overwhelmingly positive. In my mind, it was because I steered the blob, reached into that "box" for one of my passions, namely, honesty above self, and I became my own weatherman.

But thankfully, it was finally *over*!

And now for the fun… My family and invited guests all headed over to Willoughby Spit to eat, drink, and hang out on the beach. But Jim had a surprise retirement gift in store for us. He showed up in a big, orange Hooters bus and told everyone to get in. Thirty minutes later, we were sitting in the Hooters on the Norfolk Waterside, with enough food and beer to feed Napoleon's army. There were mountains of crab legs, wings, clams, and more, and a constant flow of ice-cold beer. Looking across the restaurant at my family and friends that day, I felt pretty lucky. Here was an SSE that was truly special. And it could only be achieved by dedicating twenty-three years of one's life to attain it. Whatever happened in Australia and beyond, every person sitting there with Andi and me would be remembered forever. With great conversation and great food, the party lasted well into the next morning; the military career of Lt. Col. Donald J. Feeney was peacefully laid to rest.

Thank you Larry, George, Emily, John, Jim, and Joe for being there for this once-in-a-lifetime event. And thank you, Andi, for being my wife, for being my friend, for this chapter of our story, and for the rest of our natural lives.

Next stop, the land "down under."

PART III

Reinvention and Pragmatism

CHAPTER SEVENTEEN

Seventeen Bottles of Wine on the Wall, Seventeen Bottles of Wine

---◆○◆---

W ith my military career now history, it was time to get our affairs in order for the next adventure. There's something scary, but also exciting, about reinventing your life every now and then. For example, the massive adjustments required to live and work in Comiso, Italy, as compared to Limestone, Maine, were totally different. Everything about your daily life changes, from weather and language, to new job stress and social life. But believe it or not, after so many moves, the abnormal becomes normal, the unknown is expected, and the fear of change dissipates into a comfort zone. Although you still have to navigate through all the steps of grief, you cut through them faster, mainly because the transitions make your skin a little tougher. But this move was different. I gave up my career—and my paycheck—to go gallivanting off to Fremantle, Western Australia. Deep down, I didn't feel real confident about studying for a doctorate. But I had the GI Bill, so I considered this move to be more like a sabbatical leave of absence. This was my seventeenth relocation (I was forty-six at the time), and one of the riskiest. I was walking the high wire without a net for the first time since I had left Pittsburgh. Thank goodness Andi was all in with me.

After a quick trip through Pittsburgh, Andi and I put our furniture in storage, sold her Toyota Camry, and finished tying up loose ends in Norfolk. Sadly, it was finally time to get rid of my 1984 Toyota van. I had that car for *eighteen years*! That's longer than I had known Andi and all of my ex-wives combined. That moon buggy was my alter ego, keeping me out of trouble. Here are some of the escapades it had been through: it was shot at twice; it was stolen twice; it was pushed off a cliff once; it was robbed twice; it towed two boats, one that weighed much more that it did; and it was taken uninsured by my brother John from Rhode Island to Los Angeles without me knowing about it.

We decided to donate the van to charity. I had the car inspected, and it cost me a paltry $13.95. We drove it to the airport, removed all our luggage destined for Australia, and signed over the title. I watched as the volunteer workers drove the moon buggy away from the parking lot. It was an emotional moment, and a definite SSE. I had owned that vehicle so long I couldn't remember driving anything else. I was a first lieutenant when I bought it, and a retired lieutenant colonel when I gave it away. I'd spent almost 40 percent of my entire life driving that van.

The plane ride to Perth, Australia, was brutal. When we arrived, there was a representative from the University of Notre Dame–Australia waiting at the terminal, and he drove us twenty kilometers south to Fremantle. As we entered Fremantle (the locals call it Freo) for the first time, Andi and I were amazed by the wide diversity of architecture and people. According to *The Fremantle Book, Western Australia, Sixth Edition,* "Today Fremantle is a thriving port city, it is a melting pot of many different cultures which all uniquely contribute to the multicultural ambience of the city. The sidewalk eateries, galleries, shops and general atmosphere all reflect the many cultures that are blended into the everyday lifestyle. There is always something happening in Fremantle, attracting around 700,000 visitors annually. Locals are either planning, participating in, or recovering from the array of festivals and activities held to celebrate this center of cultural creativity."

With a population of just 24,267, Freo is a "large" small city, due in part to tourism. One-third of its population are immigrants from around the world. And with one hundred countries represented in Freo, only seven nationalities make up more than 1 percent of the population. No one country or culture stood out. It was an amazing place. I have never seen a city offer such a large variety of attractions in just a few square kilometers. It felt like being in one of Disney's theme parks.

In a way, Fremantle was like America in the 1950s. Everybody had a job, a car, a nice house, and two chickens in every pot. The neighborhood families were friendly, and front doors were unlocked. Children played in the parks, without hover parents watching their every move. Overpopulation wasn't an issue, and immigration problems were almost nonexistent. The economy was very stable, taxes were low, and patriotism was strong. I kept expecting to see Sheriff Taylor and Opie fly-fishing down by the ole Round House. (It jokingly sounds like an old country song—"Down by the Ole Round House" by someone like Conway Twitty.)

Since we knew nothing about the area, we agreed to let the school administrators set up temporary housing. That lasted one night. We hit the pavement the next day and found an excellent apartment at One High Street. High Street runs through the middle of Freo, with shops and restaurants on both sides of the avenue. Our apartment, built right on the ocean, was designed to house the entrants for the America's Cup Yacht Races in 1987. However, it wasn't completed on time. (Across the street was the Round House—a prison in the seventeenth century and the oldest building in Western Australia. From our balcony, we could also see excellent views of downtown Fremantle, the Fishing Boat Harbour, and the Indian Ocean.) Our new home was a three-story townhouse, with three bedrooms and three baths, fully furnished, with a garage. Bather's Beach was right across the street. It was perfect for us. In my opinion, the West End was the best location in Freo—period. And with the US dollar worth almost twice as much as the Aussie dollar in 2000, it was even better. Not only did my GI Bill cover classes, books, labs, and so on, but it paid our rent as well! For the first time since I was fourteen years old, I would spend the next year or so without working a single day! It was great.

The University of Notre Dame–Australia had moved into numerous former warehouses and wool stores in the West End, and beautifully restored them to blend perfectly with the local architecture. This area of town is considered to be one of the best examples of a Victorian port street scape in the world. The university offers the traditions and practices of Catholic higher-education institutions. They have degree programs in twelve disciplines. I set my sights on the doctor of education program. I figured my teaching experience, along with the opportunity to live and study in Australia, created a great educational combination. But alas, things didn't work out well.

My first meeting with my mentor—a British doctor of education—was less than stellar. I was prepared to discuss dissertation topics, toss around ideas in education, and self-actualize on academics. Instead, I received the cold-shoulder treatment and was advised that my entire first year would be spent studying research techniques. I was forty-six years old and had been teaching for over fifteen years. There was no scenario in my mind where I would spend twelve months practicing how to do research. He gave me a week to settle in and told me to return with a greater commitment to his research curriculum model. I spent the next several days checking out the campus and reading up on potential approaches to research development at the school library. I decided then and there that I wasn't doctoral material. (As I mentioned earlier, I wasn't fully committed to the doctoral degree in the first place. But you never know until you try.) I returned a week later and withdrew my candidacy for the doctor of education program. My mentor wasn't surprised and didn't try very hard to change my mind. I still get a cold chill up my spine when I think about this strange, albeit short, relationship.

Although I would lose one year of GI Bill eligibility, I didn't care. This north-side kid was never meant to be a doctor of education.

On the bright side, my tuition for the remainder of the semester was covered, and we had already paid the twelve-month lease at One High Street. It was time to see the continent!

We started with our new hometown. A few minutes away, on South Terrace Street, was the Cappuccino Strip. It's an exciting avenue full of brightly colored umbrellas that expand onto the wide sidewalks from bars and cafes of every type. It's a great place for a Hemingway Afternoon and to watch the tourists. On weekends, you might see antique cars rolling by or a parade of some kind appear out of nowhere. We'd stop at

Café Marconi for some pasta and wine, or at Benny's across the street for lunch. Or drop into the Sail and Anchor Bar or Rosie O'Grady's for a cold beer. There were Italian, Mediterranean, Mexican, Indian, and Japanese restaurants nearby serving full menus as well. I never got tired of hanging out there. (Throughout my life, I have been drawn to gathering places like the Cappuccino Strip. There is something synergistic about people hanging around outside cafes and restaurants that's absent in stuffy dining rooms.) But this little town had much more to offer. The Fremantle Marketplace was loaded with local vendors and neat things to buy; the tram ride, although a little tacky, was still cool to try once; and the seafood on the Fremantle Boat Harbour was legendary. Just next to the harbor was a microbrewery called Little Creatures. On Friday afternoons, it was customary for men from several countries to go there for beer and avid discussions of world events. Sort of like an informal League of Nations. Our landlord, Tony, and I would show up every week "ready to rumble." Since I was the only Yank, I got beat up pretty good at times, especially by Tony. But I held my own overall—it's hard to keep an American like me quiet—and I really enjoyed the lively discussions.

We needed transportation, so Andi and I went to the local auction looking for a car. We were getting outbid pretty badly until the last vehicle of the day came out. It was a white, two-door Hyundai Accent. We made the final bid, and the car was ours. With traffic on the left side of the road and the steering wheel on the right, it took some getting used to. It was hilarious to watch Andi drive that car. Although I had some experience driving on the left during a few of my IG trips, it was totally new to her. She got the hang of it quickly, though. We drove that car all over Western Australia, and then sold it for the same price we bought it for a week before leaving the continent.

Perth, Western Australia, is the most remote capital city in the world. It's north of Fremantle, on the Black Swan River. (Western Australia is huge— it can easily engulf Britain and all of Europe as well.) The unique location of Perth allowed it to develop at a pace and style uninterrupted by other Australian provinces. You can take a ferry from Freo to the Barrack Street Jetty, right in the middle of the city. There was also a train from Freo that followed the river line into Perth. The electric train was unmanned, and payment of fares was left to the honor system. That's right—no one checked tickets, and everyone paid anyway. (America in the fifties?) Andi and I used both transportation systems. We liked taking the train in the morning, and returning by ferry in the afternoon as the sun set on the Black Swan River.

Perth was the place to shop, and the only large town within thousands of miles. Northbridge, in the heart of Perth, was definitely the place to go for culture, shopping, business, and nightlife. After hours of walking and shopping, a cold drink at the Brass Monkey always hit the spot. (I still have a T-shirt from there, but it's so beat up I'll have to toss it soon.) High above the town center is King's Park, encompassing over four hundred hectares. It provides sweeping views of the city, the south bank of the Black

Swan, and the hills that surround Perth. King's Park hosts a wide variety of restaurants, and a beautiful array of botanical gardens, heritage walks, and seasonal wildflower and bush tours. With spotless beaches a few kilometers away and dozens of wineries within an hour's drive, Perth is one beautiful city—plain and simple.

One weekend Andi and I drove south to Margaret River, located amid native forests and rolling pastureland. This little town is world-renowned for its wineries and has a huge artist population. There are galleries everywhere, and vineyards to see in all directions. We met a couple there— Damien and Melissa—who would become our friends for the rest of our time in Australia. He was Aussie, and she was from the United States. We hit it off right away and vowed to get together back in Perth. They introduced us to another couple—Noe and Liza, both Aussie—and the six of us became inseparable. We'll never forget how graciously they treated us and how much fun we had together. They taught us so much about their culture, and they loved to have a good time.

The six of us were always doing things together. There were happy hours on the Cappuccino Strip, microbrewery tastings, dinners on the Boat Harbour, barbeques at Noe and Liza's house, and some serious parties at our place. We even rented a cabin for a weekend in Margaret River, and hit something like fifteen wineries in one day. (I still have a headache. I tell everyone I know that if we stayed in Perth for another year, I'd have to bring my liver home in a box!)

On New Year's Eve, it's a tradition in Australia to start partying early in the day, and to put the living room furniture out on the lawn. Noe and Liza had a party, and we were invited. As you know, from time to time throughout this book, we smoked a little grass. I know it was risky in the military, but that's another story... So here comes Noe, with a joint reminiscent of a Cheech and Chong movie. At about the same time, shots and beer were flying everywhere. In what seemed like seconds, we were already wasted. I mean like never before—and we lost track of time. (Note: Since we hadn't smoked pot much over the last several years, we were amazed how potent it had become.) Sitting on a living room sofa in the middle of the front lawn, Andi and I looked at each other, laughing like crazy, and had a conversation something like this: "Man, I'm stoned."

"Me too," said Andi. "I don't think I've ever been this high before." I was thinking the same thing.

"Wow, I hope we can make it to midnight for the New Year's celebration," I said doubtfully, assuming it was at least 7:30 or 8:00 p.m. and we still had a ways to go. "What time is it, anyway?"

"It's 4:20 p.m.," she said. And we both started howling laughing. We still had over seven hours to go! We couldn't believe it. How on earth were we going to make it to midnight? What kind of pot was that? And we were so hungry, but didn't want to risk standing up and walking over to the buffet. Looking back on that day, we had a blast, and did make it to midnight. But we both agreed to never let ourselves get that wasted again.

One of the neatest things we ever did was fly to Sydney, New South Wales, visit for a few days, and then take the transcontinental train all the way back to Perth. Sydney is one of the world's great cities. The Sydney Opera House is staggering in its beauty and architecture, and has over three thousand performances each year—many outdoors and free of charge. The majestic Harbour Bridge, which towers over the city, is nicknamed the Coathanger. It stands 134 meters high and is 502 meters long. The BridgeClimb, a three-hour hike across the top of the structure, takes you to the summit of the world-famous icon. This high-elevation walk is not for everyone. The Circular Quay next door is always bustling with activity, with ferries coming and going every ten minutes. And there are many great beaches—Manly Beach is just a ferry away from the harbor; Bondi Beach, Australia's most famous coastal resort, is right in the middle of everything; and Coogee Beach, just to the south of Sydney, can easily be reached via a beautiful cliff walk over rolling hills and scenic valleys. For entertainment and dining, you can't beat the Rocks, located under the Harbour Bridge. From *Sydney, The Official Guide*: "Nestled beside the modern city, the historic Rocks are full of life and have the best of Sydney's lifestyle. Settled by convicts and troops in 1788, it's full of stories of Sydney's colourful past—but it's anything but a museum." Packed with quaint stores and eateries, and sprinkled with outside cafes, the Rocks have HA written all over them. There is so much more to Sydney. If you get there, you'll discover your own favorite corner of the city.

When it was time to head back to Western Australia, we were very excited about our rail trip across the country. The train was called the *Gandy Dancer*—part of the Indian Pacific Railroad—and was the only single-car transcontinental train in the world. The train would be our home for the next four days. We checked in and headed to our cabin. It was small, but quaint. The furnishings were all tightly meshed together to allow for as much room as possible. During the day, the rectangular cabin had room for two reclining chairs, one fold-down dining table, a mini-refrigerator, and a small bathroom. The huge window made the room bright and allowed for excellent views of the world passing by. It was so romantic sitting at our table, sipping red wine purchased from the bar car, and watching an entire continent pass by our window. In the evening, after repasting in the dining car, we'd return to the cabin, stow the chairs and table away, and lower two bunk beds from the side panel of the train car. Abracadabra—instant bedroom.

Our agenda was as follows: the train departed Sydney, went up over the Blue Mountains, part of the Great Dividing Range, down the plains to Broken Hill, New South Wales, and then on to Adelaide, South Australia. From there, we headed west to Cook, South Australia, through the Nullarbor Plain Desert, and on to Kalgoolie, Western Australia. On the fourth day, we arrived back at Perth.

It was quite a sight watching Sydney disappear behind us as we climbed the Blue Mountains.

According to www.bluemts.com, "The Blue Mountains are a magical place any time of the year. Glowing in autumn, cool in winter, colourful in spring and refreshing in summer. The Blue Mountains are densely populated by oil bearing Eucalyptus trees. The atmosphere is filled with finely dispersed droplets of oil, which, in combination with dust particles and water vapour, scatter short-wave length rays of light which are predominantly blue in colour. The Greater Blue Mountains were inscribed on the World Heritage List in 2000." The views were fantastic, and the slow, grinding climb of the train into the clouds was ethereal. But it was quite different hours later, as the train came barreling down the western side of the range while we were trying to sleep. The twists and turns were reminiscent of a roller-coaster ride. I remember Andi bouncing all over the place on the top bunk and smashing into the side of the car. We switched bunks, since I weigh much more than she, but I still got pretty banged up through the night. It was fun …

Broken Hill was like visiting a lost world. It was an isolated mining town, located in the outback of New South Wales. BHP Billiton, the largest mining company in the world, once operated here. According to www. brokenhillaustralia.com, "Today, Broken Hill is a living, breathing time capsule: an artifact that survives in the desert and waits to be re-discovered. Art Deco shop fronts welcome customers straight out of a bygone age, and all over town are monuments to men and women who suffered and died so the town could survive." Needless to say, it was eerie walking the streets, viewing the old mining equipment and semi-urban infrastructure. The strange thing about Broken Hill was the abruptness of it. You can stand on the edge of town and view a sprawling array of buildings and homes designed to house over twenty thousand people. Turn in the opposite direction, and you'll see nothing but desert for hundreds of miles. It defies logic that people actually lived and thrived in an environment so geographically removed from the rest of the world.

When we pulled into the Adelaide Train Station, we knew we were definitely back in civilization. It's a beautiful city, nestled scenically on the Gulf of Saint Vincent and framed by the Yorke Peninsula to the west and the Mount Lofty Range to the east. Kangaroo Island lies about fifty miles south, and one ferry ride away. The worst part about stopping in Adelaide? We only had eight hours to enjoy it. We hustled downtown to Gouger Street, the center of activity in this culturally diverse city. The superwide avenues, well-designed for outside cafes and a multitude of restaurants, were a joy to stroll and to observe the sights. Adelaide is known as the wine capital of Australia. The excellent soil, coupled with cool summers and rainy winters, are the perfect formula for red wines. They are particularly famous for their Shiraz and richly flavored Cabernets. Andi and I wasted no time sampling the local wares. That afternoon, during an unbelievable dining experience on Gouger Street, we put away two bottles of the best Cabernet we had ever tasted. Talk about Hemingway Afternoons! As we floated back to the *Gandy Dancer,* we vowed to return some day. (I guess you could say it's still lingering on our bucket list.) As we pulled out of the station, the setting sun was hugging the mountaintops, creating a halo over the city. It was quite unusual ...

Cook, Western Australia, makes Broken Hill look like Manhattan. It's also a ghost town. In decades past, it served as a railway station and crossing loop for the Trans-Australian Railway from Port Augusta to the east and Kalgoorlie to the west. Named after the sixth prime minister, Joseph Cook, today it has a current population of four! According to Wikipedia, "Cook is the only stop on the Nullarbor Plain for the Indian Pacific passenger train [yes, that's us] across Australia and has little other than curiosity value for the passengers." When we passed through Cook in 2000, there were only two residents. I was possessed. I wanted to find the two people who actually lived in this deserted world. It was like a *Twilight Zone* episode. There were schools, hospitals, four-way intersections, row houses, shops, and so on, but not one soul! While most of the passengers stayed on the train (it was a million degrees in the desert that afternoon), Andi and I walked the abandoned streets until we finally saw something quite extraordinary—a small open shop, with a postcard rack fluttering in the desert breeze. I am not kidding—a postcard rack! We tentatively entered the store, expecting to see a Martian or maybe Elvis ...

"Hello. Is there anybody in there?" (Pink Floyd reference aside, I was on a roll.) "Is there anyone at home?" (I couldn't help myself.) No response. So we started walking around the room, wondering what type of alien could live like this. Then we heard someone rustling in the back room.

"Yes, may I help you?" a younger gentleman asked. He looked normal enough. "Hi, we're just a couple of people on the train out there, and we were hoping to meet the two residents who live here. What's it like? What do you do to pass the time? Are you the mayor or something?" I asked somewhat sarcastically.

"I don't live here," he replied, not very enthused about my attempt at humor. "My wife and I are just filling in while the real residents are vacationing in the United States." You can't make this stuff up. *Filling in doing what? Greeting the weekly train hoping to sell a postcard or some bottled water?* "She is having a baby, and they will be back in a few weeks."

"So, they are moving back with a brand-new baby?" I asked.

"Something like that."

"That's a 50-percent increase in population in one day. Will that cause any major urban problems here in Cook? How will that affect traffic patterns in the area?" I asked, determined to get this guy to lighten up.

"Can I get you anything?" *A real conversationalist.*

"What the hell. Two bottled waters ... and these postcards." We headed back to the train. I couldn't help thinking about the idea of a new baby living in Cook. How will he or she turn out? It would be a very interesting anthropology experiment, right? Will the child be comfortably numb? Or more like *Rosemary's Baby*?

Back in our cabin, we were now howling across the Nullarbor Desert on the longest stretch of straight railway in the world. It looked like the moon outside our window. But it was very peaceful and intoxicating. Then all of the sudden, I saw two plumes of dust way off on the horizon. They looked like water spray behind jet skis. The train began to decelerate, and the jet skis got closer. Finally, they came into view. Two huge Land Rovers, covered with extra tires and gas cans, stopped at a tiny rail post at the exact time the train came to a stop. A perfectly timed meeting point in the middle of a moonlike prairie. A lady jumped out of one of the vehicles, tossed two bags on the train, and then hopped aboard just as the *Gandy Dancer* began to pull forward. I was stunned. It was like something out of an *Indiana Jones* movie… Imagine, riding on a railway in the middle of the Western Australian Desert, which spans over 237,840 square miles, and having a car drop off a passenger.

Where did they come from? Obviously there were no roads. I asked around, but no one knew anything about our new female addition. (Out of curiosity, I walked from car to car trying to locate her. It felt a little like a Hitchcock scene.) Even more amazing—how were they able to time their arrival at the exact time the train stopped? Portable GPS systems and cell phones were still on the drawing board. Who was that gal? Amelia Earhart? Helen of Troy? Sister Mary Oswald with her "ozzie hold"? Dagney Taggart? I'll never forget that moment. From nothingness to roaring Land Rovers to nothingness again—all in a matter of a few seconds. Australia, you are so strange and wonderful. We were honored to travel across your fantastic continent. You are an original, my friend, plain and simple.

But we weren't home yet. Our last stop was the mining town of Kalgoorlie, Western Australia. According to Wikipedia, "The Super Pit is an open-cut gold mine approximately 3.6 kilometres (2.2 mi.) long, 1.6 kilometres (1.0 mi.) wide, and 512 metres (1680 ft.) deep. The mine blasts at 1:00pm each day, unless winds would carry dust over the town. Each of the massive trucks carries 225 tonnes of rock and the round trip takes about 35 minutes, most of that time being the slow uphill haul. The mine is expected to be productive until about 2017. At that point, it is planned to abandon it and allow the groundwater to seep in and fill it. It is estimated it will take about 50 years to fill completely." This area is part of the "Golden Mile"—a large grouping of gold mines considered to be the richest piece of real estate on earth.

Walking along Hay Street, we were surprised to see so many brothels. Especially since the town population was only about 28,000. So Andi and I went in one to check it out. The place was clean; it had a nice bar and restaurant menu, and the employees were very professional. They answered our questions and told us about the history of the brothels in Kalgoorlie. The miners came from all over the world to work in this relatively deserted area. They were wandering workers, and not exactly pillars of the earth. The brothels probably did more to reduce crime than local law enforcement did. In fact, one of the brothels on Hannan Street—the main artery in town— now serves as a museum to the world's oldest profession, and a major tourist attraction. Unlike the United States, prostitution is accepted here and is considered to be just another business.

As the *Gandy Dancer* lurched forward, I took one more glance back at Kalgoorlie. Again I marveled at the effort it must have taken to build towns like this in the middle of the desert. They're barely connected to the world by a thin water pipeline from Perth. In that rigorous environment, they were able to lay thousands of miles of train track designed to carry heavy loads from the goldfields, to the Kalgoorlie refineries, and then to the rest of the world. I wondered what will happen when the Super Pit dries up. Will the town survive? With the miners gone, can the brothels stay in business? Time will tell ...

Chugging west toward Perth, the scenery began to change. A tree or two here, a small stream there; then a few kangaroos frolicking in the sporadic grasses. We were leaving the desert. Slowly but steadily, life was returning. Browns were becoming greens. Water—sweet water—emerged. Even an occasional road appeared through our cabin window. There was civilization nearby, and we were enjoying the transformation. Suddenly, almost magically, we were rolling past real towns like Southern Cross, Merredin, and Northam. The lonely wonder of the desert was being replaced by lush, arable land. A small part of me will always remember the vastness of the Australian desert and the sheer volume of nothingness that surrounded us. The contrasts were amazing—from the modern city of Sydney, to the absolute opposite in Cook. From the beautiful streets of Adelaide, to the mind-numbing decay of Broken Hill. Taking it one railway meter at a time, Andi and I traveled over 4,452 kilometers. When we finally arrived at the Perth train station, it hit me. I would never do anything like this again.

Back at home in Freo, we settled into the idyllic lifestyle we enjoyed so much. A typical day for us would start at sunrise, sipping scalding hot coffee on the balcony, watching the sun rise over the Indian Ocean. Later in the morning, Andi and I would take long walks—at different times—encompassing the surrounding Fremantle area. Both of us treasure each other, but also treasure our alone time. Back in high school, I had a friend who once said to me, "Alone time is growing time." I think she was right, and I've never forgotten it. Walking alone allows your mind to operate without interruption, and to develop and nourish ideas that you may not even know you are contemplating. I think Richard Carlson says it best in his book *Don't Sweat the Small Stuff ... and It's All Small Stuff*, when he talks about your back burner. "The Back Burner of your mind works in the same way as the back burner of a stove. While on low heat, the cooking process mixes, blends, and simmers the ingredients into a tasty meal. ... In much the same way, we can solve many of life's problems—serious and otherwise—if we feed the back burner of our mind with a list of problems, facts, and variables, and possible solutions. Just as when we make soup or a sauce, the thoughts and ideas we feed the back burner of our mind must be left alone to simmer properly... It puts our quieter, softer, and sometimes most intelligent source of thinking to work for us on issues that we have no immediate answer for." In all honesty, much of this book was written using the back-burner approach, that is, tossing ideas around until they are just right, and then writing them down.

Our long walks were scenic as well as enlightening. Directly south of One High Street, there was an excellent walking path. It ran past the Round House, the Fremantle Marketplace, the Fishing Boat Harbour, and the green expanse of the Esplanade—a large park across from Challenger Harbour. Heading south, the walkway passed the Fremantle Yacht Club and eventually ambled down to South Beach. From there, you could continue along cliffs of trees and granite, and eventually end up at an abandoned mine. Other times, you could walk in the opposite direction, around the Fremantle Harbour and north past the Fremantle and Stirling Bridges. The walkways are wide and scenic as well.

The Fremantle Harbour was huge and very interesting. There were always cruise liners, military ships, container ships, and so on, loading and unloading everything from cars to sheep. Sadly, watching the sheep march up the cantilevered walkways and onto the ships always depressed me. These poor animals were headed to the Middle East and had to be sold alive. During the six-week journey, roughly 30 percent would die en route so some medieval slaughtering ritual could survive. And we're the ones with the brains…

After our very long walks—both of us now famished—Andi and I would hit the streets in the late afternoon ready to dine. After food and wine, along with people watching, we'd hook up with our friends, or just casually stroll back to the house for the sunset. I remember one such day, when we met Damien, Melissa, Noe, and Lisa at a place called the Left Bank, just past the Stirling Bridge. We talked, ate, laughed, and joked our way through seventeen bottles of wine! Australia is something else—we had seventeen empty bottles of wine on the table, and no one even noticed. Try that at a soccer-mom restaurant in the United States.

To this day, I don't think Andi and I were ever more relaxed than when we were living on High Street, in that eclectic village of Fremantle.

But there's nothing perfect in life. The American stock markets were heading south, and we agonized from afar as our lifetime savings went up in high-tech smoke. Our nest egg had decreased by 40 percent, and we were getting very nervous. Both of us agreed that it was time to plan our return to reality. Since we still had some time left on our lease, though, we put our problems on the back burner to simmer for a while and prepared for our next escapade.

My brothers, Larry and John, were coming to Australia …

After a few days in Sydney, they arrived at Perth International Airport. Two hours later, we were dining on Cappuccino Strip and planning our itinerary for the next several days. This visit would be the best time the three of us ever spent together.

We started with a train ride to the Perth rail station. They were amazed by the beauty of the city—from the views along the Black Swan River to the extraordinary mountaintop scenes at Kings Park. We dined at a place called Frasers while I tried my best to point out all the sights of the city below. We took a taxi to Northbridge for shopping and people watching, and then strolled southward past many of the city structures, including Perth Town Hall, London Court, and Supreme Court Gardens on Riverside Drive. From there, it was a short walk to the Barrack Street Jetty and a serene ferry cruise back to Freo.

I haven't mentioned this earlier, but Australia has some very crazy animals. You know about the kangaroos and dingoes, and the koalas and the emu. But there are tons of outré animals there. These include the platypus, the wombat, the quokka, the potoroo, the numbat, the woylie, and the chuditch, just to name a few. So we wanted to do something different than just visit the zoo. (However, we actually did go to the Perth Zoo—you can't miss seeing the koalas, kangaroos, wombats, and emus.) Andi and I took Larry and John to Rottnest Island for a day—the only place in the world to see the unusual quokkas. The Aborigines call the island *Wadjemup*, meaning place across the water. The Dutch explorers of the seventeenth century christened it *Rotte-nest*, meaning rat's nest, having mistaken the local marsupials (quokkas) for huge rats. The quokka is really a nocturnal animal, with a rounded body, gray-brown coat, short tail, and rounded ears. They were really cool little critters and very used to tourists. We fed a few and just watched them hopping around the island. During lunch on Rottnest, a giant peacock snuck up behind John and stole food right off his plate. It was very funny. I didn't know they were that quick.

A few days later, keeping with the animal theme, we headed to Penguin Island. According to *Your Guide to Perth and Fremantle*, "Penguin Island boasts spectacular coastal scenery and diverse wildlife. This is the largest colony of little penguins, also known as fairy penguins in Western Australia, containing an estimated 500 to 700 breeding pairs." Being the great outdoorsmen that we were, Larry and I decided to take kayaks over to the island. We had no idea what we were getting ourselves into. The current was very strong, and that short eight-hundred-meter trip practically wiped us out. While John and Andi were watching penguins do what they do, we were grinding sideways trying to avoid sidling past the entire island! Safely on dry land, we collapsed for a few minutes, celebrated our great conquest, and then went looking for the others. It was great fun watching all the penguins chattering with each other and swimming around in a large, indoor structure set up like a big cave. We got some great pictures, John and Andi took the ferry over to the mainland, while Larry and I rowed with the current easily back to terra firma.

On John and Larry's last night in Fremantle, we hooked up with our friends and had a great farewell dinner and party for my brothers at the Mexican Kitchen on Cappuccino Strip. Andi and I had a blast—our family was there, and our friends were there. We knew all of this had to end soon, so we cherished the evening and will always remember Larry and John's visit fondly. The next day, they were gone.

It was 2001, and we were winding down our Australian experience, beginning to prepare for the angst of returning to the United States. It was almost time to face the reality that we were 45-percent poorer than we had been twelve months earlier. Reluctantly, we had to cancel our eighteen-day cruise back to the United States on the *Oriana*, deciding that it was cheaper to get airline tickets. On the day of the cruise, Andi and I staked out on a big hill nearby and watched the *Oriana* sail right past us. It was disheartening to admit we couldn't afford it anymore. To me, that day signified the end of the innocence. It was time to put the toys away and return to the real world. We decided to look for a place to live, set up a short-term lease, and then plot our next reinvention.

The last two months were nice, but not great. We had one-way tickets home, and like writing on water, our time in Freo was disappearing as if it never happened. We continued to see friends, go to nearby beaches like Cottesloe (yes, the most dangerous shark beach in the world) and Coogee, and even take in an occasional Fremantle Dockers' Australian Rules football game. We took one more trip to Margaret River, hoping it wouldn't be the last time we ever saw it. But we knew it would be. It was time to go—we couldn't keep our thoughts about the future on the back burner any longer. The sauce had simmered long enough.

With one week remaining, we sold the Hyundai and cherished a few last-minute HAs on Cappuccino Strip, our favorite place in Fremantle, Australia.

And then, like yesterday's footprints in the sand, the Feeneys were gone.

CHAPTER EIGHTEEN

Wherever You Go, There You Are, Book Title by Jon Kabat-Zinn

———————◆○◆———————

I t was a chilly afternoon in Fremantle, Australia, and my final day on the continent. My buddy Damien drove me to Perth International Airport for the last time. It was 2001, and I'd just finished my first full year of retirement. We talked energetically about getting together again in the United States, or perhaps back in Freo in a year or so. But we knew it never would happen. The tragic tale of Gathering No Moss is that people come and go. It's unbearable to lose touch with friends whose friendship could have lasted a lifetime. There is absolutely no antidote for the feeling of emptiness and loss. Over my lifetime, I spent many hours remembering friends that I'll never see again, and spent just as many hours trying to forget them. It's a zero-sum game in the end. *(Perhaps that's one of the main reasons this book has been so hard to write.)* But like I said in the introduction, experiences (blob) can get out of hand at times, and even overwhelm us. So we constantly strive to make sense of our lives (steer) as we move through time. Why do we subject ourselves to this type of nomadic lifestyle? Who the hell knows? But I do know this—the human mind will never let you understand the human mind.

As we passed Victoria Park along the Canning Highway heading to the airport, my mind was already back in the States. We had taken a huge hit on the market, and I knew our life had to change. With half of our life savings up in smoke, there were some tough decisions coming our way. The next year would be one of the toughest of our lives.

Our departure from Australia was quite unusual. I left one day before Andi and traveled west over the Indian Ocean, and then onward to JFK in New York. The second leg—a nonstop flight from Johannesburg, South Africa, to New York City—lasted twenty-two hours! (Note: There was a short stop in Cape Verdi for petrol, but passengers were not allowed to disembark.) The flight had six movies, and about a hundred meals. From

New York, I headed to Pittsburgh to pick up a car that my brother-in-law Frank found for us at an auction. Andi, on the other hand, flew west over the Pacific Ocean to Hawaii, so she could visit her sister in Maui, who was getting married. After a short stay, she headed through Los Angeles down to Atlanta, Georgia. In essence, we departed from one point on the globe, that is, Fremantle, flew in opposite directions, but still ended up in the same place! Our flights were almost the exact same length. I guess mother ship earth isn't that big after all, huh?

In Pittsburgh, it was good to reunite with family. Mom was doing well considering her age, and Pat and John were keeping a close eye on her. My decision to give up on the doctoral program at the University of Notre Dame–Australia was already forgotten. It was summer in the "burg", so I hung out downtown, took in a couple of Pirates games, and waited for Andi to return from Hawaii.

But my mind was racing with doubt. Did I call it quits too early? Will we have enough money to survive retirement? Will Andi and I have to reenter the workforce? What happened to the markets? I was sure I had them figured out (TMYKTMYDKS). The next big thing, as they say, would be to find a place to live in the United States. Andi knew I always wanted to live on the ocean, so we decided to start there. I poured over maps of the East Coast, from South Carolina to Florida. For people who traveled as much as we did, finding the right place was difficult. There is no perfect place to live. It would be nice to cut and paste the best parts of all the places we had resided in, and then put them in one location. But that would be impossible. Every place had its strengths and weaknesses. The key was to maximize the strengths and minimize the weaknesses. On our list we included the following: affordable living on the beach, great weather year-round, proximity to a military base, no state income tax, and an international airport close by. In addition, find a location with good boating options.

The plan was to drive our new car to Atlanta, pick up Andi, and head to the East Coast to start our house-hunting adventure. When I met her at Hartsfield-Jackson Atlanta Airport, she was wiped out from the long trip. (Coincidently, her sister had called off her wedding.) After some much-needed rest at a hotel east of Atlanta, we set out the next day to find our home.

The next few weeks were a blur. In South Carolina, we looked at Myrtle Beach, Charleston, and Beaufort. But nothing seemed right. Either there were no places on the beach we could afford, or the places were too small, or they were too rural, or they were too far from military bases and airports. And we really didn't want to pay the state income tax if we could avoid it. In Georgia, we looked at Savannah and Brunswick. Although they were both very nice, we knew right away they were not real contenders. Truth be told— both of us felt that Florida was the best choice. But we wanted to survey our options before we headed to the Sunshine State.

Since Andi and I had both spent a lot of time in Florida, we felt more comfortable house hunting there. (Andi went to high school in Orlando.)

From Fernandina Beach on the north border of Florida to South Miami, we slowly but surely narrowed down the ideal location for our retirement home. It really was a game of elimination. Although Miami was full of life and had plenty of places to live (especially during this down-market period), we couldn't tolerate the traffic. The best thing about retirement is the ability to avoid those things you dislike the most. I hated traffic, and still do. On the other end of the state, we looked closely at Jacksonville. It had almost everything we liked. But beachside living was too expensive, and the traffic was also a problem. Many of the small towns south of Jacksonville were nice, but too far removed from urban living. Daytona Beach was definitely out— not our type of town. Vero Beach and Sebastian were too remote for us. So, by process of elimination, we decided to settle in the Space Coast region.

After we signed a six-month lease on a beachfront place in Cocoa Beach, we decided to give the real estate market a try. Our goal was to find an affordable beachside condo in one of the following towns: Cocoa Beach, South Patrick Shores, Satellite Beach, Indian Harbour Beach, or Indialantic.

After driving the realtor crazy for weeks, we finally found a great condo in Indialantic, barrier island just east of Melbourne. It was called Silver Palm, and we bought a southeast corner unit one floor below the penthouse, with a wraparound balcony and a location directly on the beach. The recession of 2000 to 2001 had one silver lining: it allowed us to buy a nicer condo than we could have otherwise. We were ecstatic. For the first time since I met Andi at Raffles in San Antonio in 1989, we had a real home. When our furniture arrived, we took our time decorating the apartment, knowing deep down that we might spend years, or even the rest of our lives, in this place. The first few months were fantastic. We worked out every day, walked the beaches, hit all the happy hours, read like crazy, and caught up on all the medical issues we'd been avoiding. We were in our mid-forties, but felt like teenagers again (similar to how it felt to live in Freo). We attended art fairs and museums, and I was even getting rid of my slice on the fairways. Our friends Joe and Janet visited from Virginia, and so did my sister Pat and her husband. Larry popped in a few times, and John came down twice—once with my mother. Everyone was congratulating us on such a nice place to live. But the other shoe, as they say, was about to drop ...

The markets continued to decline, and our worth was sinking fast. Although I had a pension from the air force, we were still in trouble. Our dream home was in jeopardy, and stress was back in my life. I felt like I had let my wife down. In fact, during one of John's visits, I lost it. I blew up for the first and only time of my life. My rant was guttural, and desperate. I had failed. I couldn't provide for my wife and myself. Like my dad, my personality is 99 percent pride and 1 percent everything else. And my pride was telling me I had failed. This mistake hit me right between the eyes. (It's funny how the back burner works. I can write this today, even though it's still very emotional. Back then, it wouldn't have been possible.) We had no choice. It was time to look for a job, and pray that we could support ourselves in the future.

Of all the reasons we chose Indialantic as our home, the one we didn't consider was the job market. It's located east of Melbourne, Florida, a midsized city with limited employment opportunities. While I was struggling to find a job, the embarrassment and loss of pride welled up inside of me. I was ready for anything. For instance, we asked Larry if we could use some of the jewelry from his company to sell in kiosks at area military base exchanges. He agreed. So Andi and I would set out to different locations and schlep jewelry in the foyers. It was humbling, and paid very little. I even tried placing gumball machines around the Space Coast, traveling daily to refill the globes and collect the change that I hoped would help with costs. It didn't. Quite simply, this was the low point of my adult life. At that time, I envisioned ending up right where I started—with nothing. Only this time, I was taking Andi down with me.

And then, with our fingernails gripping the edge of the cliff, we were tossed a rope. Andi found a job! She was hired as the human resources administrator for a company called Trademark Metals Re-cycling (TMR) in nearby Rockledge. The company collected discarded metals of all types, put them through a recycling process, and then resold them. It was a great company and paid well for the area. But even more importantly, TMR saved our condo in Silver Palm. Writing about this now, I can't help thinking about Colorado and how important it was for Andi to complete her college education. Without it, she wouldn't have found this job. We probably would have left the area, and by doing so, I wouldn't have known about the State Department. To this day, I believe that education is *never* wasted.

Job interviews weren't going well for me. I was either overqualified for entry-level jobs, or didn't have enough experience in career-specific positions. (I suspected a hint of ageism discrimination, but it's almost impossible to prove.) One day, while I was sitting nervously in a hallway waiting to interview for a manager position at a Catholic church, I had this conversation with another applicant:

"How long have you been looking for a job?" I asked.

"Almost a year," he said. *Yikes.* He told me about his background, and I did the same.

"I tried to retire, but the market is eating me up. In retrospect, maybe I should have stayed in the United States government." (I had never admitted this to myself or Andi until that moment.)

He said, "You know, with your DOD background, why don't you apply for a position with the Department of State (DOS)? The pay is very good, and you're already used to traveling. I have the website right here."

For the next several days, I tuned up my resumes (work and teaching), lined up references, and completed the exhaustive online application. I had to be pragmatic here. My options were slim in Florida, and I had to jump on any opportunity I could find. About a month later, I received an official letter inviting me to Washington, DC, for a formal interview. The process consisted of three parts. First, in front of a panel of diplomatic corps officers, I was asked a wide variety of questions from current events and travel, to management style and foreign employee issues. This was very draining and really centered on the "whole person concept." Since every candidate already had at least a master's degree, discussions of educational requirements were unnecessary. Second, all the applicants were placed in a large computer room and given a short paper to read about a complex subject. Then, each applicant had forty-five minutes to write a response in essay format. I enjoyed this part—I have learned to trust my writing skill (and I hope you do too!). Finally, all but three of us were ushered out of the room. We sat eerily in silence as the large crowd dwindled down to just us. Then the door opened, and several employees entered, clapping and flashing American flags. The lead panel member declared, "Congratulations, you have been selected for employment in the Department of State. Shortly, you will receive formal employment contracts in the mail. Barring any negative security information or major medical issues, you will become diplomats representing the greatest country on earth. Again, congratulations!"

Back in Florida, I was feeling great. Another reinvention of our lives was out there awaiting us. Becoming a diplomat? Can you believe it? In a few weeks, I would get the employment contract, and off we'd go.

But I waited. And waited. Months went by, and I still heard nothing from the Department of State. During this same time frame, I was offered a teaching job, albeit part-time, with Webster University on Merritt Island. I was happy for the opportunity. But I was also compelled to tell them the truth: that I was hoping to hear from the DOS soon about full-time employment. They couldn't have been more accommodative, and agreed to give me some time to get this right. But finally, the school administrator couldn't wait any longer. He needed an answer. So I promised them I would accept the position if I didn't hear from the DOS by the end of the week. Again, they were super-accommodating. (In fact, I'm teaching for them right now. I never forgot getting that first job offer when I needed it the most and how understanding they were about my situation. As we speak, the staff at Webster University remains excellent, and I'm happy to be a part of it.)

As you may expect, I spent the next few days trying to get my recruiter in Washington, DC, to release an employment contract. I explained my predicament with Webster, and pointed out that I had already been waiting several months. It started to feel hopeless, and I resigned myself to the fact that the State Department was not in my future. On Thursday of that fated week, just one day before I accepted the Webster University teaching position, a Department of State FedEx package arrived in the mail. I got the job. I would be a foreign service officer—a diplomat—in the Department of State. Again, this slow learner would be pulled along by people and events, barreling forward again in this exciting, but nomadic, lifestyle. I couldn't help thinking, *Here we go again! Good-bye to Silver Palm. And hello to our old friend, the siren, the "moss-free" lifestyle seducer.*

I guess it was around this point in my life when the germination of an idea to write a book was born. Somebody up there was going to bat for me again. I was reminded of a line from the song "Why Me, Lord?" by Kris Kristofferson, which says, "What have I ever done, to deserve even one, of the pleasures I've known?" Surely there was some meaning to all this madness. Maybe I'd write about it someday.

But I had one more hurdle to cross before accepting the offer—Andi. After all, she had a great job at TMR and really loved our oceanfront condo in Indialantic. In addition, like me, I assumed she was tired of all the travel. So I was pacing back and forth when she came home from work that afternoon.

"I'm home," Andi said as she burst through the door.

"Hi, Andi." Pause. "Uh, do you have a minute?" I asked.

"Yeah. What's up?" She sat down beside me.

"I heard from the State Department today. I got the job. All the details are in the FedEx package on the kitchen table." Her body language remained very still. "As you know, I promised you I would turn down the job if you don't want to leave Florida." Here it goes...

"Don, that's great. Let's do it. When do we leave?" I was speechless—a rare feat for me. Talk about one of the pleasures I've known ... My bride, my wife, and my friend was ready to give up her career *again* for mine. But I knew her mind was full of doubts, including: *Where are we going this time? Will I find employment? What about my current job? TMR was really depending on me. How will they take this?* With all these thoughts and more bouncing around in her head, this is what she said:

"You're the one who's tired of traveling, not me. If you're ready to go, I'm ready to go." So that was it. The Feeneys were hitching up the wagon again. These rolling stones were gathering no moss again. (I was trying to come up with *three* clichés but could only think of two that apply.)

Like all of our moves, there was much to do. I withdrew my application from Webster University, and of course, they were very understanding. We put our condo in Silver Palm up for sale. (Made a killing, by the way.) Andi informed TMR that she would be leaving in a few months and then stayed on to help with the transition. They loved her there and had various luncheons, gifts, and going-away events for her. Looking back, the one negative that came out of this move was robbing Andi of her chance to develop her skills with TMR. We just couldn't have it both ways.

I was offered a diplomatic position as a human resources management (HRM) officer. This career field fell under the Management "cone," as it is called in the DOS. There are four other cones: Consular, Economic/Commercial, Political, and Public Diplomacy. I was drawn to the Management cone for two reasons: my background was best suited for management, and this cone had the most opportunities to try different jobs. (As you'll see later, I definitely took advantage of this feature.)

The employment orders directed me to report to Washington, DC, and to attend the George P. Shultz National Foreign Affairs Training Center in Alexandria, Virginia. Most employees just call it the Foreign Service Institute, or FSI. According to the State Department website, "The Foreign Service Institute is the Federal Government's primary training institution for officers and support personnel of the U.S. foreign affairs community, preparing American diplomats and other professionals to advance U.S. foreign affairs interests overseas and in Washington… Ranging in length from one day to two years, courses are designed to promote successful performance in each professional assignment, to ease the adjustments to other countries and cultures, and to enhance the leadership and management capabilities of the U.S. foreign affairs community."

I was slated for a four-month training program covering a wide variety of subjects. The first segment, and the most dramatic, was the Foreign Service Orientation Program. This four-week course introduces you to the State Department, provides security and classified information to new students, and outlines policy directives and objectives of the federal government of the United States. More specifically, the orientation examines the State Department organizational structure, as well as the inner workings of a typical embassy overseas. Much of the course was also dedicated to logistical subjects, like travel, pay and benefits, living conditions, language requirements, family programs, and so on.

But there is *nothing* like the Flag Day ceremony, held at the end of the third week of orientation training. On this day—drumroll please—your assignment (country) is announced in front of ninety-two other students, and you are presented with a miniature flag of your new nation. Imagine how nerve-racking it was to sit there in the classroom wondering where you'd be for the next two years. It went something like this:

"Joe Blow, General Services Officer, Paris, France." Much shouting, especially by Mr. Blow, as he sprints to the stage to collect his flag.

Jane Doe, Financial Management Officers, Feetown, Sierra Leone." Silence. Ms. Doe walks ever so shakily to the podium to receive her flag. She is destined to live and work in one of the poorest countries on earth.

And so on… There were seven HRM officers in my orientation class. We all had an idea what the possible choices were, but none of us knew for sure where we were going. Seconds before my name was called, I looked down and noticed that my hand was bleeding. Without realizing it, I had dug my ngernails into my palm so hard that I drew blood. And then, just like that, it was over.

Donald Feeney, Human Resources Management Officer, San Salvador, El Salvador."

Okay, where the hell was El Salvador? I had transplanted Andi from a beautiful beach home in Florida just to drag her to fucking El Salvador? I accepted the flag and wandered past several students, who looked at yours truly with a "better you than me" expression. When class ended, I bolted over to the Overseas Information Center to find out what I could about the country. It's a small Central Amercian nation on the Pacific Ocean, surrounded by Guatemala, Honduras, and Nicaragua. The last decade had been unkind to El Salvador, with a civil war, a military coup, and three major earthquakes. Crime was very high, and poverty levels were disheartening. Welcome to the State Department…

I called Andi at the Washington Suites in Alexandria, Virginia, where we stayed while in training. As usual, she took it better than I did. Since she knew El Salvador was a possibility, she had already spent hours researching the country. She was determined to find positive reasons to go there. And she did. Listening to her, you'd think we were heading to Italy or Spain. Anyway, what was done was done. It was time to move forward.

Over the next few months, it was a whirlwind of training courses, including among many others: Overseas Security Seminar, Basic Administrative Management, American Human Resources Management, Foreign Service National Human Resource Management, Foreign Service National Position Classification, EEO/Diversity Training, several other HRM courses. I even took a Financial Certifying Officers Course designed to allow me to back up the financial management officer at my new post.

School went right through the Christmas holiday and into the new year of 2002. We traded in the Toyota Camry and bought a new Honda CRV. (Too bad we only drove it for twenty-seven miles before the DOS required us to ship it early to Central America.) Oh well, we still had a rental car. Andi did all the paperwork to move our household goods from Florida to San Salvador, El Salvador. The beach at Indialantic seemed a solar system away. Through this nebula, the blob was steering me, and I needed to figure out how to get control of my life again. My brash days of pride and confidence were behind me. I was forty-eight years old, and recent events of my life were still being controlled by others. Thank God for Andi—who, except for her first overseas excursion in 1990, handled the endless minutiae of moving and relocating better than I did.

On a freezing Washington, DC, morning in February 2002, my wife and I headed to Dulles International Airport for our flight to San Salvador. It was one of several times in our lives that we moved to a new country— *sight unseen*—to start over again. The moss, which had just started to grow, was displaced again by the rolling movements of the nomadic Feeneys.

On the plane, I let my mind wander to Richard Carlson's book *Don't Sweat the Small Stuff ... and It's All Small Stuff*. In one chapter, entitled "Understand the Statement, Wherever You Go, There You Are," his words helped me to get on with my life en route to El Salvador:

"Something wonderful begins to happen with the simple realization that life, like an automobile, is driven from the inside out, not the other way around. As you focus on becoming more peaceful with where you are, rather than focusing on where you would rather be, you begin to find peace right now, in the present. Then, as you move around, try new things, and meet new people, you carry that sense of inner peace with you. It's absolutely true that Wherever You Go, There You Are."

When the wheels touched the ground at Comalapa International Airport, we were both excited and nervous. There was no turning back now. Retirement was a thing of the past. We were hoping the words from Hank and Bea Weiss in their book *On Your Own In El Salvador* were true. They state: "Visits to the quiet colorful towns, volcanoes, cloud forests, and beaches still leave us in awe of the beauty of El Salvador's people and places.

El Rincon Magico (The Magic Corner), as the country is lovingly known by Salvadorans, is one of Latin America's best kept secrets."

As we taxied up to the Jetway—hearts pounding with nervous excitement— our fate rested just outside the passenger window.

PART IV

Diplomacy and Restartment

CHAPTER NINETEEN

The Dead Man of Illopango

———————◆○◆———————

Before I embark on telling of life and work in San Salvador, I'd like to take this opportunity to invent a new word—*restartment*. It can be a noun or a verb, an adjective or an adverb. It means "the next logical step after retirement for those who seek it." With the fifty-five to seventy-five age group demographic now the largest in the United States, it stands to reason that not all people will retire after retirement. America doesn't need that many couch potatoes. *Restartment* is the act of reinvention that can, and does, take place at any age. In fact, the decision to write this book is driven by the axiom of *restartment*. Show me one person who is perfectly happy doing nothing in retirement, and I'll show you ten who aren't. As I stated previously, the human mind will never let you understand the human mind. That may be so, but with *restartment*, you have to try anyway. Retirement is for baseball uniforms or stud horses, not for people. All of us crave *restartment*, even if we don't realize it. (Okay, I'm off the soapbox now.)

Many of you are probably asking, "What is the Foreign Service?" In the book *Inside a U. S. Embassy*, John Naland explains:

"The first responsibility of the federal government is to safeguard the security of the nation. The first line of defense in achieving that objective is our foreign service, which staffs America's embassies and consulates around the globe. U.S. Diplomats began with Benjamin Franklin, Thomas Jefferson, John Adams, and others who were dispatched abroad to promote our nation's vital interests." (Yeah, me and Thomas Jefferson, like two peas in a pod!) "Today that tradition continues. There are 259 embassies and consulates around the world, staffed by roughly 6,000 Foreign Service Diplomats. The Ambassadors report directly to the President, and are the highest ranking American in their respective countries."

But what is the mission of the staff that serves under the ambassador? Again, from John Naland:

"Diplomacy is an instrument of national power, essential for maintaining effective international relationships, and a principal means through which the U.S. defends its interests, responds to crises, and achieves its international goals. Foreign service members proudly promote and protect American interests by managing diplomatic relations with other countries and international institutions; promoting peace and stability in regions of vital interest; bringing nations together to address global challenges; opening markets abroad to create jobs at home; helping developing nations establish stable economic environments; helping ensure American business-people have a level playing field on which to compete for foreign investment and trade; screening out undesirable aliens who apply for visas to visit our nation; and assisting U.S. citizens who travel abroad." But it's not just hobnobbing with foreign ministries or enjoying the perks of diplomatic service. Mr. Naland continues:

"A Foreign Service career imposes significant demands. Typically, Foreign Service members spend two-thirds of their careers overseas, sometimes in unhealthy or isolated locations. They live for extended periods of time far from parents, siblings, and old friends, and sometimes without familiar amenities or access to modern medical facilities. Due to international terrorism, Foreign Service members face physical danger and are sometimes required to remain at their duty posts in harm's way while their families are evacuated to the United States." Ironically, due to a recent earthquake and civil unrest in El Salvador, I didn't have final approval for Andi to travel to post until the last minute. For weeks I thought I was going to my first mission without her.

As we gathered our baggage, it hit me like a ton of bricks. I was now part of the legacy of diplomatic service. I couldn't help thinking that I was in way over my head. Franklin? Jefferson? Now Feeney? Are we really tied by common diplomatic service to our nation? I guess some things just can't be explained.

Our sponsors, the Dunkleys, picked us up in a government vehicle and took us to our new home. The first impression was a bit scary, with fifteen-foot cement walls surrounding the house, along with a giant bulletproof metal driveway gate. Above the walls, barbed wire was strung everywhere, and it looked like a small prison from the outside. The house itself wasn't bad. It was small, but had three bedrooms and three baths. A waterfall trundled down next to the staircase in the living room. In the backyard, there was a huge fountain that stood over thirty feet high. But the best asset about this house was the location—it was directly across the street from the embassy! My commute was four minutes on foot from the front door to my office. (In comparison, it would take me over an hour to get to FSI from my hotel in Alexandria, Virginia, which was only about twelve miles away.) The vacant lot next door was seedy, with plenty of undesirables mulling around. But when our management counselor offered to move us for security reasons, we decided the location was too good to pass up, so we stayed where we were. (Note: Because of the sensitivity of diplomatic issues and in respect for those who depend on anonymity to function at embassies around the world, I will refrain from using real names when appropriate.)

After a good night's rest, we had Friday off and decided to go see our new digs. The Dunkleys gave us temporary ID cards, and we entered through the main gate from our house across the street. It was definitely an SSE to discover our first US embassy compound. And it was terrific. There were two huge, identical buildings that dominated the grounds. One was the Chancery (where the US embassy was located), and the other was the home of the US Agency for International Development (AID). According to their website, "USAID plays a critical role in our nation's effort to stabilize countries and build responsive local governance... We also ease the transition between conflict and long term development by investing in agriculture, health systems and democratic institutions." All these, and more, were current challenges for the Salvadoran people.

The rest of the compound was beautifully laid out, with soccer fields, a swimming pool, the ambassador's residence, a modern gym, and a walking/ running trail that circled the entire post. The social center of the compound was the Marine House, which hosted great Friday-afternoon happy hours. All embassies, and many consulates around the world, are staffed by marines. Their primary mission is to protect classified material and equipment vital to the national security of the United States. Their secondary mission was less structured—preparing marine birthday balls, having cookouts, working Fourth of July celebrations, hosting family events, and of course, providing legendary happy hours on Fridays. (Case in point—even though I would bolt to the Marine House at exactly 5:00 p.m. every Friday when I was in-country, I never beat the ambassador to the bar!) Andi and I spent our first afternoon in San Salvador at one of the happy hours. That single event helped us acclimate to our new lives. Everyone we met was so accommodating.

Wherever we've traveled in this zany life, we've learned one very important axiom: *First impressions are worth their weight in gold!* (Remember Comiso, Italy?)

El Salvador, meaning Republic of the Savior, is the smallest and most densely populated country in Central America. The country's capital is San Salvador. It's had a rough time over the last thirty years or so. The Salvadorans had to deal with the coup d' etat by the Revolutionary Government Junta of El Salvador that occurred around 1980. Unable to hold power, they fell to a second revolutionary entity—the BPR (*Bloque Popular Revolucionario*), which conducted death squads that killed ten innocent people each and every day. One of my employees saw the death squads firsthand. While driving to work one morning, two cars stopped abruptly right in front of her. Guerrillas jumped from the first car and shot everyone in the middle vehicle while she watched in horror. They turned their automated weapons on her, paused a second, then ran to their car and fled. Finally, in 1992, with the help of the United Nations, the government of El Salvador and the commanders of five distinct guerilla groups finally signed a peace agreement that ended the bloody twelve-year civil war.

But their troubles weren't over—it was Mother Nature's turn to step in. According to Wikipedia, "El Salvador lies along the Pacific Ring of

Fire, and is thus subject to significant tectonic activity, including frequent earthquakes and volcanic activity. The San Salvador area has been hit by earthquakes in 1576, 1659, 1798, 1839, 1854, 1873, 1880, 1917, 1919, 1965, 1986, 2001, and 2005." Just to cite one example of the damage to the population, again from Wikipedia: "The 5.7 earthquake of 1986 resulted in 1,500 deaths, 10,000 injuries, and 100,000 people left homeless." Throw in the droughts, floods, hurricanes, landslides, and famine caused by any or all of the above, and it feels like the Savior wasn't necessarily watching the republic.

The demographic development of the Salvadorian population is also very interesting. Over the centuries, the African descendant population remained very low, making it quite unique among the Central and South American regions. Unlike the countries around it, El Salvador didn't import many slaves during the colonial period. The long sea journey made transportation of slaves cost-prohibitive. In addition, the short, two-month indigo harvest season didn't provide enough incentives from a farming perspective. In essence, the country developed from European roots, with most of its African population a product of voluntary migration from neighboring countries. In essence, the melting pot of El Salvador was formed without many of the atrocities associated with slavery.

San Salvador's embassy (actually located in Santa Elena) was large, with a State Department population of 550 employees, consisting of US diplomats, Foreign Service nationals, American family member employees and their families, and US citizen residents. My office worked with fifteen different US government entities, from AID and the Drug Enforcement Agency (DEA), to the IRS and the Peace Corps. Our HRM staff consisted of eleven female Salvadorans who definitely spiced up the daily routine and were a pleasure to work with. (A happy hour with this group was a riot!) That said, my first few weeks on the job were not very good. I was disappointed to learn that I wouldn't be in charge of my own section. After all those years as a manager and leader, supervising hundreds of people, I was slated behind another, more-senior person (a regional human resources management officer), who had much less experience than I did. I felt like my skills were being wasted. Lucky for me, the management counselor picked up on my disappointment and called me into his office a month or so after I arrived.

"Don, I just got off the phone with the Western Hemisphere Affairs (WHA) Office in DC, and they are starting a new initiative. It's called the WHA Volunteer Temporary Duty (TDY) Program. I'd like to nominate you for this project. It will require a lot of TDY travel, but I think you can handle it. Look, I've spoken to your supervisor, and I know you are disappointed about being the number-two guy in the section. Here's your chance to make a name for yourself, while at the same time help other posts with challenging problems. What do you think?"

It was like manna from heaven. "I'm in. What do I need to do?"

"Call the office listed here on this cable, and throw yourself into the mix." I did exactly that. Over the next fourteen months, I went on eleven

TDYs directly related to the WHA TDY Program. Of the eighteen months I spent in El Salvador, I spent over 35 percent of my time on the road. It was exciting but tiring, informative but lonely. Since I had asked for this opportunity, I had to capitalize on it. Let the travel begin …

In Bogota, Colombia, I spent several weeks managing the largest HRM section in the entire State Department. The hours were long and the work was difficult, but I loved it. In the community, narco-terrorism and drug trafficking were the norm. The apartment I stayed in sat across the street from a vacant lot. It had been a grade school, but was blown up by terrorists, killing many children, including Americans. One month after I left Colombia, a local bar and restaurant where I had dinner with the financial management officer was also blown up. (It makes you wonder how effective Plan Columbia really turned out to be. It was established in 1989 to quell the drug trade and violence, and to protect the people of Columbia. The program has cost the United States billions of dollars. I'm not sure how history will judge it.)

With so much tension in the Bogota office, I managed to negotiate an early release of my staff one Friday to have a social function. We used a few vans from the motor pool and headed north to Chia for an early dinner. (Note: Traveling in any other direction by car was too dangerous, and prohibited by the regional security office.) In the van, I asked the senior HRM employee the following: When was the last time you did something like this? Her answer—never, in twenty-eight years! That was the hardest-working post I ever visited. During my stay, we worked every Saturday, without exception, in addition to elongated weekly schedules.

My trips to Managua, Nicaragua, were also difficult. The embassy guard force, usually contracted out, was made up of local Foreign Service nationals (FSNs). That places all responsibility for managing over one hundred guards directly under the regional security office, which was supported by the management section. This program was a fiasco. On a regular basis, guards were abandoning posts without warning, falling asleep on duty, and stealing ammunition. What a nightmare it was for the financial management officer, who was dual-hatted as the HRM officer. In addition, fraudulent hiring practices and nepotism were rampant. I did my best during those visits, but I'm not sure how effective I was in the long run. Because my TDY responsibilities involved so many Spanish-speaking countries, the WHA Bureau sent me and Andi to Spanish-language "immersion" training in Antigua, Guatemala. We stayed in an old monastery that was converted into an inn, and spoke nothing but Spanish eight hours a day for three weeks. It was hard work, but very effective. And since Guatemala was also part of San Salvador's regional responsibility, I traveled to Guatemala City on several occasions to take on the tougher HRM issues. I always stayed on the top floor of the Clarion Hotel in the town center (diplomatic privilege?). It was great, until the week a 7.2 Richter scale earthquake hit Guatemala City. Pictures fell from walls, my computer smashed to the floor, and furniture bounced around like something from *The Exorcist*. The worst feeling was the eerie swaying of the building, which was tall and round like a silo, and the creaking sounds that the infrastructure made. Quite hair-raising, to say the least.

In Tegucigalpa, Honduras, HRM problems were real. One of the issues was nepotism. Mothers and fathers, brothers and sisters, sons and daughters, and uncles and aunts were working all over the embassy. Relatives were hiring relatives, and this was unacceptable. The inmates were running the asylum, so to speak. It got so bad that the diplomatic security team in "Teguc" required all new employees to complete sworn affidavits listing all relatives currently working in the embassy. One of my jobs was to toss out the employees who had lied under oath and weed out new applicants who had relatives already working in the mission. Another problem, among many, was the violence against the local national consular workers. In Honduras, the turndown rate for visas was very high, mainly because the applicants were suspected of trying to enter the United States illegally. When these people got rejected, they sometimes waited outside for the consular workers who handled their cases. There were fights, injuries, damage to property, and life-threatening situations. Since Teguc had no secure parking for these employees at that time, they took great risks to do their jobs. Eventually, post had to use security escorts to walk employees to their cars.

One of the nicer TDY trips I had during my tenure in San Salvador was to Curacao in the Dutch Antilles. (Note: I would later be assigned there.) The Department of State had designed an updated, computer-based job classification system for all its FSNs. I spent two weeks classifying every job description on post. I used computer-weighted measurements to assess job responsibilities, knowledge, intellectual skills, communication, and working environment. Lucky for me, many of the positions were under-classified, resulting in pay and grade increases. This definitely helped when I returned as the management officer several years later.

During this period of constant travel, I was developing quite a reputation in WHA for handling a wide range of problems at several Central and South American locations. I was thrilled when I was asked to speak at the 2002 entry-level conference held in Guatemala City. I gave a presentation to over two hundred officers on the complexities of the management section, concentrating on current and future DOS issues. Nothing speaks to the problems of the region better than someone who was there, in-country, to witness them.

There were many other TDYs, but I'll concentrate on just one more. Working with the WHA TDY Program Office, I was selected to attend the Advanced Human Resources Management Workshop at FSI. This was significant, because I needed a grade waiver to be eligible to attend the workshop. Since I was still an FS-04 (the grade scale goes from FS-09 to FS-01, with FS-01 being the highest), I was considered too junior for this advanced seminar. But with WHA pulling strings in DC, I got in the course. There were guest speakers from around the world, discussion groups, management modeling exercises, Myers-Briggs personality tests, 360-degree evaluations, class presentations, panels answering questions, in-class discussion formats, and such that really helped me to understand the State Department mission.

Coming from the DOD, I was used to taking charge, accepting a challenge, and completely finishing a job without delay or assistance. However, while I was going about my business, I couldn't understand why other diplomats were procrastinating. I failed to realize that the State Department was a different kind of animal. Let's call it nonconfrontational. Many of the attributes of being a military officer fell on deaf ears in the State Department. I had to learn to slow down and to not always expect tasks to be completed. Some things just remained undone. I found that many diplomats were brilliant, but a little flaky. They would decide not to complete certain tasks and would provide no explanation for it. I surmised that since it was a political organization, many things happened for unknown reasons. My exuberance to get things done was interpreted as coming on too strong. I thank my career development officer in DC and my management counselor in El Salvador for easing me back into my lane.

As usual, Andi had no trouble finding work in the Chancery. She got hired as an assistant program manager with the Bureau of International Narcotics and Law Enforcement Affairs (INL). She was the INL primary point of contact for administrative issues affecting the Public Affairs, Regional Security, Financial Management, and Drug Enforcement Agency offices. She drafted monthly INL flash reports, news-related stories, and quarterly financial management reports. She would occasionally travel to Guatemala on business, but couldn't tell me anything about it. It was a challenging position, and I was glad she found such a great job utilizing post's family-member employment program.

Unfortunately, El Salvador fell way short on the things-to-do list. Most of the downtown area was off-limits, mainly because of high crime, trafficking in persons, and drug-related matters. Strangely, as we have learned in all of our travels—the more austere the location, the more you depend on coworkers for your social entertainment. This was definitely true in San Salvador. Like the Marine House happy hours, house parties and employee get-togethers were the main form of interaction. In addition, there were several good restaurants in the Santa Elena area that we all enjoyed. Put simply, we needed and depended on each other and circled the wagons to find things to do when not in the embassy. For example, the nearby Zona Rosa was a collection of open-air restaurants, chic clothing stores, cafes, and so on spread out over eight square blocks in Colonia San Benito. Our favorites were Tre Fratelli, an excellent outdoor Italian restaurant; Basilea, a beautiful spot on the second floor with a lush landscape overlooking Zona Rosa; La Pampa Argentina, near the embassy, which served the best steaks in Central America; and Tony Roma's, when a craving for American food was in order. The Sunday brunch at the Princess Hotel was also memorable. Because of the limited options in San Salvador, these restaurants became important parts of our off-duty enjoyment. (To be honest, up until this assignment, I had never really focused on the importance of restaurants in our social lives. We made every meal count—they were our temporary escape from diplomacy.)

Golf was another diversion. Although I hadn't played much in the last few years, I hooked up with a couple of fellow employees for regular rounds at the golf course in Illopango. The course was laid out along the contours of *Lago de Illopango* (Lake Illopango), which borders the provinces of San Salvador, La Paz, and Cuscatlan. It's a beautiful setup and is surrounded by mountains and active volcanoes. The lake itself, however, was nothing more than a large septic tank. The waste from the capital city funneled into the water for disposal. If you hit a ball in that water, you left it there. The course was basically located in the middle of nowhere, hidden behind unpaved rutted roads and tricky blind bends. I played there at least fifteen times and couldn't find it again if you paid me. It was a good course—long, with plenty of water holes. One day we were bouncing along the road, and I noticed a dead body lying in a nearby clearing! I was shocked, and instantly pointed this out to my two golfing buddies. They hardly even reacted. "Dave," a senior officer in the embassy and an expert on Central and South American cultures, said it best: "It happens all the time. Probably a drug-related or gang-related hit. They drive the bodies out here, leave them at a designated spot in a remote location, and then notify the authorities to come and pick them up. We've seen others in this area as well."

I was stunned by his response.

But then I began to think it over. For the police authorities, it worked. The gangs and drug traffickers were eliminating each other, keeping the killings out of the limelight, and even notifying them when and where to pick up the bodies. The hit men were left alone to carry out their crimes, were rarely physically connected to the scene, and were long gone before they divulged where the bodies were dropped. Quite simply, it was a strange symbiotic relationship. The authorities got rid of criminals, collected the bodies, and closed the cases quickly. The criminals were left alone to take out undesirables without risk to innocent citizens. I often think about the Dead Man of Illopango. Who was he? How did he get himself into this predicament? Even though he may have done bad things, was it fair to drop him off on the roadside like trash, waiting to be picked up? Or was it just another circle-of-life example, albeit a morbid one? One never knows, does one?

At times, we felt a little trapped in our mini-prison, and needed a getaway to reenergize. It was important for us to break out of El Salvador—and we did. The easiest place to travel to was Miami, which received the majority of Central American flights. (This was a big pain in the neck for me. For most of my regional trips in Latin America, I had to go through Miami first. So a one-hour flight to Honduras took me several hours. I was well-known at the Miami airport, especially at the Islander Bar and Grill.) So we headed to South Beach a few times—a great place to hang out, dine, and hear some high-octane music. The people watching was pretty good too. (But you'd better brush up on your Spanish.) Sometimes we'd head over to the Bayside Market Place on Biscayne Bay, do some tourist shopping, and have a cold one at one of the many establishments. Other times we'd just stroll down Miami Beach, take in the beauty of our home country, and reacquaint ourselves with the greatest nation on earth.

Another escape from Salvador involved a seven-day Caribbean cruise from Miami, going to San Juan, Curacao, Aruba, St. Thomas, and St. John. It was nice, but cruising was becoming very predictable. It was our fourth voyage, and we were losing interest in the concept. (Note: Our fifth cruise, from England to the Western Mediterranean, ended our cruising interest for life.) Maybe it's just me, but you can only eat so much on a ship. And if you do find a great port with lots to do, you only have five or six hours to enjoy it.

The constant lines, faux Broadway productions, tacky dining rooms, and the extra-small cabins get to you after a while.

One of the greatest things we ever did—easily on my all-time top-ten list—was transiting the Panama Canal. Since we didn't want to waste four or five days on a cruise ship just to see the canal, we tracked down a company called Ancon Expeditions, which did one-day full-transit tours monthly. So we headed to Panama City for a few days and spent one of the best twelve hours of our lives touring the wonders of the Panama Canal. We left Amador Causeway bright and early on a beautiful Panamanian morning. The boat was nothing special; it held about fifty people, and had food, a bar, and a sundeck I didn't leave for the entire trip. (Like the pale Irishman I am, I paid for that the next day.) Once at sea, the Bay of Panama was in full view, and nicely accented the Bridge of the Americas as we passed underneath. Soon we came upon our first set of Pacific-sector locks—the Miraflores Locks— which elevated the vessel so it could seamlessly enter Miraflores Lake. The lake is artificial and consists of collected freshwater, and it separates the Miraflores Locks from the upcoming Pedro Miguel Locks. The lake was created to reduce the water-level differences between the two. But as we entered the Pedro Miguel locks, we still had to rise almost thirty feet in order to move forward. As we exited, we traveled through the Gaillard Cut (also known as the Culebra Cut, because it resembles a snake). The Gaillard Cut is very interesting because it's carved right through the Continental Divide. There is a lot of history and geological marvels around this area of the canal. Maintaining the cut requires thousands of man-hours and continuous maintenance to avoid the potential of massive landslides.

In my opinion, the real jewel of the canal is Gatun Lake, which was formed by erecting the Gatun Dam across the Chagres River. It is the engine of the canal, because it uses gravity as its power source. Lake Gatun rests just above sea level, which allows downward water flow to operate all the canals from the Pacific to the Atlantic. Amazing, huh? The power of water… And the lake is huge, with beauty in all directions. I always thought the Panama Canal was, well, a canal. But it's much more. When you pass through Gatun Lake, you could be anywhere in the world. It's wide and beautiful, and meticulously maintained. (I'm getting pumped just writing about it.) Much of this area is historic, so it didn't surprise me to see a Smithsonian Research Station there, in a section called Barro Colorado.

Of course, what goes up must come down. The Gatun Locks, the only ones on the Atlantic sector, cascade down over eighty feet, using three distinct chambers. Soon afterward, with our boat now at sea level, we entered the Atlantic Ocean and finished our incredible voyage at Cristobal, Colon. We disembarked, and returned via bus to the Sheraton Four Points Hotel in Panama City. I'll never forget that day. Even though we enjoyed our stay in Panama City, it was the canal expedition that made the trip so special.

Back at home, Andi and I spent a lot of time in our Santa Elena mini-prison across the street from the embassy compound. We barbequed often, and planted tons of flowers and plants in the backyard. I hit about a million golf balls into a golf net, worked constantly on the inside waterfall trying unsuccessfully to stop it from leaking, and giggled with glee when San Salvador had one of its incredible downpours. I love the rain. I always have. I can just sit there and take it in. It "sends me," as the old song goes. The sound, the smell, the power, the rush of swift changing winds, and so on are addictive. (Maybe that's why I liked the Panama Canal so much.) I had never seen the power of monsoon rains before. It was breathtaking. I'd love to can it, put it in six-packs, and drink it every time I need a lift.

Singularly significant events (SSEs) can occur at the strangest times, for totally unexpected reasons. One afternoon while I was tinkering with the waterfall in the backyard, I noticed a small nest in one of the trees. It was perched at eye height, and the mother looked like a song sparrow. In the coming weeks, we watched each other very closely. She would fly in my face, cackling and causing a disturbance if I went anywhere near the nest. After the two nestlings were born, she became even more territorial and pecked me on the head a few times. Then one day, as I was inspecting her nursery, one of the nestlings was gone. At the same instant, I heard chirping on the ground. I assumed one of the chicks had fallen into the grass. Remembering my youth, I was careful not to touch the bird, because my scent would scare off the mother. (Is this true? I didn't know, but I wasn't going to risk it.) So I ran into the house, grabbed a large pan and a soup ladle, and returned ready to scoop up a baby bird. Of course, Mom was pissed. She kept buzzing me and pecking me on the head. You have to give her credit. I weigh 235 pounds; she weighs two ounces. And she's attacking me! After several attempts, I got the little tyke into the pan, and eventually put it back in the nest. And Momma was giving me holy hell the entire time. I left them alone and went back into the house.

The next morning as I approached the nest, I was glad to see both youngsters were doing well. And then the strangest thing happened. Mom sat there, even when I was very close to the nest, and just looked at me complacently. No squawking, buzzing, or chirping. Just the look... I came to the only conclusion I could. After I rescued her nestling, she had accepted my presence in her personal zone and no longer felt the need to protect her family from me. She had weighed the facts and come to a logical conclusion. I was stunned. It was an ethereal experience, a rare moment of understanding between man and animal. The days passed, and soon one, then the next young bird flew the coop. And then Mom was gone as well.

I thought it was over. But not yet. About a week later, as I was putting new flowers in the fountain, I looked up at the nest one more time, and she was perched on the branch above it. The matriarch had come to say good-bye. She looked right at me and then flew away for good. Even today, writing this story years after it happened, I still get goose bumps. I'll treasure this little SSE for life...

During our last several months in El Salvador, Larry and John came down to visit. Andi and I knew it would be a challenge finding things for them to do. It wasn't Australia, that's for sure. Larry brought some extra jewelry from his company with him to give to my staff. So I had all the Latino ladies from the office over to the house for food and drinks. It was a blast. We had a very good time, and all of the ladies enjoyed the jewelry. (I can't remember one day after that when the ladies weren't wearing Larry's jewelry. As I mentioned to him several times, it must feel good to get such positive feedback.)

We hit a couple of the local restaurants and headed to the coast to check out the sights. La Libertad (the Freedom) is the commercial and fishing town closest to San Salvador, and is a popular weekend getaway for Salvadorans. It's not a beautiful spot; La Libertad is full of rocky, unusable beaches, and insistent locals peddling a wide assortment of wares. (It kind of reminded me of Tijuana, Mexico.) But just thirteen kilometers west from the Freedom is the town of Playa Sunzal. It has a nice beach and has become a surfer's paradise. A variety of surfing movies were shot there. At the top of the cliff, there's a restaurant and bar called Café Sunzal. According to *On Your Own in El Salvador*, "Since Café Sunzal opened in January 2000 this is, without a doubt, one of the best restaurants around and has one of the best views in El Salvador. The décor, the surf and exquisite food all blend into a great romantic ambience." It was one of our favorite escapes from the overpopulated city. But it didn't impress Larry and John that much. (I guess we aimed low living in a place like El Salvador.) I think they were expecting more of a Caribbean resort, and were somewhat shocked by the unadorned coast of the Republic of the Savior.

Determined to find something my brothers would enjoy, I booked a weekend at Playa El Cuco, about 120 kilometers east from Santa Elena. Again according to *On Your Own in El Salvador*: "The road to El Cuco twists its way up and over the coastal mountain range, with a great view of the San Miguel Volcano on the right. The beach itself—once you get away from the little town at the end of the road—is another one of El Salvador's hidden coastal gems."

We stayed at a place called El Tropi-Club Cabanas, with a nice pool and restaurant. However, it wasn't near as nice as I had hoped. But we enjoyed each other's company, shared food and drink, hit the beach, and found the makeshift restaurant to be pretty good. After we returned to our house, we had one more night together. (That was good, because Andi and I were out of options.) The next morning, they were both glad to depart San Salvador.

Even though it wasn't a great vacation, we really appreciated them visiting us in Central America.

As our time in El Salvador wound down, I was eagerly expecting a new posting. The WHA TDY Program was a great success. My position in San Salvador had moved to Fort Lauderdale, where the WHA regional headquarters was located. It would be a permanent traveling billet covering several Central and South American posts. So I was free to leave Salvador early and was not surprised to get a call from my career development officer. Usually all entry-level officers got "directed assignments" for their first two postings. That means they don't negotiate or network with posts for their own assignments. Selections are made by the Entry Level Assignments Section in DC. But my case was different, since my billet was being transferred to Florida. I was free to leave early and had established quite a record in the bureau. So my CDO called me one afternoon and offered me a Regional HRM position in Bahrain. I was crushed. From Central America to the Middle East. Where were all the Madrids? Romes? Pragues? Sydneys? I came home dejected and broke the news to Andi. Over the course of the next few days, she did massive online research and convinced me that Manama would be a great fit. So I called my CDO back and accepted the assignment to Manama, Bahrain, nestled right in the middle of the Arabian Gulf.

Our short stay in San Salvador (eighteen months) was over. I must admit, the time went pretty fast. Since I spent so much time traveling in the region, the time spent in-country didn't seem that long. On the last day in our mini-prison, I distinctly remember feeling very lucky that we were in the Department of State. This great organization reached out to us when we needed it most. Our lives were back on track, the stock market was recovering nicely, the rearview mirror was discarded, and our future was full of opportunity. I was steering the blob. I will always be thankful for this second chance.

So long, *El Rincon Magico* (the Magic Corner). And keep an eye out for the Dead Men of Illopango.

CHAPTER TWENTY

Working in Manama and Playing in Egypt, Greece, India, Spain, Italy, Gibraltar, the Med, the United Arab Emirates and the Sultanate of Oman

———◦———

L et me start my saga into the Gulf state of Bahrain by thanking you again for staying with me through this journey. As I said earlier, writing this book was one of the hardest things I have ever done. No person can capture every thought and emotion associated with living in Manama, or anywhere else for that matter. (Try this experiment—write down everything you did last year. Difficult, isn't it?) It was a constant challenge to decide what to leave in and what to leave out, what I remembered and what I had already forgotten. How to decide what topics are more interesting to you? Did I spend too much time on lesser details, while skimming over the more interesting vignettes? In the end, I guess it's up to you to decide.

Like many Americans, I had the tendency to stereotype the Middle East prior to going to Bahrain. I think *The Lonely Planet: Bahrain, Kuwait, and Qatar*, a book authored by Gordon Robison and Paul Greenway, emphasizes this well:

"Many of the rather unfortunate images associated with it [meaning inferences from the Oil Sheikh] —gold-lined sinks, expensive cars abandoned in the desert at first sign of mechanical trouble, garishly painted statues at a Beverly Hills mansion—date from the '70s. Today's Gulf defies the stereotype and presents the visitor with a set of contradictions. It's both cosmopolitan and insular. It honours ancient traditions amid an overly modern, even plastic society. It professes deep-seated conservatism, while reaching for the products of the liberal, Western world. Its governments often talk as though they are part of the developing world, while their citizens enjoy some the highest living standards on earth."

We left Pittsburgh in August 2004, passed through Frankfurt, Germany, and then headed to Manama. It was a real perk to fly diplomatic business class for the first time in our lives—especially on Gulf Air. Bahrain, along

221

with most of the neighboring countries in the Gulf, has a genuine respect for US diplomats. We were always treated well. As I was lying flat in my seat-bed, zooming toward the Middle East, my mind ran all the way back to high school and the creative writing paper I had written for Mr. Bradley's class. If you recall, the story was about waking up one day and finding myself standing on the ceiling, instead of the floor. I went through a lot of gyrations trying to move about on the ceiling, but I couldn't change my fate. I ended the story by staying home, too afraid of falling upward. But this was not entirely true. In my dreams, which still arise on occasion, I do step out of the house, and I do jettison skyward. The terror is shocking, but fortunately, I wake up before I find out how it ends … (I liken it to the feeling of doom a fish must feel when it's scooped out of the ocean by an osprey. Think about it. One minute it's swimming around in the ocean; the next moment it's airborne 200 to 250 feet in the air! Talk about fright. The last two images it will ever see as it's asphyxiating in midair are the sky, and the earth below— two dimensions it never saw before.)

Why am I bringing this morbid stuff up? Because I was feeling the same sense of uneasiness entering the next phase of our lives. The lifestyles we had in Fremantle, Australia, and Indialantic, Florida, had been erased. The replacements? The "garden spots" of El Salvador and Bahrain. The contrast couldn't be ignored. As I sat up to flag down the flight attendant for yet another red wine, it hit me. Consciously, my high-school story ended by staying home (safely in the United States?). Unconsciously, in my later dreams, I stepped out, and shot upward like the fish in the talons of the osprey. Did I choose this life to prove I was not afraid to step out of that house? Or did I secretly wish I'd stayed in that room, with its comfortable surroundings and family nearby? As I finished my wine, I had to face it. There was no turning back. I just hoped our fate would be less terrorizing than the fate of the flying fish.

Our sponsors picked us up at Bahrain International Airport in Muharraq, and drove us to our new home in Hani Gardens, just off the Budaiya Highway, in Barbar, Bahrain. Barbar is a suburb in the northeast section of Bahrain, and near the Shaikh isa Bin Salman Highway, the causeway to Dhahran, Saudi Arabia, and points west. Although our house was kind of dark inside—with dull tile everywhere, and nondescript furniture sporadically placed here and there—it was still much better than El Salvador. The high walls and barbed wire were gone, and the backyard was big enough to barbeque and set up my trusty golf net. The biggest drawback was the long commute to the embassy. Even though we listed "close to the embassy" as our top priority in housing preferences, we found ourselves far from post. The housing committees at embassies are very powerful. Members are either elected from the general population (I served in this capacity in Athens) or appointed based on their particular US agency. Housing selections are decided, among other things, by the grade of the diplomat or US employee, school-age children, pets, allergies, and so on. Usually, the larger families got the bigger residences. Andi and

I were just two. So our appointed homes were sometimes, but not always, smaller than most of the others.

The shock factor upon our arrival in Manama was palpable. The harshness of the language; the floor-length shirtdresses called *thobes,* and the accompanying *gutras* (loose head scarves) worn by men; the traditional women's dress, which was little more than an enormous, all-covering black cloak; the outrageous contrasts between Bahraini citizens and the lower-class expatriate workers who catered to them; and the mosques with architectural *minarets* (towers), *mihrabs* (niches in the wall facing Mecca), *minbars* (pulpit chairs), and *kursi* (stands for the Quran) located on almost every block. The terrain of the island was flat and drab, and the elevation of Manama was an ear-popping two meters above sea level. And the heat, OMG, the heat!

The first night was very rough for each of us. We had no car, personal belongings, or TV. We sat quietly on strange furniture and wondered what the hell we were doing in the Middle East. It was dark and hot outside, and we had no idea where we were. We knew no one and were exhausted by the long trip. On top of everything else, I couldn't sleep. I broke into a cold sweat worrying about the next day—when I had to report to a new job, in a new embassy, in a new country *again.* This SSE came down on me pretty hard. I handled it worse than Andi and broke down and cried— something I've done maybe five times in my life. Without her beside me as we transitioned into the State Department, I never would have left that upside-down room. I would have stood on that ceiling forever.

As they say, this too shall pass... I sprang out of bed the next day and was raring to go when my ride showed up. (We were already moving through the stages of grief.) It's amazing what one day can do to your psyche. Andi and I had handled another low point together, and I was eager to get to know Manama.

Again from *The Lonely Planet: Bahrain, Kuwait, and Qatar,* Bahrain is "the only island-state in the Arab world. Bahrain is about the size of Singapore, but with a fraction of the population. Although comprising 33 islands, the country is often referred to simply as 'the island.' Bahrain is unique in several ways: Gulf Arabs and foreign expatriates mix more easily here than elsewhere in the region; it's the easiest of the Gulf countries to visit; and, although it is not cheap, it offers good value for those on a budget... In Arabic, bahrain means 'two seas.' Since the dawn of history Bahrain has been a trading center, and, until about a generation ago, virtually all trade came and went by sea. Occupying a strategic position on the great trade routes of antiquity, with good harbours and abundant fresh water, the Bahrainis are natural traders."

The strategic position of Bahrain in the Gulf—surrounded by a cast of characters that includes Saudi Arabia, Syria, Iraq, Kuwait, and Iran—was not lost on the United States. In one capacity or another, the US Navy has been in Bahrain since 1971. In 1992, the navy activities in the region were renamed the Administrative Support Unit Southwest Asia. From 1997 through 2003, propelled by the Gulf War with Iraq, the facility grew, and eventually became Naval Support Activity (NSA) Bahrain. Today, NSA Bahrain is the home to the US Naval Forces Central Command and the US Fifth Fleet. This NSA was a great perk for embassy employees. It contained a small but well-stocked commissary and NEX (Navy Exchange). Andi and I visited often, especially when our desire for American food and staples kicked in. Unfortunately for us, a new facility, known as the "Freedom *Souq*," opened just days before our tour ended. It had a huge NEX and commissary, along with a wide variety of popular American restaurants.

The country of Bahrain knew exactly what it was doing when it allowed the United States to station there. This is a tiny country, but possesses a big stick—military protection by the United States—as part of its regional stability.

My job in the embassy was twofold. While in-country, I was charged with the administration of all areas of Regional Human Resource Management (RHRM), and to provide timely, accurate, and professional counsel for the following: the ambassador and his or her immediate staff; American direct-hire employees; locally employed staff, including Foreign Service nationals; American service members; US citizen residents; and third-county nationals. (Third-country nationals are neither US nor Bahraini, but employees on contract or work visas from countries like India and Pakistan.) Talk about an eclectic group of customers! I thought managing Americans was tough. Try keeping Indians and Pakistanis from going at each other. Or try to arbitrate disagreements between Sunnis and a Shiite someday. There were levels of hatred and animosity in that embassy that definitely made it a complex workplace.

The second part of my job was regional. I was charged to provide regional supervisory oversight to US embassies in Oman, Qatar, and Yemen. When I met my supervisor for the first time—the management counselor—she added this comment to my job requirements:

"The RHRM position requires frequent travel in the Middle East, which can be difficult and dangerous. Regional opinion displays strong doubts about US policy regarding the Arab-Israeli dispute. In addition, the war in Iraq has created renewed negative sentiment in the entire region."

Yikes. It makes you want to book a ticket to Yemen for the holidays, right? But embassy life turned out to be pretty good. I had two very capable management counselor supervisors, the second of which turned out to be extraordinary. He didn't know it, but he would become a mentor of mine. I had a great HRM staff, who worked very hard to keep the blob moving in a steerable direction. Andi, of course, found a job quickly as the office manager for the Office of Military Cooperation (OMC). She did everything from maintaining office procedures and preparing recurring and nonrecurring reports, to coordinating meetings and conferences and tracking procurement and contract maintenance requirements. The OMC mission was to manage the security assistance programs between the United States and Bahrain. On the home front, things were looking up, and we were getting settled into a routine. Our household goods and car arrived, and we bought Andi a second car locally. Slowly but surely, Andi and I started to discover the interesting, but unusual, aspects of Bahrain. We started with the Manama *Souq*. It's a bazaar located right in the heart of the city. Vast in area, it has everything from traditional Middle East fare to modern shops. As hellobahrain.com states: "One can see and buy all kinds of spices, fabrics, kaftans, thobes, handicrafts, souvenirs, dry fruits, nuts, and any other thing one can imagine." The Gold *Souq* (18K and 21K gold items) was also very interesting, and so were the pearl shops. Bahraini pearls are all natural and represent some of the only non-cultured pearls left in the world.

Although most of the traders were Bahrainis, there were also many ex-pats, including Indians, Pakistanis, Bangladeshis, and Egyptians, as well as vendors for all the neighboring Gulf countries. It was a blast navigating through the crowded pathways and alleyways, realizing that you might not come out where you went in. Once in the *souq*, haggling was an art form. In my opinion, the vendors really enjoyed the give-and-take with customers, and would go through all kinds of gyrations intended to elicit the best price. But it was all in good fun, and most traders gladly offered a cup of *cha* (tea) and a comfortable seat to take the load off. (But if you are claustrophobic like me, be prepared. It gets pretty tight in those narrow passages. And there was also a ripe odor in the air, a combination exponentially created by hot weather and heavy clothes.)

Our next escapade was the long drive to see the Tree of Life. It's over four hundred years old and stands naked in a sea of desert, with no evidence of any water supply. Over fifty thousand people visit the site each year. It's a mesquite tree, near a town called Jebel Dukhan. There are stories placing the tree at the site of the Garden of Eden. Other tales document the history of the Tree of Life back to the Dilmun civilization (circa 2300 BC). Currently, the Tree of Life is ranked number four on the Official New Seven Wonders of Nature. It's not easy to find, and the stark barrenness of the immediate surroundings makes the tree stand out even more.

We also checked out a couple of forts and the Grand Mosque. Bahrain Fort, once the capital of Dilmun, has some of the richest remains of the period, and is a very important site for ancient civilizations in the Gulf. It's well maintained, with excellent stonework, and provides great views of Manama. Riffa Fort, built in 1812, was built during Persian rule, and was later converted into a royal residence for Shaikh Salman bin Ahmed, one of the Bahraini rulers. It's a good glimpse into royal life in the 1800s, with tons of architecture and wall carvings. Perhaps the best thing about Riffa Fort is the functioning Wind Tower. This tower was designed to catch the slightest breeze and then funnel air down into the house. We were very impressed with the functionality of the Wind Tower, which was very critical before the advent of air-conditioning. One of the must-see attractions in Bahrain is the Grand Mosque. The Al Fateh Islamic Center (Grand Mosque) has the world's largest fiberglass dome and can hold over seven thousand worshippers. Inside and out, the architecture is amazing, with great Arabic detail and imagination.

As I mentioned several times in this book, restaurants and bars are a big part of the nomadic experience. Finding favorite dining spots and popular watering holes definitely helps allay the feeling of isolation. Near our house was a place call Brenigan's—an ex-pat bar that provided an oasis for this Irish-American and his spouse. It was a great place to go after a hard day at the embassy. I spent many happy hours there with coworkers, trying in vain to solve all the world's problems. (The rarity of a place like this in the Middle East made it even more attractive to me.) It was fun to watch the Saudi men drop in for a quick cocktail before heading back home via the nearby causeway. Saudis are not allowed to drink, so they can't go to liquor stores. To get around this, they would buy a couple bottles of whiskey in Brenigan's, but had to pay the full shot price, or somewhere around six hundred dollars per bottle! Safely tucked away in their sports car, and sometimes accompanied by secret compartments to hide pork (another no-no for the Saudis), they would race away. In my opinion, I found the Saudis arrogant and hypocritical. The men would leave their women at home, unable to drive, work, or even be seen in public without them. They, of course, would head to Bahrain to party, that is, drinking and hitting the brothels. Finally on the way home, they would smuggle goodies hidden in their cars. I never understood those people.

Although the options were pretty limited, we did find a few really good restaurants. Our favorite was a place called Zoe's, in Adilya, near the diplomatic area. It had a Mediterranean and Italian menu, and was set uplike a New York loft-style restaurant. They knew us well there, and even asked patrons to move tables on occasion so we could have our favorite spot. Over at the Ritz-Carlton was another great hangout—Trader Vic's. It was located on Manama Bay, just outside the city center. The menu was a little pricey, but the appetizers were legendary. We loved watching the boats, or *dhows* pass by, or catching the tourists walking along the water and even feeding the fish in the large koi pond. On special occasions, we'd go with friends to the Bambu Restaurant, an Oriental establishment located in Adliya, just down the road from Zoe's. You'd pay one price, and they would bring an endless flow of well-presented samplers until you couldn't eat another bite. It was fun—but watch out for the heartburn afterward.

Ever since we lost Kismet while living at Willoughby Spit, Andi had been hoping to get another cat. So she did some checking around and found a shelter associated with the Society for the Prevention of Cruelty of Animals (SPCA). One day we both went to the shelter, and Andi fell in love with an abandoned brownish -gray-and-white tabby. We adopted her, made sure she had all her shots, and scheduled her for spaying. We decided to name her Kismet as well. (Actually, she is officially known as K II.) While I was gone to Yemen on business, Andi picked up our new addition, increasing our family size by 50 percent. Today, K II is still with us in Florida, fat and happy, living like a queen. She's more rooster than cat, and wakes us up every morning before the sun rises; she'll only eat tuna—don't even try to sneak anything else into her dish. And this cat has a foot fetish as well. Every time I try to put on my shoes, she darts at me expecting to get her pets. I spend many mornings sneaking around and playing hide-and-seek, hoping to lace my shoes in peace.

Back at the embassy, I was up to my ears in complex program management issues. Just a few of the initiatives (I don't want to bore you to death):

- Interpreting the constant changes to Bahraini immigration law. This had a huge effect on residency requirements for expatriate family members, complex restrictions on visiting visas for Americans, and legal interpretations of Non-Objection Certificates for exceptions to policy.
- Serving as the management officer for Bahrain's first-ever International Institute of Strategic Studies "Gulf Dialogue," I had to integrate several visits simultaneously, including the US national security advisor, three US senators, the CENTCON four-star general, various other admirals and generals, a dozen former ambassadors, and a host of US House members. The logistics were complex, and every decision had far-ranging effects. (I also handled two secretary of state visits—work intensive and not very fun.)
- Development of a Foreign Service National Retirement Contribution Plan for embassy employees. Since 50 percent of the embassy staff were third-country nationals (TCNs), they had no retirement plan. It took over twelve months to build a case for this program, including comparator studies, Separation Liability Trust Fund computations, cost databases, and so on. When Main State finally approved the plan, post had an immediate 100-percent enrollment of its TCNs.
- Regional long-range objectives for Doha (Qatar), Muscat (Oman), and Sana'a (Yemen). The majority of my visits were spent developing a workforce hierarchy based upon computer-based job measurements, improving the recruitment models in each totally different country, and dealing with job-performance issues. I expanded the region's ability to develop benefit surveys and comparator analysis, integrated a Department of Commerce Agency into the Department of State, and developed in-house training seminars for Foreign Service nationals in performance reporting, time and stress management, and effective performance management/feedback.

Perhaps my biggest contribution to embassy life remains forgotten today. Shortly after my arrival in Manama, I was confronted with a systematic morale and communication breakdown that started at the deputy chief of mission (DCM) level. Our DCM, a brilliant diplomat, for one reason or another was losing control of the embassy staff. The DCM is the number-two person behind the ambassador, and is the chief operating officer of the embassy. (I was even contacted by a principal deputy assistant secretary from Washington, DC, who had heard rumors about our predicament.) In no time, I was up to my ears in complaints about her. I had a plan, but needed the ambassador's permission. So here I am, a new Foreign Service diplomat, untenured, asking the ambassador to stand down and allow me to evaluate his handpicked DCM. (This was a big risk—and I wouldn't have been upset if he had thrown me out of the office.) I convinced him that his involvement would skew the results. He acquiesced, so I went to work.

I met with the DCM one-on-one for almost two hours, heard her side of the issues in question, and then tried to fairly address the concerns of the various sections heads—Political, Economic, Management, Regional Security, Consular, and so on who were unhappy with her leadership style. She was hurt, even embarrassed—and wept at times. But I convinced her to agree to an open session with all concerned. I promised to keep it on point and assured her that the ambassador was onboard. The meeting was brutal. As we went around the room, small complaints grew bigger, and they really let her have it. They questioned everything from how she managed people to her ability to lead. But she surprised them all. The DCM stoically took it all in—much of the criticism lacked maturity, if you ask me—and vowed to work on their concerns. And she did.

Over the next few months, I conducted a series of group and individual facilitations. What I discovered was a pattern of communication problems that were debilitating, but repairable. Using formal and informal feedback sessions, I began to see and hear improvements in morale and effectiveness. In the end, I was very proud of how the Manama team pulled together.

(Postscript: That DCM is now an ambassador, and truly deserves it. I was then—just as I am now —very impressed by how she handled this situation. She developed into a great listener, and even more importantly, she became an even better leader. Much of the criticism that was meant to hurt her made her stronger. For the rest of my time in Manama, we never spoke about it again. Tacitly, we understood there was nothing more to say, and we were both happy about that. I've wondered many times if she even thinks about those difficult times. Maybe someday I'll find out if she reads this.)

A few months later, I was selected to attend a conference in New Delhi, India. It was great to get out of Manama for a while. When the five of us foreign service officers arrived at Indira Gandhi International Airport, the shock of overpopulation hit us like a tsunami. We gathered our bags and left the controlled area. Just outside, the masses of people in both directions were suffocating. Add that to an eight-hour flight in a cramped plane, and you know this "claustro" was sweating bullets. Thank goodness, we spotted a gentleman with a "US Embassy" sign and were able to forge our way through the crowds to a waiting van. It took forever to creep through the massive traffic, but we eventually arrived at our hotel in central New Delhi. After I got settled into my room, my plans involved room service and a bottle of red wine. When I was told that liquor was not served, I was given directions to a nearby bottle shop.

It looked innocent enough—just a few dozen people milling around outside. So I went inside, grabbed a bottle of red, and headed to the counter. In a matter of seconds, the store filled to capacity, and Indians were pushing to get to the front. I was literally crushed against the wall, with people shoving me into a smaller and smaller space. I was really sweating, and verging on the brink of violence. I never felt that paranoid before. I'm a pretty big guy, and it was time to act. Leaving the wine behind (poor choice, I know—but I was freaking out), I lowered my shoulders and tore through a mass of humanity until I was in the fresh air. I walked swiftly back to the hotel, and forgot about wine. I needed solitude—period. I don't think I would have let Marilyn Monroe in my room that night. Okay, maybe ...

The conference was located in the same hotel and was tailored to entry-level officers (I was on my second posting at the time), and it was great. There were many guest speakers; we broke up into leadership and management teams to solve problems, and discussed post-specific lessons learned and concerns. I enjoyed it a lot. Like most conferences I've attended over my lifetime, it's always the interaction with peers that's the most useful learning outcome. Many of the problems you think are unique to your post are shared by others. This common-core experience helps bring things into focus.

India is fascinating and scary at the same time. New Delhi has a population density of 15,164 people per square mile! The current population of India is over 1.2 billion, which is already more than one-sixth of the world population, and it is projected to reach 1.6 billion by 2050. They will pass China in total population by 2025. Think about it—Indians populate countries everywhere, and in unknown amounts. For example, there are more Indians in Bahrain than Bahrainis. It's not unreasonable to assume that the worldwide Indian population dwarfs its nearest rival. It could currently be as high as 26 to 28 percent of the entire planet! It's fascinating to me that the biggest demographic shift in world history is happening and it goes largely unnoticed. Also consider the Indian lifestyle outside of India... They remain insular to change, marry almost entirely within their own nationality, are usually not interested in learning the language or culture of their country of residence, and live very austerely so they can send the majority of their earnings home instead of investing in local economies. Although countries like China and the United States are at or near zero population growth, India is exploding with humanity. Over 50 percent of India's population is under the age of twenty-five—prime childbearing years. What does this mean? Who knows, but its enormity blows me away. What will the effects be on world population? Food supply? The balance of military and political power? Natural resources? The environment as a whole?

On the third night of the conference, I was itching to try my luck again on the streets of New Delhi. Although we had a few group outings, I wanted to venture off on my own. After failing to rustle up an accomplice, I took off on a solo mission. The concierge told me about a restaurant with international flair (can't remember the name), so he called me a cab, and off I went. At every stoplight, indigent people were groping at the windows and begging for food or money. Some held very sickly looking children, and they really got to you. But my cabbie insisted that I ignore them, and said most of the beggars were not even Indians (I didn't believe that). When I arrived at the restaurant, I chose a table outside—as far away from crowds as possible. Just as I was about to start my meal, a cow walked by me and took a shit right on the terrace floor! I swear he was laughing at me when he did it. He had that "I can do anything I want here—I'm sacred" look about him. As you may know, cows roam freely anywhere they want in India. They are considered holy and untouchable to the Indians. Am I the only one who sees the irony of this situation? On one corner you have people begging for food; on the next corner you see a six-hundred-pound cow lazily relieving itself or napping in the middle of a busy intersection. Obviously, the restaurant meal was less than stellar. Maybe if they would have cleaned up the mess before I ate, it might have been better. (Believe it or not, there are dozens of Indian websites that track cow movements around the clock.)

Anyway, I left a McDonald's Big Mac coupon as a tip (just kidding). When the conference ended, many of the participants left India. I stayed behind with about thirty others to take a trip to the Taj Mahal in Agra, India. After we left town, we headed south on our ninety-minute bus ride. Between claustrophobia in the bottle shop and the cow shit, I was expecting something strange to happen. And it did. Somewhere near a town called Palwal, in the middle of the countryside, traffic came to a screaming halt. Drivers began to beep horns and scream at each other. It was like two hundred degrees, and most vehicles were open-air. Filled with road rage, drivers started pouring over the median from both directions and bearing down on oncoming traffic. It didn't take Einstein to figure out what happened next. The wrong-way drivers met up with oncoming traffic. Four lanes and four rows of traffic each facing one other. It was awful. It took over four hours for the police to oversee the backing up of five miles of cars, one at a time, so the vehicles could finally proceed on the proper side of the highway. During this time, we were greeted by hucksters displaying bored monkeys performing tricks, and horn blowers rousing very tired and unhealthy cobras from their frayed wicker baskets. PETA would have been appalled. Finally, six hours later, we arrived in Agra.

Borrowing from my trusty Wikipedia source:

"The Taj Mahal is a white marble mausoleum located in Agra, Uttar Pradish, India. It was built by Mughalemperor Shah Jahan in memory of his third wife, Mumtaz Mahal." (What happened to the first and second wives?) "The Taj Mahal is widely recognized as 'the jewel of Muslim art in India and one of the universally admired masterpieces of the world's heritage.' The Taj Mahal is regarded by many as the finest example of Mughal architecture, a style that combines elements from Persian and Indian architectural styles. In 1983, the Taj Mahal became a UNESCO World Heritage Site. While the white domed marble mausoleum is the most familiar component of the Taj Mahal, it is actually an integrated complex of structures."

The Taj Mahal sits by the River Yamuna, and provides a striking silhouette from all directions. It took over twenty-two years to complete, and at its core is a huge rotunda. In the center of the white marble mausoleum lie the remains of Mumtaz Mahal and Shah Jahan. It's a huge expanse, with a circular walkway around the tombs, making them appear to be very small. The ornate craftsmanship on the tombs, and everywhere else for that matter, highlighted the extraordinary feel of the place. After lining up outside, and paying a servant for some booties to wear over your shoes (no soles of shoes allowed), you enter the mausoleum. At your own pace, you take the circular route around the resting places, then back out again. That's it. The rest of the time is spent wandering around the grounds, taking pictures, and visiting some of the other structures. Before leaving Uttar Pradesh, I bought a beautifully adorned vase made from the same marble pit as the Taj Mahal. The vase was cut from a single piece of marble—and not glued together like so many others. The best way to check this is to hold the opening of the vase under a lightbulb. If it's been sectioned together, you'll see it immediately.

The bus ride back to New Delhi was uneventful. Later that evening, we all met one more time in the lounge, then hit the sack. The next morning at the crack of dawn, we arrived at Indira Gandhi International Airport. With the long flight back to Manama ruining my breakfast, I decided to implement one of my tactics to get an upgrade. I purposely boarded last, well after my compadres, betting that the airline overbooked. They did. I then pulled my diplomatic passport and gave them a bunch of BS about all this important stuff I needed to get done in Manama. Delaying my flight was unthinkable. They huddled together, discussed my predicament, and decided to give me a first-class ticket to Manama. I was chuckling when I looked back at my colleagues *shoehorned* into their economy seats. I had guaranteed them that I would get a first-class ticket—and I did.

Back in Manama, it was time for some regional travel in the Gulf, one of the requirements of my position. Traversing to Doha (Qatar) and Muscat (Oman) were relatively painless visits. They were both pro-American countries, and the embassy staff integrated well into the society.

And then there was Sana'a ...

Yemen was, and is, one of the most volatile countries on earth. As they say, it may not be the asshole of the universe, but you can see it from there. I remember my first visit to Sana'a, in 2004, very well. The roads were disastrous, with large craters everywhere, traffic lights were sporadic, and building debris remained untouched from the civil war waged over a decade earlier. The country was very dangerous; I realized this quickly when I arrived at my hotel. As it turns out, the danger for Americans in country was so great that our State Department Regional Security Office commandeered the building. I was told that there was no other way to bring official travelers into Yemen safely. (Ironically, as I write this passage, Americans were recently evacuated from the embassy due to viable terrorist threats.)

The next morning, I was picked up by an armored car—complete with armed guards—for my commute to the embassy. The tension at the post was real. These US patriots worked very hard, and were reminded daily about local attacks, threats, roadblocks, crime, and so on. I did my best to assist where I could, but it was obvious that the issues in Yemen were much too complicated to be addressed during short visits. For example, with strong US support, the Yemeni government had agreed to build a new, safer hotel near the embassy. But even this was becoming problematic. Every time building materials arrived for construction, they were stolen. So the government hired a large security force to provide 24-7 protection against theft. So what happened? The guards stole all the materials! When I left after my last visit, the hotel was unfinished—a shell of steel without the mortar and glass needed to complete it.

(Yemen, sadly, is no longer a nation-state. It's a puddle of nondescript terrorist factions, with separate and violent agendas ranging from murder to piracy. All through the 2000s, the country has been rife with uprisings and rebel groups. The Arab Spring of 2012 exacerbated the problem. Today Yemen is in a full-scale uprising. Insurgencies and tribal struggles are pitting armed opposition and terrorist groups against the government, and more worrisome, against the Yemeni people themselves. God help them ...)

On a different tack, I'd like to speak positively about the westernization of many of the Middle Eastern countries. Our US media loves to scare us with horrible stories about the Arab world. Recently, someone said this to me about the press—"If it bleeds, it reads." But American notions about the Middle East are not always accurate. Countries like the United Arab Emirates, Qatar, Bahrain, Oman, and even Kuwait have taken measurable steps toward limited democracy and improved US relations. (I admit that the Arab Spring may have detoured some of the progress.) These countries are embracing many of the practices of trade and business that our allies depend upon. Much of this change has happened in the last twenty-five years—that's the speed of sound for Western development anywhere, especially in the Middle East. Become informed; separate the media from the facts. Yes, you have Syria, Iran, Yemen, and to some extent Egypt doing their destructive best to harm US interests. But I urge you not to clump all the regional governments into one pot. It will take a long time for light to come through the darkness of the Middle East. But it definitely has begun ...

In all honesty, Bahrain wasn't my favorite stop along the changing pathways of my life. Yes, I found restaurants and ex-pat bars (like a true Irishman), and even hunted down limited tourist attractions. And the Riffa Golf Course— although very expensive—was one of the best courses I ever played. But our daily lives in Manama became very mundane. Lucky for us, the United Arab Emirates (UAE) was nearby. Two of our favorite getaway cities were Abu Dhabi and Dubai.

Abu Dhabi is the capital of the UAE and has one of the most perfectly laid-out downtown areas in the world. We always stayed at the Hilton, with the beachfront Hiltonia across the street. It was a Western escape in the Middle East—with bars, music, sand and beach, Western bathing suits, and so on. From there, we would walk the corniche—kind of like a cement boardwalk—along the beach and take in the beauty of the city. The corniche has been awarded coveted Blue Flag status—the internationally renowned eco-label for beaches and marinas that guarantee clean and safe bathing water. Take a short walk to the central business district, and you'll find over 130 of the world's most renowned stores. While in town, the hardest part of our carefree stroll was deciding where to eat. Restaurants and cafes were everywhere. At night, we'd take in a sunset cruise, which highlighted the beauty of the city even more under starlight. When our short stays ended, we'd come back home refreshed.

Dubai was a completely different animal. It's a Las Vegas–type city, with anything and everything. During one visit, we had a cabbie tell us that over 10 percent of all the world's cranes were in Dubai! This city has it all: the tallest building in the world (Burj Khalifa, towering 2,722 feet), together with twenty-two other skyscrapers; twenty-three shopping malls, one with an indoor ski slope; the largest marina in the world; the only seven-star hotel on earth (Burj al Arab); nine *souks*, with everything from gold to camels; and ten man-made islands rising from the sea. The really cool thing about Dubai is that it's divided—the older section, with all its traditional charms, and the newer section, which can feel like you're in New York City. We'd spend one afternoon riding a traditional dhow in the Old Town, with the Dubai Creek full of watercraft activity. Then we'd spend the next day in New Town, marveling at the size and scope of all the sparkling man-made islands. If anyone questions the Western slant of the Middle East, send them to Dubai. This place could just as easily be in Texas.

Andi and I also went to Muscat, Oman, for a few days. I don't remember a lot about it, but we enjoyed long walks along the corniche, hit several of the little shops, visited a mosque or two, and actually found a four-star hotel with a bar! The Omanis were very pleasant and pro-American. The trip was designed to decompress, and it did.

Now that I think about it, Bahrain brought lots of extra travel opportunities to Andi and me. Aside from UAE and Oman, we did take two longer vacations—one unforgettable week in Cyprus, and a twelve-day Western Med cruise out of South Hampton, United Kingdom.

My senior FSN, Selia, had a house in Limassol, Cyprus. At the time, it was empty, and she suggested that we vacation there. We'd stay rent-free, and she would have someone to check out the place and make sure everything was okay. So we headed to Cyprus. Limassol is the capital of the Greek side of Cyprus. (Several years ago, while Andi and I were in Izmir, we also visited the Turkish side of Cyprus.) The city is located in the south-central part of the island and is a perfect spot for exploring east and west. It's the second-largest city and is home to the main port of the country. Limassol is also a huge tourism and wine center. Outside cafes are everywhere along the main streets, and the food and people watching are great. But be prepared—the hucksters outside the restaurants can be pretty pushy. On our third day there, Andi and I headed to Larnaca, which is located on the Mediterranean Sea east of Limassol. We strolled around the souvenir shops, marveled at the panoramic seafront view, and visited Larnaca Castle, among other sites. But it was a gloomy day and the rain wouldn't quit, so we were shuffling around with no clear purpose.

And then it all changed. I saw a sign outside a small tourism shop offering two-night, three-day trips to the pyramids! I entered the store, and the conversation went something like this:

"Excuse me, I noticed your sign outside. How do the pyramids trips work?" "Twice a month, we offer short cruises to Port Said for those who want to see the pyramids, but don't want to spend a lot of time in Egypt." This was a great idea. Egypt is not for everyone. And although I have lived on five continents, Africa was never going to be one of them.

So I asked, "Just curious, but when does the next voyage take place?" Knowing that we only had four days left on Cyprus, I wondered why I even asked this question. I'll never forget her answer:

"What time do you have?"

"What?"

"I have a ship leaving from Limassol in forty minutes. Are you interested?" I couldn't believe our luck, and ran outside to locate Andi in another store and told her the situation.

"How long of a drive is it from here to the port?" I asked, returning with Andi by my side. "About a half hour. Are you staying in Limassol? Can you get to the port in forty minutes?"

I looked at Andi; she nodded. So we paid the passage fee and sprinted to our rental car. I drove like a bat out of hell. We stopped at Selia's house to pack as fast as humanly possible, then took off for the ship. Judging by my watch, I didn't think we were going to make it. When we screeched into the parking lot, the boat was still there, and an employee was waiting for us. It was definitely fate.

"Are you the Feeneys?" We nodded. "Great, let's go, we're already late. Leave your car where it is. I'll call the dockmaster and explain. Come on— the pyramids await."

Safely on the ship, Andi and I felt fantastic. Less than one hour earlier, we were walking in the rain in Larnaca. Now we were asea in the Med, bound for one of the great wonders of the world. We dined lavishly with other passengers, and hit the sack. It was going to be a huge day tomorrow.

The next morning, after docking in Port Said, Egypt, we were preparing to disembark. What happened next was really otherworldly. There were several white buses lined up on the dock, enough to carry all of us. Police and Egyptian military were everywhere. After boarding was complete, the buses charged through Port Said at fifty to sixty miles an hour! There were roadblocks at every intersection, with military guards to enforce them. All the stoplights were turned off. We had a motorcade with dozens of armed police leading the way. The city was literally shut down until we cleared the town limits. We found out later that a legitimate terrorist threat was aimed toward our convoy. Egypt's unrest was really hurting tourism, so they were bound and determined to make sure these tourists got to see the pyramids.

Of course, the pyramids were everything we thought they would be. These world-famous millennia-old monuments of the Nile Valley took your breath away. Quoting from Wikipedia:

"This complex of ancient monuments includes the three pyramid complexes known as the Great Pyramids, the massive sculpture know as the Great Sphinx, several cemeteries, a workers village, and an industrial complex... The pyramids, which have historically loomed large as emblems of ancient Egypt in the Western imagination, were popularized in Hellenistic times, when the great Pyramid was listed by Antipater of Sidon as one of the Seven Wonders of the World. It is by far the oldest of the ancient Wonders and the only one still in existence."

It was eclectic and wonderful. I climbed down into the Ramses Pyramids through a small one-meter-by-one-meter opening. Being the "claustro" that I am, it felt cramped and humid. At the bottom, of course, was a crypt. The pyramids are just really big graves. (There was a KFC and a McDonald's right at the entrance—I ordered a Pyramid Burger, and Andi had the Sphinx Salad.)

Next it was off to the Cairo Museum, with outstanding pieces like the solid gold mask of King Tut, the remains of Ramses III, and artifacts from the Valley of the Kings. (For nearly five hundred years, from the sixteenth through the eleventh centuries BC, tombs were constructed for the pharaohs and powerful nobles in the Valley of the Kings.) We then headed to a papyrus factory, where local merchants made paper from reeds, just like they did thousands of years ago. We bought a replica of the first calendar ever invented, and it was expertly constructed entirely of 100 percent papyrus paper. (It's hanging in our house right now.)

All good things must come to an end. After another five-alarm rush through Port Said, we reboarded the ship and enjoyed a great dinner with excellent wine selections. The next morning, we were back in our car heading to Selia's place. We spent the last day on Cyprus in Paphos, on the west end of the island. It's a beautiful seaside town, with lots for tourists. Andi and I enjoyed the Coral Bay and visited the Tomb of the Kings. The beach area at Petra tou Romiou was very beautiful, and we dined later in a restaurant high on a cliff, providing an awesome view of the Paphos Castle and Aphrodite Hills. What a trip—and what a lucky break catching that ship to Egypt. If it hadn't been raining that day in Larnaca, we would have never seen that tiny tourist shop, and the grandeur of the pyramids would have bypassed us …

Our final diversion from Manama—a twelve-day Princess Cruise to the Western Med—was a big mistake. We stayed in London for a few days— always nice and always expensive—and then took a cab/train/cab eighteen kilometers to South Hampton to catch our cruise boat. (The cost was 172 pounds—I should have known right there that this cruise would be the love boat from hell!) We piled onboard, and off we went.

Although the itinerary was amazing (Barcelona, Seville, Majorca, Sardinia, Rome, Florence, and Gibraltar), we figured out early that our thirst for cruising would end here. We had cruised several times already, and life at sea—not to mention in our pint-sized cabin—was losing its appeal. Plain and simple: we weren't getting enough time on land. How can you enjoy Barcelona in six hours? Or the Island of Sardinia for a half day? Our cruise became a fidgety countdown to the next time the ship stopped. We always tried to be the first ones off and the last ones on. I marveled at the amount of cruisers who would stay on the ship even when we were in port. You can only eat so much, right? And how many hours can someone lie around the pool with classic Mediterranean locations a staircase away? We especially grew to dislike the days at sea, where getting a chair by the pool was practically impossible. People would get up at 5:00 a.m., run down to the pool area, and claim all the seats with towels, shoes, or whatever they could find.

The logistics and the itinerary for this Princess Cruise were not optimal. For example, to visit Rome and Florence, we had to take ninety-minute bus rides each way. Unless you were on a guided tour (we never were), you had to constantly measure what you wanted to see versus the time you had remaining. Since we'd been to Rome a few times, we skipped the places we'd seen before (mistake) and tried other venues. In an effort to maximize our short time there, we missed some of our favorite sites. (Let's face it—they wanted cruisers on the boat, and spending money.) It killed us to leave Majorca and Gibraltar, two really nice stops, before 5:00 p.m.! Imagine taking a trip to Bourbon Street in New Orleans, and leaving just as the happy hours start. At every port, most of the clubs and restaurants were not even open while we were ashore.

But the cruise schedule wasn't the most annoying part. It was the British. According to the concierge, more than 95 percent of the passengers were from Great Britain. For the next twelve days, we saw stinginess—I call it cheapness—that would assault the generosity and ingenuity of Americans. There were several examples, but I'll just point out three of them.

Compensation for the crew: Having been on many cruises, we learned that the common practice was to leave envelopes in your cabin for tips. The envelopes were for the waiters, bartenders, room service, housecleaning staff, and so on. But Princess Cruise Lines was struggling with a real morale problem—Brits don't tip. And since all or most of the crew's compensation came from tip revenue, they were forced to try something different to rectify the problem. So on this cruise, they tried automatically charging the minimum requested tip to all passengers for each day of the cruise. The Brits went nuts. The lines at the bursar's office were gigantic. The natives rebelled, and Princess had to acquiesce. When word got around that the staff was working for nothing, the service went to hell. (Andi and I got to know an American couple working the dining room, and they kept us abreast of all the happenings.) The morale sucked, and many employees would not return after this voyage.

Yanks like us worked around the cheapness. (I must say, in all my travels on this globe, I have always been proud of Americans for our generosity.) Since all the dinner seating was open, we simply gave our Maitre'd fifty dollars and asked him to reserve a corner table for us each night by the window. Some nights it was just Andi and I, and other nights we brought people we'd met with us. Each time when we arrived at the dining room, we saw long lines of passengers waiting for their free table. We, however, were escorted directly to our corner location overlooking the sea. We dined relaxed and unrushed for twelve nights—for a measly $50.00. You see, with open dining, the waiters and staff get different people every night. This makes it very difficult to establish a rapport that usually leads to compensation at the end of the cruise. The staff was amenable to the open seating *until* the Brits spurned the automatic tip initiative, leaving them with nothing. (Not to worry—we definitely took care of our servers at the end of the cruise.)

Overwhelmed by the cheapness of these passengers, we finally decided to cancel our automatic tip assessment as well. But for a whole different reason. The staff was upset, and it showed in many of the sections of the ship. So we decided to track those who did a good job and tip them. In fact, we ended up tipping twice as much as we were suggested to give, but we didn't care. Let's call it "a value for a value," as Ayn Rand professed in her classic *Atlas Shrugged*. I didn't want one penny of our money to go to those who didn't earn it. Ayn Rand likens her theory of Objectivism to a trader: "A trader is a man who earns what he gets and does not give or take the undeserved. A trader does not ask to be paid for his failures, nor does he ask to be loved for his flaws." It seemed to me that if the cruise staff provided a service to the passengers (a value), then the passengers should trade that value for another value (in this case, compensation). The majority of the passengers couldn't care less.

In a true socialist approach—and desperate to squeeze some compensation from the tightfisted passengers—the ship decided to mandate that deserving employees who did receive tips had to turn them in to the supervisors, who would arbitrarily "split them evenly among everyone." (Ayn Rand was turning in her grave—reward the undeserved by taking from the deserving? Are we talking about income redistribution here?) On our last night, we found those who deserved our compensation and worked out ways to trade tips for good service *without* forcing them to turn over hard-earned dollars for central distribution. (The key was to tip them when the watchful eyes of the supervisors were looking elsewhere.) Why do this? Because we chose who deserved our compensation—not some faceless staff member. The true genius of "a value for a value" philosophy is in its simplicity. If trades become complicated or get watered down by policy or poor performance—watch out. Many nations have dissolved over the millennia by taking from those who produce and giving to those who don't.

Barcelona: We arrived at Barcelona and were really excited about seeing this wonderful city. We had heard so much about it and were itching to get off the damn boat. As soon as we hit the stairwell, we found ourselves in stagnant lines queuing seven floors above the ship exit. (The Brits love to queue up. Believe it or not, I faked a queue one night near the theater, and people actually lined up behind me—even though they had no idea why they were standing there. So, tongue in cheek, I asked a few of them—why are you standing behind us? They had no response.)

The longer we stood in that stairwell, the hotter I got. Our precious little time was dwindling away. That's it—I couldn't take it any longer. A staff member explained to me that the passengers were waiting for a low-cost shuttle to town, a mere five kilometers away! It turns out they had some sort of coupon. (If you need a coupon to travel three miles, perhaps cruising is not for you.) I grabbed Andi's hand and drilled my way through the hordes of passengers. Finally I saw daylight. As we attempted to disembark, we were stopped by a crewman and told that we had to take the shuttle. I dared him to stop me—he didn't. All of these people were packed like rats with one goal in mind—to save a few euros on the shuttle. Directly across the street, there were several cabs standing idly by. For the equivalent of five dollars, our taxi dropped us off at the Gran Via de les Corts Catalones, the main thoroughfare that runs through the entire city from southwest to northeast. The last thing I saw as we drove away from the ship was dozens of people standing in the sun, waiting for an unseen trolley that would save them approximately $1.50 US. For that bargain price, they were losing precious time touring one of the great cities on earth. I told Andi if I ever got that cheap, divorce me, or better yet, send me back to the upside-down room and leave me there!

Captain's cocktail hour: On every cruise, there's one night when the ship offers complimentary cocktails and snacks in the main lobby near the lounges. It usually lasts one hour and is designed to allow passengers to meet the captain, take pictures, and so on. On the night of the captain's shindig, scheduled to start at 5:30 p.m., Andi and I were hanging around the main lounge waiting for dinner. It was just past five o'clock, and the place was practically empty. Our favorite waitress was taking care of us, and we were reminiscing about our day on the Rock of Gibraltar. At 5:29 p.m., the most amazing thing happened. Totally unchoreographed, hundreds of Brits arrived seemingly out of thin air. The second the free drinks came out, the servers were deluged with grabbing passengers. It looked like one of those old CARE commercials, with starving kids reaching for handfuls of rice. It was humiliating. I saw people with drinks in each hand and appetizers under their arms, heading to tables to store their stash, and then hustling back to the servers for more.

Miraculously, at exactly 6:30 p.m., they were all gone. The place felt like a wheat field just after the locusts departed. As Andi and I sat there quietly, I felt like I needed a shower. Throughout this book, I have tried to stay as neutral as possible about most of the things that happened to us around the world. In this case, I couldn't do it. In fact, I left out several other examples of embarrassingly frugal behavior. Reflecting back, maybe because the British pay so dearly for government programs and entitlements, there isn't any disposable income for gratuities. Or maybe this is the norm for citizens of Great Britain. I can't say; I've never spent twelve days at sea with them before. And I won't again.

But this I will say: *generosity*—especially for those whose livelihood depends on serving you— will always be repaid in other ways. And *cheapness*, like sloth and laziness, is a sin against the body and soul.

Our tour in Bahrain was ending soon, and I was in the middle of bidding on my next assignment. Since I had recently got tenured and was no longer considered an entry-level diplomat, I was free to bid on my own posting. This process was very complicated. The Standard Operation Procedure (SOP) was over one hundred pages! In simple terms, you went on the website and reviewed worldwide openings, both overseas and domestic. After you narrowed down your post preferences, making sure you followed the SOP guidelines, you began the networking process. This required sending a detailed e-mail to the points of contact at your desired posts, with resumes, Department of State Employee Profiles, Employee Performance Reports, and so on. The post would then request names for a 360 evaluation. A 360 evaluation considers supervisors, peers, and subordinates. The interested post contacts all of these employees and attempts to get a good feel on whether you'd fit in their organization. At some point, when a post agrees to hire you, they offer what's called a handshake. This nebulous term means that if all goes well at the assignment panel in Washington at the appropriate time in the bidding season, you are actually given an official assignment. (I know, it sounds more complicated than ObamaCare.)

My goal after Bahrain was to step up and bid on a management officer position overseas. However, when we left Manama in 2006, the available positions at my grade were very limited. So after a lengthy discussion with Andi, taking into consideration my mother's health and our long stint overseas, we decided it was time to return to the United States.

Ironically, I was drawn to the counseling and assignment officer position in the Career Development and Assignments Division in Washington, DC. This is a key part of the bidding process I mentioned above, that is, the assignment panel operations. Since I had done something similar when I worked in the air force, I decided to bid on this job. After going through all the networking steps, providing names for 360s, and so on, I was told that I would be going to panel, and to stand by. (Later, when I actually sat on the assignment panels, I developed a greater appreciation for their complexity and effectiveness.) But we were leaving Manama soon and were getting pretty anxious about the slowness of the panel. The problem is, while you're waiting for officials in DC to make decisions, many other potential preferences are getting filled. When handshakes appear on the website, the bidding for those vacancies is discontinued. In essence, the list of desired locations was getting smaller, making it harder to wait for a final decision.

On one of our final weekends, we decided to forget about future assignments and headed to Sakhir for the 2006 Bahrain Grand Prix. This facility was immense, and the race tower looked like something out of *War of the Worlds*. I have to give the Arabs in the Gulf region credit—when they do something, they do it big. The complex has six separate tracks, including a test oval and a drag strip. The surface is Graywacke aggregate, shipped in from England, and is very popular with the drivers because of the grip the cars experience. (If you recall, I enjoyed Grand Prix races in Europe when I was a young enlisted guy.) It was the first race of the 2006 Formula One Season, and as usual, the weather was hot, hot, hot. And since the racetrack was right in the middle of the desert, blowing sand became a real concern. The race officials avoided this problem by spraying an airborne adhesive on the sand surrounding the track. It worked well, and Fernando Alonso (Spain) won for the second year in a row, barely edging out Michael

Schumacher (Germany) by a mere 1.246 seconds. It was a powerful event, and one of the last things Andi and I did in the Middle East.

The following Tuesday, my assignment to Washington came through. We shipped our SUV early so it would be waiting for us in DC. And we drove Andi's car up until the last day, and then sold it to my replacement. Our last connection to Bahrain was detached.

Andi and I, a couple of moss-less stones, were heading home. Counting Australia, we had been living overseas for six of the last eight years. We were drained, and felt a little alienated. It was time for a change.

CHAPTER TWENT Y- ONE

Back for a Cup of Coffee in the United States

———————————◆○◆———————————

It was special that sunny morning when I felt the vibration of the wheels going up as our plane gently rose above the Manama skyline. The plane creaked and moaned over Muharraq and seemed to tip its wing to the Fifth Fleet at NSA Bahrain on the shores below. As we rolled out of our departure pattern, I could see central Manama—specifically, the Al-Fatih Mosque, which is the largest building in the country, and the famous Bahraini Pearl Monument. As we headed northeast toward Europe, I saw the small island of Umm al-Na'san for the last time. This tiny ait is the dividing line—and final checkpoint—for the King Fahd Causeway to Saudi Arabia. Finally it was just the Gulf over the horizon, saying good-bye to a couple of misfit residents.

The final departure from any country is a singularly significant event. For Bahrain, I knew I would never be back. It was an okay posting, but there was too much to do and not enough time in life to return. As I looked at the sea below through my tiny oval window, I marveled again at the amazing human mind. I was already data dumping thoughts of Manama and thinking about our next chapter in the United States. In essence, I was already starting what would be a short—but necessary—exercise through the stages of grief. Even though we were heading to our home country, it was somewhat foreign to us. The pace of Washington DC, is fast, and people are always preoccupied with multitasking and time management. Over the past several years, our lives had been the opposite, that is, simplified and at a slower pace. As my mind continued to replace yesterday with tomorrow, I thought about the scene in *2001: A Space Odyssey,* where Dave, the crew member, was slowly draining the intelligence from HAL, the ship computer. HAL was at first upset, then curious, and finally resigned to the fact that he wouldn't remember his past much longer. His last words of intellect were, *"Dave, will I dream?"*

In a similar fashion, I was wondering why humans are so eager to let go of their past. Why was I already mentally displacing two years of my life in the Middle East? Is it the basic skills of survival from lost millennia? Are we programmed to move forward or die, like sharks? Are we all Italian drivers, throwing away the rearview mirror, resolved in the knowledge that what happens behind us is not important? Or is it simply cognitive dissonance, where the mind does its rebalancing to allow movement forward without too much baggage? Anyway, Bahrain, like HAL, I'll see you in my dreams ...

The flight was very long and tedious, especially since we were dragging Kismet along with us. After a stopover at Heathrow in England, we finally arrived at Dulles International. The taxi ride to our hotel was brutal. We had a thousand bags and the cat carrier and all her paraphernalia, and we were delirious with exhaustion. Of course it was rush hour—welcome to DC— and we crawled down the highway. Mercifully, we finally arrived at our hotel. We unpacked, had some food delivered, and crashed. Tomorrow, we would wake up refreshed, begin our home leave, and start the first day of our new lives. Manama was already forgotten.

One of the great benefits about being in the State Department is the Home Leave (HL) Program. As Foreign Service diplomats travel from country to country, they can easily become disconnected from their roots in America. The HL program, which is mandated by Congress, requires Foreign Service officers to take time off in the United States between postings. This HL period is designed to reacquaint employees with the country they represent worldwide. (You'd be surprised how many diplomats don't like this program. They would prefer to avoid the United States altogether. In my opinion, too many diplomats lose touch with the United States. If it weren't for HL, the disassociation would be even worse.) It's not just the diplomat. The family members, especially children, also face adjustment hurdles. In frequent cases, children may reside in the United States an average of one year per decade! Imagine attending high school in DC, for example, after never experiencing the US educational system. The norms would be unknown, and the stress onerous. The State Department does have a good program focusing on teaching American children how to live in America. (I often think of Andi moving to a new city her senior year in high school and how difficult it was for her. But at least she was in the same country...)

We loved HL. We were authorized up to twenty days, and we decided to use all of it. Our number-one mission: to find a place in Washington, DC, that was close to the Department of State Building, which is located in Foggy Bottom. More importantly, I was adamant that our apartment had to be within walking distance of Main State, as it's called by DOS employees. The commute in Bahrain had worn me out. I couldn't handle the DC traffic every day.

Moving to Washington had one big advantage. We were moving to a place we knew something about. While in the air force, I often went to DC (Andrews AFB and the Pentagon) for official business. On the State Department side, a large part of my career development, that is, training and leadership programs, were held at the Foreign Service Institute in

Alexandria, Virginia. And with my sister living off Wisconsin Avenue in Tenleytown, we visited her often as well.

We usually stayed in Georgetown on business. It's my favorite part of the city. So Andi and I decided to concentrate our search in the Georgetown/ Foggy Bottom/West End area. But it didn't take long for sticker shock to set in. Every two-bedroom apartment we looked at was either too expensive or too small. Many were below ground level or in lousy condition, while others were nothing more than dormitory rooms. (George Washington University is right next to the Department of State complex, making apartment rentals even harder to find.) Even some of the renowned brownstone apartments were tiny, dark, and damp. We were disheartened and began to face the reality that commuting was in our future.

On our fifth or sixth day of house hunting, we stumbled upon our dream apartment. It was a top-floor penthouse, with two bedrooms and two and a half baths. It had a fireplace and was perfectly located at 2401 Pennsylvania Avenue, across the street from the Melrose Hotel. The West End location was ideal, and the walking commute to my office would be twelve minutes. The unit had five balconies, with the main one facing west toward M Street, the center avenue in Georgetown. The building was shaped like a large piece of cake. Our apartment was at the pointed end of the cake, with rounded balconies maximizing the view. The facility was expertly managed, and the security was solid. There was only one problem—we couldn't afford it. Even with my USAF pension and the assumption that Andi would also work, we couldn't get there from here. We left dejected and continued our search.

Several days later, tired of finding nothing, we decided to go back to 2401 Pennsylvania and try to negotiate a better price. The building manager had done some calculations and was expecting to see us again. As it turned out, we were able to lock in a first-year rental discount as long as we agreed to established increases the following two years. It was well over our budget, but we now had a full year to adjust to the rate increase and plenty of time for Andi to find employment. (As it turned out, we were gone after one year anyway, so the increases never materialized.) With great excitement, we now had a penthouse apartment between Georgetown and Foggy Bottom, right on Pennsylvania Avenue. The unit was in perfect condition, with wood floors and a brand-new kitchen. The Feeneys, and Kismet, had a home.

Our vehicle had arrived, so we decided to spend some time in Pittsburgh. It was a great perk for us to live just four hours away. (Note: We would never live this close to my hometown again.) And with Susan's family in DC as well, we finally had some real opportunities to reunite with relatives.

Back in Pittsburgh, everything was the pretty much normal. John was still there, and Pat and Frank lived in a small hamlet called Sarver, Pennsylvania. Mom was Mom. She was getting pretty old—she was seventy-nine—and you could sense she was gearing down and getting ready to leave us. Just four years earlier, when Larry had a big seventy-fifth birthday bash for her in Rhode Island, she was full of life and looking like she would live forever. (I have a photo with Mom and us five kids, and she really looked happy.) I guess in a morbid sense, Bob Dylan says it best: "He who is not busy being born is busy dying." My mother was now disinterested and had an air of resignation that I hadn't seen before. But we enjoyed each other's company. At this point of our lives, the bumps in the road were meaningless. And she always got excited to see Andi. We'd go out for dinner, and she would keep telling me how lucky I was to have Andi in my life. After a few wines, the subject would invariably lead to Dad. In my mind, I felt she was trying to subconsciously atone for some of the harsh words said in anger, even if Dad did deserve them at times. There were no winners in that situation.

In Washington, our furniture had arrived, and for the twenty-second time in my life, I was unpacking in new environs. I still had a few days of home leave left, so we devoted the rest of our vacation to getting the apartment squared away. We were stoked. An incredible apartment, a stint in the United States, and a new job I was sure I would enjoy.

My new office was in SA-3 (State Annex-3) on Virginia Avenue, just across the street from Main State. Ironically, it was just a few short blocks from the mall where my Toyota van was robbed in 1990! Avoiding Main State was a huge break. The Department of State Building is among the worst-designed structures this side of Istanbul's Grand Bazaar. It has halls going nowhere. And others that abruptly end for no apparent reason. Honestly, you needed GPS to find the tucked-away elevators. I don't think Lewis and Clark could have avoided getting lost in that maze. I hated that building. Watching thousands of employees navigating through the hallways reminded me of George Orwell's *1984*. It was especially bad in the morning, when commuters were already worn down by traffic and humidity. Needless to say, I was happy to be across the street in a smaller place. SA-3 was an easy-in, easy-out facility, which made my walking commute through the campus of George Washington University even better.

My job title was Deputy Assignments Officer, and I was attached to the Office of Career Development and Assignments. According to my official work requirements, I "counseled, represented, and assigned officers for the Western Hemisphere Affairs Bureau (WHA), the Bureau of Consular Affairs (CA), the Bureau of International Narcotics and Law Enforcement Affairs (INL), the Bureau of Intelligence and Research (INR), and the Bureau of Information Resource Management (IRM)." In short, my job was to get the best officers I could for the bureaus listed above. I lived on the phone and reviewed the resumes and job histories of hundreds of employees. I had stacks of 360 evaluations to read on a daily basis. Since WHA was by far my largest customer, I spent most of my time—having both good and bad days—working with the executive section of the Western Hemisphere Affairs Bureau.

As I said earlier, the State Department Assignment System was extremely complex. But there was one clear checks-and-balances system in place at SA- 3. While assignment officers (AOs) like me supported the bureaus, the career development officers (CDOs) attached their allegiance to the individual officer. Many times, the AO and the CDO were on the same page. And many times, they weren't. Many times, the different bureaus were on the same page. And many times they weren't. All assignments, especially those where bureaus and individual preferences were not in agreement, went to panel for resolution.

The mid-level panels, and to some extent the entry-level panels, were absolutely the most fun part of the job. The panels had members from a variety of sources. Every bureau had representation, and all the assignment officers and career development officers were also there. Senior-level and entry-level officers were voting members as well. And there were many other nonvoting officers present for a variety of reasons. (To be honest, I never knew why so many of them were there to begin with.) The panels were chaired by former ambassadors or soon-to-be ambassadors. At the central table, thirteen voting thirteen members, including myself, decided... whether John Doe went to Paris or to Manama. It was very much like a courtroom. Cases were presented and discussed in a formal style, ending with a vote. And like a trial, most of the work was done prior to the panel meeting. Like F. Lee Bailey, the famous lawyer, once said, "The case is won or lost before you enter the courtroom."

The best way to explain a case at panel is to use an example. Let's say WHA needed a Dutch-speaking political officer for Suriname. My bureau's only qualified in-grade candidate wanted the assignment, but another bureau argued that he was needed in Tashkent and that other qualified candidates were available for Suriname. This contradiction was called a shoot-out and would be settled by final vote at panel. My job was to build a case for my candidate, using every angle I could. Why was he so critical to Tashkent? What other officers could fill this slot? What about all the money the USG spent to get the appropriate Dutch-language level needed for Suriname? Did the other candidates have the right level of Dutch-language proficiency? Were there family issues to consider? Where have both officers been assigned? (Usually, but not always, the officers who served in hard -to -fill locations like Haiti or Iraq would get some preferential treatment in the final vote.) And on it went.

Armed with all the information I could muster, I presented my case in panel. The other bureau presented their case. The CDO spoke for the individual's preference. If there were medical or personal problems, these were addressed as well. Perhaps the language officer would add some input on the effects of assigning non-Dutch-speaking officers to Suriname. After all arguments were laid out, the floor was open to questions from voting and nonvoting members. When all discussion was completed, the chair called for a vote, and it was seconded by a voting member. All in favor of this officer going to Suriname, say aye. Opposed, say nay. If I won the shootout, our candidate was placed on assignment to Suriname, and my WHA Bureau was happy. If I lost, my candidate was released from assignment and might very well appear on an upcoming panel projected to Tashkent. It was high drama to say the least. The panel decisions were very competitive, and the final decision had a huge effect on an officer's life. With well above fifty people in the panel room—many with highly differing opinions on what made a good assignment—the conversations definitely became confrontational. I've seen panel members almost reduced to tears...

Now that I was settled into my new job, it was time for us to become familiar with our new neighborhood. Of course, this wasn't very difficult. We were near everything. In one direction was the National Mall, with all the presidential monuments, Smithsonian museums, and war memorials. In the other direction rested Georgetown, with dozens of restaurants and watering holes. And of course, there was the Georgetown Waterfront, easily my favorite weekend spot in DC. After a long week at panel, I loved walking down to the waterfront on the weekends, especially in the summer. There were tourists everywhere, pleasure boats docked two and three deep, and shuttle boats and dinner boats passing by. My regular haunt was Nick's Riverside Grill. I liked being a regular, something I never had the opportunity to experience overseas. I always felt like Norm walking into Cheers. It was a great feeling. (For years, each time I returned to DC on business, I would invariably wander down to Nick's. And in most cases, the usual suspects were still there.)

One of my best buddies at Nick's had a story I have to tell you. If he knew I was writing about this, he'd get embarrassed and ask me not to share it with you. But I have to. It's too powerful to ignore. Andrew is a bachelor, and an Irish Catholic who works as an investment broker in DC. Several years ago, he went to New York City on business and was walking back to his hotel.

As he passed an alleyway, he saw five guys, all armed, attempting to rape a young girl. Without hesitation, Andrew rushed into the alley. He grabbed the first rapist by the neck and broke it. He fell dead. While this was happening, another guy came up behind him and slit his throat. (You should see the scar.) As Andrew fell to the ground bleeding, perhaps thinking he would die there, the hooligans ran. He was rushed to the hospital, and miraculously, he survived. The girl was unharmed.

About a year later, he got a call from the girl's father. As it turns out, she was getting married. The father of the bride asked Andrew to attend the wedding and to give his daughter away! The father knew—and so did the young bride—that she would have died in that alleyway if it hadn't been for Andrew. With plane tickets, hotel reservations, and such in place, Andrew went back to New York to give away the bride. I know him pretty well. Every time this story comes up, he downplays it—mainly because he is modest and doesn't seek attention to himself. It would embarrass him when I told this story at Nick's. But he is a hero—period. What would you have done in that situation? Would you have walked past quickly, pretending not to notice? Or maybe called 911, convincing yourself that you did a good deed? Or yelled to passing pedestrians for help? Or would you have put a total stranger's life first, dropped everything, and run unarmed into the alley where five armed men were waiting? I talked to Andrew about this several times. Obviously I hope this never happens to me, or anyone else for that matter. But if it did, I pray that I would have the courage he displayed.

Right up the street from the waterfront was M Street, which is the center of Georgetown. Andi and I spent countless hours dining on that wonderful street. At J Paul's, we always took the corner seat by the window. It was our spot to enjoy a good meal, meet up with friends, and watch the world go by. When we felt like Italian, we headed straight to Paulo's, just north of M Street on Wisconsin Avenue. When American fare was preferred, Old Glory, right on M Street, was the place to go. But you'd better be hungry; the portions are huge.

A few blocks east, in or near our building at 2401 Pennsylvania, were a few more of our favorites. The best thing about 51st State was the outside patio, where we would sit and enjoy the wide variety of appetizers. It was also cool to look upward and see our penthouse apartment perched high in the building across the street. We couldn't wait to show family and friends our place from the 51st State patio. At 2401 Pennsylvania, below street level, was McFadden's, a truly great Irish Pub. The food was excellent, there were plenty of football games blasting on the weekends, and the bartenders treated us very well. We're not late-night people, but I recall long lines in front of McFadden's, which was a very popular spot for the students of George Washington University. And right across the street, the Melrose Hotel had a nice outdoor lanai area that was perfect for a good Cabernet after a long day at the office. I would meet Andi there often. All of these great hangouts made me feel at home, a rare treat for a Foreign Service diplomat.

The Mall is legendary. Most Americans already know this. We covered every part of it, from the Lincoln Memorial to the US Capitol, and from Lafayette Square to the Jefferson Memorial. All of the Smithsonian Institutions are classics—you just have to find your favorite ones. To try to list all the great points of interest in the Mall would be overzealous. My suggestion—buy some good walking shoes, and come to DC to break them in.

The absolute greatest thing about living in the West End was the luxury of walking. Having the ability to do almost anything you wanted, and do it on foot, was simply priceless. On my twelve-minute walk to work, I saw hundreds of frustrated drivers sitting motionless in their cars, with stress on their faces as they anxiously inched down the avenue.

Andi and I walked everywhere. We enjoyed the simple things, like hiking over to Union Station and then riding the Circulator Bus back to Georgetown. Or walking to the Southwest Waterfront, where a colleague of mine lived in a tugboat! Or heading up to DuPont Circle for lunch, or strolling Massachusetts Avenue, where all the foreign embassies were located. But my favorite walk of all was my cardiovascular workout. Starting from 2401 Pennsylvania, I'd go south past the Watergate Hotel and the Kennedy Center until I reached the Rock Creek and Potomac Parkway. There I'd head along the Potomac River until I reached the Arlington Memorial Bridge. After crossing the bridge, I'd vector down onto the wide walking/biking path and head north past Theodore Roosevelt Island up to the Key Bridge. I'd cross the bridge, turn right, and eventually end up back in Georgetown. To this day, I still think it's the finest urban walk in the country. There are national treasures on every turn. Of course when I had the time, I would conclude my circuit with a stop at Nick's. From there, it was ten short minutes back to the apartment.

Financially, things were going well for us. My pension covered the rent, and I was making more money than I ever had before. And as usual, Andi found a great job in Main State. I am always amazed how fast she finds employment no matter where we live. She was hired by the Office of the Legal Advisor for Consular Affairs (L/CA). Her position as office manager placed her directly under the secretary of L/CA. Working with ten lawyers and two paralegals, she was the focal point for establishing, updating, and maintaining effective and efficient operations for all administrative and procedural responsibilities. Andi loved this job. And she was treated very well. I was always happy to stop by her office and witness personally the important role she played in L/CA. (Again when she left, they poured accolades on her, from luncheons to gifts.) As I mentioned earlier in this book, one of the least popular unintended consequences of a diplomat's career is the strain it puts on his or her spouse. There's no way around it: one spouse has to take a backseat when it comes to career development. And when that spouse does find challenging employment—like with L/CA—he or she may have to give it up at a moment's notice.

As you know by now along this journey, curveballs always come along when you don't expect them. After six months in DC, two major events occurred that would change our lives again. One involved my supervisor, and the other involved me. I'll start with my supervisor.

"Phillip" was a career diplomat, with twenty-six years of service in the State Department. He was a quiet, almost bashful man, and a great boss. He was courteous and hardworking, and he didn't hesitate to stand up for you when needed. We were a two-man shop. He worked the senior-level panels, and I handled the mid-level panels. We were a good team—maybe the best team on the floor—but something was bothering him. Little by little, he was becoming more withdrawn. I sensed something was wrong, but I decided not to pry.

A few months later, in the summer of 2006, all hell broke loose for Phillip. As it turns out, he was accused of sending threatening e-mails to the president of the Arab American Institute (AAI) and of violating the civil rights of the employees there. According to an AAI statement, "The threats were both intimidating and frightening—and the fact that the defendant was a 20-year career officer at the Department of State made it of even greater concern." Many of Phillip's comments were profane and related to the 2006 Lebanon War. Since Philip had served two different tours in Beirut, Lebanon, it became apparent that his discrimination and hateful language against Arabs had gotten the best of him. Looking back, I do remember Phillip ranting about Persians (Iranis), citing examples as a consular officer that deepened his dislike for Iran, and Arabs in general. He was forced to retire, and his career was over.

But the story wasn't.

The AAI continued to push for a trial. They wanted jail time. In August 2007, Phillip was indicted with a violation of Title 18 of the United States Code, Section 875 (c), threatening messages in interstate commerce to injure an individual, and a violation of Title 18 of the United States Code, Section 245 (b) (2) (C), by threat of force or use of force, to interfere with the civil rights of the founder and employees of the Arab American league. Phillip pleaded guilty in June 2008 and was sentenced to one year in jail, a $10,000 fine, and three years of post-release supervision.

I always found Phillip to be a very soft-spoken and likable person. I guess only he can explain what tormented him so much and why it led to criminal behavior. One never knows, does one?

In our weekly panels, the other life-changing issue began to surface. The management officer position in Curacao, part of the Netherland Antilles, went suddenly vacant. Rumors were that the chief of mission (COM) was incorrigible, and the incumbent had curtailed her assignment. Since it was a short-notice vacancy, that is, they needed someone ASAP, that limited the available pool, with issues like school-age children and tour-length restrictions to navigate. My boss, and a couple of the other team chiefs, were encouraging me to apply for the position. They knew I was interested in a management officer job after DC and felt it was a good fit. And since I had just gotten promoted to FS-02, I had the right grade for the assignment.

I was immediately torn. On one side, we had a great apartment in DC, where we had been living for barely seven months. And Andi had a great job that she really liked. On the other side, I did want a management officer slot, and the thought of living on a Caribbean Island for three years was definitely tempting. At our next panel, even my panel chair was pushing me to take the job, asking me to "get the COM off my back." I decided to talk to Andi about it. We drew a "T," with pluses and minuses, and placed it on our refrigerator:

- *Pluses:* It was a management officer position; we'd live on a Caribbean Island; financially, we'd save money by avoiding rent payments; I'd get a consular commission and General Service Officer Training, which are two distinct, critical sections in a large embassy; because of the length of training, the COM would be long gone by the time we arrived at post.
- *Minuses:* We'd have to leave DC and our apartment in less than one year; Andi would have to quit her job, which she really liked; I'd have to leave my job, which I really liked, and head to FSI for immediate training; upon arrival at post, I'd quickly be back into a supervisory position, which I was hoping to avoid; we'd be living far away from family again.

When the Curacao job hit the assignment system, it became apparent that the training would place the selectee in the summer cycle and that the current COM would be long gone. Suddenly we were getting a lot of interest from management officers. Andi and I decided to go ahead and interview for the job. The way I saw it, we couldn't lose. If I got the job, it was off to the Caribbean. If not, we were very comfortable in DC.

I met the incoming COM, Ambassador Dunn, at Main State for an interview. He was very cordial and seemed like a good person to work for. My plan was simple—be as honest and direct as I could, and let the chips fall where they may. (A trait I still jealously protect in my "box" of untouchable tenets.)

The key part of the conversation went something like this:

"How do you see your role as my management officer?" he asked. I was ready for this one.

"Ambassador, the way I see it, you would deal with Washington, the ministries, VIP visitors, official functions, and so on, and I'd take care of everything else." I noticed a quick flicker of his eyes. He hadn't expected that response. I continued, "My biggest concern with any job is micromanagement. If I can't carry out my responsibilities autonomously, I might as well be golfing." This comment was a big risk. One of two things was going to happen: either he appreciated my honesty and liked the idea that I volunteered to do much of the day-to-day management of the consulate, or he would feel threatened by my direct approach. The rest of the interview was pretty normal, and he left without showing his hand. As I was walking back to SA-3, I had a good feeling about our discussion. Although I didn't think I'd get the job, I felt the satisfaction of being very clear and very honest— which is rarely done when networking for a job in the State Department. It was a risk I was in a position to take. After all, the worst-case scenario would mean that Andi and I would stay in Washington.

A few days later, I was offered a handshake and accepted it. I guessed right that Ambassador Dunn appreciated having a management officer openly willing to assume responsibility. In my opinion, I'd rather have to slow down an overachiever, than push an underachiever. (During our entire three years together in Curacao, he did allow me the autonomy necessary to do my job. I've always appreciated that about him.)

One week later, I found myself back at the Foreign Service Training Institute (FSI). For the next 140 days, I became a student. My two major objectives were to learn the general services officer career field and to get a consular commission.

The general services officer (GSO) is the backbone of every embassy and consulate. He or she usually has the largest staff and manages several difficult and highly visible programs. My job was to shotgun through the entire portfolio in ten weeks. Some of the largest responsibilities included:

Contracting: Anyone who has worked with government contracts knows how complex they can be. Time lines, delays, cost overruns, and so on. A mind-numbing process.

Procurement and Supply: This area was a huge responsibility. Large amounts of money, contracts, real estate, legal limitations, financial restrictions, purchasing of goods and services, highly restrictive regulations, and so on.

Property: By far, this was the biggest headache for the GSO. Maintaining the COM residence and all the other buildings on post is a never-ending chore. Even worse, managing the residence housing program was a thankless job. Complaints about individual housing were an everyday occurrence. And of course, the maintenance staff was too slow, or they didn't do the work correctly, and so on. It always amazed me how difficult USG officers could be with their housing. *It's free, for Pete's sake!*

Travel and transportation: The GSO had a hand in anything moving, that is, from shipment of household goods and automobiles, to official travel and vehicle purchasing and leasing. I remember sometimes thinking, *why in the hell did I volunteer for this job?*

Customs and clearances: This responsibility was almost unmanageable. Import/export laws and regulations were always changing overseas. Working with seaports and airports was a source of constant frustration. Damaged and missing materials during the customs process were also problematic. And of course, everything was the GSO's fault.

Believe it or not, there were many other responsibilities, including supervision of a large number of employees and management of a host of internal controls.

The GSO course was long and thorough. Although it was impossible to be prepared for everything that might happen at post, the course gave you the tools to solve most problems, and it taught you where to go if you needed help. I met several people in that class whom I still consider friends. But friendships, unfortunately, are hard to maintain when everybody is spread out all over the globe.

As tough as the GSO course was, it paled in comparison to the consular course. According to the Family Liaison Office, which concentrates on opportunities for the families of USG diplomats, the "Consular Course is divided into four modules: U.S. Passport and Nationality, Immigrant Visas, Non-immigrant Visas, and American Citizen Services. Coursework in Security, Accountability, Fraud and Ethics (SAFE) as well as consular systems training is also built in. The Course is of graduate-level difficulty, involving a substantial amount of highly technical reading. There are several hundred pages of reading material for each module, supplemented by readings in Foreign Affairs Manuals (FAMS), and the Immigration and Nationality Act (INA)."

Our bible was *Benders's Immigration and Nationality Act (INA),* which provided an excruciatingly detailed breakdown of US Immigration policy. Written in a legalese format that was almost unreadable at times, it held all the answers. Luckily for students at FSI, we were given self-instruction guides for each of the four modules, which helped to "translate" the INA into readable parts.

Each module was intense, and the exams lasted several hours. The complexity of the test questions required thorough understanding of the INA and the ability to accurately adjudicate your findings. Many officers were set back during the course, and others never finished. It was intense, to say the least.

The US passport module helped us understand the requirements process, application procedures, documents and fees needed, types of passports, identification of legal and illegal passports, and so on. Although this module was very informative, passports were usually issued by passport centers and not posts—except for temporary, emergency passports. Similarly, the immigration process (permanent status into the United States) was long and complicated, and not really an issue at the consulate in Curacao.

That left two *gigantic* consular programs—the Non-Immigration Visa (NIV) and American Citizen (AmCit) Services.

NIVs allow foreign nationals to apply for entry into the United States for a *temporary* purpose. This is how a preponderance of illegal immigrants enter the United States each year. Currently there are forty-five classifications of NIV visas, each with key elements, document requirements, and derivatives. Our job, in a nutshell, was to determine if the individual applying for the visa had intentions to remain illegally in the United States. Our INA was complicated, but very clear on one overarching issue: consular officers were to assume presumption of status, that is, "Every alien shall be presumed to be an immigrant until he establishes to the satisfaction of the consular officer, at the time of application for a visa, and the immigration officers, at the time of application for admission, that he is entitled to nonimmigrant status" (*Bender's INA*, Section 214).

What does this mean? It means that consular officers should assume illegal entry until proven otherwise. I was amazed the first time I read this section. It's the application of the negative to derive the positive. But it makes sense when you think about it. Not only does this law put the burden of proof on the applicant; it gives the officer the ability to refuse a visa because he or she isn't convinced the alien is entitled to entrance into the United States.

The great part about this module was the role-playing portion. One area of the school had a faux consular section set up, and we all took turns being the applicant and the adjudicating officer. Sometimes the applicant was legal, and sometimes he or she wasn't. It was fun watching the consular officer try to figure out if the applicant deserved a visa or not. After each round, we'd have a sit-down and discuss what happened or what should have happened.

The other major area of concern at post is American Citizen Services. This module concentrates on assisting Americans traveling around the world. In Curacao, for example, we dealt with deaths on cruise ships, lost children, fights between US citizens and locals, visiting military members getting arrested, and more. During the class, we visited a staged prison at FSI and interviewed an imprisoned American being held there. We learned that visits are complicated and require tact and diplomacy, as well as a firm knowledge of each country's penal system.

I was very happy to get my consular commission, because that meant I was finally done with FSI! Andi and I went to Paulo's to celebrate and to discuss our next move. The Honda CRV was already on its way to Curacao, and so was some of our furniture. (The rest was placed in storage at the Hagerstown Storage Facility.) We moved into a nearby hotel for our last two weeks and were getting excited about another totally unexpected destination. After all, how many people get to live on a Caribbean isle and get paid in the process?

After a short trip back to Pittsburgh to say good-bye, we tied up all our remaining loose ends and crashed for one final night in Washington, DC. It had been a short, but sweet, home stand. I felt like the journeyman baseball player who spent his whole career in the minor leagues. Then one day, he finally makes it to the majors. But he doesn't last. After his cup of coffee in the big leagues, he's sent away again.

As I lay in bed too excited to sleep, my mind wandered. For the first time in my life, I was getting tired of my nomadic existence. Where were our roots? Where were we from? Over the years, it hadn't really mattered much. But now, as I was aging, I was beginning to wonder why we were still on the road. Gathering moss couldn't be that bad, right? Lots of people seem to be happy doing it. Were we missing the greener grass of the Joneses? Had we traveled so much that we'd never be comfortable staying in one place? Or even living in the United States for that matter? Had we become travel junkies? Should we have stayed in DC?

Thankfully, the sweet nothingness of sleep rescued me from my thoughts… Good-bye again, America. I enjoyed the cup of coffee. I'll be in the minors if you're looking for me.

CHAPTER TWENTY-TWO

"Luck enters into every contingency. You are a fool if you forget it— and a greater fool if you count on it." —PHYLLIS BOTTOME

L uck… What is it? Do some people really have it? Or is it just early preparation? According to the *Webster's Ninth New Collegiate Dictionary,* luck is "a force that brings good fortune or diversity" or the "events or circumstances that operate for or against an individual." What is that force? What are the events or circumstances that generate good or bad luck? Is it something to joke about, like Rodney Dangerfield's quote "The way my luck is running, if I was a politician, I would be honest"? Or is it something to worry about, like Tom Hanks's comment "As an actor, I am always waiting for my luck to run out"? Can we affect our own luck?

Why am I asking these questions? Because for the next three years, luck— both good and bad—would be a major part of the Feeney experience. Onward to the Dutch Antilles …

For a change, the flight to our new post wasn't bad. After a short stop in Miami, Andi, Kismet, and I flew directly to Curacao in just about three hours. I was nervous and apprehensive as we circled the small island, which is part of the ABC Islands (Aruba, Bonaire, and Curacao). My first thought—*what in the hell are we going to do on this rock for three years?* In our moss-less lifestyle, three years in the same place seemed like a sentence, not an assignment. Other than Willoughby Spit in Norfolk, we hadn't lived anywhere that long since the Air Force Academy in the early nineties.

You'd think I'd be used to moving to new places by now. Instead, I always get nervous. I usually lose sleep weeks before arriving at a new posting, tossing and turning in a cold sweat worrying about tomorrow. (Will my luck run out this time?) I'm guessing this paranoia comes from a combination of Irish Catholic guilt and the skillful mismanagement of my brain by the military. Although I understand the differences between these two opposing forces, the end product—anxiety—is often the result.

255

Ironically, when we finally touched down at Hato International Airport, these very same values helped to allay my doubts. In other words, the strong influence of church and military gave me the very courage I needed to pursue a life of constant reinvention and paranoia. I guess this dichotomy will always be part of me, sort of like an internal yin and yang thing. Luckily, Andi was willing to share this migrant lifestyle with me.

Two of the GSO foreign nationals from the consulate were waiting for us just outside the baggage area. During the drive southward, they did a wonderful job making us feel at home, and pointed out areas of interest along the way. (I didn't realize it then, but I would work side by side with Armino and the guys for the next three years.) Curacao rests about thirty miles north of Venezuela, with Aruba to the west and Bonaire to the east. It is cigar-shaped, with Willemstad, the capital, in the center of the island. It is divided by the largest natural port in the Caribbean, with Punda on the eastern side and Otrobanda on the western side. The port is constantly busy with cruise ships, US military vessels, Dutch military vessels, oil tankers, yachts, submarines, and container ships. There are three distinct ways to travel from one bank to the other. The oldest route across St. Anna's *baai* (straight) is the Queen Emma Pontoon Bridge. It's a revolving bridge and swings open to let passing ships in and out of the port. Originally designed by the US consulate general in 1888 and renovated in 1939, it uses hinges and diesel engines to open and close the structure. When not in use, it rests parallel to the shore. When closed, it provides a wide walking lane for passage. High above the pontoon bridge is the Queen Juliana Bridge. At 495 feet, it's the highest in the Caribbean. The views are spectacular, with all the multicolored buildings and historic forts nicely framed by the Caribbean Sea. (The architecture and bright splashes of color reminded me of Amsterdam.) Lastly, along each shore, there are constant water shuttles available for passage across the baai.

Curacao is a very interesting island. According to www. environmentalgraffiti.com, "Take one third European heritage, one third native Caribbean ancestry, and one third African culture, shake and sprinkle with a handful of other ethnic influences and you get Curacao, one of the world's most diverse communities... For centuries, people have come from all over the world to this tiny speck in the South Caribbean Sea to try their fortune. Amerindians, Caiquetios, Spanish, Dutch, African slaves, traders from all over the world—all have left their ethnic footprint on an island that is today a well-connected microcosm of the world." Andi and I were really looking forward to immersing ourselves into Curacao's melting pot. From day one, we were impressed by this small island and how people from many cultures blended together in peaceful coexistence. Is there something to be learned here?

Unfortunately, the make-ready on the vice-consul residence wasn't completed, so the guys took us to the Kura Hulanda Hotel on the Otrobanda side of Willemstad. This five-star hotel provides a boutique-village atmosphere, even though it's situated right in the middle of Willemstad. The hotel is spread over an eight-block area and has a little bit of everything. There are pools, bars, restaurants, shops, an anthropological museum, spas, courtyards, gardens, and so on, all cleverly presented in seventeenth-century Dutch architecture. This area of Willemstad is a UNESCO World Heritage site. Our room, however, left something to be desired. It was a loft, with a very narrow spiral staircase. In fact, we couldn't get our luggage up the steps. There was no air-conditioning, and many of the windows didn't have panes; the heat and the insects were a bit too much for us. (I guess seventeenth-century Dutch living wasn't our thing.) But we loved the complex, and went back many times for dinner and happy-hour functions.

The next morning, we moved to a hotel just out of town in Piscadera. It was less flashy, but had air-conditioning and suite-style rooms, and allowed pets. After a day of getting settled, we picked up our car and dined that evening at the Marriott just down the road. The next day, it was time to get to work.

The US consulate is located high above Willemstad, on John B. Gorsiraweg Street, just east of the Queen Juliana Bridge. It sits on the edge of a cliff, with a panoramic view of the city and the sea beyond. It's a small post, with the Roosevelt House (chief-of-mission residence), a busy consular section, two office buildings, a couple of warehouses, several garages for the government vehicles, assorted storage areas, and an adjoining parking lot for visitors. In 1793, the consulate was opened in Curacao to facilitate trade in the region, making it one of the earliest posts in US history. In 1950, the government of Curacao donated the Roosevelt House to America as an expression of gratitude for military protection during World War II. By today's standards, the COM residence in Curacao would be inadequate, mainly because of its small size. But since it was donated to the United States and remains a historic building with political ties, future chiefs of mission will remain there. Although the old landmark is a hassle to maintain, the lush grounds behind the residence make it all worthwhile. There are several cascading levels, with seating areas, open spaces for official functions, a huge pool and lanai, outside bars, and beautiful pathways—all perfectly positioned for the best views of Willemstad below.

The American consulate staff was made up of three US diplomats, six Drug Enforcement agents, a five-person DOD force protection team, and approximately twenty-five US Customs and Immigration officers at the Queen Beatrix Airport in Aruba. For administrative duties, the post employed fourteen local Dutch nationals, and thirteen of them worked directly for me. (There was also an embedded CIA agent, but he transferred shortly after my arrival.) All of the local staff spoke at least four languages— English, Spanish, Dutch, and Papiamento. Watch out on your birthday. You had to listen to "happy birthday" in four languages.

As the management officer, I served as a kind of de facto deputy chief of mission. My job was to make sure the day-to-day operations were supporting the mission, and to fix them when they weren't. Yes, I was basically steering the blob. There were local conditions that made this job harder than you would expect. The USAF Forward Operating Location (FOL) at the airport was heavily involved in drug-interdiction operations throughout the Caribbean; our DEA staff was constantly monitoring and detecting criminal drug activity as well; and a continual flow of US military vessels into Curacao's port created complex force-protection challenges. Add to this the other five islands under our responsibility—Aruba, Bonaire, Sint Eustatius, Saba, and Sint Maarten—and you have a small, but jumping, post. (Not to mention the constant irritation of Hugo Chavez—just thirty miles south—one of the most ruthless leaders in the Western Hemisphere.)

The main difficulty serving as a big fish in a small pond was the wide variety of responsibilities that came with that distinction. Not only was I the management officer and vice consul, but I was also the backup consular officer, GSO, funds control officer for our $2-million annual budget, real property manager for all USG structures, contracting and acquisition officer for local and international contracts, and acting chief of mission when Ambassador Dunn was away. Although the responsibility was huge, I thrived on it. By challenging our Dutch employees through delegation and empowerment, I was able to continually improve post operations and morale without getting bogged down with time-consuming activities. (They were a great team, and often made me look better than I deserved. The staff was diversified, much like the demographics of the island, and they brought many different ideas and approaches to the table.)

After our second week in Curacao, we finally moved into the new vice consul's house, just above Spanish Waters on the eastern end of the island. Located at 52 Kaya Vivaldi, Cas Grande, it was the highest residence in the area and had ocean views in multiple directions. The place was very big, with six bedrooms and four baths, a gigantic living area, and an immense outside sitting area. The house rested peacefully amid beautiful grounds in the front and in the back. (I always felt it was nicer than the Roosevelt House.) The pool was very large, and the patio and cabana layout could easily accommodate fifty people. We had fruit trees everywhere, and iguanas the size of small alligators traipsing around the place. I couldn't believe a poor kid from Pittsburgh could ever end up in a place like this. (Good luck?)

Armino and his staff took very good care of us. The place was immaculate, and everything was in perfect order.

As we started to settle into a routine, it was time to find out a little bit about our new home. We gravitated to Punda, in Willemstad, to watch cruise ships and other vessels enter and leave the harbor. This activity became one of our favorite pastimes, so we spent many weekend afternoons talking to tourists and enjoying the show. Our favorite hangout was the Iguana Café, with outside tables right on the Sint Anna Baai. At the mouth of the baai, there were two forts—Riffort across the water in Otrobanda, and Fort Amsterdam to our immediate left. They stand as vigils for sailors entering the port. Both have been cleverly modernized to accommodate hotels and shops without losing their historic appearance. When large cruise ships or oil tankers passed by, you felt like you could touch them. To our right was the famous postcard display of multicolored Dutch buildings that are associated with Curacao. Just behind us was the district of Punda, where most of the island's tourist shops and restaurants were located. It's an easily walkable area and provides an excellent chance to see the ornate Dutch architecture. I spent many lunch hours just strolling around Punda, taking in the ambience. A few blocks south of the Iguana Café takes you to the De Boogjes, or water fort arches. Here, along the base of another fort (couldn't find the name), were several waterside restaurants and bars tucked between the arches. Very different, to say the least.

A short walk across the pontoon bridge brings you to Otrobanda, a bustling area because of the cruise trade. Cruise passengers are funneled through Riffort Fort when they embark and disembark from the Mega Pier, which is located just outside of the port. Of course, this route is full of shops, watering holes, and even a casino. Otrobanda also has several docking wharfs along the baai, and sometimes berthed as many as five ships at the same time. We received regular docking schedules from one of my employees, so we knew when to be in place to watch the action. It was a blast. (Note: We still do this today at Port Canaveral.) Sadly, the inner port, or Schottegat, has not been maintained very well, and the pollution is horrific. It's too bad—the right development of this area would have been a gold mine. Now it's just a polluted refinery stop for Venezuelan oil.

Back in Rhode Island, my older brother Larry—who had been married to Bonnie for thirty years—filed for divorce several months before we arrived in Curacao. (Bad luck or an opportunity taken?) Needless to say, it caused quite a rift among the Feeney siblings. Bonnie was like a sister to us all, so Larry took a lot of heat from the family. Anyway, he wanted to know if he could bring his new friend, Sandy, down for the new year (2008). Andi and I had no problem with that. The way I see it, who wants someone who doesn't want you? I voiced this opinion to Bonnie a few times. In other words, had this gone the other way around—and it was Bonnie filing for the divorce—I'd say the exact same thing to Larry. If there's anyone who could give advice about overcoming a divorce, it was me. Who needs the aggravation? Let it go. Like William James says:

"The greatest discovery of my generation is that a human being can alter his life by altering his attitude."

My mother said it a million times: the "best way to hold on is to let go." If someone leaves you, isn't that better than holding on to someone who wants to leave you?

We met Larry and Sandy at the airport and couldn't wait to show them our new digs. Andi and I really liked her, but had to convince ourselves that that didn't mean we stopped caring for Bonnie. The next three or four days were a blur. We went snorkeling on a two-mast sailing ship, hit a couple of nice beaches—Jan Thiel and Mambo— hung out poolside at our house, and frequented a few of our favorite restaurants. On New Year's Eve, I had reserved a table at Bistro Le Clochard, a French restaurant in Fort Amsterdam, right across the baai from the fireworks. It was an all-you-can-eat and all-you-can-drink evening, and we did some serious damage.

(Don't worry, I had a taxi scheduled for two o'clock in the morning.) At 11:00 p.m., the pontoon bridge opened, and the largest tanker ship I ever saw entered the harbor. From where we were sitting, actually below street-level, it looked like the ship was going to roll right over us. We were amazed how close it got before it turned to starboard and scraped past the old fort walls. Maybe it was the wine talking, but I'll never forget how cool that was. Anyway, we had a blast, laughing and talking for hours and enjoying the fireworks.

As for Larry, he was the happiest I'd ever seen him. (He had met Bonnie in tenth grade and had been with her ever since. So I'd have to flash back to fifth grade to remember Larry *not* being with Bonnie.) He was sixty, going on eighteen! His renewed energy sparked a conversation that we still have today. I said to him—by my calculations, given our ages and how seldom we saw each other—that we'd get together maybe ten more times in our lifetime. This profoundly affected him, and he vowed to prove me wrong. (And he did. We have gotten together thirteen times in the last four years.)

But did he prove me wrong? Or did I use a little psychology to keep in touch more often? It doesn't matter, does it? TMYKTMYDKS. We saw them off at the airport and promised we'd come up to Rhode Island soon.

Island life was becoming very agreeable to Andi and me. Months melted by. There were soft breezes, palm trees swaying in the wind, and rainstorms converging on Kaya Vivaldi like storm troopers in World War II. We awoke to unbelievable sunrises and sipped wine to romantic sunsets. Sometimes in the evenings, I'd swim laps down at the pool, with the stars above and rock and roll blasting on the stereo. Except for finding an occasional dead iguana at the bottom of the pool or having one dart by your face at night— quite startling—it was a very relaxing way to exercise.

We were tanned, healthy, and content with life. (Talk about luck, huh?) At about the same time, my brothers Larry and John came to visit. It's a small island, so we did the usual things, that is, snorkeling, beaches, restaurants, hanging at the port watching ships, barbequing at my pool, and so on. It was fun. But I was bound and determined to find something memorable and different to liven up their visit. And I found it. I decided to rent a helicopter for a day! The itinerary included transit to Kleine Curacao, a small deserted island to the east; an entire day on the island, with plenty of food and refreshments; then a return trip back to Willemstad. I know it was expensive and somewhat wasteful. But I didn't care.

We rose slowly from the heliport and hovered for just an instant, and then off we went. The young pilot was crazy, and he went zooming here and there to make sure we saw a wide range of scenic views. When I told him I worked at the consulate, he flew us right over it! When I mentioned we lived near Spanish Waters, he said, "Let's take a look." But the craziest part of the flight occurred moments later, when I told the pilot that I had left the hose running in our pool. So what does the pilot do? He zeros in on our house, drops the helicopter to about seventy feet, circles the pool, and tilts the chopper for a better look. Andi was freaking out, but my brothers enjoyed it. Thank goodness, the water wasn't running. What if it was?

Would he have gone down to twenty feet and dropped me in the deep end? Then lower the struts so I could grab hold of the chopper James Bond–style and pull myself into the cockpit? I would have liked that.

Kleine Curacao was deserted for most of the day. The four of us spent the hours swimming, eating, drinking, walking, talking, and so on. It's not often that you have an entire island to yourself. Right around dusk, a yacht moored nearby, and we saw some people walking toward us.

"Hello," said the captain as he looked in all directions for our watercraft. "How in the hell did you get out here?" At that exact moment, the thumping noise of helicopter blades became audible.

"Funny you should ask. Here comes our ride right now," I said with just a little smugness. You should have seen the looks on their faces as we jumped aboard and whooshed upward. On the way back, I asked the pilot to fly under the Queen Juliana Bridge. He would have been grounded by the FAA if he did something like that in the United States. But he obliged. We startled a few tourists and irritated some dockworkers, but it was great fun. We landed shortly afterward, gathered up our stuff, and headed home. What a day.

Back at work, I was on a hot streak. I managed to get salary increases for our local staff for the first time in five years; convinced bureau counterparts in DC to upgrade electrical systems on post and to fund the repaving of the entire compound; had a kitchen built in our office building, which was a big morale lift for my staff; built several new garages for our armored vehicles, which greatly diminished the sun damage to their polymer windshields; and remodeled additional space for our growing DEA staff. In the role of acting chief of mission (yes, that's right), I attended government meetings, ran country team-staff meetings, and met with VIPs from ship captains to aircraft commanders. I hosted a Status of Forces Agreement (SOFA) conference between the Netherlands Antilles and the United States, involving the ministry of foreign affairs, the solicitor general, the minister of defense (legal), and the attorney general of Aruba, and a US DOD negotiation team that flew in from Washington, DC. In the end, both countries successfully extended the SOFA document.

And even though employment was almost nonexistent for spouses at post, Andi still managed to find part-time work as a special projects coordinator. She handled a variety of different programs. One of her most important roles was managing our inbound and outbound classified pouch operations and other nonscheduled classified equipment and correspondence. She'd drive right on the tarmac at the airport and greet the diplomatic courier at the bottom of the steps, exchange IDs and materials, and deliver or receive classified information. It was quite clandestine. She also handled our retail price survey, acted as an escort in controlled-access areas, and honchoed many consulate activities, including Curacao's International Bazaar, Caribbean Navy Days, and Independence Day celebrations.

As a vice counsel and consular officer, I stayed very involved in many American citizen cases that arose during my time in Curacao. Here are a few of them.

Throughout my tour, we remained actively involved in the Natalee Holloway case in Aruba. As you recall, she disappeared while on vacation in 2005 and was never found. The primary suspect, Joran van der Sloot, continued to haunt her family and local authorities with wild-goose chases. Every time the case would fall off the front pages, van der Sloot would make up another outrageous story about the location of her remains, or that he had sold her into sexual slavery, or some other insane statement. This would reopen wounds in the family and create all kinds of havoc with the FBI, divers, ships, the Dutch government, Greta Van Susteren of Fox News, and so on. Of course, his dribble never led to anything. Over in Curacao, these gyrations really put our consular officer in a tough position. As much as we tried to assist at every turn, the end result was that we could do little to help. It's ironic, isn't it, that he met his waterloo in Peru, where he was convicted and incarcerated for murder? I hope he rots in jail and gets plenty of unwanted conjugal visits.

I was directly involved in a case where four American citizen dancers were being held captive at a nightclub in Aruba and were being forced to prostitute themselves. I sent police to the location and carefully tried to subdue an armed club manager over the phone until help had arrived. When the police raided the club, they were able to catch the owner by surprise, disarm him, and gain custody of the dancers. I could hear him in the background threatening the girls with violence. (I told the club manager over and over again that I didn't call the police—maybe he bought it.) Next, I had them transferred to an unnamed hotel, mainly because I believed they were in real danger. Within hours, I found their next of kin and secured funding to get them out of Aruba. The following morning, I initiated a police escort to the airport, where I had arranged for Aruba's preclearance facility employees to meet them outside the concourse. My goal was to make certain that the dancers were *never* left unaccompanied. Everyone involved sighed in relief as the plane headed skyward. It was very gratifying to hear from the girls in the United States expressing how thankful they were for our assistance.

But nothing rocked this small post harder than the next American citizen case. In the fall of 2008, our consular officer, James Hogan, disappeared. As his supervisor and vice consul, my role changed immediately. I met with the police commissioner and lead inspector to open the case and to ensure that the disappearance had the highest priority; that the rules of engagement for eventual US involvement were understood; and that armed guards and roving patrols, including a victims' expert, were dispatched to his home and family. Everyone from Ambassador Dunn and the force protection guys to the DEA staff and my GSO employees were combing the small island trying to locate him. A lost diplomat is a big thing in the State Department. (Just look at the consulate in Benghazi.) Within days, our post was overridden with diplomatic security personnel, FBI agents, a

Western Hemisphere Affairs cadre, local police, and TDY personnel from around the Caribbean region. I arranged to fly in the adult children so they all could be with their mother. I also brought in the regional psychiatrist and set up a series of outreach sessions for the family.

After several weeks, the strain of this effort was getting to us all. Jim was a good friend to me and to many of the DEA agents. As his supervisor, I probably spent more time with him than his wife did. And even though we tried everything we could to find him, there was a definite sense of dread in the consulate. And much of it rested on his spouse, Abby. As the case moved on, many of her comments to authorities seemed contradictory. From the first day, some of our DEA agents suspected that Abby was involved in the disappearance. There were too many things that didn't add up. As the case went on, more and more of us felt that she was hiding something. But what could we do? Without proof, we had to continue to support her and her five children in the best manner possible.

For several months, the Hogan investigation continued in vain. The USG, and the Dutch government, did everything they could to assist. We had divers combing the location where some of his clothes were found, and air assets flying all around the east end of the island. There were literally hundreds of police and military on foot scouring the area for signs of Jim Hogan. We used scent dogs and boats of all sorts to widen the search. In the end, he was lost forever. One year later, Secretary Clinton's office declared James Hogan, a US diplomat, deceased. Gone, but not forgotten.

(Postscript: Abby Hogan was found guilty of obstruction of justice in the case of the disappearance of her spouse, James Hogan. She received a one-year prison sentence for repeatedly providing false information to US law-enforcement officials. It was later determined that she had deleted over three hundred e-mails that may have been valuable to the case, including information about her extramarital affair.)

In an odd way, the disappearance of Jim Hogan highlighted a streak of events—most of them unlucky—that stayed with us until we left Curacao.

It started innocently enough. In 2008, just before Christmas, Kismet II disappeared. As you recall, we had lost Kismet I in Virginia, and Andi never recovered from it. (Remember, she rescued that kitten from under a car on a busy street in Turkey.) We paced every block in our community looking for her, hung signs everywhere, and offered a five-hundred-dollar reward. I felt so bad for my wife, but there was nothing else we could do. Then on Christmas Eve, while I was in the shower, I heard Andi shriek. "It's Kismet. Don, it's Kismet at the front door!" Nine days after her disappearance—at half her previous body weight—our cat was back. (Good luck to find the cat, or bad luck to lose it— or both?)

In early 2009, Andi had one of her worst diabetic incidents ever. Her blood sugar was so low that my glucagon injections couldn't bring her back from hypoglycemic shock. She was having convulsions and sweating profusely. So I called an ambulance. When they arrived and checked her blood sugar, they sent me down the hall to get some clean towels. When

I returned, the nurse was seconds away from giving Andi an insulin shot! This would have killed her in minutes. I grabbed her hand.

"What in the hell are you doing? She doesn't need insulin; she needs glucose. You could have killed her!"

The nurse replied, "Her glucose level is 332. She needs insulin." I was stunned. In twenty-plus years of marriage, I had to resuscitate her at least fifty times, and she was *never* high in glucose. I knew this lady was bonkers.

"No way, lady. Check it again. Look at her. She's in hypoglycemic shock," I screamed. She finally agreed to recheck her sugar level. It was 32, not 332—a life-threateningly low glucose level. As it turns out, the nurse had forgotten her glasses and had misread the monitor! This could have been a piece of bad luck that proved fatal.

Just a few months later, my mother, Theresa Kachinko, died in her sleep at the age of eighty-two.

She was found in her normal sleeping position by my brother John. On the day she passed away, my brother Larry was on the phone with Andi when I came home from work.

"Don, it's your brother. I'm sorry, but your mother has passed away," Andi said as I walked through the front door.

Larry and I talked for a long time, discussing our migration to Pittsburgh for the funeral, memories of our mother, and so on. He was the perfect person to call me at this juncture. We were the closest to each other, and he knew all about my up-and-down relationship with Mom. I shared with Larry how much fun I had on my last trip to Pittsburgh. It felt like our mother was trying to make up for lost time. Her conversations had an underlying message: "Good-bye, no hard feelings, right?" The message was received loud and clear. No hard feelings, Mom. I love you. *Didn't I always come home when the streetlights came on?*

With both parents gone, the Feeney kids were orphans now. Reluctantly, we had to admit that this was probably a blessing. As I mentioned earlier, Mom was ready to leave this earth, and no one was going to stop her.

Back home, the five siblings rode in a black limousine right behind our mother, who was in the hearse in front of us. We were on our way to the burial site. I was glad the service was over, because I couldn't enter the funeral home. I didn't want my last memories of my mother clouded up by a casket and some eerie makeup. It just didn't add up for me. (Note: I couldn't attend the funeral service for my dad either.)

And just when I thought I had handled things pretty responsibly, I lost it in the limo. My brothers and sisters were pointing out new restaurants on the eastside, talking about capital-gain strategies for the modest amount of money Mom had left us, and other subjects I felt were inappropriate.

"WHY DON'T YOU ALL SHUT THE HELL UP? WE'RE TAKING MOM TO HER BURIAL, AND YOU'RE TALKING ABOUT RESTAURANTS AND CAPITAL GAINS AND SHIT? JUST SHUT UP. JUST SHUT UP AND SHOW SOME REMORSE. JESUS ..." I was not happy. I was trying to use my silent moments to pray and to honor my mother for everything she had done for us. But I couldn't concentrate because of all the banter in the limo.

Looking back, maybe I was out of line. But I didn't care. Everyone stopped jabbering, and we rode quietly to the cemetery. After the service, all was forgotten, and we bonded together as siblings. The next day, like the four winds blowing, we all went back to our normal lives. We knew the pain of losing our mother would dissipate over time, but in the immediate future, the process would be difficult. Each of us needed to grieve and to navigate the stages of grief at our own pace.

Just a few months later, I awoke one day with ringing in my right ear. I assumed it was a head cold and didn't think much of it. After a trip to DC for business, I stopped by Pittsburgh to visit the family. It was weird without Mom, but John and I were getting along pretty well then. He convinced me to get my ear checked and set up an appointment with an Ear, Nose, and Throat doctor, who prescribed a magnetic resonance imaging (MRI). MRIs are designed to use radiology to visualize structures in the body. The diagnosis was tinnitus, caused by hyperactivity in the brain. This activity caused the ear to involuntarily emanate high-pitched noises. But I must admit I felt a little uneasy when the doctor mentioned that there was something else in my brain! He suggested a magnetic resonance angiogram (MRA), which uses magnetic files and pulses of radio-wave energy to provide pictures of blood vessels. Since I was leaving for Curacao the next morning, I decided to get the MRA done there. And then the fun really began ...

After tracking down the lone MRA machine on Curacao, I was told it was broken, and no one had any idea when it would be fixed. So I tried to get an appointment with the only neurologist on the island. I even left my MRI results from Pittsburgh in his office. He never touched them. Weeks went by, and I started to wonder what the hell was going on. I e-mailed our DOS regional physician and explained my situation. He hooked me up with a doctor in town who recommended a computer tomography (CT) scan. This procedure uses X-rays to make detailed pictures of the structures inside the body. I'll never forget his phone call after the local hospital released the scan results:

"Mr. Feeney, this is Dr. Jones [not his real name]. I don't want to alarm you, but you need to listen carefully. You have a brain aneurysm, a quite large brain aneurysm, and you need to see a neurologist immediately." Coincidently, our regional physician was arriving in Curacao the next day. So I met with him and explained the scenario thus far; he decided to refer me to our regional medical office in Fort Lauderdale. The decision was immediate. I was to be MEDEVACed (medical evacuation) to Baptist Medical Center in Miami and see a neurologist the next day.

As it turns out, I had a football-shaped aneurism resting atop three large arteries in my brain. The recommended neurologist told me bluntly that brain surgery was impossible due to the location of the aneurism. Ten years earlier, that would have been my death sentence. However, at 8:00 p.m. that evening—with me present—he called a top-of-the-line vascular neurosurgeon on his cell phone and explained my situation. (I listened very intently, since my life was on the line.) Even though the doctor was out of town at a conference, he instructed me to bring the CT scan to his office the next day. At this point, I wasn't sure if I should feel lucky to get a quick consult or worried that I needed a quick consult.

Back at my hotel, I called Andi, explained everything to her, and advised her to catch the first flight to Miami. She was crying, and I was crying— nothing like a little adversity to spice up one's life, huh?

The results were crystal clear. The CT scan clearly showed a massive aneurysm. (I was later told that if the aneurysm broke, I would be unconscious before I hit the ground. And to think that I had waited almost two months for that doctor in Curacao to look at my MRI.) Dr. Smith (not his real name) went on to say that I needed surgery the next day. I was told to go back to my hotel and remain as motionless as possible, that is, in a Zen-like position, prior to the surgery. He worked in the Cardiac and Vascular Institute, which is part of Baptist Medical Center. His recent success neutralizing aneurysms using arteries for entry to the brain was highly experimental. The plan was to run surgical instruments through my leg, up the carotid artery into the brain. While there, he would fill the aneurysm with platinum and apply a porous stent to the area to allow tissue to grow over the entrance, essentially sealing the membrane. The operation was very risky, with a 30 to 40 percent chance of death. In addition, since Dr. Smith had never attempted a triple stent, he would be forced to sever one of my cerebral arteries and try to construct a risky double stent. This probably would mean a stroke on my left side.

One of the disadvantages of government-run health care is that it settles for the lowest common denominator. Reduced fees, aging equipment, hidden taxes, long lines, extended reimbursement periods, higher costs, loss of choice, and so on all lead to declining medical care. The medical staffs that remain under these conditions tend to become facilitators, collecting small government-mandated fees and spending most of their time referring difficult cases elsewhere. Is it fair to pay $400,000 or $500,000 to complete medical school, and then have the government tell you what your expertise is worth? (The lines in our visa section seeking US entry for medical care were a constant reminder of the failed Dutch health system in the Netherlands Antilles.) For example, not only did the neurologist purposely avoid looking at my MRI, but he also knew he was unqualified to do anything about it. So he did nothing. Since he only received $35 per patient, why bother with anything requiring real medical expertise?

Another example: when I was considering bidding on a management officer job at the consulate in Toronto, the incumbent asked me if I had any medical issues. At the time, I was fine, but we did have Andi's diabetes to worry about. He told me flatly to forget about coming to Canada. The government-run medical care program was a bust, and consulate employees waited months for appointments. In fact, many times they were denied care altogether by administrators. The post was forced to rely on regularly scheduled trips to Buffalo just to get the care they needed. It reminds me of the Jay Leno quip:

"If ObamaCare passes in the Congress, where are Canadians going to go for medical care?"

Despite it all, with Andi at my side, I felt calmer than at any other time in my life. It was wildly serene. My fate would be determined, hit or miss, lucky or unlucky, and I had no control over it. To me, all the pressure was on Andi. Under the effects of anesthesia, if I didn't make it, I'd never know it. If I came out of this with a stroke, she would become an instant 24-7 caretaker. I couldn't help feeling that she was getting the lousy end of the deal. I cautioned her to prepare for the worst, told her I loved her, and off I went.

As I was being wheeled down the corridor, I thought about my life and about God, and wondered whether to pray to him for my survival or not. As a rule, I don't usually pray for things from God. The way I see it, there are millions of people who need his help more than I do. I've never prayed for a promotion, money, luck, or anything like that. I remember thinking, *God, if you decide to let me hang around a little longer, I'll take it.* (I've always believed the Big Guy had a sense of humor and didn't mind a little patronizing.) *Who knows, maybe you have something else in mind for me (a book, maybe?).* Either way, I was prepared to accept his decision. Looking back, I'd had a pretty good life so far. The road to this moment had been eventful, to be sure, and I had a blast. If it was over, so be it.

Seven hours later, I awoke in the recovery room. My first thought was about the stroke. (My dad had a stroke, and it had been permanent. He would burn his fingers with cigarettes because he didn't feel the fire melting his skin.) I moved my left hand and wriggled my fingers. No stroke. Then I thought, *maybe the surgery hasn't begun yet.* At that exact moment, Andi came bursting into the recovery room, tears of joy in her eyes. "Did I have the surgery?" I asked.

"Yes, and everything went perfectly." She beamed. "Dr. Smith was so excited by the results that he was actually giggling."

"Can you move your left arm?" Andi asked.

"Yes. Thank God." *He picked the correct artery*—how lucky was that? There were many follow-up procedures over the next three years, all of them producing the same result—the aneurysm was gone! It was just scar tissue now. Over the years, I couldn't resist some self-deprecating humor about the operation. Here are my two favorite gag lines:

Don't let them cremate me before digging out the platinum. At $1,500 an ounce, I'm worth a lot more now.

And you thought I was hardheaded before …

Let's review the wreckage: Kismet II had been lost, just like Kismet I, I had developed tinnitus, Jim Hogan had disappeared, Andi had narrowly avoided a lethal injection, my mother had died, and I had survived brain surgery. A pretty good posting so far …

Were these events lucky or unlucky? Think about it. As I mentioned above, is it lucky to find a cat that's lost, or is it unlucky to lose one? Was I lucky the tinnitus MRI located my aneurysm? Or is a lifetime of ringing in my left ear caused by the tinnitus an unlucky result? Was Jim's disappearance unlucky or just plain criminal? Were we lucky to avoid a diabetic catastrophe, or unlucky that Andi has suffered from diabetes since the age of twenty-five? Is it unlucky that my mother died, even if that's what she wanted? Am I lucky to have survived brain surgery, or would I be luckier if I never had a problem to begin with?

Back in Cas Grande, Andi and I were doing our best to put past incidents behind us. We needed to get out of the house and enjoy the island again. Although Curacao wasn't overwhelmed with activities, it had a pretty eclectic selection of interesting spots. One of our favorites was Zanzibar's, located on Jan Thiel Beach. It's the classic outside, beachfront restaurant, with straw roofing and a cantina-type ambience. This was our "Dutch" place, that is, one of the few places predominantly frequented by locals. Just a few miles to the west was Mambo Beach, the exact opposite. It catered to tourists, and that's just what we liked when we hung out there. I already mentioned the Kura Hulanda complex, as well as Iguana Café, two mainstays when we went into Willemstad. Near our home was a place called the Boathouse, which provided excellent food and wonderful views overlooking the Spanish Waters. When we felt like being around Americans, we headed to the Marriott Hotel and hung around the pool bar talking to folks from the United States. We were occasionally drawn to Tony Roma's near Willemstad for the Kickin' Shrimp, and to Cravings nearby for the edamame.

Andi and I met a lot of nice people in Curacao. But my best buddy was Brad, our military liaison officer at post. He had a huge job, trying to balance the needs of the DOD (his chain of command) with the needs of the ambassador (a job delegated to me). We worked well together, mainly because Ambassador Dunn was very supportive, and so were the FOL commanders at the airport. Brad and I spent many hours at the Kura Hulanda, talking about work and life in general. I was glad to have him around.

One weekend, Brad had talked me into hiking Mt. Christoffel, the highest peak on the island at 1,227 feet. It was a steep and challenging climb, especially since it had just rained and the rocks were wet. Near the top, it got very steep, and the footholds were definitely slippery. But we made it, and the summit was beautiful. With 360-degree views of Curacao and flora and fauna everywhere protected by a natural refuge park, I was glad Brad talked me into this climb. But he wasn't done. Next he led me to a small town on the western side of the island, where his favorite cliff-diving spot was located. The ledge had to be at least ninety feet high. He jumped and waited for me to follow. After a few nervous moments, I took a deep breath and leaped. It felt like slow motion on the way down. I hit the water hard, but I was okay. Why is it always uplifting to confront one's fears and then conquer them?

Years later, Brad and I still get together when we can. He is an American Airlines pilot, and a USAF aircraft commander (KC-135 tanker). I don't see him much these days because he's always going back and forth to Afghanistan to support US airpower.

As our posting was coming to an end, I would be remiss if I didn't mention the other ABC Islands, Aruba and Bonaire.

Aruba is a short eighteen-minute flight from Hato International. It's much smaller than Curacao and has a very arid climate. Tourists love it because of its beaches, the dependable sunny weather, and the fact that it lies outside the hurricane belt. On the downside, it's very densely populated and offers very little outside of the tourist areas. I always looked at Aruba this way: if you visit for a few days, go to Aruba. If you stay longer, go to Curacao. The beaches in Aruba are nice, with many hotels, bars, and restaurants. Oranjestad, the capital, is quaint, with some shopping and tourist activities. However, beyond that, there is very little to do inland. Every time we went there, it was just to hang out on the beach, eat and drink, and decompress over a long weekend.

Bonaire, on the other hand, was a totally different experience. Although, like Aruba, it depends on tourism to support the economy, that's where the similarity ends. Bonaire is midsize compared to Curacao and Aruba, has very few beaches, and caters to scuba divers and snorkelers. Because of its location in the Caribbean Sea, it is world-renowned for scuba diving and consistently rates as one of the best diving locations in the world. (Note: When my tinnitus started kicking up, I abandoned diving. No one could convince me that the atmospheric pressure from diving hadn't created or contributed to the ringing in my ear.) Lac Bay, in the south part of the island, is the sailing center, with boats from all over the globe. Overall, Bonaire is very laid-back and has the feel of the old tropics, that is, rustic small towns like Kralendijk, the capital, nestled among homey neighborhoods, devoid of mass development and large hotel chains.

We rented a dune buggy and covered the entire island, from gigantic salt farms in the south, to Washington-Slagbaai National Park in the northern corner of the island. The happy hours were calm and very relaxing. We loved hanging out at the Rumba Café, especially since it had Feeney's Whiskey on the shelf (no relation, though) . We also loved to stroll from our regular hotel—Divi Flamingo— down to the City Café, one of the few places where people gathered. It was a wonderful diversion from the crowds of Aruba and Curacao.

While all this excitement was going on, I was actively bidding on my next posting. Since Andi and I were pretty sure this would be our last embassy, we decided to concentrate more on location and less on career progression. Both of us were slightly surprised when I was offered a handshake for our top preference—Athens, Greece. (With twenty-six bidders for one opening, I didn't think it would happen.) Pretty lucky, huh?

During our last few months in the Netherland Antilles, we were already preparing for Athens, Greece. We scoured the Internet for anything we could find, and bombarded our sponsor with questions about Athens. But even though I had my hand on the rearview mirror, I wasn't ready to throw it away yet. This whole concept of luck kept me from activating my usual "what's behind me is not important" approach.

What is luck? I still didn't have a clue. Is it really something measurable? Can it be influenced by fate, or perhaps early preparation? Can you make your own luck? When someone is down on their luck or out of luck, where does it go?

Maybe Socrates had it right when he said:

"True wisdom comes to each of us when we realize how little we understand about life, ourselves, and the world around us."

Am I nuts, or is TMYKTMYDKS saying the same thing? I guess I'll ask Socrates when I get to Greece. Maybe luck is just life—plain and simple. As your life ebbs and flows, just like the Feeneys', perhaps you also seek explanations for the unknown. Focusing on good luck or bad luck may be a healthy way to get past changing events in our lives. But be careful—I think problems can arise if we dwell too much on luck, especially bad luck. I'm reminded of a quote by Sydney J. Harris, an American journalist from Chicago, who once said:

"When I hear somebody sigh, 'Life is hard,' I am always tempted to ask, 'Compared to what?'"

Armino was waiting outside the house on Kaya Vivaldi, our bags were packed, and I had Kismet's carrier in my hand. (I swear, I've been toting that damn cat carrier for decades.) A moment later, Andi and I left our vice consul house for the final time. We had gotten through some tough times on that little island. The memory of my mother's death was fading steadily, but it still crept into my dreams. Andi's diabetic problems have continued, and they scare the hell out of me. Jim is long gone, Kismet is still with us, the upside-down room still haunts me, and my tinnitus would drive me to drink if I didn't already.

But we'll survive ...

Crossing the Queen Juliana Bridge for the last time, I finally did reach for that rearview mirror, and symbolically tossed it behind me as we gazed at the lights of Willemstad below. Luck or no luck, life goes on, and the events of the last three years might as well be from the Dark Ages for all I care. Life — what a precious commodity. If luck is part of it, so be it. If it isn't, that's okay too. In the end, no one says it better than Irving Berlin:

"Life is 10 percent what you make of it, and 90 percent how you take it."

CHAPTER TWENTY-THREE

From the Cradle of Democracy to the Birth of Restartment (WhereDoes Space End?)

———————◄○►———————

Our plane dipped, then thrust forward. The morning light hovered over Curacao like a halo. As usual, leaving a place for the last time creates an SSE in my life and generates a free flow of thoughts. In particular, I was wondering why we are so quick to forget our past. Is it some form of survival ritual from lost millennia? Is it a way for the subconscious to simplify complexities in our lives by moving pain and trauma to the back of our minds? Are we all Italian drivers, eager to throw away the rearview mirror? Are we doomed to repeat the past if we ignore it, like Churchill said? Does time really heal all wounds? Does adversity make us stronger? Or is it still just cognitive dissonance—the brain's way of rebalancing our lives and minimizing the baggage? I couldn't answer these questions then, and I can't answer them now. But I do know this: whether you believe in God or not, your ability to think is the most godlike gift that you'll ever give or receive. It's the brain that generates feelings in the heart and depth in the soul. It's boundless, just like space. And like space, no one knows where it ends. (Try getting an atheist to explain mysteries like these.)

Andi and I were going to be okay. We've survived a few scares, but who hasn't? Although the future is uncertain, it's great to have the brain along for the ride. After all, like Bob Dylan says, "Yesterday is just a memory, and tomorrow's never what it's supposed to be."

I vowed then and there to be grateful for my life with Andi, to be thankful to God for allowing me to survive, and to accept the lucky and not-so-lucky experiences as part of the mix.

It was the summer of 2010, and it was time for home leave (HL). For the last thirty years, every time I changed locations or took a vacation, I always went home to visit family. I spent many months bouncing in and out of distant airports, from Australia to the Middle East and from Turkey to Hawaii. I estimate that these reuniting trips cost us more than

271

$100,000. It was time for a change. Andi and I decided to rent a condo in Fort Myers Beach, Florida, and announced to all our relatives that we'd have a spare bedroom for visitors. We suggested they lock in their dates early, so we could get some kind of schedule going. We flew into Miami International for the thousandth time, rented a car, and headed west to the Gulf of Mexico. The place was right on the beach. As much as we loved the Atlantic side of Florida, we thought using HL to feel out the Gulf Coast would help us determine a retirement location at a later date. It was a quiet, fun month. We worked out every day, took long walks on the beach, and hung out at beachside establishments talking to anyone and everyone. We used our rental car to cruise up and down the coast, and took in the beauty of Florida. (We both knew we wanted to retire there, but we didn't know when or where yet.)

Unfortunately, no one came to stay with us. Initially I was hurt by this. After all those years of tracking down relatives and doing my best to keep in touch from light-years away, I felt it was someone else's turn to reach out. But this soon passed. Everybody had their lives to worry about, and few people in this world have the freedom and financial ability to travel like we did. And in some ways, I expected this. I predicted that after my mom died, my brothers and sisters would drift further apart. It was only logical, since most of our get-togethers were in Pittsburgh and centered around my mother. With her no longer with us, traveling home lost some of its appeal. During the funeral services, there was talk about annual get-togethers, but I knew that would never happen.

After HL was over, it was off to Washington, DC, again. I was entering a new geographic region of the State Department—the Bureau of European and Eurasian Affairs (EUR)—and had several consultation meetings in Main State. In addition, I was also required to complete some mandatory leadership training. Andi and I loved the short trips to DC the best. Get in, do your thing, then get out. We stayed in Georgetown (of course), and found all our favorite restaurants. We met with old friends, and made some new ones in the EUR bureau. I enjoyed my Memorial-Bridge-to-Key-Bridge walks, and started right where I had left off at my favorite watering hole— Nick's Riverside Grill. All the usual characters were there.

We didn't think much about it, but when we boarded the plane from Dulles International to Athens, it would be our final nomadic journey …

And it started poorly. Our flight from DC was delayed by three hours, and our connection in Madrid was going to be close. For some reason, we had decided to carry Kismet II on the plane with us—big mistake. Halfway to Spain, she chewed right through the cat carrier! So I spent the next three hours playing jack-in-the-box with her. Her head would pop out, I'd push it back in, her head would pop out, and I'd push it back in … You get the message. (I wonder how mischievous she would have been if we hadn't given her a tranquilizer.)

After our arrival in Spain, we gathered all our bags, got through customs and immigration and security screening, and then had to hustle to another terminal for our connection to Greece. There were stressful signs along the way saying "fifty minutes to the gates," then "forty minutes to the gates." We weren't going to make it. I told Andi to run for it and try to hold the gangway open long enough for me to check all the bags. With our cat popping in and out of her carrier and bags hanging from both arms, I ran as fast as I could. Exhausted, physically and mentally, I arrived at the gate. Thank goodness, Andi was standing there with a flight attendant at the Jetway door. They were waiting for me and our crazy cat.

After a second sedative, Kismet was inert when we landed at Eleftherios Venizelos in Athens. Our sponsor met us at the baggage claim, the driver loaded up our bags into the embassy van, and off we went to our new home. The apartment was located on the side of Lycabettus Hill, in the Kolonaki section of Athens, just a few blocks northwest of the US embassy. It was smallish by US standards—but did have three bedrooms and two and a half baths. The bedrooms were on the second floor of the building, and the living area was on the third. The Kolonaki area was popular and crowded, and had high-rise apartment buildings on every street. Our apartment—located at 50 Kleomenous—was well-maintained, with hardwood floors, a nice-sized kitchen, and a fireplace. The unit also had off-street parking, a real plus in any Athens neighborhood. Our sponsor left us food and supplies, including cat food and a litter box. Andi and I felt comfortable almost immediately.

In general, our lives were always about contrast. A short time ago, we had been living in a big house on a small island, with only one road to the consulate. Now we were in a small apartment, in a crowded neighborhood, living in a huge city, surrounded by dozens of multilane highways. I was no longer a big fish in a small pond, serving as the number-two guy under the chief of mission, with direct responsibility for thirty-five people. I was now a small fish in a big pond, inheriting a human resource management position with policy oversight encompassing over five hundred embassy employees. Ocean views were replaced by balcony views, the pool was an afterthought, and the iguanas were long forgotten. Our Honda CRV—critical in Curacao for transportation—was practically useless in Athens, since we walked 95 percent of the time. If it wasn't for weekend trips and once-a-week treks to the grocery store, we could have easily survived without an automobile. Even the fish and vegetable market, the *laiki,* was just one block away.

We awoke fresh on a Friday morning and couldn't wait to see Athens. I had the day off and wasn't expected at the embassy until Monday. (Our cat had an interesting night—I think we over-sedated her. At one point, she passed out while she was eating, and plopped headfirst right into her bowl! But she came around eventually. I must admit, it was funny watching her bumping into things and stagger around like a college freshman at his first frat party.)

Acting on the advice of my sponsor, we started our Greek experience with Mount Lycabettus. At 908 feet, it's the highest point in the city and an ideal location to view the entire Athens panorama. As we ascended up Kleomenous, we noticed an opening between apartment buildings.

There— framed perfectly—we saw the Acropolis for the first time. It was like a dream. She rose above Athens, perched on a nest of stone. Although the Parthenon dominated the view, we also noticed many other structures, including the Temple of Athena Nike (built to commemorate the Athenians' victory over the Persians) and the Propylaia (main entrance to the enchanted city).

Andi and I rode the Funicular, a railway that ascends to the summit via an underground track. According to myth, Lycabettus was created when Athena accidently dropped the mountain she had been carrying from Pallene for the construction of the Acropolis. At the top is a small church, Ayois Georgios, an amphitheater, two restaurants, and a couple of large outside sitting areas. In a way, the mount hovered over Greece like a helicopter. The unrestricted 360-degree vista was breathtaking. What a magical start to our new posting.

We were speechless when we saw the Acropolis in its entirety, seeming to float atop the city. We also located Hadrian's Arch, the Ancient Temple of Zeus, the Ancient Agora, the National Gardens, the Neo-Classical Parliament Building, and the National Historic Museum. After some serious searching, we finally pinpointed the Plaka, which is the oldest continuously inhabited area of the city and rests upon what used to be the center of Athens centuries ago. The area sits just below the Acropolis, on the north side of Athens, and would become our favorite place in Greece. Full of tourists and Athenians alike, it's shoehorned amid ancient ruins and archaeological sites, but still retains an undeniable charm. There were *tavernas* (restaurants) everywhere, and thousands of outside seating areas for dining and people watching. Musicians could be heard in all directions, and tour groups traipsed by in large numbers. The most amazing thing about the Plaka is that it continues to maintain its ancient feel, even though it sits right next to downtown Athens. We ended our first full day in Greece with dinner at Café Peros, in Kolonaki Square, which is a chic shopping and dining area near our house.

We awoke the next morning as excited as five-year-olds on Christmas. Our plan was to spend the weekend walking around Athens—a recon mission if you will—to size up our new neighborhood. It was a breeze strolling down Lycabettus Hill, through Kolonaki Square, and down to Vas Sofias, the main street into Athens. (The US embassy is located on the same street, just a short twelve-minute walk away.) We passed two museums, the Benaki and the Cycladic (our favorite by far), crossed the street, and entered into the National Gardens. The garden area is massive, with Parliament and Syntagma Square on the northwest side of the park, and the Zapion Exhibition and Congress Hall in the center. The Zapion hosted many historic events, including the signing of the EU Treaty, the start of the Athens marathon, and some outrageously good wine fests. On the south end of the National Gardens are two ancient structures—the Temple of Olympian Zeus, and Hadrian's Arch. Temples were the most important public buildings of ancient Greece. The Temple of Olympian Zeus was built in Doric style and is the largest temple in Greek history, exceeding even the Parthenon. It took 650 years to complete. Hadrian built his arch in a strategic location, carefully placed to mark the boundary between ancient Greece and the "new" Athens under Hadrian's rule. (Note: Hadrian's Library near Monastiraki Square was also quite impressive.)

We strolled down Ermou Street, where shopping outlets of every kind can be found. A short trek across the Plateia Lysikratous, and we arrived on Adrianou Street in the Plaka. The plaza is so named for the monument of Lysikrates that dominates the area. The monument is the best-preserved choragic structure in Athens. These monuments were built in ancient Greece to house trophies. Lysicrates, a local citizen, built this one in the fourth century BC. Adrianou Street is the main artery that passes through the Plaka. (It became part of our weekend walking ritual, rivaled only by the DC Memorial/Key Bridge walk, and I enjoyed it each and every time.)

Andi and I decided to walk in a circular route, ending up back on Adrianou near Monastiraki Square. This entailed walking up the south side of the Acropolis on the Dionysos Areopagitou (DA), a cobblestoned arcade protected from vehicle traffic. The DA was full of wonders. We passed the brand-new Acropolis Museum, the Theatre at Dionysos (birthplace of the Greek tragedy, and the first theater built of stone), and the Odium of Herodes Atticus (still in use today). We crossed the apex, and started down the Theorias Alameda on the northwest side. This part of the promenade was beautiful, with great scenes of the Acropolis above and very nice outside tavernas along the way. At the bottom of the hill, we were back on the other end of Adrianou. A sharp right, and we passed the Museum of the Ancient Agora, the Ancient Agora (marketplace), and the Stoa of Attalus (covered arcade used for merchants, artists, and religious gatherings). After the first of many leisurely lunches near the Ancient Agora, we circled back through Monastiraki Square, and then back to our apartment in Kolonaki. (The only downside involved topography. The walk from our apartment to the Plaka was all downhill. On hot days, the uphill return was brutal. I recall a few times wimping out and calling a taxi.)

Needless to say, we were energized by our new posting, and confident that we would treasure our tour in Athens. It was now time to concentrate on my new job at the embassy.

The Regional Human Resources Management position was a huge responsibility. My staff and I oversaw 195 USG employees, three hundred locally employed (LE) staff, and eleven ambassador and deputy chief of mission residence personnel. We had direct HR management over twenty-two different government agencies, and also supported the US consulate in Thessaloniki. I had eleven employees on my staff, with a mixture of LE and American positions. Our office was charged with being the subject-matter expert for all HRM programs. In short, this meant that we represented the ambassador, and the United States, on a wide variety of issues, including US visa policy for mission members, legalities of local labor law, compensation packages, recruitment, hiring, orientation, career development, position classification, promotions, awards, performance evaluations, separations, and retirements. It was a grind to say the least. (Of course, there were many unspoken responsibilities that never appeared on a diplomat's job description. I'll just leave it at that.)

The US embassy is located on Vas Sofias, approximately one mile from the Acropolis. The mission covers an entire city block and rests on a trapezoid-shaped section of real estate. The chancery was built in the front, and another large annex was constructed right behind it. The chancery's design resembles the Parthenon, but built in a modern manner. It's covered in Pentellic marble, stands three stories high, with a fourth floor underground, and has a large outside courtyard in the center. To protect it from sunlight, a dramatic façade extends twenty feet around its square structure, making it the most dramatic feature of the building. With over five hundred people working in the compound, many other amenities were added. The mission has a cafeteria, gym, Navy Exchange Store, medical facility, and very large parking garage. It wasn't El Salvador's spacious compound, but all in all, it was a reasonable facility.

When I accepted this assignment, I had a good buddy and colleague who told me I was crazy. He said only a sadist would take on the problems in Athens. By the end of the first year, I began to realize he was right. The problem areas were threefold. First, the chaotic economic situation, where Greece faced constant threats of a government default. Second, the Peter Principle—in a hierarchy, individuals tend to rise to their levels of incompetence—reared its ugly head. And third, the Greek employees were some of the most ungrateful local nationals I have ever worked with. I'll touch on each of these briefly.

The Greek economic collapse was the canary in the coal mine for the European Union (EU). Years of spending money on government pensions and other benefit programs, coupled with the inability to collect enough taxes to compensate for their extravagant spending, put Greece in this predicament. The Greeks endured thousands of federal worker layoffs and watched as hundreds of businesses went under each month. The unofficial unemployment rate was well over 24 percent. For young workers—ages eighteen through twenty-five—the rate was as high as 45 percent. Many employees were furloughed indefinitely or forced to work reduced hours. Like any culture, a combination of no jobs and too much free time breeds problems. Crime was soaring by the time we left. In our two years in Athens, we had our car broken into twice, and the heating oil from our basement stolen three times. On the medical front, two government-run hospitals closed blocks from the embassy. Although the state was still collecting revenue for health care, it was a failure, like every other place I have been. The primary care was so bad that most Greeks paid extra for private health care, in addition to the mandatory cost of a broken public-health system. I personally dealt with doctors and dentists who refused to issue receipts—an obvious attempt to avoid paying taxes. The Parliament kept raising taxes, trying in vain to cover up their overspending with even more spending. It didn't work. (Hear that, America?)

If it weren't for the EU—especially Germany—stepping up to bail out Greece, it would have definitely collapsed. The aftershock might have been deafening. Average hardworking people couldn't make enough money to cover current tax levies, let alone the constant flood of new ones. The Parliament continued to raise property assessments, and created new revenue streams like the ambiguous "austerity tax." (If you failed to make payment, your electricity was shut off. This from the cradle of democracy?) Salaries were cut across the nation. All investment money fled the Greek marketplace, companies relocated, and the wealthy moved private fortunes elsewhere. Bonds were practically worthless, and were downgraded to junk level. Prices continued to go up as supply dwindled, while revenues were speeding downward. Amazingly, Ayn Rand predicted this exact scenario in *Atlas Shrugged*. Who is John Galt?

Simply put, it was a lose-lose scenario. If it weren't for the EU, the government would have crashed, taking down the Continent, and to a lesser extent the United States, with it.

Were the Greeks appreciative of this bailout? Hardly. They were constantly griping about the Germans. It wasn't uncommon to see pictures of Chancellor Merkel with a Hitler-type mustache in magazines or pasted on buildings and windows. Or witness self-indulgent demonstrations in Monastiraki Square demanding that Germany and the EU rescue them. What was their leverage? We failed, so you have to help us! If we default, so does the EU. It was a borderline shakedown—the only tactic they had left. The sense of entitlement was almost unbearable. Talk about biting the hand that feeds you! A large majority of Greeks felt it was Germany's responsibility to bail them out. After all, they had the money, so why shouldn't they?

Back in the embassy, the Peter Principle was in full regalia. Although there were many examples of incompetence to cite, I'll just mention a few closest to my neck of the woods. The two officers in my direct chain of command— management counselor and deputy chief of mission—were diplomats who surpassed their level of incompetency well before they arrived in Greece. The management counselor, although pleasant and intelligent, was well past her competency level. Focused on doing the least amount of work possible, she shifted and redirected every difficult situation to the sidelines or to somebody else to avoid confrontation. I'm not sure if it was because she was facing mandatory retirement, or that she just decided not to rock the boat. For whatever reason, her management style frustrated me to no end. In addition, she was a managing-up type of boss, and couldn't or wouldn't even think about questioning her supervisor's decisions, even when they adversely affected the mission. I saw a lot of potential in her, but it wasn't coming out.

The deputy chief of mission (DCM) was another story. As a former English teacher and public affairs officer, he was simply unqualified to lead. Our incoming ambassador took a risk and selected him because of his ability to speak fluent Greek. His usefulness ended there. He was emotional like a child, and pouted like one as well. When I disagreed with him, he'd lose it like someone with sand kicked in his face. He would regularly meet with small cadres of the local staff and gather all the scuttlebutt he could. And like an old crone in the park, he'd use the gossip against American officers. It never mattered if it was true or not. His wife was Greek, and worked in the management counselor's section for a while. When he became the DCM, she had to be removed under our nepotism regulations. He held that against me from that day forward. (Ironically, during an IG inspection of the mission, the fact that we acted quickly to fix this situation saved the ambassador from a direct hit that could have changed our overall rating.)

As I said before, SSEs come at the strangest moments. It was time for my performance evaluation, and the DCM was my formal reviewer. Since he wasn't a very good writer, I helped him edit portions of my evaluation. After several tries, he still couldn't get it right. The sentences were sporadic and didn't flow very well. Finally it came to this:

"John [not his real name], I've read your portion of my evaluation, and would like to make a few suggestions," I said. Since senior leaders rarely knew your day-to-day activities, employees were expected to assist them to ensure the evaluation was as strong as possible. Promotions depended on it.

"What suggestions do you have?" he asked skeptically.

"Well, the final few paragraphs are unclear and don't really address the issues accurately. If you'd like, I can draft an update for you, or send you two or three suggestions that would improve the clarity a little bit."

"No, leave it the way it is. Anything else?" I had nothing else, so I left.

In my line of work, everyone walks on water, and 95 percent of performance evaluations are excellent. Because of this anomaly, any deviation from excellence knocks you out of promotion consideration for years. I was moving pretty fast in the organization, and finished high in my class when I made FS-02. I knew, and so did he, that any tepid comments would slate me into the middle of the pack. He never liked me, but I didn't care. The code is simple: if an employee does good work, and the rater and reviewer have no reason to question his or her performance on or off the job, then they should ensure he or she gets a strong rating and a clear promotion recommendation. (My management counselor gave me a strong evaluation, due in part to her willingness to consider a few changes here and there.)

Put simply, the unclear message he sent me was in direct contrast to the clear message he conveyed to the promotion boards: *don't promote this guy. I don't like him.* His immaturity took over, and he knew his childlike refusal to improve my evaluation would affect my career. (I reviewed hundreds of performance appraisals in my line of work, and was more qualified than he would ever be. I can't tell you how many times I helped other supervisors upgrade the overall ratings of their employees.) Luckily, this type of behavior by senior leadership in the State Department didn't happen very often.

Unfortunately, there were many other examples of the DCM's inability to lead. When I think about how outstanding other DCMs have been in my career, I wince when I compare them to this guy. The SSE was formed then and there. I would retire early, after this assignment. I would tell Andi soon, but not yet. I would *never* work for an inferior supervisor again, nor let an incompetent person determine my future in any organization.

The negative effects of that conversation turned out to be a blessing in disguise. A small part of me considered staying in the State Department for another tour. But after meeting with the DCM, the small part was squashed like a bug on a sidewalk. The SSE had landed. I decided to tell Andi that I had had enough of the USG. Our finances were secure, and my health wasn't. I explained to her that I was very nervous about continuing to work and using up the last of my healthy years. Not many things scared me in life, but that one sure did. Of course, she understood immediately. She saw the apathy in my eyes, watched every morning as I slouched through the door on my way to the office, and was acutely aware of the toll it was taking on me mentally and physically. My decision to retire didn't surprise her—she was expecting it. (Like I said before, she's the smart one in this family.)

When motivated, we can move fast. After Andi and I agreed that the Space Coast (Indialantic, Florida,) was still our favorite retirement preference, she hit the Internet hard. We knew exactly what we wanted—beachfront condo, top floor, three bedrooms, three baths, corner unit, wraparound balcony, garage, and so on—and found a realtor who understood. Then we flew back to Florida several months before our tour was up, mainly to take advantage of the bottom in the real estate market. After several days of searching, we found the one and only place that met all our desires. So we bought it. With the house of our dreams secured—bought ridiculously low, at just the right time, with all-time low interest rates—our remaining months in the State Department would be tolerable. We had a plan in place, and our eyes were already focused on the finish line. The dull ache of embassy life in Athens was steadily being replaced by expectation and hope.

Besides the Greek economy and the rush of underachieving Peter Principle supervisors, the last off-putting area of frustration was the locally employed (LE) staff. The LE employees in this embassy were by far the hardest people to work with in my thirty-five-year government career. Many were professional, but many were not. Their sense of entitlement bordered on arrogance, and they constantly demanded compensation and benefits afforded to US diplomats. For some reason, they couldn't grasp the concept of local-hire employment. As I mentioned earlier in this book, diplomats have it tough. They deal with constant movement (gathering no moss?) and are forced to live for decades outside the United States. In many cases, they take postings in unwanted countries, and have to leave children behind or place them in boarding schools far away. They have no local community or family near them, and deal with danger on a regular basis. On the other hand, the LE staff stay in-country, put their kids in good schools, and earn more money than 75 percent of their counterparts nationwide. Even with their economy collapsing around them, they constantly demanded more salary and benefits. The local nationals failed to recognize the irony of the situation, that is, that tens of thousands of fellow Greeks were thrown out on the street by their own government. (My HR staff understood this and tried in vain to convince the Greek nationals how fortunate they were to be USG employees.) You'd think that one glance outside the front gate at the economic devastation of Greece would have reminded them how good they had it. But it didn't.

Let me take a second to explain a few things here. Reading this book, you have been with me through most of my life. It hasn't always been pretty, and I've made my share of mistakes. But except for a few rare situations, I've tried to avoid negativity as much as possible. But I couldn't take that approach here.

I felt compelled to honestly reflect on embassy life in Athens. The morale was like a black cloud hanging over the place. The level of distrust was high, unverified rumors abounded, and most fellow diplomats were eager to get the hell out of Dodge. At one time or another, many colleagues I trusted and admired mirrored my opinion. I don't know why synergy goes bad, nor why the US embassy in Athens was such a hard place to work. (Note: I have never felt this way about any other posting I've been assigned to or have visited on temporary duty.) I'll tell you this—the day Andi and I left that compound for the last time was one of the highlights of our two-year diplomatic tour.

But don't confuse the negative work environment with the country of Greece. We absolutely loved living in Athens and touring around the country. Even with all the economic turmoil and uncertainty, Andi and I found the Greek people *outside* the embassy to be pleasant, humorous, and for the most part pro-American. At times it felt like the embassy was on another wavelength.

During our last several months in Greece, I started to develop some abdominal problems. After a few weeks of antacids and Zantacs, I wasn't feeling much better. When I started to pass blood through my intestines, I got really nervous. The medical unit at the embassy sent me to a private hospital for a colonoscopy and a CT scan. (The embassy medical section wouldn't even consider using a government-run medical facility.) The results were frightening. The doctor said I had cancer in my colon and it had to be operated on immediately. His primary concern was simple—had it spread to other parts of my body or not? I knew that colon cancer, with the exception of pancreatic cancer, was the deadliest type of this hideous disease. The intestines wrap around everything in the pelvic and abdomen area. Any movement of the cancer outside the colon was potentially fatal.

You have to be kidding me, I thought! *I'm still recovering from brain surgery for God's sake. The surgeons weren't sure if my aneurysm was contained or not, and now this?* It's like the old *Hee-Haw* TV show lyric, "If it weren't for bad luck, I'd have no luck at all."

I was MEDEVACed again, with Andi, back to the Baptist Medical Center in Miami. After a few consults, it was obvious that surgery was imminent. The doctor laid out my options, and they weren't good. First, the chances that the cancer had spread were high, since it had grown so much already. Second, the growth was near my rectum. Any operation that required removal of this area of the colon meant a colostomy bag forever!

And third, the incision in my pelvic region would be very large and might cause some collateral damage (it did, but I still can't talk about it). Wow. Great news, huh?

Before we left Athens, I sent my family an e-mail covering the latest details about the cancer. My brother Larry came down to Florida to help in any way he could and to be there for us. (I asked family not to come down for the brain surgery. This time, I welcomed Larry's company, especially for Andi's sake.)

Hours before the operation, sitting in a waiting room, the nurse practitioner from my brain surgery last year came bursting into the room and headed right toward us.

"Don, I read about your upcoming cancer surgery. I can't believe it. You poor thing. You just had the brain operation a year ago. But you know what? You're a superstar, and the prize pupil of our Vascular Surgery Institute. And you're the talk of the lecture circuit as well. I know you'll do fine. Good luck, Don," she said. With a tear in her eye, she gave us a big hug and took off. She had more lives to save.

As she headed toward the door, I took a quick look at Larry. I wasn't sure he, or my family in general, really believed us when we told them how dangerous and complicated my brain surgery really was. In two minutes, the nurse did it for me.

I was prepped for surgery and lying in a stretcher awaiting my medical escort. Andi and Larry were by my side. As calm as I felt the first time, that's how nervous I felt this time. I was pressing my luck. (There's that word again.) *How could a cancer that's so advanced not have invaded the rest of my body? How can a person with any dignity walk around with a bag of fecal material around his waist? Did I cash in all my chips with the brain surgery?*

I decided not to pray for God to save me. I still believed there were too many others less fortunate than myself. So I prayed for Andi, just in case I'd never see her again. I thought about wearing a colostomy bag for the rest of my life, and decided I'd rather die on the table. And if the cancer did spread all over my body, how much time did I have left? Maybe a quick exit might be the best option. As you can see, I was quite morbid, when Larry said something that really lifted my spirits and still does today:

"Don, look at it this way. No matter what, at least you know you're coming out alive this time, right?" He couldn't have said anything that did more for my psyche than those words. He was right. I'd live to fight another day, regardless of the outcome. Even if the cancer were in an advanced stage, I'd have options. So I decided to worry about tomorrow later.

The operation was intense, and left me with one less foot of intestine. The cancer was only two centimeters from my rectum, approximately three quarters of an inch, but was far enough away to be removed without my needing a colostomy bag. The surgeon tested twenty areas of my lymph nodes—the true highways of cancer travel—and all were negative. The growth was so close to spreading, the doctor compared my colon to the skin on his arm. According to him, the cancer had eaten through the colon and was just a thin derma layer away from breaking loose. The incision was deep and wide and would be painful for a long time. Follow-ups would be necessary. I was not out of the woods yet. But it didn't matter. For the second time in my life, I had run through a car wash and didn't get wet. I was released from the hospital a few days later and didn't even need chemotherapy. For some reason, I had survived two life-threatening operations in fifteen months, each by the skin of my teeth. What did it mean? Why was I the lucky one again? I read about people dying from aneurysms and cancer all the time.

Even today, while writing this book, I still can't get my head around it. Am I still here for a reason? Has God chosen me to remain and take care of Andi and her diabetic problems? Or is it just random luck—some make it and some don't? Is there a higher power driving me to write this book, even though it's one of the hardest things I've ever done? Perhaps someday I'll understand, or maybe I won't. Either way, I'll keep looking for answers. But I'm not too confident they'll be found. After all, *the human mind will never let you understand the human mind.*

We drove away from Baptist Medical Center for the last time. I had mixed emotions. That place had saved my life twice, so I felt attached to it somehow. Behind those walls remained professionals with the power to heal and the ability to save lives. On the other hand, I never wanted to see that hospital again!

After my second narrow escape, we returned to Athens. Our lives started to settle into a routine. We decided to try to enjoy this great country while we could. Although my dislike for the embassy persisted, our enjoyment of Greece made it tolerable.

Since the operations ate up all of my medical leave, and most of my personal leave, we had to be frugal when planning vacations. We started simply, with a three-island trip to Aegina, Poros, and Hydra. From the port of Piraeus, Aegina is the closest island to the mainland. Because it's not a victim of mass tourism, it retains much of its Greek charm. Most visitors are locals, who come over to Aegina for the weekends to escape the hectic city lifestyle for a while. Relaxing and very charming, Aegina is a real living and working island. As you walk the streets, you are instantly impressed with the authenticity of the place—something rarely seen on Greek island excursions.

Poros rests on the Sardonic Gulf close to the Peloponnesian mainland. Once a tourist destination, its popularity has declined due to regional locations of airports closer to the more touristy islands. The port is one of the most scenic in all of Greece, with a narrow inlet splitting the small town in two. Cafes and shops still abound, and visitors are warmly welcomed. What makes Poros different from the other Greek Isles is the lush pine forest that still covers much of the island. We walked along the water's edge, popping in and out of stores and shops, and generally taking in the ambience. It's a special place—my favorite of the three.

Hydra is a different ball game altogether. This island relies heavily on tourism, and benefits from numerous bays and natural harbors. It's small in size, very arid, and devoid of automobiles. The inhabited area is so dense that most people walk or ride burros. The only vehicles on the island are rubbish trucks. It's the in place to be, with many movie stars and famous people owning villas on the crest line above the town. The Kamini Yacht Club welcomes ships from around the globe. The crescent-shaped town center of Hydra is loaded with the usual tourist amenities. We grew fond of this island and returned again before we left Greece.

With a taste of the Greek Isles under our belts, we turned our concentration back to the mainland. Without a doubt, one of the greatest mythical sites on earth is the Oracle at Delphi. Resting seemingly on the top of the world, sloped against Mount Parnassus, it provides an unbelievable view of the Pleistos Valley below. Delphi is the home of the Sanctuary of Apollo and the Pythian Games (second biggest behind the Olympic Games), and the site of the ancient oracle. The Greeks considered Delphi to be the middle of the earth. Rulers and kings came from all directions to seek guidance from the oracle. According to Wikipedia:

"Apollo spoke though his Oracle; the sibyl or priestess of the oracle at Delphi was known as the Pythia; she had to be an older woman of blameless life chosen from among the peasants of the area. She sat on a tripod seat over an opening in the earth. When Apollo slew Python, its body fell into the fissure, according to legend, and fumes arose from its decomposing body. Intoxicated by the vapors, the sibyl would fall into a trance, allowing Apollo to possess her spirit. In this state she prophesied."

We walked the hallowed grounds and trod the Sacred Way to the Pythia's tripod seat next to the Temple of Apollo. We visited the amphitheater used for the Pythian Games, along with the massive athletic fields farther down the mountainside. We stood at the Stoa of the Athenians and wondered how they reacted to the omens delivered by the Oracle. We also passed many large buildings, called treasuries, where countless millions in gold and jewels were stored for the oracle's safekeeping. It was a unique place. Andi and I visited Delphi three times—once with my friend Brad, who came to Greece to spend a few days with us. We were never disappointed.

Andi and I found out quickly that you could drive in any direction from Athens and stumble upon amazing history. I like the Corinth Canal, cut through solid rock to connect Corinth with the northern edge of the Peloponnese. Begun by Nero, it wasn't finished until the early 1800s. Too narrow for today's superliners, it's still functional. A bridge spans the middle of the channel, and the boat trip though the canal is memorable.

Instead of going on and on about the seemingly endless places to go in Greece, I'll just list a few that we enjoyed to whet your appetite:

- *Nafplio*—Marble pavements, looming castles, waterfront dining and hiking, and a large plaza similar to what you might see in an Italian village.
- *Sounio*—Home to the Temple of Poseidon. Huge pillared structure on top of a mountain overlooking the sea. Awe-inspiring. (We still

have a small statue of Poseidon in our living room. It's carefully placed so he's always facing the sea.)

- *Marathon*—Location of the historic battle of Marathon; large burial mound for casualties; a soldier ran twenty-six miles back to Athens to warn of possible attack, then collapsed and died.
- *Ancient Olympia*—At the confluence of the rivers Alfeios and Kladeo; enjoyed over a thousand years of esteem as a religious and athletic center.
- *Mycenae*—Fortified palace complex; one of the earliest examples of sophisticated citadel architecture; abandoned in 1100 BC; its reconstruction is remarkable.
- *Epidauris*—Renowned for the perfect acoustics of its amphitheater; if you sit in the top row of the arena, you can hear whispers from center stage.
- *Pindos Mountain Range*—vast and beautiful range extending from the Greek border of Albania south beyond Metsovo. It trundles east toward Macedonia and out to the Ionian Sea.

This is by no means a complete list of wonders to see. Since we only had two years in Greece—shortened even more by medical issues—we tried our best to see what we could while we were there.

On a few occasions, we were able to get away from the embassy and visit more of the Greek Isles. One of our excursions, to the Island of Rhodes, was a real capstone event. It personified the thrill of living amid the gods of Greece.

The Island of Rhodes is located in the Eastern Aegean Sea. It's one of the largest Dodecanese Islands and is shaped like a spearhead. Positioned northeast of Crete and just off the Anatolian coast of Turkey, it's known as the Island of the Knights. Rhodes is also known for the Colossus of Rhodes, one of the Seven Wonders of the Ancient World.

The Colossus of Rhodes was a statue of the Greek titan Helios, and was erected to protect the port city. It stood over thirty meters high, easily one of the tallest statues in the world. According to ancient writings, Helios stood with one foot on each side of the harbor entrance, glaring at any possible foe considering entry. The statue collapsed during an earthquake in 226 BC. The harbor is still there, now protected by the Statues of the Rhodian Deer, strategically placed at the former footholds of the great Titan. The old town in Rodos is quite spectacular. Spanning over twenty-four centuries of history, it houses a medieval-like city behind fortress walls.

According to www.rodosisland.gr, "you enter the Old Town of Rodos through the Gate of Freedom." From there, you pass "medieval fortress-like buildings, narrow alleys, minarets, old houses with their balconies, decorative, drinking or ablution fountains, and tranquil or busy squares with shady trees." Added to the UNESCO World Heritage List in 1988, the Old Town of Rodos covers 58.37 hectares of land (over 132 acres). The website continues, "The cobblestone Street of the Knights, one of the best-preserved medieval streets in existence, is flanked by medieval Inns of the various 'tongues' of the countries represented by the Order of the Knights of St. John. At the foot of the Street, in Museum Square, stands the Hospital of the Knights, which houses the Archaeological Museum."

Nearby, in the newer part of town, rests the strikingly beautiful Rodini Park. It's thought to be the site of the School of Rhetoric, where many scholarly icons studied. Among them were Julius Caesar, Cato the Younger, Cicero, Pompey, Brutus, and Mark Antony. The park is a labyrinth of streams and paths, shaded by maple, cypress, and pine trees. I would have loved to wax philosophic with those guys. Who knows? Maybe they could tell me where space ends. Or where Jimmy Hoffa is buried. Or why hot dogs come in packs of ten, but hot-dog buns come in packs of eight.

Not far from the Old Town is the historic jewel of Rodos—the ancient city-state of Lindos. It was the home of the ruler Cleovulus, and was admired throughout its ancient history as a city of wealth, beauty, and strategic position. Located down the mountainside to the Aegean Sea, it's easy to admire the view from today's modern motorway. It's a stout hike downward through villages, ancient houses, cobblestoned streets, mansions, churches, tourist shops, restaurants, and so on. The streets are too narrow for automobiles. Once at sea level, the water views are excellent, and the hills come alive with color. If you desire, you can take a donkey upward past the motorway all the way to the ancient Acropolis of Lindos, situated well above anything else in the area. The Island of Rhodes is a blueprint for the development and cross-cultural coexistence of humans through the millennia. People from every part of the globe reside there. They stand unified as the protectors of this special place, much like the Colossus of Rhodes did many centuries before them.

Back at the embassy, my office was as hectic as ever. During the Arab Spring of 2011, much of the Middle East was under duress. Egypt was no different. By 2012, when military leaders announced that President Mohamed Morsy had been removed from power, it started a chain of violent and deadly events. Our citizens were in grave danger, and we had to get them out of there. Fearing for the worst, the State Department began the largest evacuation of Americans in US history. Athens was named as one of the evacuation centers. I was given the job to represent the ambassador and greet our countrymen. My assignment was simple—to ensure that our embassy was there to provide whatever assistance we could. It was quite extraordinary.

One of my key roles was to meet the planes on the tarmac and represent the United States. I may not remember it exactly, but it was something similar to this:

As the frightened and weary Americans departed the planes, we led them to a series of buses. I entered the first full bus. "Hello, everyone, and welcome to Athens." A huge roar of applause greeted me, almost knocking me over. "My name is Don Feeney, and I'm with the US embassy here in Greece. We'll take you to the reception center in a few moments, where you'll receive transportation, hotel rooms, food, and anything else you may need. You're safe now." Another huge burst of applause. I repeated this scenario with each of the buses, and literally felt goose bumps every time. The raw emotions of appreciation and relief almost overwhelmed me. They were us—Americans— and needed help. I was able to assist in a small way, and it felt great.

The terminal was bustling with activity. We had reception stations everywhere—assisting with children, verifying visa and passport information (many evacuated Egypt without proper IDs), making plane reservations, scheduling hotel accommodations, passing out food, attending to injuries, and so on. I remember thinking this was America at its finest. People helping people in need without hesitation. Unfortunately, some of the passengers were not Americans, but aliens attempting to enter Greece illegally. The customs officials anticipated this, and were on hand to broker these situations. All in all, it was quite hectic for several days and nights. And it was also one of the few times I was glad to be posted in the Athens embassy.

In the HRM business, one of the constant overseas complexities is the management of US residence policies. Different in each country, they are extremely complicated and politically driven, and require just the right amount of tact and compromise. Two huge disagreements arose between the Ministry of Foreign Affairs (MFA) and our embassy. The first involved length-of-stay visas for American family members. The Greek government was adamant that all visitors to Greece—not on government orders or possessing a diplomatic or official passport—must depart after ninety days. This was problematic. Many of our classified contractors remained well over three months. In addition, today's US families are much more complicated. They include a wider variety of family combinations. The current immigration laws prohibited certain family members from residing with diplomatic families, and this didn't sit well with the ambassador or the post population. After over a year and many visits to the MFA, we were able to create a new visa category for family members. It was complicated and time-consuming, but it worked. One of the limiting factors of any US exception to current immigration law is the fear of showing favoritism to Americans. All the other embassies and consulates watched us closely and were eager to express opinions about advantages given to the United States. The MFA was well aware of diplomatic differences and had a tendency to proceed very slowly, hoping to avoid confrontation and to shelve initiatives like this one. But this time, we wouldn't let them.

The stakes really increased when posts worldwide were asked to gauge in-country reactions to a very complex scenario—providing full diplomatic status to same-sex partners. The MFAs around the world responded differently. In countries like Sweden and France, it was an easy adjustment to diplomatic policy. In other countries, especially in the Middle East, it was an impossible goal. Greece was somewhere in between. Greece is a very religious country, with an overwhelmingly high percentage of Christians. Providing same-sex partners with full diplomatic status amounted to treating them the same as married spouses. We had nothing in the Vienna Convention on Diplomatic Relations to assist us. At first, the Greek government refused to consider providing diplomatic status at all.

Eventually, we were able to get the MFA to use a little-known nonimmigrant visa (NIV) category to allow same-sex partners to stay in the country under the guise of a work visa. This was a good start, because work visas could be renewed yearly if the diplomatic partner remained in Athens. But shortly afterward, the Ministry of the Interior (MI) overturned this exception and insisted the use of the NIV waiver was unlawful.

Interestingly, the timing of the Greek economic collapse may have helped us turn the tide on this issue. Massive layoffs of government employees affected all the ministries, and jobs changed hands. My ally in the MFA moved up in the organization, while his counterpart in the MI moved out. Shortly afterward, post was given the go-ahead to process our first request for a same-sex Greek diplomatic card. Of course, we still needed the diplomatic visa, which is issued in the United States, and the MI refused to waive this requirement. We were getting snowballed. The MI and the MFA both knew that once we secured that initial visa, they couldn't delay this process any longer. So they implemented a stalling tactic that really strained our relationship with the ministries. Since I was heading back to the United States for my retirement seminar, I decided to try to break the stalemate. I carried the passport of a life partner back to DC and was standing at the door the next morning when the Greek embassy opened on Massachusetts Avenue. I refused to leave that embassy until the visa was approved. Five hours later, after many back-and-forth phone calls to Athens, I walked out of there with the approved visa! With precedent now on our side, future cases like these would be much easier to process.

Most of my days as an HRM were overwhelmed with complexities. Just to name a few: our regional psychologist died suddenly while working in Germany, generating a host of complications; I had to fire several employees, some for criminal acts and some for poor performance; the consulate in Thessaloniki was identified for closure, which created a myriad of management challenges; our office withstood two IG inspections, which put the entire post on edge; one employee charged me with racial discrimination—a very serious offense—even though I never met her (maybe it was bias by telepathy?); and I was fired from the Housing Committee—even though I was elected by my peers—because I voted down a weak appeal from the general services officer to move to a bigger place. All of these challenges, and others, were just normal events in that place. We needed a vacation ...

Santorini (*hiraT* in Greek) is one of the Cycladic Islands, located in the south Aegean Sea, and is considered by many to be the most beautiful spot on earth. Formed by twelve volcanic eruptions, each approximately twenty thousand years apart, Santorini rests on the caldera, or volcanic rim, like President Reagan's shining city on the hill. Andi and I were very excited about seeing this worldwide jewel. According to the *Santorini Island Guide (2011-2012)*, it's "a White fantasy... the perfect blending of earth and heaven. Aromas and flavors refined by the sun. Wind, lava, and time embraced by the sea. A precious, enchanting, and passionate lover cloaked in a veil of mystery." Okay, the quote is a little over the top, but you get the picture.

This was going to be our last extended vacation in Greece, and we were determined to make it a good one. The first thing we noticed upon landing at Santorini National Airport was the stark contrast of colors. The deep blue sea accentuated the dark and rugged sides of the caldera. Atop the rim, Fira—a city of white with sky-blue domes and roofs—seemed to float on the ether. The skyline was intense in its simplicity. The volcanic rim has an inverted "C" shape, with the rest of the volcano, including the crater itself, buried under the sea.

When we arrived at our hotel in Fira, the capital city, we knew we were in for something special. From our hotel balcony, the entire panorama of Santorini was laid out before us. To the northwest, the city of Oia, with its *capetanospitas* (captains' houses) and *yposcafas* (dwellings carved in rocks) offer sea views, architecture, and world-famous sunsets. The best part about Oia is that it's not as crowded as Fira, and the marble promenades are wider and cleverly cut into the mountainside. (We bought a fish sculpture made of quartz and bronze that appears to be leaping into the air. And I don't know why. Every time I look at it, I can hear it saying "sucker." Anyway, since it was our last vacation in Greece, I guess we had to come back with something besides refrigerator magnets.)

On the opposite end of the crescent, in the southwest corner, is the town of Akrotiri. It's just a small fishing village, but it boasts over fifteen centuries of human inhabitants—and an archaeological settlement of the prehistoric Thira that's worth a visit. We rented a car—a Smart Car, which was a piece of shit, I might add—and drove to Akrotiri to visit the Red Beach, nestled well below the caldera. Perhaps the best part of this town was the fantastic views of Santorini, especially the islands off the main volcanic rim—Thirasia, Neo Kameni, Palia Kameni, and Aspronisi. Each stood defiantly above the waterline, refusing to succumb to the fate of the rest of the underwater volcano. On the way back to town, we passed a small, very exquisite hotel dangling on the edge of the southern rim (can't remember the name). Even though we weren't guests, the concierge allowed us to hang out at the beach bar for a while and gaze at the beauty that is Santorini. If we ever return, we'll find that place, and definitely stay there.

Fira is the center of the island. The densely built homes zigzag down the caldera, providing narrow residential walkways between them. Shops and cafes are everywhere along the small sidewalks, especially at Theotokopoulos Square, the main gathering place for tourists on the island or for those arriving by ship. At sunset, Fira gets very crowded, and the lights of the night blaze over the darkness of the sea. Sunset parties are the norm, but you'd better get to your favorite spot early.

Well below, the ever-present cruise ships appeared every morning. Looking like ants from the top of the caldera, the excited cruisers would start their trek up to Fira, which in Santorini, isn't an easy proposition. They had three options for ascension to the mountaintop:

1. Take the cable car, which is small and slow and usually has long lines.
2. Walk 587 steps to the summit. One of our favorite hangouts was near the top of the steps. There were some tired, sweaty people passing by. The cold beer in my hand definitely drew attention from those thirsty hikers.
3. Ride a *barron*, or donkey, up a switchback into Fira. I'm not an animal activist or anything, but it was sad to see how hard those donkeys worked to carry out-of-shape people and luggage up that steep precipice.

Our time in paradise was over. So we loaded up our stuff—including the fish—and headed back to Athens. Our remaining few months would be a cinch. With no future postings to worry about and an oceanfront penthouse waiting for us in Indian Harbour Beach, Florida, we were feeling pretty good about ourselves. These last days were blissful. We never missed a weekend doing our favorite thing—walking among the paths and alleyways of the Acropolis and the Plaka. Then stopping at Postale's or Moma's on Adrianou Street for lunch and people watching. Or lounging at my favorite place in Monastiraki Square—Metro Café—with tables right in the middle of all the activity. There was always something going on there, from student demonstrations and African drumbeats, to live stage music, jugglers, mimes, clowns, and so on. I think it was the weirdness of the area that attracted me most. Our Armenian waiter really got to know us well, and even gave us a going-away gift (which made Andi cry). He was a poor, hardworking immigrant—much like our ancestors—who asked for nothing but a chance to work and take care of his family.

For the first time since I was seventeen years old, I was going to live where I *wanted* to, not where life took me. Full of expectation, the winding down of my professional career in Athens was very therapeutic. Since I knew exactly what I wanted to do with my life, and was lucky enough to have a loving spouse sharing the same dream, I realized an astonishing fact—I was happy! Past medical catastrophes were just a memory, and I was bound and determined to enjoy our lives together while I still had healthy years left. I was fifty-eight, and gambling that I'd already had my share of bad luck (brain surgery and colon cancer) for a while. I felt like karma was on my side.

We weren't interested in going-away parties or retirement dinners. Andi and I decided to get together with our friends on our own terms, and begin the distancing process away from the black hole of the US embassy. I did, however, take my entire staff out to lunch (we didn't return that afternoon— what can they do to me, give me a bad performance rating?). We were hoping to keep in touch with many of our State Department friends, but were not optimistic. It's hard for them to look back when they're constantly moving forward. No one knew that more than us. Pledges to get together in the future eventually became wishful afterthoughts. We understood this and were okay with it.

After all, like Thomas Jefferson said, "I like the dreams of the future better than the history of the past."

On my final morning in the State Department, sitting on our balcony at 50 Kleomenous in Athens, the complexity of my life hit me like a cold Korean wind. One brain aneurysm, two careers, three divorces, one moon buggy, two deceased parents, four marriages, one parade float, four siblings, two tragic deaths of close friends, one coin toss, twenty-four moves, five continents, one song sparrow redemption, fifty-two countries, one airborne Pontiac Firebird, two commander jobs, one missing consular officer, five passports, one colon cancer, two Kismets, one military AWOL, and one gift from heaven—my wife, Andi.

Later that morning, for the last time in our lives, we loaded bags— and Kismet II—into a government van and headed to the airport for our departure from Greece. When we land in Florida, the moss will begin to grow. The *restartment* process will commence in earnest.

As we crossed over the eastern seaboard of the United States, I couldn't help thinking about all those places, all those moves, all the excitement, and all the loneliness that finally brought me to this point. Looking at America below the horizon, I could almost hear her say, "Welcome home; we've been waiting for you for a long time." And finally, for the first time in my adult life, I'd cease living like a rolling stone.

The track was long and exhausting, and took its toll on myself and my small family. Simply put—this diplomat was tired of the race.

My life—my race—had barreled through the following laps:

- Pittsburgh, Pennsylvania (North Side and Avalon)
- Clarion, Pennsylvania (college)
- Pittsburgh, Pennsylvania (Belleview after college graduation)
- San Antonio, Texas (Basic Training and Tech School)
- Zweibrucken, Germany (air force—enlisted)
- Limestone, Maine (air force—enlisted)
- San Antonio, Texas (Officer's Training School and Tech School)
- Honolulu, Hawaii (air force—HRM)
- Rolla, Missouri (ROTC instructor)
- San Antonio, Texas (Military Personnel Center—Air Staff assignment)
- Comiso, Sicily, southern Italy (CBPO chief)
- Colorado Springs, Colorado (Air Force Academy instructor and commander)
- Honolulu, Hawaii (Inspector General staff)
- Izmir, Turkey (commander)
- Norfolk, Virginia (Joint Task Force)
- Fremantle, Australia (sabbatical for PhD)
- Indialantic, Florida (retirement, sans PhD)
- Washington, DC (State Department orientation and Foreign Service Institute)
- San Salvador, El Salvador (regional HRM officer)

- Manama, Bahrain (regional HRM officer)
- Washington, District of Colombia (career counseling and assignment officer)
- Willemstad, Curacao, Netherlands Antilles (management officer)
- Athens, Greece (HRM officer)
- Indian Harbour Beach, Florida (restartment begins)

So, my friends, the story of the nomadic Feeneys has ended. I am deeply touched by your willingness to stay with me through this outrageous project. I simply could not have toiled this hard if I didn't believe I had something to say. I hope I guessed right.

I've written things in this book I've never said out loud. The changes along the way have been difficult to write down on paper. At times, I had to trick myself into thinking I was writing about someone else. But in the end, I tried to honestly tell my story, warts and all, because to do otherwise would be unthinkable. The very thing that made this book so hard to write is the reason I wrote it to begin with—the search for meaning, clarity, spirituality, love and closure. And just as importantly, to expose this search to you, the coveted reader, for judgment. I hope you sensed this as well.

Finally, the power of thoughtful people like you—eager to learn and digest differences among us all—motivates me greatly. Although humans share many similarities, it has always been my belief that each of us is different. The vastness of the brain can lead me to no other conclusion. It's time to listen to mine. And it is telling me the following:

Learn to live well, or fairly make your will;
You've played, and loved, and ate, and drunk your fill:
Walk sober off; before the sprightlier age
Comes tittering on, and shoves you from the stage.

—Alexander Pope

End

CPSIA information can be obtained
at www.ICGtesting.com
Printed in the USA
LVHW031108020322
712194LV00004B/59